THE MEN OF BARBAROSSA

THE MEN OF BARBAROSSA

Commanders of the German Invasion of Russia, 1941

Samuel W. Mitcham, Jr.

CASEMATE PUBLISHERS
Philadelphia & Newbury

Published in the United States of America in 2009 by
CASEMATE
908 Darby Road, Havertown, PA 19083

and in the United Kingdom by
CASEMATE
17 Cheap Street, Newbury, Berkshire, RG14 5DD

ISBN 978-1-935149-15-6

Cataloging-in-publication data is available from the Library of
Congress and from the British Library.

Printed and bound in the United States of America.

10 9 8 7 6 5 4 3 2 1

For a complete list of Casemate titles, please contact:

United States of America
Casemate Publishers
Telephone (610) 853-9131, Fax (610) 853-9146
E-mail casemate@casematepublishing.com
Website www.casematepublishing.com

United Kingdom
Casemate-UK
Telephone (01635) 231091, Fax (01635) 41619
E-mail casemate-uk@casematepublishing.co.uk
Website www.casematepublishing.co.uk

CONTENTS

MAPS

PREFACE

The purpose of this book is to tell the story of Operation Barbarossa and the men who directed it. This objective is massive in scope because Barbarossa, the German invasion of the Soviet Union, was massive in scale, arguably the largest military operation in history. In the single Battle of Kiev, for example, the Red Army lost twice as many men killed as the United States suffered during the entire Vietnam War. Soviet losses in prisoners alone exceeded the size of the entire U.S. Army in Vietnam at the height of its deployment. The Soviets suffered nearly as many losses a month later, at Bryansk and Vyazma, as the Germans closed in on Moscow. Launched across a north-south axis that spanned the width of Eurasia, Operation Barbarossa involved millions of soldiers and countless fighting vehicles. It also changed the world forever.

Before Barbarossa, the German Wehrmacht (German armed forces, 1935–1945) seemed invincible, and its supreme commander, Adolf Hitler, seemed to be an unstoppable force of nature. No one, it seemed, could check the Fuehrer, much less defeat him. (The Battle of Britain, of course, was seen as a defeat for the Luftwaffe, rather than the Wehrmacht. The German Army was still undefeated, and it was by no means clear in the spring of 1941 that the German pilots would not yet finish off the United Kingdom.) Barbarossa changed all of that. By the end of 1941, Allied victory seemed to be a very real possibility. Few would have bet on it 16 or 17 months before.

Operation Barbarossa was truly staggering in its magnitude. Wars, however, are not fought by numbers; they are fought by men, and this is where *The Men of Barbarossa* comes in. Its goal is not only to tell the story of the invasion, but to tell the history of some of the men behind it. Very often, writers stereotype German officers into two categories: Prussian gentlemen or Nazi monsters. There were, of course, both—but there were also varying shades of gray. I hope that my humble efforts contribute to a deeper understanding of what happened in 1941, why it happened, who made it happen, and what went right or wrong.

I would like to thank Melinda Matthews, head of the Interlibrary Loan Department at the University of Louisiana at Monroe (also known as the Cultural and Intellectual Center of the Western Hemisphere) for all of her help, as well as various employees at the Bundesarchiv/Koblenz, the Bundesarchiv/Freiburg, the U.S. National Archives, the War College, the United States Army Military History Institute, and the U.S. Air Forces's Air University Archives. Thanks also go to the late Theodor-Friedrich von Stauffenberg, who left me his papers, as well as dozens of German Army "201" files (i.e., personnel records). Thanks also go to Colonel Ed Marino, Colonel John Angolia, and the late Dr. Waldo Dalstead for sharing their photographs with me and for allowing me to duplicate them. I alone am responsible for any mistakes.

Last but not least, thanks go to my wife, Donna, and to my children, Lacy and Gavin, for putting up with my literary efforts all of these years.

Dr. Samuel W. Mitcham, Jr.
Monroe, Louisiana
March 9, 2009

CHAPTER I

SETTING THE STAGE:
THE WEHRMACHT, 1933–1941

When Adolf Hitler came to power on January 30, 1933, the German *Reichswehr* (armed forces) had two branches: the *Reichsheer* (army) and the *Reichsmarine* (navy). According to the Treaty of Versailles, which ended World War I, the army was limited to 100,000 men (4,000 of whom could be officers), while the navy was limited to 15,000 officers and men. Of the four innovative weapons of World War I—tanks, airplanes, poisonous gas, and submarines—the Reichswehr was denied all four.

Hitler began his secret military expansion almost as soon as he achieved power. On March 9, 1935, he announced the existence of the Luftwaffe, which his cronies Hermann Goering and Erhard Milch had been building for some time. The reaction of Germany's potential enemies (primarily the United Kingdom and France) was so tepid as to be almost nonexistent. This encouraged Hitler, who renounced the Treaty of Versailles (which the Germans called the *Versailles Diktat*) a week later. He was now free to pursue his military buildup in even greater earnest.

Because he and his Nazi paladins considered themselves revolutionaries, he also tended to embrace revolutionary military concepts, such as terror bombing and the *blitzkrieg* (lightening warfare). The same day Hitler renounced the Treaty of Versailles, the German Army activated the first three panzer divisions.

The military entity Hitler used to expand, recruit, and train his armies was the *Wehrkreis*–the German military district, which had served the Second Reich well. (Its counterpart in the Luftwaffe was the *Luftgau* or air district.) By August 26, 1939, when the Home or Replacement Army was created to control the *Wehrkreise* (also spelled

Wehrkreisen), four "waves" of divisions had been created. These Hitler used to conquer Poland. Thirty-one more waves would be formed and sent into action by January 1945, along with several divisions that did not belong to specific waves. By 1943, there were 18 Wehrkreise forming and/or training German divisions: I, II, III, IV, V, VI, VII, VIII, IX, X, XI, XII, XIII, XVII, XVIII, XX, Bohemia and Moravia (in what had been Czechoslovakia), and the Wehrkreise General Gouvernement, in what had been Poland. Map 1.1 shows the Wehrkreise and their territorial responsibilities in 1939. Map 1.2 shows the Wehrkreise after the conquests of Poland, Belgium, and France.

In early 1938, it was discovered that Field Marshal Werner von Blomberg, the defense minister, had married a prostitute. He was forced to retire in disgrace. Heinrich Himmler and his deputy Reinhard Heydrich chose this moment to bring trumped-up charges of homosexuality against the non-Nazi commander-in-chief of the army, Colonel General Baron Werner von Fritsch. Although later exonerated, Fritsch was also forced to resign.[1] Hitler took advantage of this situation to end the corporate independence of the army, place it solidly under Nazi control, and simultaneously set up Germany's command structure for the next war. On February 4, 1938, he named himself Supreme Commander of the Armed Forces (*Wehrmacht*). His new chief executive officer would be General of Artillery (later Field Marshal) Wilhelm Keitel, who held the title commander-in-chief of the High Command of the Armed Forces (*Oberkommando der Wehrmacht* or OKW).

Despite his impressive title, Keitel was a nonentity and became a notorious yes-man for Adolf Hitler. The real brains of the OKW was its chief of operations, Major General (later Colonel General) Alfred Jodl.[2] (Appendix 1 shows a table of equivalent ranks between German and American armed forces.)

Under the OKW in the German organizational structure were the High Command of the Army (*Oberkommando des Heeres* or OKH), the High Command of the Navy *(Oberkommando der Kriegsmarine* or OKM), and the High Command of the Luftwaffe (*Oberkommando der Luftwaffe* or OKL). This, of course, was the formal chain of command, which was largely theoretical. In practice, the navy and air force went their own way, and their commanders, Grand Admiral Erich Raeder and *Reichsmarschall* Hermann Goering, tolerated no interference from Keitel or the OKW. This was a policy the OKH could not adopt.

To gain effective control of the high command of the army, Hitler had to control the commander-in-chief of OKH. To accomplish this goal, he had to find a general with enough gravitas to command the respect of the senior generals, but who would also submit to the will of the Fuehrer. For this purpose, he selected General of Artillery Walter von Brauchitsch.

Heinrich Alfred Hermann Walter von Brauchitsch was born in Berlin on October 4, 1881, the son of Prussian General of Cavalry Bernhard and the brother of Major General Adolf von Brauchitsch (1876–1935), who retired in 1929. From his very earliest days, it was clear that Walter was a Prussian general-in-training, and his career progressed more or less normally for a general-elect. He grew up in the Imperial Court and for a time was personal page of Empress Augusta Victoria. Educated in cadet schools, including Gross Lichterfeld (Germany's West Point), he was commissioned second lieutenant in the elite 3rd Foot Guards Regiment on March 22, 1900, at the age of 18. The following year, he transferred to the 3rd Guards Field Artillery Regiment and was associated with the artillery branch most of the rest of his career.

His positive contributions and innovations in that branch have largely been overlooked by historians; however, Brauchitsch played a major role in the development and adoption of the 88mm anti-aircraft gun as an anti-aircraft and anti-tank weapon. The 88mm was later mounted on the PzKw V "Tiger" tank, and was feared and respected by a generation of American soldiers, who generally considered it to be the finest tank gun used in World War II. Brauchitsch, meanwhile, became a battalion adjutant (chief administrative officer) in 1906 and regimental adjutant in 1909. He married Elizabeth von Karstedt, described as an unattractive woman, in late 1910.

Lieutenant von Brauchitsch began his General Staff training in 1912 and was transferred to the General Staff of the XVI Corps when World War I began in August 1914. Meanwhile, he was promoted to first lieutenant in 1909 and to captain in 1913.

Brauchitsch spent the entire war on the Western Front, serving with the XVI, the 34th Infantry Division (1915–17), Higher Construction Staff VII (1917), the 11th Infantry Division (1917–18), the 1st Guard

Reserve Division (1918), and the Guards Reserve Corps (1918). He emerged from the war as a major (1918) and a member of the Hohenzollern House Order. He was accepted into the Reichsheer as a matter of course.

After the war, Brauchitsch was transferred to the staff of Wehrkreis II in Stettin (1919–20) and the staff of Artillery Commander II (Arko 2), also in Stettin (1920–21). He then did a year's troop duty as a battery commander in the Prussian 2nd Artillery Regiment, which was also stationed in the Pomeranian capital. After spending three years in the *Truppenamt* (1922–25), as the clandestine General Staff was called, he served two more years of troop duty as commander of the II Battalion, 6th Artillery Regiment in Muenster (1925–27). (Map 1.3 shows Germany's major cities, and Map 1.4 shows the regions of Germany.) He became chief of staff of Wehrkreis VI, also in Muenster, in late 1927. On February 1, 1930, he became chief of the Army Training Department (T 4) and chief of the Artillery Inspectorate on March 1, 1932.

On March 1, 1933, shortly after Hitler took power, Brauchitsch was given one of the most important positions in Germany: commander of Wehrkreis I and the 1st Infantry Division. In this post, he commanded the province of East Prussia, which was separated from the rest of the Fatherland by the Treaty of Versailles and surrounded on three sides by an unfriendly Poland. In this position, Brauchitsch's attitude toward the Nazis varied from cool aloofness to outright hostility. He dealt firmly with Erich Koch, a rabid Nazi, and went so far as to eject SS units from Wehrkreis maneuvers when they displeased him. When Goebbels spread an unflattering rumor about him, Brauchitsch challenged him to a duel. He professed to be a deeply religious Evangelical Christian and was known to keep a Bible by his bed. Certainly none of his colleagues considered him a Nazi collaborator at this stage of his career.

Brauchitsch's career progression was proceeding on schedule. He was promoted to lieutenant colonel (1925), colonel (1928), major general (October 1, 1931), lieutenant general (October 1, 1933), and general of artillery (April 20, 1936). It was known that Baron von Fritsch, the commander-in-chief of the army, considered Brauchitsch his "best horse" and looked upon him as a possible successor.[3] In April 1937, he became commander-in-chief of Army Group Four, and was placed in charge of all of Germany's mobile forces, including the panzer divisions.

It seemed to outside observers that he was earmarked for greater things in the future. Far from believing he was on the verge of a great career, however, Brauchitsch thought he was at the end of the line. He faced the prospect of retirement in disgrace, forced to eek out a living on inadequate financial means, ostracized by his friends and the officer caste, and separated from everything he held dear. The reason for this bleak prognostication was a woman or, more accurately, two women.

According to General Curt Siewert, Brauchitsch's wife was an unattractive "governess type," lacking in femininity and human warmth.[4] She and the general had been living apart for five years, although Brauchitsch had at least one extramarital affair before they separated. The other woman was a beautiful, sexy divorcee named Charlotte Rueffer, the daughter of a Silesian judge. They had met in Berlin in 1925 or 1926, and Brauchitsch had asked his wife for a divorce at that time, but she refused. His relationship with Charlotte then cooled, and she married a bank director named Schmidt, but he drowned in a bathtub during a business trip; she was thus able to resume her liaison with Brauchitsch when he returned to Berlin in 1937.

Brauchitsch was determined to free himself from his wife and marry Charlotte by early 1938, but his wife was unwilling to grant him a divorce without a large lump-sum cash payment. Brauchitsch could not meet her demands and knew that she would contest the divorce if he did not. A divorce was bad enough in the late 1930s, but a scandal was something that the Prussian Officers' Corps would not tolerate, even from its generals. Brauchitsch knew that if he proceeded, his 38-year military career would be destroyed; he was nevertheless determined to forge ahead, even though it meant professional ruin.

Then, suddenly, he received an offer that would leave him happily divorced, his ex-wife financially secure, and himself promoted to colonel general and commander-in-chief of the German Army! Personal considerations aside, this represented quite a jump for Brauchitsch, who was tenth on the seniority list at the time. Unfortunately, there were strings attached. Brauchitsch would have to meet a series of demands put forth by Adolf Hitler. These included accepting the new command structure, renouncing the army's traditional position as "first among equals" vis-à-vis the navy and Luftwaffe, and retiring or transferring a great many of his friends and fellow generals.

Walter von Brauchitsch had to struggle with his conscience. Certainly he had little use for the Nazis—until Hermann Goering, acting as intermediary for Adolf Hitler, offered him a way out of his marriage without destroying his military career. The details of the negotiations of January 31 to February 3, 1938, were never fully revealed and now must be regarded as lost. The results, however, are known. Brauchitsch "sold out" to the Nazis. "To achieve his new position," Telford Taylor wrote, "Brauchitsch stooped to the meanest concessions and put himself under permanent obligation to Goering and Keitel as well as to Hitler. For this dismal surrender of principle for position, the officer paid soon and dear."[5] Taylor was certainly correct in his description. Brauchitsch was promoted to colonel general and was named C-in-C of the German Army on February 4, 1938, and the army lost its previously unquestioned hegemony in German military affairs. Frau von Brauchitsch received a cash payment, variously reported as 80,000 to a quarter of a million Reichsmarks, and was quietly divorced from her husband, who then married Charlotte Schmidt, a fanatical Nazi who constantly reminded her husband of "how much we owe the Fuehrer." And every general Hitler did not like was either transferred or forced into retirement.

The first to go was Lieutenant General Victor Schwedler, the chief of the powerful Army Personnel Office (*Heerespersonalamt* or HPA), who had consistently rejected Nazi attempts to obtain the best appointments for sympathizers of the NSDAP (*Nationalsozialistische Deutsche Arbeiterparti*).[6] Transferred to Dresden, where he assumed command of Wehrkreis IV, Schwedler was succeeded by Colonel Bodewin Keitel, the brother of Wilhelm.[7] Both of Schwedler's deputies, Colonels Adolf Kuntzen and Hans Behlendorff, were also transferred.[8] Future Field Marshals Ritter Wilhelm von Leeb and Ewald von Kleist were also forced into retirement, along with dozens of lesser lights. All were succeeded by Nazis or officers favorably inclined toward National Socialism. Among those arbitrarily sacked was Oswald Lutz, the chief of the Panzer Branch and the first general of panzer troops, who heard about his dismissal on the public radio. He was replaced by his deputy, Heinz Guderian, who did not utter a word of protest on behalf of his longtime defender and mentor, and seems to have been delighted to assume his vacant chair.[9] Only General of Artillery Ludwig Beck, the chief of the General Staff, and General of Mountain Troops Wilhelm Adam, the commander-in-chief of Army Group Two, registered significant objections to the Brauchitsch purge. Both were retired before the year was out.[10] To replace Beck as the chief of the General Staff and chief planner of the army, Hitler and Brauchitsch promoted his deputy, General of Artillery Franz Halder.

Between them, Brauchitsch and Halder—along with Hitler and his entourage—would command the ground forces on the Eastern Front during Operation Barbarossa.

Franz Halder was born in Wuerzburg, Bavaria, on June 30, 1884. By his own declaration, the males in his family had been soldiers for more than 300 years. He graduated from the Theresien Gymnasium (High School) in Munich on June 30, 1902, and joined the Royal Bavarian Army as a *Fahnenjunker* (officer cadet) in the Bavarian 3rd Field Artillery Regiment on July 14. He attended the War School in Munich and was commissioned *Leutnant* on March 9, 1904, and spent most of his career in the artillery. Selected for the Bavarian War Academy in Munich, he underwent General Staff training from 1911 to 1914. He was promoted to *Oberleutnant* (first lieutenant) in 1912.

Halder left the War Academy on July 31, 1914, and joined the Bavarian III Corps as an orderly officer. He spent most of World War I on the Western Front, serving as Ib (Chief Supply Officer) of the Bavarian 6th Infantry Division (January 1915–December 1916), Ia (Chief of Operations) of the Bavarian 5th Infantry Division (December 1916–March 1917), General Staff Officer (GSO) with the 2nd and 4th Armies (March–July 1917), and Ia of the Bavarian Cavalry Division on the Eastern Front (July–October 1917), before becoming a GSO to the commander-in-chief, East, where he was a senior planning officer. He was sent back to the Western Front on December 24, 1917, as General Staff officer to Bavarian Crown Prince Rupprecht's Army Group. When the war ended, he was sent to Munich as adjutant of the Central Office of the Bavarian General Staff. He was selected for the Reichswehr in 1919.[11]

A captain since 1915, Franz Halder worked in the training department of the Reich Defense Ministry in Berlin (1919–20), was on the staff of the 7th Infantry Division in Munich (1920–21), the staff of the commandant of Munich (1921) and again on the staff of the 7th Infantry (1921–23). He spent the period from October 1923 to December 1925 at Landsberg am Lech as commander of the 4th Battery/7th Artillery Regiment. He was promoted to major in 1924.

Already earmarked for greater things, Franz Halder became chief of operations (or Ia) of the 7th Infantry Division on December 1, 1925. (Appendix 2 shows the abbreviations for the German staff positions used during World War II. Appendix 3 shows the German ground units and their approximate strength during the first three years of the Second World War.) Four months later, he was back in the training department (T 4) in Berlin, where he remained until 1931. He was promoted to lieutenant colonel in 1929 and colonel in late 1931.

Halder transferred to Muenster on October 1, 1931, as chief of staff of Wehrkreis VI. Exactly three years later, he was promoted to major general and became Artillery Leader VII and deputy commander of the 7th Infantry Division in Munich. He became a lieutenant general on August 1, 1936.

General Halder continued his rise to the top in the fall of 1936, when he returned to General Staff in Berlin as head of the maneuver staff. He became deputy chief of the General Staff for training (Senior Quartermaster II or O Qu II) on October 12, 1937, and deputy chief of the General Staff for operations (O Qu I) on February 10, 1938. He was promoted to general of artillery on February 1, 1938.

In 1938, Hitler demanded that Czechoslovakia return the Sudetenland to Germany. Against the firm opposition of Ludwig Beck, the chief of the General Staff, he pushed the world to the edge of war. When Hitler could not be dissuaded, Beck resigned. Halder officially became chief of the General Staff on September 24, 1938.

Halder was a competent but unimaginative chief. He tried to restrain Adolf Hitler, but without positive results. In the process, he earned Hitler's contempt. For his part, Halder came to consider Hitler mentally unbalanced. He dabbled in the anti-Hitler conspiracy and even smuggled a concealed pistol into Hitler's presence, but could not use it. As a Christian, he declared with tears in his eyes, he simply could not bring himself to murder an unarmed man.

As chief of the General Staff, Halder was responsible for training and educating General Staff officers; representing them to the head of state; organizing higher headquarters; supervising the army's supply, communications, transportation, and administrative services; advising the army commander-in-chief and the head of state; and assisting in the execution of the decisions of the C-in-C and head of state. Unlike the World War I and Prussian chiefs, however, he did not have troop command functions. One could hardly imagine a more difficult and stressful job.

Halder played a positive role in the Polish campaign of 1939, but his plan for the conquest of France and the Benelux countries was an unimaginative rehash of the Schlieffen Plan which had failed in 1914, and Hitler eventually rejected it in favor of a plan advocated by Erich von Manstein, the former deputy chief of the General Staff and the chief of staff of Army Group A in 1939–early 1940. Brauchitsch and Halder got rid of Manstein by promoting him and giving him a corps command in the east, but the damage had been done. Halder further undercut his standing with the dictator by opposing the Western campaign of 1940 and the Russian campaign of 1941. He had a strong sense of ethics and opposed invading Belgium and the Netherlands on moral grounds. Hitler lamented that the Nazi *Gauleiters* (party leaders of regional branches of the NSDAP, roughly equivalent to U.S. governors) could not command armies; otherwise, he would rid himself of certain generals, including Brauchitsch and Halder. Hitler realized that he had to depend upon the technical expertise of the General Staff officers; he did not have to like them, however, and he did not. He also did not have to listen to their advice on strategic matters, and he did not.

The manner in which Brauchitsch and Halder sent Manstein into professional exile in early 1940 exhibits one of Halder's major character flaws. He was hardworking and demanding on both himself and others, but he was no genius and resented those who were. He demanded loyalty above all else, including originality and innovation. He especially resented Erwin Rommel, the "Desert Fox," whom he conspired against and whom he tried to have dismissed, but without success. Despite his professed Christianity, Halder definitely had streaks of pettiness and mean-spiritedness in his character.

Following the fall of France, Halder was promoted to colonel general on July 19, 1940, the same day Brauchitsch and 11 other officers were promoted to the rank of field marshal. He oversaw the planning for

Operation Barbarossa and tried unsuccessfully to convince Hitler that Moscow should be the primary objective of the campaign, but failed. After France, Halder also overestimated the abilities of the German Army. Like Hitler, Jodl, and others, Halder was convinced that Moscow could be captured before the onset of winter; he therefore did not ensure that the German ground forces were provided with enough winter clothing. Tens of thousands of men lost fingers, toes, and limbs as a result of this shortsightedness.

With the army firmly under his control, Hitler had removed the last force that had the physical power to overthrow him and end his dictatorship. Now free of all restraints, he pursued his policy of *Lebensraum*—acquiring "living space" for the German people in the east. In Europe, of course, this could only be accomplished by resorting to war, which Hitler ignited on September 1, 1939, when he invaded Poland. Only his former economics minister, Hjalmar Horace Greeley Schacht, raised strenuous objections. He called upon Brauchitsch to meet with him to discuss the illegality of Hitler's actions, but the C-in-C of the army replied that Schacht would be arrested if he even set foot on army property. Not surprisingly, Schacht ended the war in a concentration camp.

For Hitler and Nazi Germany, there followed an almost unbroken string of victories: Poland (1939), Denmark, Norway, Luxembourg, the Netherlands, Belgium, France (1940), Yugoslavia, Greece, Crete, and much of North Africa (1941). Except for the campaigns in Denmark and Norway, all of the campaigns were directed by the OKH (i.e., by Brauchitsch and Halder). The C-in-C of the army and the chief of the General Staff, however, lost a great deal of their status with Hitler because they opposed going to war against Czechoslovakia in 1938 and because their plan to conquer France was unimaginative and was eventually rejected in favor of one proposed by Erich von Manstein. Meanwhile, from September 1939 to June 1941, only Great Britain's Royal Navy and Royal Air Force (RAF) denied the Fuehrer the complete mastery of non-Soviet Europe, and even that was a near-run thing. Then, in July 1940, Hitler turned down a path that would end in a fatal mistake: he ordered the OKH (Brauchitsch and Halder) to initiate planning for the invasion of the Soviet Union.

CHAPTER II

THE PLANNERS

While General Erwin Rommel, the "Desert Fox," struggled to take Tobruk with fewer than two German divisions, 75 percent of the German Army secretly deployed in assembly areas in northern Norway, Finland, East Prussia, Poland, the Protectorate, and Romania for Hitler's invasion of the Soviet Union. The planning for this operation began in July 1940, and was initially entrusted to the highly capable Colonel Bernhard von Lossberg.

Bernhard Viktor Hans Wolfgang von Lossberg was born in the Berlin suburb of Wilmersdorf (referred to as Berlin-Wilmersdorf) on July 26, 1899. His father, Friedrich-Karl von Lossberg, was a war hero and one of the few men to earn the *Pour le Mérite* with Oak Leaves during World War I. (The *Pour le Mérite*, or "Blue Max," was Prussia's highest military order until the end of World War I.) He served as chief of staff of the 2nd and 6th Armies on the Western Front and retired as a general of infantry, commanding Group Command One (also sometimes translated as Army Group One) in Berlin in 1926.

Young Bernhard was educated in a variety of schools in Hanover, Charlottenburg, Danzig, Eisenach, and Stuttgart, and entered the service as a *Fahnenjunker* in the elite 2nd Foot Guards Regiment in July 1916. He was sent to the Eastern Front a year later and fought in Galicia, along the Sereth River, in the Battle of Riga in Estonia, and in the subsequent pursuit of Russian forces. He was seriously wounded on September 13, 1917, and received his commission 13 days later, in the hospital. He returned to active duty with the 2nd Foot Guards in January 1918 and was sent into action again in March, this time on the Western Front. He took part in the great Ludendorff Offensive and was wounded again on March 28, but remained with his regiment. A more serious wound on

April 7 landed him back in the hospital. He did not return to duty until late August, when he joined the staff of the General Quartermaster in Berlin—a rare and prized assignment indeed for a second lieutenant without General Staff training. He was still here when World War I ended on November 11, 1918.

As a result of his wounds, Lossberg had a distinct limp for the rest of his life. He was assigned to the 115th Infantry Regiment in July 1919, as the former Imperial Army (now called the *Uebergangsheer* or Transitional Army) downsized into the Reichsheer—the 100,000-man army allowed to Germany under the terms of the Treaty of Versailles, which ended World War I. He became part of the Prussian 5th Infantry Regiment at Stettin when it was activated on October 1, 1920. From 1923 to 1926, Lossberg commanded the regiment's signals platoon. He was promoted to first lieutenant on April 1, 1925. He became adjutant of the II Battalion, 5th Infantry Regiment (II/5th Infantry Regiment) in early 1926, and was transferred to the staff of the Commandant of Berlin in early 1929.

Lossberg remained in Berlin until 1936, officially serving on the staff of the 3rd Infantry Division (October 1, 1930) and of the Commandant of Berlin; in fact, he was undergoing clandestine General Staff training. From 1933 to 1935, he worked in the T 1 Department of the Troop Office, as the secret General Staff was called. This office was responsible for operational planning, which indicates that he was highly thought of by "the powers that be." He was, in fact, physically and intellectually imposing, and was viewed as both a talented staff officer and bridge player. He was promoted to captain on April 1, 1933.

Lossberg married Ella Schmidt (who was nine and a half years his junior) in Berlin on July 15, 1934. She gave him two sons. They moved to Bartenstein in northeast Wuerttemberg (in southwestern Germany), where Lossberg assumed command of the 14th Company of the 44th Infantry Regiment (11th Infantry Division) on October 6, 1936, despite the fact that he had been promoted to major on August 1. Strangely, for a future general, it was to be his highest and last command.

In July 1937, Major von Lossberg became Ib (Chief Supply Officer) of Wehrkreis I in Koenigsberg, East Prussia, but returned to Berlin in the spring of 1938 as a member of the 4th (Training) Department of the General Staff. In mid-August of that year, however, he was detached to the OKW' s Special

Staff W, which was involved in the transport of military equipment and war volunteers to the Condor Legion, which was fighting on Franco's side in the Spanish Civil War. He again excelled in this post and, as a result, was named deputy chief of the OKW's operations staff on April 1, 1939. He and his chief, Alfred Jodl, were deeply involved in planning the invasions of Denmark and Norway, which began on April 9, 1940. During this period, Lossberg ran afoul of Adolf Hitler for the first time.

The strategic key to the Norwegian campaign was the northernmost Norwegian port of Narvik. Although German forces under Major General Eduard Dietl seized the city on April 9, the Royal Navy quickly sank all ten of the German destroyers there and threatened Dietl's battle group with defeat or with internment in Sweden. For the first time, Adolf Hitler exhibited panic and indecision in a military situation. "The hysteria is frightful," Jodl reported in his diary. On April 14, the dictator ordered Dietl to evacuate Narvik, despite the lack of an imminent military threat. An ever-obedient General Keitel gave the coded message to Lossberg, who angrily refused to relay it to Dietl. Instead, he appealed to Jodl and then Brauchitsch, who signed an order (apparently drafted by Lossberg), which congratulated Dietl on his promotion to lieutenant general and added: "I am sure you will defend your position [i.e., Narvik] to the last man."[1] Lossberg, meanwhile, met with Jodl and tore up Hitler's original (and unsent) dispatch in front of the chief of operation's eyes.

Hitler, however, was still nervous, so he sent Lossberg to Oslo, Norway, to meet with General Nikolaus von Falkenhorst (the overall commander) and to observe the situation. Lossberg returned on April 22 and reported that the British had only landed 5,000 men in the northern sector. Hitler responded by nervously declaring how Falkenhorst should dispose his forces. The fearless lieutenant colonel contradicted him. He pointed out that every key position was in Falkenhorst's hands and that Hitler should leave operations to him—i. e., that the Fuehrer should mind his own business. Hitler resented being lectured to and shortly thereafter decreed that Lossberg not be allowed to come into his presence. Lossberg's estimation of the situation turned out to be completely accurate, however.

Despite Hitler's dislike for Lossberg, the colonel was nevertheless the first man selected to write a feasibility study vis-à-vis an invasion of the Soviet Union. Lossberg submitted a 30-page report in July 1940, which he code-named "Fritz," after his oldest son. Lossberg concluded that the primary objectives of the invasion should be in the north—i.e., against Leningrad and then Moscow. The key to success, Lossberg felt, would be the encirclement of the Soviet armies in the frontier areas by rapidly moving armored and mechanized units. He argued that the focal point of the battle should be in the north, because the Soviets would not abandon the Baltic region, which they had seized only a few months earlier.

All future planning for the invasion of the Soviet Union was based on the Lossberg Plan. Lossberg, however, did not provide for an offensive role for the German-Romanian forces to the south. Future planners quickly changed that.

Meanwhile, Halder delegated the task of producing another plan for the invasion to Colonel Hans von Greiffenberg and Lieutenant Colonel Gerhard Feyerabend.

Hans von Greiffenberg was born in Tschebiatkow, in the Buetow district of Pomerania (now the Bytow district of Poland) on October 12, 1893. He was educated in cadet schools and joined the Imperial Army as a second lieutenant in the 14th Infantry Regiment on January 20, 1914. World War I began less than eight months later. Greiffenberg spent the entire war with his regiment or in various hospitals, serving as a battalion or regimental adjutant. He fought in Belgium (where he was wounded on August 20) and in Russia (November 1914), where he was seriously wounded in December 1914. He did not rejoin his regiment until August 1915. The 14th Infantry returned to France the following month, and Greiffenberg fought at Verdun, Champagne, and the Lys. He also spent ten days as an acting battalion commander in June 1916. He was promoted to first lieutenant on August 18, 1917.

After the war, his division (the 4th Infantry) was sent to Kolberg, West Prussia, where it defended Germany's eastern border against the Poles. After serving as adjutant of the 7th Infantry Brigade (also of the 4th Infantry Division) from May 1919 to March 1920, he joined the Reichswehr as an orderly officer with the 4th Infantry Regiment, which headquartered at Kolberg (now Kolobrzeg, Poland). From October

1920, he was adjutant of the III Battalion at Neustettin (now Wejherowo, Poland) and the II Battalion at Deutsch Krone (now Walcz, Poland). On October 1, 1923, he was detached to the Headquarters, Wehrkreis II, at Stettin, where he began his General Staff training. Later, he served as a GSO in the Reich Defense Ministry (1926–28), then served a year detached to the Finnish Army (October 1928–October 1929), and the Spanish Army (October 1929–October 1930). After undergoing further training, he returned to the 4th Infantry Regiment as a company commander from October 1931 to August 1932. He was promoted to captain in 1925 and to major in 1932.

From August 1, 1932 to October 1, 1933, Greiffenberg was an exchange student and attended the U.S. Command and General Staff College at Fort Leavenworth, Kansas. Germany and the United States had made an agreement whereby they could exchange two students per year. The American school was considered so inferior to the War Academy in Berlin, however, that Germany did not exercise its option thereafter. The Americans, on the other hand, always sent two men to the German course. One of them was Lieutenant Colonel (later General) Albert C. Wedemeyer, who later commanded the U.S. China Theater.

After returning to the Fatherland, Greiffenberg spent another year in the Defense Ministry. He was promoted to lieutenant colonel on June 1, 1935, and was named commander of the I Battalion/103rd Infantry Regiment in Ohrdruf, Thueringen (Wehrkreis IV). He attended the short-lived Armed Forces Academy from October 1937 to February 1938, and was promoted to colonel on January 1, 1938. The following month, he was assigned to the T 4 (Army Training) Department, where he remained until October 3, 1938, when he became chief of the T 1 (Operations) Department of the General Staff. When Germany mobilized on August 26, 1939, however, Greiffenberg became a department head in the Operations Branch of the OKW. Halder nevertheless selected him, along with Lieutenant Colonel Gerhard Feyerabend, to draw up a plan to invade the Soviet Union.

Gerhard Feyerabend was born on April 29, 1898, in the Dopsattel District of East Prussia, near the provincial capital city of Koenigsberg. He was educated in the cadet schools and entered the service as a *Faehnrich* (senior officer cadet) in the East Prussian 82nd Field Artillery Regiment on March 29, 1916. He was in action in France by late June and fought in the Upper Alsace, on the Aisne, at St. Gobain, Picardy, the Aisne, the Marne, and Verdun. He was commissioned on December 5, 1916. He returned to East Prussia after the war, applied for the Reichsheer, and was assigned to the 1st Artillery Regiment in Koenigsberg in 1920. He remained here as a battery officer and battalion adjutant until 1929, when he was detached to the headquarters of the 1st Infantry Division (also in Koenigsberg) to begin his clandestine General Staff training. He later trained in Stettin, Berlin, and Munich, and was admitted into the General Staff on April 1, 1933—the same day he was promoted to captain. (He had been promoted to first lieutenant in 1925.)

Captain Feyerabend returned to Koenigsberg and served on the staff of Artillery Command I (1933–34), became Ia of the 1st Infantry Division (1934-35), was on the staff of Wehrkreis I (1935–36) and commanded a battery in the 1st Artillery Regiment (1936–37). He finally left East Prussia in October 1927 to become Ia of the 24th Infantry Division in Chemnitz, Saxony. After serving with the 24th Infantry in the Polish campaign, he was Ia of the General of Artillery at the OKH Headquarters in Zossen, a town about 30 miles south of Berlin (October 1939–January 1940), and, after a leave, was named Ia of the XXXX Motorized (later Panzer) Corps on February 5, 1940. He fought in Belgium and France, and was promoted to major (1936) and lieutenant colonel (March 1939), before being recalled to Zossen as a member of the operations department of the OKH. Here he assisted Greiffenberg in planning the invasion of the Soviet Union.

The Greiffenberg-Feyerabend plan was similar to Lossberg's, except that it called for a major thrust across the Ukraine to Kiev. The invasion, therefore, would have three major objectives: Leningrad, Moscow and Kiev.

Halder did not like the idea of sending a third thrust toward Kiev, so he ordered a third feasibility study, this one to be conducted by Major General Erich Marcks.

Erich Marcks was born in Schoeneberg, a suburb of western Berlin, on June 6, 1891. His father was a prominent history professor and Bismarck scholar at the University of Berlin. Young Erich studied law and philosophy at the University of Freiberg before joining the 9th Field Artillery Regiment as a *Fahnenjunker* on October 1, 1910. He was commissioned second lieutenant on December 19, 1911, and served with his unit in the invasion of Belgium, the Battle of the Marne, in the Aisne sector and in Champagne, and in the Battle of the Somme. Lieutenant Marcks was severely wounded in the face and bore the scars the rest of his life; his nose was particularly disfigured.

After his recovery, Marcks was transferred to staff work and became a member of the General Staff in 1917. Later, he was active in forming *Freikorps* (Free Corps) units to protect the Weimar Republic from unrest, and especially against leftists and Communists. He became press chief in the Armed Forces Ministry in 1929, and left the service in 1932 to become press chief for General Kurt von Schleicher's puppet chancellor, Franz von Papen. Later, when Schleicher was chancellor (1932–33), Marcks was his press secretary. (General Schleicher was succeeded by Hitler on January 30, 1933, and was murdered by the Gestapo in June 1934. Hitler, OKW, and the Nazis never fully trusted Marcks because of his association with Schleicher.)

Marcks rejoined the service in 1933 as a major and battalion commander in Muenster, and, in 1935, became chief of staff of Wehrkreis VIII (later VIII Corps), a post he held when the war broke out in 1939. He became chief of staff of the Eighteenth Army in late October 1939. After the fall of France, he was on detached duty in Berlin, where he authored the plan to invade the Soviet Union that would become the basis for the final form of Operation Barbarossa.

Marcks looked like the stereotype of a studious college professor, right down to his wire-rimmed glasses. He was, however, a highly capable General Staff officer. His final plan, ready on August 5, envisioned a campaign of two phases: First, the Soviet armies close to the frontier would be destroyed in battles of encirclement; then, the most valuable industrial regions in the Soviet Union would be occupied, including Leningrad, Moscow, and the Donetz Basin of the Ukraine. To accomplish this task, Marcks proposed that two army groups, North and South, be created. They would be divided by the Pripyat Marshes (a vast swamp 150 miles from north to south, and more than 300 miles long), and their mission would be to attain the line Archangel-Gorky-Rostov. Moscow, he stated, "constitutes the economic, political, and spiritual center of the U.S.S.R. Its capture would destroy the coordination of the Russian state."[2]

One of Germany's most solid and advanced strategic thinkers,

Marcks did not believe that the Soviet Union could be conquered in a single campaign—unlike Brauchitsch and Halder. He also expressed his fear of an Anglo-American-Soviet coalition and a two-front war. His concerns were ignored.

Halder accepted Marcks's basic ideas and turned the detailed planning over to Lieutenant General Friedrich Paulus, the new deputy chief of the General Staff for operations, on September 17.

Friedrich Wilhelm Ernst Paulus was born on the evening of September 23, 1890, in the parish of Breitenau-Gershagen, in the province of Hesse-Nassau, in southwestern Germany. Although he is often incorrectly cited as "von Paulus," he was not of the aristocracy; his father, in fact, was a bookkeeper in the civil service. He was "a man of the people," to use Third Reich jargon. He did, however, marry a Romanian countess and often put on aristocratic airs.

The future field marshal was educated at the Wilhelms-Gymnasium at Kassel. He graduated in 1909 and applied for a cadetship in the navy, but his application was rejected. He briefly studied law at the University of Munich before joining the 111th (3rd Baden) Infantry Regiment at Rastatt in 1910. He was commissioned *Leutnant* on October 18, 1911.

Paulus married Countess Elena "Coca" Rosetti-Solescu in 1912. She was beautiful, graceful, strong-willed and ambitious, especially for her husband. She gave him three children: Olga (born 1914) and twin sons, Friedrich and Alexander (1918). Both became captains. Friedrich was killed in action during World War II and Alexander was wounded during the Stalingrad campaign. When his father began working with the Russians in 1944, Alexander was arrested by the Nazis and spent the rest of the war in a detention camp.

When World War I began, Paulus was a battalion adjutant in the 3rd Baden. Later he was on the staff of the 2nd Prussian *Jaeger* (light infantry) Regiment (1915) and on the operations staff of the Alpine Corps (1917). He was promoted to first lieutenant in 1915 and to captain in 1918, and fought on the Eastern and Western Fronts and in Romania. After the war, he helped organize and apparently fought with *Freikorps Grenzschutz Ost* (Free Corps Border Guard East) in the Eastern Marchland.

Accepted into the Reichsheer, Captain Paulus was adjutant of the 14th

Infantry Regiment at Konstanz, in southern Baden, on the Swiss border. He began his clandestine General Staff training in Berlin in 1922. The following year he was on the General Staff of Group Command Two in Kassel. He was a GSO with Wehrkreis V in Stuttgart from 1924 to 1927, and remained there as a company commander in the 13th Infantry Regiment (1928-29).

Although his fitness reports noted that he lacked decisiveness, they praised his work as a General Staff officer. Paulus was, indeed, one of those men who was an excellent staff officer, but a poor to mediocre commander. This did not impede his advancement in the peacetime army at all. He was promoted to major (1929), lieutenant colonel (1933), colonel (1935), and major general (January 1, 1939). Meanwhile, he was appointed tactics (i.e., General Staff) instructor with Wehrkreis V (1930); commander of Motor Transport Section 3, an experimental panzer/ reconnaissance battalion (1934); chief of staff to the commander of motorized forces (General Oswald Lutz) in Berlin (1935); and chief of staff of the XVI Motorized Corps (1938).

When Germany mobilized for World War II on August 26, 1939, Paulus was named chief of staff of the Tenth (later Sixth) Army. Here he worked for the brutal but dynamic Walter von Reichenau. The two made a very effective team: Reichenau hated paperwork and Paulus, who hated dirt, might have been chained to his desk at headquarters. They were very successful in Poland, Belgium, and France, leading to Reichenau's promotion to field marshal and Paulus's promotion to lieutenant general on July 19, 1940. Shortly thereafter, in September 1940, Paulus was named Oberquartiermeister I (O Qu I), deputy chief of the General Staff for operations. He carried out a multitude of duties in this post, but his most important job was to conduct a strategic study for the invasion of the Soviet Union.

Paulus retained Marcks's basic concepts, but added a third army group and specified that three major thrusts take place: Army Group North to Leningrad, Army Group Center to Moscow, and Army Group South to Kiev. Moscow was to remain the primary objective.

After Paulus completed his study, the chiefs of staff of the three army groups then in existence, A, B, and C, were ordered to make their own studies. They were General of Infantry Georg von Sodenstern, General of Infantry Hans von Salmuth, and Lieutenant General Kurt Brennecke, respectively.

Kurt Brennecke was born on December 16, 1891, in Ringelheim, Lower Saxony, in the foothills of the Harz Mountains. He joined the Imperial Army as a *Fahnenjunker* in 1910 and was commissioned second lieutenant in the 15th Infantry Regiment (of the 13th Infantry Division) on August 18, 1911. By the spring of 1914, he was adjutant of the II Battalion. He fought on the Western Front in WWI in 1914, was seriously wounded in October, and did not return to active duty until June 2, 1915, when he was named regimental adjutant. He was given command of a battalion in the 353rd Infantry Regiment at Lake Drisvisty (on the Lithuania-White Russia border) 11 days before the armistice.

Brennecke served as staff commandant (headquarters company commander) of the ad hoc Corps von Bergmann, and adjutant of Location Command Duesseldorf in 1919. Accepted into the Reichswehr, he was assigned to the 17th Infantry Regiment in Brunswick as the regimental signals officer (1920–23). He then commanded a company in the same regiment (1923–24), spent a year with the Prussian 2nd Cavalry Regiment at Osterode and Allenstein (1924–25) and became welfare officer on the staff of the 2nd Infantry Division at Stettin (1925– 30). Apparently he also underwent his secret General Staff training at this time. After a tour of duty in the Defense Ministry in Berlin (1930–33), he was assigned to the 2nd Motor Transport Battalion at Stettin. He commanded the battalion from January 1934 to May 1935.

Brennecke was chief of staff of Wehrkreis VII in Munich from 1935 to 1938. He became chief of staff of Army Group Six at Hanover in late 1939. This HQ became Fourth Army when the Third Reich mobilized on August 26, 1939. On October 25, 1940, he assumed the post of chief of staff of Leeb's Army Group C, which became Army Group North when Germany invaded Russia. He was promoted to first lieutenant (1915), captain (1918), major (1930), lieutenant colonel (1933), colonel (1935), major general (August 1, 1939), and lieutenant general (August 1, 1940).

Hans von Salmuth was born in Metz (then a German garrison town) on November 21, 1888, the son of Anton von Salmuth, who retired as a captain. Hans entered the service as an officer cadet in 1907 and was commissioned in the 3rd Grenadier Guards Regiment in 1909. During World War I, he fought in Belgium and France, and served as a battalion adjutant and then as a General Staff officer. He joined the Reichswehr and became a company commander in the Prussian 1st Infantry Regiment at Koenigsberg (1920–22). He served on the General Staff of the 1st Infantry Division at Koenigsberg (1922–23), on the General Staff of Artillery Command I (1923–24) and was a company commander in the elite Prussian 9th Infantry Regiment at Potsdam (1927–30).

He returned to the Staff, 1st Infantry Division (1930-33) and became Ia of the 2nd Infantry Division in Stettin, Pomerania on December 1, 1933. Later he became chief of staff of Wehrkreis II (also in Stettin) (1934–35) and was chief of staff of Army Group One in Berlin from 1937 to 1939. He served as chief of staff of Army Group North (later B) during the invasions of Poland and France (1939–40), where he performed brilliantly. He was promoted to general of infantry effective August 1, 1940. Earlier he had been promoted to first lieutenant (December 1914), captain (August 1916), major (1928), lieutenant colonel (1932), colonel (1934), major general (1937), and lieutenant general, to date from August 1, 1939.

Georg von Sodenstern was born in the Hessian city of Kassel on November 15, 1889. Educated in cadet schools, he joined the Imperial Army as a *Faehnrich* on March 13, 1909, and was commissioned in the 62nd Infantry Regiment on January 27, 1910. He fought on the Western Front during World War I, served in the Reichsheer, and chief of staff of Army Group Two in late 1938. He replaced Erich von Manstein as chief of staff of Rundstedt's Army Group A on February 6, 1940. He held this post until October 1, 1940, when he became chief of staff of OB West in Paris. Rundstedt wanted him back, however, and he was appointed chief of staff of Army Group South on June 10, 1941. He was promoted to lieutenant colonel on October 1, 1932, colonel on September 1, 1934, major general on March 1, 1938, lieutenant general on February 1, 1940, and to general of infantry on August 1, 1940. Sodenstern had a reputation for talking excessively, but he knew about the anti-Hitler conspiracy as early as 1938 and kept his mouth shut.

Salmuth and Brennecke produced plans similar to that of Paulus. General von Sodenstern, who was very pessimistic about the prospects for the invasion, advocated a rapid and immediate advance on Moscow, which was to have priority over even the destruction of the armies in the frontier. His plan had no influence on future OKH planning.

Paulus's final study (which included input from the work of Brennecke and Salmuth) concluded that, if Germany was to defeat Russia, the Wehrmacht could not allow the Red Army to retreat into the interior: it must be decisively defeated in or near the frontier zones. It called for opening gaps at critical points, battles of encirclement with the panzer forces forming the spearheads, and a principle thrust north of the Pripyat Marshes toward one vital objective: Moscow. The campaign must be concluded by late October, Paulus warned in writing, before the Russian rainy season began. His report, however, failed to convince Hitler that the capture of Moscow was of critical importance.

Brauchitsch and Halder presented the Paulus plan to Hitler on December 5. Hitler had only one major objection to it, but it was one of the greatest significance: he wanted to defeat the Russians on the northern and southern wings first and take the Ukraine and Leningrad. "Moscow," he said, "is of no great importance."[3] He was more concerned with capturing the Baltic States and the agricultural and industrial complexes to the south. The loss of the Ukraine and its Donetz Industrial Basin, he believed, would wreck the Soviet economy and cause the people to turn against the Communists. Then, he felt, the capture of Moscow would be an easy matter.

The OKH generals did not protest when Hitler changed the fundamental focus of their plan. They had learned that remonstrating with the Fuehrer did no good; nevertheless, they continued to regard Moscow as the main objective, for both political and military reasons. It was, after all, the transportation and communications hub of the Soviet Union. They believed that a thrust toward Moscow would compel the Red Army to oppose it with most of its divisions, which would give the German Army an opportunity to encircle and destroy them.

Apparently Halder and von Brauchitsch felt that, once the campaign was under way, events would dictate the correct course of action. "A conspiracy of silence descended on the subject," Cooper wrote.[4] According to Major General (later General of Artillery) Walter Warlimont, the deputy chief of operations at the OKW: "It later became known that their reasoning was that, in time, the course of the campaign would compel even Hitler to go back to the original army concept. This was, to a certain extent, taking the easy way out and it proved to be no more than self-deception."[5] As a result, the campaign would begin with the Fuehrer and his senior generals divided over the issues of what was the major objective of the invasion. The seeds of disaster had been sown.

One of the people who surprisingly opposed the invasion was Hitler's notorious yes-man, Field Marshal Keitel.

Wilhelm Keitel was born on the family estate of Helmscherode, in the province of Hanover, on September 22, 1882. Although he would have preferred to spend his life as a farmer, his family's farm was not large enough to support his and his father's family, so he joined the army as a *Fahnenjunker* in the 46th Field Artillery Regiment in 1901. He became regimental adjutant in 1908. In September 1914, he was severely wounded by a shell splinter on the Western Front during World War I. Upon recovery, he briefly resumed his duties as adjutant before being given command of a battery in November 1914. He held this post until March 1915, when he posted to the General Staff of the X Reserve Corps. He became Ia of the 19th Reserve Division in 1916, and fought in France, Russia, Flanders, and on the Meuse. In late 1917, he was named chief of operations of the Naval Corps in Flanders, a post he held at the end of the war. He then served as the chief supply officer of the II Corps (1919), tactics instructor at the Cavalry School (1919–22), and commander of a battery in the 6th Artillery Regiment at Wolfenbuettel (1922–25).

Although later known as "Lakeitel" (*lakei* means "lackey" in German), he definitely had organizational talents. Except for a troop commander tour as leader of the II/6th Artillery Regiment at Minden (1927–29), he served in the Defense Ministry from 1925 to 1934, rising to the head of the Organizational Branch of the army. After serving as Artillery Commander III and deputy commander of the 3rd Infantry Division (1933–34) and commander of the 22nd Infantry Division in Bremen (1934–35), Keitel returned to Berlin in October 1935 as head of the Armed Forces Office of the War Ministry. When the war minister, Field Marshal von Blomberg, fell from power in February 1938, the position of war minister was abolished and Keitel became commander-in-chief of the High Command of the Armed Forces (OKW) on February 2, 1938, precisely because he did not have a strong personality. He nevertheless rose rapidly in rank, from major in 1929 to field marshal on July 19, 1940—seven promotions in 11 years. Throughout his adulthood, he was intellectually dominated by his more ambitious wife. His younger brother Bodewin (1888–1953) became a general of infantry and was head of the powerful Army Personnel Office from 1938 to 1942. As a sign of his displeasure with Wilhelm Keitel, Hitler sacked Bodewin in September 1942. Later, the younger Keitel commanded Wehrkreis XX (March 1943–late 1944).

Rather than risk another scathing dressing down, such as Hitler had given him in October 1939, when he opposed invading France in the winter of 1939/40, Keitel sent him a written memorandum in August 1940. Hitler, who now surrounded himself only with yes-men, summoned him to his office and gave him a vicious reprimand. Deeply wounded, Keitel suggested that the Fuehrer find an OKW chief whose judgment he trusted more. Hitler flew into a rage and heaped a torrent of abuse on Keitel's head. He did not have the right to resign, the dictator shouted, but would serve until he had no further use for him. The humiliated field marshal left the room without saying a word. Now he saw clearly part of the price he would have to pay for accepting promotions he did not deserve and a position for which he was intellectually not qualified. His reaction to this impossible situation was to submit completely; he would carry out the will of the Fuehrer, no matter what entailed.[6]

In May 1941, Keitel signed the infamous Commissar Order, in which he commanded that German soldiers shoot Communist Party officials immediately after they were captured, without courts-martial or trials of any kind. Several generals protested against this criminal order, which directed them to shoot unarmed prisoners of war, but Keitel insisted that it be obeyed to the letter. This order, which originated with Hitler, can be traced to a speech he made to his commanders on March 30, in which he ordered that all Soviet officials, civilian or military, were to be shot when captured, even if they surrendered. In Russia, he said, the German soldier was not to be bound by the ordinary rules of war. This speech set the tone for one of the cruelest conflicts in modern history.

FLAWED INTELLIGENCE

Another major weakness in the German plan was the fact that its intelligence was faulty. This statement does not apply to tactical intelligence—i.e., that of the immediate combat zone—but it most certainly applies to strategic intelligence. German aerial reconnaissance and short-range radio interception kept the German ground commanders well informed as to the Soviet units located at or near the border. The vast interior of the Soviet Union, however, was a mystery to Halder's planners.

While the Soviet intelligence and espionage network formed a clear picture of the Wehrmacht's intentions and a fair idea of its dispositions, German military intelligence failed disastrously. Two German military organizations were responsible for obtaining data on the Soviet armed forces: O Qu IV, the military intelligence staff of the Army High Command, headed by Major General Gerhard Matzky, and Admiral Canaris's Abwehr.

Gerhard Matzky, who became director of O Qu IV, army intelligence, on January 5, 1941, was born at Kuestrin/Oder in Brandenburg Province on March 19, 1894. His father, Rudolf Matzky, later retired from the Imperial Army as a major. Young Matzky joined the Kaiser's Army as a *Fahnenjunker* in the Upper Silesian 63rd Infantry Regiment on March 26, 1912, and was commissioned on August 18, 1913.

Except for the first four months of 1917, when it was on the Russian Front, the 63rd Infantry spent the entire war in the West as part of the 12th Infantry Division. It fought no major battles in Russia, but was in extremely heavy fighting north of the Somme, where the 12th Infantry faced a major British offensive alone and suffered 61.5 percent casualties.

Matzky survived this battle and ended the war as a first lieutenant, with both grades of the Iron Cross and the Wounded Badge in Black. Promoted to captain in 1923, he was commander of a company in the Prussian 2nd Infantry Regiment at Allenstein (now Olsztyn, Poland) in 1931. Promoted to major the following year, he became a lieutenant colonel in 1934 and a full colonel in 1937. He joined the military attaché branch and from September 15, 1938 to November 30, 1940, was military attaché to Toyko. He then returned to Germany and on January 5, 1941, became O Qu IV in the High Command of the Army, controlling the attaché branch, as well as the Foreign Armies East and Foreign Armies West departments.

O Qu IV was divided into two main sections: Foreign Armies West under Lieutenant Colonel Ulrich Liss and Foreign Armies East under Lieutenant Colonel Eberhard Kinzel. These titles are somewhat misleading, since Liss was responsible for gathering information concerning the armies of Western Europe exclusively, while Kinzel was responsible for the rest of the world, including Scandinavia, China, Japan, the United States, and South America.

Gathering intelligence concerning the Red Army was only a minor part of Kinzel's duties prior to 1941. Since the OKH had not designated the Soviet Union as a major potential target, Kinzel's section devoted little time or money to it. Even less was done in 1939 and 1940, because Hitler had forbidden either the Abwehr or the OKH to collect and evaluate data on the Red Army. Finally, Kinzel was not particularly well qualified for his duties. He was an infantry officer by trade and not an intelligence expert; he had no specialized knowledge of the Soviet Union; and he could not speak Russian. Canaris and his Abwehr performed equally miserably.

Eberhard Kinzel was born in Berlin-Friedenau on October 18, 1897. He joined the army as a war volunteer in the 20th Infantry Regiment. Sent to France, he became an officer cadet in 1915 and commanded a mortar platoon at Verdun, where he was wounded in May. He returned to the field in July and was promoted to second lieutenant later that month. In April 1917, he was promoted to company commander, and in August was an orderly on the staff of the II Battalion. He ended the war on the staff of the III Battalion. In 1919, he joined the Freikorps von Oven, where he fought Communist insurrectionists and rose to battalion adjutant. He joined the Reichsheer in 1920 and was sent to Stettin, where he served with the Prussian 5th Infantry Regiment, and was adjutant of its training battalion from 1923 to 1926. Selected for General Staff training, he worked in the Defense Ministry from 1929 to 1933, when he became assistant military attaché to Warsaw (1933–36). After spending a year with the 66th Infantry Regiment at Magdeburg (1936–37), he became Ia of the 19th Infantry Division at Hanover (1937–38). He became chief of the Foreign Armies East Department at the OKH on November 10, 1938. He was promoted to captain (1932), major (1936), lieutenant colonel (1939), and colonel on February 1, 1941.

The man who was to head the Abwehr, Wilhelm Franz Canaris, was born in Aplerbek, a village in the Ruhr near Dortmund, on New Year's Day, 1887, into an upper class family of businessmen, coal mine executives and industrialists. He was a taciturn man of below average height and unmilitary bearing, which led people to underestimate him. He was described as "inscrutable . . . volatile and abrupt . . . quiet . . . reserved and uncommunicative," and he had few friends.[7] Well educated, he had a talent for languages and became fluent in French and Spanish, good in English, and fair in Russian.

He broke with his family tradition due to his love for the sea and entered the navy as an officer cadet (*Seekadett*) on April 1, 1905. He trained on the cruiser-corvette *Stein*, the toughest training ship in the Kaiser's Navy, and at the Kiel Naval Academy. He became an ensign on September 28, 1908. He served primarily in torpedo boats and cruisers prior to World War I, but was transferred to South America, where he set up an effective spy network for the German Navy. Canaris was on the light cruiser *Dresden* from 1911 until the war began. The *Dresden* was the sole survivor of the Battle of the Falkland Islands, but the British finally ran it down in the Pacific Ocean and sank it in March 1915. Canaris was interned in Chile but escaped and, after a number of adventures, successfully made his way back to Germany. He later set up a naval intelligence network in the Mediterranean, where he was captured and severely beaten by the Italians. He nevertheless managed to escape before he could be executed. He later commanded a torpedo boat, a transport submarine (which doubled as a minelayer), and two U-boats, with which he sank three enemy ships (16,174 tons) and severely damaged another.

During the "war after the war," Canaris served with the Freikorps and was on the personal staff of Gustav Noske, the tough and dynamic defense minister, where he helped a Freikorps assassin to escape. In 1920, he was accepted into the Reichswehr and was assigned to the staff of Naval Station Baltic Sea (1920–23). He was successively first officer on the cruiser *Berlin* (1923–24), on the staff of the Naval Command (1924–28), first officer of the battleship *Silesia* (*Schlessien*) (1928–30), chief of staff of Naval Station North Sea (1930–32), commandant of the *Silesia* (1932–34), and commandant of the naval base of Swinemuende (1934–35). On January 2, 1935, he became chief of the Abwehr, a post he held for nine years. He was promoted to lieutenant, j.g. (1910), lieutenant (1915), lieutenant commander (1924), commander (1929), captain (1931), rear admiral (May 1, 1935), vice admiral (April 1, 1938), and admiral (January 1, 1940).

Canaris was generally "over his head" as chief of the Abwehr, and German intelligence estimates during World War II were generally wrong. In the airborne invasion of Crete, for example, Admiral Canaris made several serious mistakes when personally took charge of the military intelligence phase of the operation. His estimate of the number of British troops on the island was only a third of the actual total. He assured General of Paratroopers Kurt Student (commander of the XI Fliegerkorps) and the other planners that they could expect little resistance on the island, and his spies informed him that the Cretans would probably welcome the paratroopers with open arms. In fact, the natives actively supported the British and even killed wounded German paratroopers with axes and pitchforks.

The aerial reconnaissance reports were also generally wrong. Many decoy anti-aircraft sites, armed with wooden guns, were reported as the real sites, while the real positions, which were very well camouflaged, went undetected. Finally, Canaris stated that the British "Tommies" (including the Australians and the New Zealanders) were "demoralized" and "wouldn't show much fight."[8] They fought like tigers.

These mistakes cost the XI Fliegerkorps more than 6,000 casualties out of 25,000 men—one-fourth of the total engaged. Crete was the graveyard of the German parachute corps. Later, the Abwehr also seriously underestimated the strength of the Red Army and the quality of its tanks. Stalin had more than twice the number of divisions the Germans thought he had.

The military intelligence professionals were not the only people who submitted estimates on the potential of the Soviet armed forces. Ernst-August Koestring, the military attaché to Moscow, Hans Krebs, his deputy, and others did as well. Unfortunately for the Wehrmacht, most of them were as wide of the mark concerning Soviet potential, as was the OKH and the Abwehr.

Ernst-August Koestring, born in Moscow, Russia, on June 20, 1876, was a true Russian expert. He was raised in St. Petersburg and became fluent in the Russian language early in life. He eventually returned to East

Prussia, where he joined the army in 1895 as a one-year volunteer in the 4th *Ulan* (Lancer) Regiment at Thorn. He was discharged from active duty in 1896 but remained active in the reserves and earned a reserve commission in 1898. He did not return to active duty until 1900, when he joined the 5th Cuirassier Regiment at Riesenburg, East Prussia.

Koestring was on the staff of the Military Riding Institute (1909–11) and was adjutant and tactics instructor at the Officers Riding School at Paderborn when World War I broke out. He immediately joined the staff of the XX Corps at Allenstein, East Prussia, and served in East Prussia, Poland, the Ukraine, Russia, and Turkey. He was adjutant of the XX Corps (1915), adjutant of the Eighth Army (1915), adjutant of Army Group Scholtz (1915–16), and orderly to General von Seeckt with the Austrian Twelvth Army. In this post he was seriously wounded in the head on October 6, 1916, and did not return to duty until December 1917. He became adjutant to the chief of the General Staff of the Turkish Field Army (again under General von Seeckt). He served with the Prussian War Ministry for two months before becoming German liaison officer to the Ukrainian War Ministry on September 1, 1918. He held this post until the end of the war. Meanwhile, he was promoted (from second lieutenant of reserves) to second lieutenant (1901), first lieutenant (1910), and *Rittmeister* (captain of cavalry) in 1913.

Koestring commanded a battalion in the 76th Landwehr Infantry Regiment from November 1918 to March 1919, when he joined the cavalry department in the Prussian War Ministry. He was a foreign armies advisor with the Defense Ministry (1919–22), served with the 16th Cavalry Regiment at Langensalza, Thuringia (1922–24), and commanded the regiment's 4th Squadron (1924–25). He rejoined General von Seeckt as adjutant to the chief of the Army Command in Berlin in 1925.

In early 1927, Koestring commanded the 10th Cavalry Regiment at Zuellichau, Brandenburg/Neumark (now Sulechow, Poland) from 1927 to 1931. He was (secret) military attaché to Moscow from early 1931 until March 31, 1933, when he retired. Meanwhile, he was promoted to major (1922), lieutenant colonel (1927), colonel (1930), and honorary major general (March 11, 1933).

Koestring was recalled to active duty on August 1, 1935, in his former position as military attaché to Moscow. He was promoted to major general (August 1, 1935), lieutenant general (August 1, 1937), and general of cavalry September 1, 1940.

Hans Krebs was born in Helmstedt, Brunswick (*Braunschweig*) on March 4, 1898. He joined the Imperial Army on September 3, 1914, a month after World War I began. He served with the 10th Jaeger Battalion and with the 78th Infantry Regiment, where he fought in Belgium and France. From December 1914 to March 1915, he attended the *Fahnenjunker* course at Doeberitz and a 30-day infantry course at Muensterlager. He then returned to his unit, which was now on the Eastern Front, and was assigned to the regiment's machine gun company, where he remained until July 2, when he was severely wounded. He returned to duty in August and remained in machine gun units until March 1917, and briefly commanded a company. Meanwhile, he was promoted to second lieutenant on June 18, 1915.

Krebs remained with the 78th Infantry until the end of the war, fighting in Galicia (Poland) and in France, including the battles in Aisne, Champagne, on the Meuse, in the Battle of Picardy, and on the Somme. He remained in the Reichsheer and was assigned to the Bavarian 20th Infantry Regiment from October 1919 to September 1920. He transferred to the Prussian-Brunswick 17th Infantry Regiment in Brunswick in 1920 and remained with it until 1923, when he joined the staff of the 6th Infantry Division at Muenster. He commanded a company in the 17th Infantry from 1924 to 1928, when he began his secret General Staff training. He was attached to the T 3 Department (the foreign armies office) of the Defense Ministry in 1931, and learned Russian. He also took a trip to Russia and the Far East. He was named assistant military attaché to Moscow in 1933. A year later, he was given command of a company in Infantry Regiment Gumbinnen, which was stationed in Gumbinnen, East Prussia (now Gusev, Russia). He became chief of operations of the 24th Infantry Division at Chemnitz, Saxony, on October 15, 1935.

Krebs joined the General Staff in Berlin in mid-October 1937 as Ia of the 11th Department (O Qu II), which dealt with service schools and officer training programs. He remained there until October 6, 1939, when he went into Fuehrer Reserve. He did not return to active duty until December 15, when he became chief of staff of the VII Corps. He fought in Belgium and France, but on October 1, 1940, returned to his old job as assistant military attaché to Moscow. In the meantime, he had been promoted to first lieutenant (1925), captain (1931), major (1936), lieutenant colonel (February 1, 1939), and colonel (October 1, 1940).

The OKH was not impressed with what little it knew about the Red Army. It had made a poor impression in Poland, an even worse one in Finland, and Koestring and his deputy, Colonel Krebs, expressed low opinions of it. The Soviets, however, through their police state and totalitarian government, had been very successful in blocking the flow of information out of their country. Encouraged by their government, most Soviet citizens were unfriendly to and suspicious of both strangers and foreigners. In addition, the travel of foreigners within the Soviet Union was very restricted. Some information could be gained from radio interception, but this was limited by the range of the receivers and by the fact that the Red Army had few radios, so it relied on telephone or telegraph cables instead. The range of the aircraft also limited the value of aerial reconnaissance.

As a result, the Germans were able to obtain a good idea of the dispositions of Soviet troops in the border zones, but had almost no idea of what to expect in the interior. It had almost no knowledge of the Soviet strategic reserves, had no grasp of the extent of the Soviet industrial complex, and no idea of the ability of the Soviet Union's economy to sustain a major war effort. All of this resulted in a number of seriously flawed intelligence estimates.

In late 1940, Hermann Goering asked General of Infantry Georg Thomas, the head of the OKW's Economic and Armament Office (Wi Ru Amt), to produce an intelligence estimate on the military-industrial capabilities of the Soviet Union.

Georg Thomas was born in Forst in the Lausitz District of Brandenburg on February 20, 1890. The son of a factory owner, he had an interest in economics and a background that served him well later in life. He joined the army as a *Fahnenjunker* in the 63rd Infantry Regiment on September 2, 1908, was commissioned second lieutenant on January 27, 1910, and served in World War I, where he was a battalion and regimental adjutant on the Western Front (1914–17). He served as a General Staff officer in

1917 and 1918, also in the West. After the war, he was liaison officer between the Reich and East Prussian provincial commissioners in the East Prussian Plebiscite Area (1919–20). After serving as a company commander in the Prussian 2nd Infantry Regiment at Allenstein (1922–24), he served on the staff of Wehrkreis I at Koenigsberg (1922–24), the General Staff of the 4th Infantry Division at Dresden (1924–27), and the Army Weapons Office in the Reich Defense Ministry in Berlin (1927–34).

He was chief of staff of the Weapons Office from 1930 to 1935, when he became chief of the Economics Office Group at the OKH. In 1938, this position was renamed the Defense Economy and Armaments Office and became part of the OKW. Thomas was promoted to lieutenant colonel (1932), colonel (1934), major general (January 1, 1938), lieutenant general (January 1, 1940), and general of infantry (August 1, 1940).

Thomas was also a member of the board of directors of Kontinentale Oel AG, an oil company whose purpose was to exploit petroleum reserves in the occupied countries, and served on the board of *Reichswerke Hermann Goering* which, among other things, was an iron and steel company. He was one of the very few German officers who opposed the invasion of Poland in 1939, not for moral reasons, but because he did not believe that Germany could win the war economically. Unknown to Goering and the Nazis was the fact that he was a member of the anti-Hitler conspiracy and had been part of the planning for the military coup against the Fuehrer in 1938.

Thomas's intelligence estimate was based mainly upon guesswork and projections from out-of-date information. Thomas estimated that, if Germany could conquer European Russia (excluding the Urals), it would eliminate 75 percent of all of the Soviet armaments industry. This report implied that the loss of the industrial areas in and around Leningrad, Moscow, the Ukraine, and the Donets Basin would finish the Soviet Union as a military power. It grossly underestimated the value of the Soviet industrial belts in the Urals and in Asia, including Sverdlovsk, Magnitogorsk, Perm in the Urals, and several large complexes in Asia along the Trans-Siberian Railway, including Omsk, Novosibirsk, Tomsk, Krasnoyarsk, Irkutsch, and others. In addition, there were several major concentrations in the southern Soviet Union, including Ashkhabad,

Samarkand, Tashkent, and Alma Ata. Unfortunately for the Wehrmacht, this report seems to have been used to form the basis of German economic strategic planning.

German estimates on the size and capabilities of the Red Army were no less erroneous. On July 22, 1940, Halder estimated that the Soviets had 50 to 75 divisions.[9] In August, General Marcks estimated that the Red Army had 151 infantry divisions, 32 cavalry divisions, and 38 motorized brigades, of which 96 infantry divisions, 23 cavalry divisions, and 28 motorized brigades were arrayed against Germany.[10] At the beginning of the campaign, however, OKH estimated that the Red Army had 200 divisions. Within six weeks, it was discovered that it had at least 360.[11]

In addition, the German General Staff did not even know the T-34 tank existed, had never heard of the super-heavy KV tanks, and had no knowledge of the terrifying multiple-barrel rocket launchers the soldiers would nickname "Stalin's pipe organs." Their estimates on the number of Soviet tanks were very low. In the mid-1930s, Guderian had been ridiculed by the senior generals for estimating that the Soviets had 10,000 tanks, and General Beck even accused him of exaggerating and spreading alarm. Guderian's estimates were, in fact, conservative. The Soviets had 24,000 tanks available when Operation Barbarossa began and enough industrial capacity to produce 1,000 more each month. German industry only produced 2,800 tanks throughout 1941.[12]

Luftwaffe intelligence estimates were also wrong. The Luftwaffe military intelligence department was, in fact, almost always wrong. It was headed by Hermann Goering's personal friend, Josef (Joseph) Schmid, who was the most colossal failure of all the intelligence officers.

Joseph "Beppo" Schmid was born in Goeggingen near Augsburg in southwestern Bavaria on September 24, 1901. A strong right-wing German nationalist, he missed World War I because of his age, but joined the Freikorps von Epp as a volunteer in February 1919 and served until 1921, putting down Communist and leftist rebellions. Here he obviously impressed Major General Ritter Franz von Epp, who used his influence on Schmid's behalf; he was allowed to enter the army as a *Fahnenjunker* in the 19th Infantry Regiment on April 13, 1921, despite the fact that he had not fought in the Great War. He underwent officer training at the War Schools in Munich and Ohrdruf (1922–24), met Hermann Goering, and took part in the Beer Hall Putsch on the side of the Nazis in November 1923. Because he had not yet achieved prominence, and was just a foot soldier in the crowd, Schmid was never punished for this, even though General von Seeckt, the commander-in-chief of the army, closed the Infantry School at Munich and moved it to Doeberitz as punishment. (Although sympathetic to the nationalists in general, Seeckt, whose wife was Jewish, had no use for the Nazis.)

Beppo Schmid was commissioned second lieutenant on December 1, 1924, and spent more than eight years (January 1, 1925–September 30, 1933) as a platoon leader in the 21st Infantry Regiment at Nuremberg. He was promoted to first lieutenant in 1928. His career, however, took a major leap forward in 1933, when he scored in the upper 15 percent in his Wehrkreis exam and was selected for General Staff training. He was promoted to captain in 1934, graduated from the War Academy on June 30, 1935 and, thanks to his friend Hermann Goering, was transferred to the Luftwaffe the next day. His rise was rapid thereafter: major (1936), lieutenant colonel (1938), and colonel (July 19, 1940). He was initially assigned to the operations department of the General Staff of the Luftwaffe and was named chief intelligence officer of the air force on January 1, 1938.

"Beppo Schmid was a complete wash-out as an intelligence officer, the most important job of all," General of Fighters Adolf Galland told his interrogators in 1945. [13] Milch agreed, stating that Schmid "was a man who trimmed his sails to the wind for fear of Goering. Besides which he wasn't an airman and didn't understand the significance of the reports he received." [14] Unlike most intelligence officers, who tend to be a pessimistic lot and overestimate the strength of their opponent, Schmid consistently underestimated the strength and production capacity of Germany's enemies, especially that of the United States and the Soviet Union. He usually confirmed the overly optimistic views of Goering and his chief of staff, Hans Jeschonnek. His underestimation of the RAF contributed to the defeat of the Luftwaffe in the Battle of Britain and also led the Luftwaffe leadership into believing that the Soviet invasion would be much easier than it actually was.

During his long tenure as chief of intelligence (January 1, 1938 until November 9, 1942), Schmid did nothing to improve the low quality of the air force intelligence service. Galland later wrote that the most so-phisticated piece of technical equipment the air force used, up until 1944, "was a pair of binoculars. The personnel consisted of some old reservists of the intelligence battalions, pensioned policemen, unfit men, or over-age civil servants . . . and a horde of female assistants."[15]

General Schmid's branch placed the strength of the Red Air Force at 8,000 airplanes, three-quarters of which were in European Russia. Actually, the Soviets had 10,000 aircraft in the western areas alone, and at least 3,000 in the East; furthermore, they were supported by an average production of 1,131 per month.[16]

The only marginally prominent officer to produce an intelligence estimate that was even close to correct was Colonel Heinrich Aschen-brenner, the air attaché to Moscow.

Heinrich Aschenbrenner was born in Krankenhagen, near the village of Rinteln in Lower Saxony, on July 8, 1895. He enlisted in the army when World War I broke out and was assigned to the Hanover-Brunswick 164th Infantry Regiment of the 20th Infantry Division. He fought in France (1914), Galicia on the Eastern Front (1915), France again (1916), back to Russia (1916), and in France a third time (1916). He was promoted rapidly to corporal, sergeant, and second lieutenant of reserves—all within 23 days in May 1915. He became a platoon leader and was a company commander in late 1916, when he was accepted for flight training. He was a pilot in the 2nd Combat Wing on the Western Front in 1918 and was promoted to second lieutenant in the active Officers' Corps in October. This influenced his selection for retention in the Reichswehr in 1919. He was also wounded at least once during the war and earned both grades of the Iron Cross.

Aschenbrenner served as a platoon leader in the 20th Motor Transport Battalion (1919–20), platoon leader in the West Prussian 3rd Infantry Regiment at Deutsch-Eylau (now Ilawa, Poland) (1920–21), and company officer in the 1st Signal Battalion at Koenigsberg (1921–26). He was promoted to first lieutenant in 1925 and officially retired from the army in September 1926. Actually, he went to the secret German air force base in Lipezk, U.S.S.R., where he was an instructor in radio communications, night (instrument) flying, and bombing. He returned to Germany in September 1929, officially returned to active duty, and was signals officer for the fortress of Kuestrin from 1929 to 1931. Promoted to captain in 1930, he retired again (this time for real) on September 30, 1931, only to be recalled to active duty in the secret Luftwaffe as a flight instructor in Brunswick on October 1, 1933.

He soon became an office group director for the technical development of communications equipment in the technical office of the Air Ministry (1933-35). He commanded the instruction battalion at the Air Signals School at Halle/Salle from October 1935 to February 1937, when he became commander of the Air Signals Instruction and Test Battalion at Koethen, Saxony-Anhalt, on March 1, 1937. A year later (April 1, 1938), he became commander of the Air Signals School and Test Regiment, also at Koethen. He was named signals leader of the 8th Special Purposes Regional Air Command when the war broke out but was sent to the Soviet Union on October 1, 1939, as air attaché at the German Embassy in Moscow. He was, meanwhile, promoted to major (January 1, 1935), to lieutenant colonel (March 1, 1937), and colonel (June 1, 1939).

Aschenbrenner was able to convince the Soviets to show him more than they showed to anyone else. A few Luftwaffe experts, led by Aschenbrenner, were allowed to visit six secret aircraft manufacturing plants in the Urals (in the interior of Russia) in the spring of 1941, and were astonished by what they saw. Some of the installations they visited employed 30,000 laborers per shift and were operating three shifts a day. After inspecting the factories, Anastas Mikoyan, the famed designer of the MiG, told the Germans: "We have now shown you all we have and all we can do. We shall destroy anyone who attacks us."[17]

Aschenbrenner and his colleagues immediately reported to the OKL that a large-scale aircraft production program was underway in the Soviet Union. They were ignored by Luftwaffe intelligence. On June 21, 1941, the Luftwaffe commanders in the field had no idea that they were about to take on an enemy that outnumbered them at least seven to one.

CHAPTER III

THE DEPLOYMENT

In the spring of 1941, the Wehrmacht deployed for the invasion of the Soviet Union. It consisted of the Army of Norway, an OKW formation under the command of Colonel General von Falkenhorst, and three army groups which were subordinate to the OKH: Army Group North under Field Marshal Ritter Wilhelm von Leeb; Army Group Center under Field Marshal Fedor von Bock; and Army Group South under Field Marshal Gerd von Rundstedt. Each army group was supported by an air fleet: the 1st Air Fleet under Colonel General Alfred "Bomber" Keller supported Leeb; the 2nd under Field Marshal Albert Kesselring backed Army Group Center; and the 4th Air Fleet under Colonel General Alexander Loehr operated in the zone of Army Group South. All totaled, the Wehrmacht deployed 3,000,000 men, 3,350 tanks, 7,184 guns, 600,000 motorized vehicles, and 625,000 horses against a Red Army, which still outnumbered them by 1,500,000 men in European Russia alone.

Hitler's decision to invade Russia at this time did not meet unanimous approval within the Wehrmacht. Field Marshal Fedor von Bock, for one, objected to the entire idea of invading Russia.

Fedor von Bock was born in Kuestrin (now Kostrzyn, Poland), a fortress city on the Oder River, in the province of Brandenburg, on December 3, 1880. His father was General Karl Moritz von Bock, who had commanded a division during the Franco-Prussian War. His mother, Baroness Olga Helene von Falkenhayn von Bock, was related to General Erich von Falkenhayn, a former chief of the General Staff, and had relatives in the Russian aristocracy.

Even as a child, Bock yearned for a career in the army. He was educated at the Potsdam Cadet School and the Gross Lichtefelde

Military Academy, and grew into a strong-willed, efficient, and arrogant young man. Although not brilliant, he became an excellent tactician and a good linguist, being fluent in French and fair in Russian and English. He was a fanatical soldier who, in later years, often lectured his men on how it was an honor to die for the Fatherland. Because of his outspoken patriotism and iron-like determination, he was nicknamed "the Holy Fire of Kuestrin."

Bock graduated from Gross Lichtefelde and was commissioned directly into the elite 5th Foot Guards Regiment on March 15, 1898. He became adjutant of the I Battalion in 1904 and regimental adjutant in 1906, despite the fact that he was still only a second lieutenant. Bock married Mally von Reichenbach, a young Prussian noblewoman, in a Potsdam garrison ceremony in 1905. They had one child, a daughter, who was born in 1907. Bock began his General Staff training in 1910 and, after graduating, was named Ib (chief supply officer) of the Guards Corps in 1913. He became Ia (chief of operations) of the corps in September 1914 and fought in Belgium, on the Marne, and in Flanders, Galicia, and Russia. He was transferred to the General Staff of the Eleventh Army on the Eastern Front in May 1915. He was detached to the 4th Foot Guards Regiment as a battalion commander in January and February 1916, and led it with fanatical courage on the Somme. He was later decorated with the *Pour le Mérite* for his bravery.

In August 1916, Bock became chief of operations of the 200th Infantry Division, which fought against the Romanians in the Carpathian Mountains. In March 1917, he "returned home" as the chief of operations of the Guards Corps, but remained there only a month before being transferred to Army Group Crown Prince Friedrich Wilhelm on the Western Front as chief supply officer (Ib). He remained here until the end of the war. One of his last acts in World War I was to meet with Kaiser Wilhelm II at Spa, Belgium, where he unsuccessfully urged the monarch to return to Berlin and crush the Kiel naval mutiny. This occurred two days before the Armistice. Bock remained a loyal monarchist and a strong nationalist all of his life.

During the upheavals that marked the first four years of the Weimar Republic, Bock was deeply involved in the army's efforts to defend Germany's Eastern Marchlands against the Poles. Using army funds, he clandestinely helped to support the Freikorps and the Black Reichswehr (a secret organization of illicit military units), and to suppress Communist revolutionaries and other agitators. He was also involved in the activities of the *Femegerichte* (Secret Court) and was almost certainly involved in the murders of a number of left-wingers who informed the Allied Control Commission about secret German military activities. Meanwhile, he served on the General Staff of Group Command One in Berlin (1919–20) and was chief of staff of Wehrkreis III and the 3rd Infantry Division in Berlin (1920–24).

After the period of civil unrest that the Germans called "the war after the war," was over, von Bock commanded the II Battalion of the 4th Infantry Regiment at Deutsch Krone (1924–26). He later commanded the regiment itself (1926–29), the 1st Cavalry Division at Frankfurt/Oder (1929–31), and Wehrkreis II and the 2nd Infantry Division, both head-quartered in Stettin, Pomerania (1931–35). Meanwhile, he was promoted to first lieutenant (1908), captain (1912), major (late 1916), lieutenant colonel (1920), colonel (1925), major general (1929), lieutenant general (1931), and general of infantry (March 1, 1935).

Adolf Hitler was impressed with the tall, thin, and highly opinion-ated professional soldier. For his part, Bock detested the Nazis, but refused to oppose them. He was, in fact, a willing tool of the regime and never uttered an official word of protest about the activities of the SS or the atrocities they committed. Of Bock, Telford Taylor wrote: "His mind was closed to everything but the most immediate consequences of 'soldiering for the King' . . . [He was] a violent nationalist, a stern dis-ciplinarian, and intent only upon strengthening the Army and advancing his own military career, in which he was distinguished by industry and determination more than brilliance."[1]

Cold-blooded, vain, and humorless, the Holy Fire of Kuestrin continued his relentless rise on May 20, 1935, when he was named commander-in-chief of Army Group Three, which he led in the occupation of Austria in March 1938. This resulted in his promotion to colonel general on March 15, but Bock's behavior and deliberate insults so badly offended the Austrians that Hitler felt compelled to transfer him from Vienna to the command of Army Group One in Berlin in November. (The events in Austria did not harm Bock's career, largely because Adolf Hitler secretly agreed with the general and also despised the Austrians.)

It should be noted here that Bock had a very irritating personality and rarely got along with anyone. He disliked the Nazis, hated Austrians, and had nothing but contempt for any and all civilians, regardless of nationality. He did not get along with Field Marshal von Brauchitsch, and felt Hitler had made a mistake in naming him commander-in-chief of the army. In Fedor von Bock's mind, only one man was good enough to hold this post—and that was Fedor von Bock. He also disliked most of his subordinates, especially Heinz Guderian, the commander of the Second Panzer Group and the "Father of the Blitzkrieg."

The following year, Army Group One became Army Group North, which Bock led in the conquest of Poland. Army Group North was re-designated Army Group B on October 12, 1939, and Bock led it with considerable skill during the conquests of the Low Countries, Luxembourg, and France. He was promoted to field marshal on July 19, 1940.

Fedor von Bock was scheduled to command the initial assault waves in the invasion of the United Kingdom in the fall of 1940; however, when the Luftwaffe was defeated in the Battle of Britain, the invasion was cancelled and he was ordered to redeploy his forces back to East Prussia and Poland. This he did in September 1940, and in succeeding months. For much of the winter of 1940/41, however, Bock was absent from duty because of severe stomach ulcers.

Cold, arrogant, vain, humorless, opinionated, aloof, and unbending, Bock was nevertheless on good terms with Hitler, who visited him on his 60th birthday, December 3, 1940, when he heard that the marshal was ill. Bock gave voice to the fears of many within the High Command concerning the vastness of Russia and Germany's lack of knowledge about its true military strength. As Bock spoke, Hitler grew aloof and uncommunicative, and obviously did not want to listen to objections to his planned invasion.

When Luftwaffe Field Marshal Albert Kesselring visited Bock on June 21, 1941, he was surprised to find the Holy Fire of Kuestrin very depressed, a marked contrast to the optimism he exhibited just prior to previous campaigns. The next day, however, Bock's headquarters became Army Group Center. It controlled the Ninth and Fourth Armies and the Second and Third Panzer Groups—51 of the 149 German divisions committed to Operation Barbarossa on June 22, 1941.

After Lieutenant Colonel Henning von Tresckow, the chief of operations of Army Group Center, received the Commissar Order instructing German soldiers to execute Communist political officers as soon as they were captured, without benefit of trial, he urged Field Marshal von Bock to protest against it in writing. Bock said that he disliked the order also, but would probably lose his job if he protested. "In that case," Tresckow said, "you will at least have made an honorable exit in history." Bock filed the protest; Hitler did not sack him, but neither did he revoke the order. "I do not expect my generals to understand me," he said, "but I expect them to obey my orders." Heinz Guderian also protested the order, to no avail. The final order, which instructed the Wehrmacht to shoot all captured commissars or hand them over to the SD for execution, was issued to the line units on June 6.[2]

Wilhelm Joseph Franz von Leeb was noted for his competence as a defensive commander, his high moral code, and humorless and forbidding personality. "If von Leeb ever tried to smile, his face would crack," Field Marshal Siegmund Wilhelm von List said of him.[3]

Leeb was born in Landsberg-am-Lech, Bavaria, on September 5, 1876, the descendant of an old Bavarian military family. He entered the Bavarian Army as a *Fahnenjunker* on July 16, 1895, attended the War School at Munich, and was commissioned in the Bavarian 4th Field Artillery Regiment on March 3, 1897. He spent a year in China as a platoon leader in the 1st Mountain Battery of the East Asian Field Artillery Regiment (1900–01) and saw action in the Boxer Rebellion. Transferred back to Germany, he was with the 4th Bavarian Field Artillery until 1903, when he began his General Staff training at the Bavarian War Academy. He was on detached duty with the Prussian General Staff in Berlin from 1909 to 1911, and then attended a course at the Artillery School at Jueterbog, before transferring to Erlangen, where he commanded a battery in the 10th Bavarian Field Artillery Regiment for two years.

He was named Ib (chief supply officer) of the I Bavarian Corps in March 1914 and served on the Western Front. In March 1915 he was named chief of operations (Ia) of the 11th Bavarian Infantry Division, which was then in the process of forming. He saw action in Galicia, Serbia, France (including the Battle of Verdun), Russia (including the

Battle of Kovel), and Romania, before returning to Alsace in the spring of 1917.

For his services in this post, Leeb was decorated with the Bavarian Max Joseph Order (the equivalent of the Prussian *Pour le Merite)*, which carried with it a non-heredity knighthood. The new knight (*Ritter*) was on the General Staff of Crown Prince Rupprecht of Bavaria from May 1917 until the end of the war, winding up as chief quartermaster (Ic) of the army group. He was, meanwhile, promoted to first lieutenant (1905), captain (1912), and major (May 19, 1916). He was accepted into the 100,000-man Reichswehr as a matter of course.

Promotions are usually slow for officers in small armies, but Ritter von Leeb was one of the exceptions. He was initially sent to Munich, where he served as a General Staff officer and as chief of the Army Department of the Bavarian Ministry for Military Affairs. He was then transferred to Berlin as a department head in the Reich Defense Ministry (1919–21). He spent the 1921–23 period on the border of hostile Poland as chief of staff of Wehrkreis II, and then returned to Bavaria as chief of staff of Wehrkreis VII in Munich, where he helped suppress Hitler's Beer Hall Putsch in November 1923. He returned to troop duty as commander of the II Battalion, 7th Artillery Regiment (II/7th Artillery) at Landsberg (1924–26), before moving to Nuremberg as commander of the regiment itself (1926–28). He was then Artillery Leader V (Arko V) at Stuttgart (1928–29), Arko VII at Munich (1929–30), and commander of Wehrkreis VII and the 7th Infantry Division (February 1, 1930–October 1, 1933). He was then named commander-in-chief of Group Command Two (one of the Reich's two army groups). Leeb was promoted to lieutenant colonel (1920), colonel (1925), major general (February 1, 1929), lieutenant general (December 1, 1929), and general of artillery (January 1, 1934).

Wilhelm von Leeb was an anti-Nazi, although not fervently so. He was, however, highly suspicious of Adolf Hitler from the beginning. On February 2, 1933, four days after he assumed power, *der Fuehrer* gave a private speech to his senior admirals and generals. General von Leeb was not impressed. "A businessman whose wares are good does not need to boost them in the loudest tones of a market crier," he declared. The astute and morally solid Leeb thought that Hitler was trying to bribe them.[4]

In addition, the general was a devout Catholic and was under Gestapo surveillance as early as 1934. During the Nazi purge of the Defense Ministry and High Command of the Army (OKH) in early 1938, known as the Blomberg-Fritsch crisis, Leeb was solidly on the side of Baron von Fritsch, the commander-in-chief of the army, who was falsely accused of being a homosexual. On February 4, 1938, the day Fritsch was replaced by von Brauchitsch, Hitler sent a courier to Leeb, asking that he submit a request to retire. Leeb dutifully did so and retired on February 28.

Perhaps realizing that he might need officers of Leeb's caliber, even if he did not like them, the Fuehrer approved Leeb's honorary (*charakterisierte*) promotion to colonel general, effective that day. Leeb was also named honorary colonel of the 7th AR, a signal honor in the German Army. After 1938, Leeb often wore the uniform of the honorary colonel of the 7th Artillery. (Like Leeb, Gerd von Rundstedt was retired in 1938 and was also given an honorary colonelcy. Unlike Leeb, Rundstedt never wore anything but his regimental commander's uniform, although he did wear field marshal's insignia on his shoulder boards.)

Hitler was right when he concluded that he might need Leeb and other retired officers in the future. In the fall of 1938, the dictator pushed the world to the edge of war in the Sudetenland crisis, when he demanded that territory be returned to Germany by the Czechs. General Ritter von Leeb was recalled to active duty as commander of the Twelfth Army. He deployed his forces along the Czechoslovakian border before the British and French backed down and signed the Munich Accords, which turned the disputed areas over to Hitler without a fight. Leeb returned to Bavaria and his retirement in October, but was recalled to active duty in 1939. This time London and Paris did not back down, but the Wehrmacht invaded Poland on September 1, 1939. World War II had begun.

In September 1939, Germany had three army groups–North, South, and C–under the commands of von Bock, von Rundstedt, and von Leeb, respectively. Leeb was charged with the task of defending Germany's western borders with an assortment of non-motorized third- and fourth-class units.

At this time, Britain and France missed one of the greatest opportunities of the war. With the best German divisions engaged in Poland, a major Allied offensive would have captured the Ruhr industrial area, without which Germany could not wage a major war. Leeb defended it with 800,000 men. A third of his 33 divisions were Landwehr, men 35 years old or older with little or no military training. Several of his divisions had no artillery and Leeb did not have a single tank. He faced a French army of 2,800,000 men in frontline units (not counting 2,000,000 in reserve), 11,000 guns, and 3,286 tanks. Leeb understood his task, however, and exhibited no nervousness, although he forbade his men from undertaking any aggressive action. The Allies launched one minor offensive, which gained an average of 1.5 miles along a 15-mile front.

To the east, the last Polish forces surrendered on October 6. Tragically, Wilhelm von Leeb's only son, a lieutenant, had been killed in action in the Battle of Lvov (Lwow). A few days later, as part of his deal with Stalin, Hitler turned Lvov over to the Soviets. One can imagine what Ritter von Leeb thought about this.

Leeb opposed Hitler's invasion of France from the beginning. He was especially opposed to the idea of violating Dutch neutrality and was horrified at the prospect of invading neutral Belgium for the second time in 25 years. Since Brauchitsch could not get Hitler even to consider changing his plan, Ritter von Leeb met with the other two army group commanders at Koblenz on November 9. He advocated that the three of them jointly resign. Presented with a united front of his army group commanders, Leeb said, Hitler just might back down. Bock and Rundstedt, however, coldly rejected the proposal, and Leeb returned to his headquarters at Frankfurt in a depressed state of mind.

Germany invaded France, Belgium, the Netherlands, and Luxembourg on May 10, 1940. Leeb's army group very much played a secondary role in the campaign. Its job was to pin down as many French divisions as possible in the Maginot Line. Leeb performed his task with success and was rewarded on July 19, 1940, with a promotion to field marshal.[5]

THE NEW WAVES

While the political maneuvering continued behind the scenes, General Fromm and the men of his Replacement Army were working feverishly, raising new divisions for Operation Barbarossa.

Friedrich (Fritz) Fromm was born in Berlin on October 8, 1888. He entered the Imperial Army on December 30, 1906, as a *Fahnenjunker* in the 55th Field Artillery Regiment at Naumburg/Saale. He was promoted to second lieutenant on June 18, 1908, and was adjutant of the I Battalion from 1913 to 1915. In 1914, he fought in the Belgian Ardennes and at Namur, before his regiment was sent to the Russian Front, where it fought in East Prussia and Poland. Sent back to France in the spring of 1915, Fromm's regiment took part in the trench warfare of 1915–1918, including the Battle of Verdun (1916), in Flanders and on the Somme. He was on the staff of the 30th Infantry Division from 1917 until the end of the war.

Fromm was promoted to first lieutenant on November 28, 1914, and to captain on April 18, 1916. He rejoined his old regiment when the war ended and remained with it until it dissolved in 1919. Selected for the Reichswehr, he served in the 7th Artillery Regiment at Nuremberg (1919–20), as a battery commander in the 3rd Artillery Regiment at Frankfurt/Oder (1920–22), and on the staff of the 3rd Infantry Division in Berlin (1922–27). He was promoted to major on March 1, 1927, and began his General Staff training that same year. Promoted to lieutenant colonel on April 1, 1931, he served in the defense ministry and spent a year as commander of the IV Battalion/3rd (Prussian) Artillery Regiment at Potsdam (1932–33). Fromm was named chief of the defense office in the Reich Defense Ministry on February 1, 1933—the same day he was promoted to colonel.

Fritz Fromm remained in this post in its various incarnations as the German Army grew from 100,000 to more than 4,000,000 men. His office became the General Army Office in the Reich Defense Ministry in 1934. The Defense Ministry became the War Ministry in 1935, and Fromm's office was transferred to the High Command of the Army in early 1938. When Germany mobilized, he became commander of the Replacement (or Home) Army on August 31, 1939. His position was renamed chief of army equipment and commander of the Replacement Army on November 16, 1939. He remained chief of the General Army Office until June 1, 1940, when he relinquished it to his highly capable deputy, General of Infantry Friedrich Olbricht. Meanwhile, Fromm was promoted to major general on November 1, 1935, lieutenant general on January 1, 1938, and general of artillery on April 1, 1939.

Fritz Fromm loved a good cigar and was an avid hunter, both activities Adolf Hitler hated. The Fuehrer, however, appreciated Fromm's competence and he no doubt played a major role in Germany's early victories. Hitler rewarded him on July 19, 1940, with a promotion to colonel general and the award of the Knight's Cross, a decoration normally reserved for combat soldiers or generals who directed major campaigns.

Hitler demanded that the army expand from 120 to 180 combat divisions for his invasion of the Soviet Union, and the Replacement Army and the Wehrkreise raised no fewer than five new waves of troops for the campaign. The Wave 11 infantry divisions were created by transferring cadres from existing divisions to the new unit and then "rounding them out" with new recruits from the draft class of 1920. Simultaneously, other new draftees were transferred to the old divisions, so that no division was too badly depleted and each division would have at least a sizable contingent of combat veterans. Each "old" division transferred three battalions back to its home Wehrkreis, where they were incorporated into a new division. All of the Wave 11 divisions were "three regiment" divisions (i.e., all had three infantry regiments).

The Wave 11 divisions were all more or less ready by October 1940; by then, the Replacement Army had already begun work on the Wave 12 divisions, which were formed in the same manner as the Wave 11 divisions. The Jaeger divisions were formed from the same cadres, but controlled only two rifle regiments and were equipped as pursuit divisions. The divisions of the 12th Wave were the 97th, 99th, 100th, and 101st Jaeger and the 102nd, 106th, 110th, 111th, 112th, and 113th Infantry Divisions. All ten Wave 12 divisions had been formed and activated by the end of December 1940.

The Wave 13 divisions were formed in a manner similar to the Wave 11 divisions. They were, however, not nearly as well equipped and were not designed for combat on the Eastern Front; rather, they were used as occupation or garrison units, in order to free other divisions for employment in the East. All were posted to France or Belgium except the 319th Infantry Division, which was used to garrison the English Channel Islands of Guernsey, Jersey, Alderney, Sark, Herm, and Jethou. There were nine divisions in the 13th Wave: the 302nd, 304th, 305th, 306th, 319th, 320th, 321st, 323rd, and 327th Infantry Divisions. All were formed and had completed their unit training by early 1941.

The Home Army began forming the Wave 14 divisions in November 1940. They were also designed to perform occupation duties in the West, and the 333rd and 335th Divisions had a high percentage of Polish soldiers in German service. There were eight Wave 14 divisions (all infantry): the 332nd, 333rd, 335th, 336th, 337th, 339th, 340th, and the 342nd.

During the five months of 1941, the Replacement Army formed 15 Wave 15 divisions, all numbered in the 700 block. All were static (non-motorized) two-regiment divisions, composed mainly of older men, many of whom were from the *Landeschuetzen* (infantry) battalions; Volks-Deutsche (ethnic Germans from occupied areas); or foreign personnel. They reflected the shortage of young men of military age in the Third Reich. In addition, their support units reflected the growing shortage of equipment in the depots of the Home Army. They had an artillery battalion instead of the usual four-battalion artillery regiment, and most of them had engineer, signal, and reconnaissance companies, instead of battalions. They had no divisional anti-tank battalions, and their infantry regiments had no 13th and 14th Companies (i.e., they had no infantry cannon, heavy weapons, or anti-tank units). The Wave 15 divisions were numbered 702, 704, 707, 708, 709, 710, 711, 712, 713, 714, 715, 716, 717, 718, and 719. They were all sent to France or the Balkans. The units sent to Yugoslavia and Greece were later redesignated Jaeger divisions.[6]

In addition to these units, the 90th Light Division was created from miscellaneous units in North Africa, the 199th Infantry Division was formed in Norway, and the 4th, 5th, and 6th Mountain Divisions were organized in southern Germany and Austria. They were not part of a particular wave.

In June 1941, four Wave 16 reserve infantry brigades were formed: the 201st, 202nd, 203rd, and 204th. All were designated security units and the 201st and 203rd were upgraded to security divisions in the summer of 1942. None of them had artillery units.

As a result of the massive reorganization in the winter of 1940/41, 84 new divisions of all types were created, at a cost of 17 of the 1,939 divisions that were converted to other types of units or broken up. In June 1941, Hitler thus had 205 combat divisions, although they were not that much more powerful than the 140 divisions which had invaded France and the Low Countries in 1940. This was because the number of panzers had not increased, even though their quality was higher, employing more PzKw IIIs and IVs and fewer PzKw Is, PzKw IIs, and tanks of Czech manufacture.[7] (See Appendix 4 for a description of the characteristics of various tanks that fought in World War II.)

General Fromm, however, issued a clear warning: at the end of May, he had only 80,000 men in the reinforcement (march) battalions and they had only three months' training. In addition, only about 350,000 men (mainly from the classes of 1921 and 1922) would be available for the rest of 1941. In other words, if German casualties in Barbarossa exceeded 430,000, the Home Army would not be able to replace them. In addition, German tank production, although it had improved slightly, was still quite low. Less than 200 had been produced per month in 1940. German industry would increase its quarterly tank production from less than 700 in the first quarter of 1941 to 1,100 in the last quarter of the year, but this would still be woefully inadequate, as we shall see.

DEPLOYMENT

The OKH had three army groups and several smaller formations at its disposal in the spring of 1941. In the north lay Field Marshal Ritter Wilhelm von Leeb's Army Group North, which included the Eighteenth Army (Colonel General Georg von Kuechler), the Sixteenth Army (Colonel General Ernst Busch), and Fourth Panzer Group (Colonel General Erich Hoepner). Its missions were to annihilate the Soviet forces in the Baltic States and to capture Leningrad. The weakest of the army groups, it controlled 29 divisions, of which three were panzer and three were motorized. It was supported by Colonel General Alfred Keller's 1st Air Fleet (660 aircraft).

In the middle of the German line lay its strongest force: Field Marshal Fedor von Bock's Army Group Center. North to south, it controlled the Third Panzer Group (Colonel General Hermann Hoth), Ninth Army (Colonel General Adolf Strauss), Fourth Army (Field Marshal Guenther von Kluge), and Second Panzer Group (Colonel General Heinz Guderian). Its initial mission was to destroy the strong Soviet forces in the Brest-Vilna (Vilnius)-Smolensk triangle, near the German frontier, and then to wheel north or continue to drive towards

Moscow, as ordered. Bock's forces totaled 50 divisions, of which nine were panzer and six were motorized. It was supported by Field Marshal Kesselring's 2nd Air Fleet, which had 1,180 airplanes.

Between southern Poland and the Black Sea lay Gerd von Rundstedt's Army Group South. It was divided into a northern wing, concentrated between the Pripyat Marshes and the Carpathians, and a southern wing in Romania. In the north lay the strike force: Walter von Reichenau's Sixth Army, Ewald von Kleist's First Panzer Group, and Colonel General Heinrich von Stuelpnagel's Seventeenth Army. To the south lay Colonel General Ritter Eugen von Schobert's Eleventh Army, as well as the Third and Fourth Romanian Armies, under Generals Petre Dumitrescu and Nicolae Ciuperca, respectively. The northern wing was ordered to destroy Russian General Mikhail Kirponos's very strong forces in Galicia and the Western Ukraine, secure the Dnieper crossings, and capture Kiev. The southern wing had the task of protecting the Ploesti oilfields and, for that reason, Eleventh Army's divisions were interlaced with the less dependable Romanian divisions as "corset stays." In all, Rundstedt had 41 German divisions, of which five were panzer and three were motorized. He also controlled 14 Romanian divisions (about 150,000 men). Army Group South was supported by Colonel General Alexander Loehr's 4th Air Fleet, which contained 930 aircraft. In addition, the Luftwaffe committed two anti-aircraft corps to the offensive: Major General Walter von Axthelm's I Flak Corps and Lieutenant General Otto Dessloch's II Flak. Three independent flak regiments were also committed.

To the north of the main battlefront, Finnish Marshal Carl Mannerheim deployed 14 divisions (500,000 men) in the Finnish sector. In July he also was to begin an offensive on both sides of Lake Lagoda in conjunction with Leeb's efforts to take Leningrad. Finland, however, was to enter the war as a co-belligerent, and not as a German ally; its orders came from Mannerheim, not from Berlin.

North of Mannerheim's divisions lay the Far North sector, where Nikolaus Falkenhorst's Army of Norway deployed four German divisions in two corps (about 67,000 men) in northern Norway and northern Finland. It also controlled a Finnish corps. The objective of the Army of Norway was to capture the Soviet port of Murmansk. It was supported by Luftwaffe Command Kirkenes (of Stumpff's 5th Air Fleet), which had only 70 aircraft. These were commanded by Stumpff's chief of staff, Colonel Andreas Nielsen. (Hitler had ordered that Stumpff keep the bulk of his forces to the south, in case the British decided to invade Norway.)

In addition, the OKH initially held 28 divisions (including two panzer and three motorized divisions) in reserve. In all, the High Command of the Army deployed 148 German divisions, including 17 panzer and 13 motorized divisions. Its Barbarossa forces included 3,050,000 men, 3,350 tanks, 7,184 guns, 600,000 motor vehicles, and 625,000 horses (excluding the Far North sector, which was an OKW theater). The OKH also earmarked a dozen additional divisions (including two panzer divisions and a motorized division) for Operation Barbarossa.

The OKH planned to conquer the Soviet Union with 160 divisions—18 more than it had employed in the conquest of France. The area of operations in Barbarossa, however, was about 1,000,000 square miles—about 20 times the size of France. In addition, although the number of panzer and motorized divisions had more than doubled, from 15 in May 1940, to 32 in June 1941, the number of tanks had only risen from 2,574 to 3,332, an increase of 758 panzers.

The German armies were, in fact, a far cry from the highly mobile, incredibly well-equipped units that Goebbels' Propaganda Ministry made them out to be, and that many people still believe they were. Only 46 of the German divisions available for the invasion, for example, were fully equipped with German arms. The rest were either deficient in equipment (mainly in assault and anti-tank guns), or were outfitted with captured arms and equipment, primarily from France and Czechoslovakia. Eighty-four infantry divisions and even three of the motorized divisions were equipped with vehicles drawn from foreign countries. In fact, counting foreign equipment, the German Army had 2,000 different types of vehicles, 70 different types of guns, and 52 models of anti-aircraft guns. As a result, maintenance would be a nightmare in the Russian campaign, and the breakdown rates in all units would be extremely high.

In addition, most of the infantry divisions were still heavily dependent upon horsepower. Some 119 divisions were still horsedrawn, and 77 of these had only horsedrawn supply units, including 15,000 Polish two-wheeled *Panjewagen* (peasant wagons).[8] Most of the divisional artillery regiments depended solely upon horses or mules. Hitler and his generals were clearly gambling on a war of short duration, although few of them seem to have appreciated the risk they were running. Most German commanders at all levels favored the invasion of the Soviet Union, because they felt that it was only a matter of time before the Soviet Union tried to "stab Germany in the back" and were stimulated by their successes in Poland, France, and the Balkans to think that they could easily defeat Stalin's legions. They were probably right on the first point, but, in retrospect, it is clear that they overestimated their own abilities and greatly underestimated those of the Soviet Union.

Overconfidence played a major role in the disaster that overtook the German Army in Russia at the end of 1941. Following the tremendous success of the blitzkrieg in France and the Balkans, the military technocrats abandoned their previous caution and were now convinced that no power in Europe could halt the Wehrmacht.[9] OKH, for example, had replacement equipment available for a campaign of only three months, but felt no need to press for the higher priority in armaments because it believed its reserves would be adequate to conquer the Soviet Union. On December 3, 1940, General Jodl, the chief of operations of the OKW, unequivocally stated that it was correct to reduce the armaments allocations for the army in favor of the navy and Luftwaffe, since Operation Barbarossa could be fought with existing equipment. General Fromm, the C-in-C of the Replacement Army and chief of army equipment, saw no reason to press for a higher priority for the army in armaments production, a sure indication that he agreed with Jodl.[10] Even more incredibly, the OKH did not even bother to prepare for the possibility of a winter campaign and only purchased enough winter clothing to supply a greatly reduced army of occupation. This overconfidence and shortsightedness would cost a great many soldiers fingers and toes, lost to frostbite in the months ahead.

While the OKH directed operations on the Eastern Front, German occupied territories would come under the control of the OKW, an arrangement that became more and more solidified as the war progressed. By 1942, it would become popular to refer to the Russian Front as an "OKH Theater" and to any other sector as an "OKW Theater," in effect creating another command division in the upper levels of the German armed forces. In June 1941, Germany had 38 divisions in western Europe, one in Denmark, seven in Norway, seven in the Balkans, and two in North Africa. All, of course, were under the control of the OKW.

SOVIET PREPARATIONS

On the other side of the frontier, Joseph Stalin, the general secretary of the Soviet Communist Party, had become the official chief of the Soviet government on May 6, 1941, when he made himself chairman of the Council of People's Commissars. Several agencies were directly subordinate to this body, including the Defense Committee of the Council of People's Commissars, which supervised and coordinated all state agencies involved with the buildup and maintenance of the armed forces. These included the People's Commissariat of Defense under Marshal Semen Timoshenko, and the People's Commissariat of the Navy (Admiral Nikolai G. Kuznetsov). The Soviet Union had no separate air force.

Within the Defense Commissariat was the Main Military Council, which was the decision-making body for the Defense Commissariat. The nominal chair of this powerful command agency was Marshal Timoshenko, but committee member Stalin was really in charge. Also on the Main Military Council were Foreign Minister Molotov and eight deputy defense commissars, including the chief of the General Staff, Marshal Georgi Zhukov. The General Staff was responsible for war plans. When the war began, it established a general headquarters, the *Stavka* (staff), which directed the war effort throughout the conflict.

The highest army field commands prior to the outbreak of hostilities were the 16 military districts. In case of war, those on the frontiers were to be converted into fronts (army groups). The day Hitler invaded the Soviet Union, five became fronts. The Leningrad Military District, under Markian M. Popov, became the North Front. The Baltic Military District, commanded by Fedor I. Kuznetsov, became the North-West Front, and Dmitrii Pavlov's West Military District became the West Front. Kirponos's Kiev Military District became the South-West Front, and the Odessa Military District became the South Front, covering Bessarabia. According to Zhukov, the Soviet strength in the border districts facing Germany, Hungary, and Romania stood at 150 divisions: 88 rifle, 36 tank, 18 mechanized, and eight cavalry divisions. Another 20 divisions faced Finland, and the Soviet Union had a further 133 in the interior and in the Far East. Other divisions could be rapidly formed when reservists were called up.

Soviet military command functions at all levels were complicated by political surveillance. Political commissars were posted to every staff down to regimental level, and *politruks* (political leadership officers) extended down to platoon level. The commissars, looking over the commanders' shoulders, had the authority to review the commanders' every decision and could revoke them if he felt so inclined. They were also trained to see sabotage in every reversal and treason in every retreat, no matter how necessary it might be. In addition, the commanders had to deal with the secret police of the People's Commissariat of Internal Affairs (*Narodnyy Kommissariat Vnutrennikh Del*, or NKVD). The NKVD had authority over state security and maintained surveillance over officers and men in the armed forces. It also had troops of its own, which often formed blocking detachments and were used to halt or prevent retreats. They could also pass summary judgments on anyone and were authorized to carry out executions. The commissars, the NKVD, and other agencies provided Stalin with a constant stream of information outside military channels concerning the actions, behavior, and attitudes of his officers.

At the beginning of 1941, the leadership of the Red Army was in considerable disarray. During the purges of 1937 and 1938, it had lost all 11 of its deputy commissars for defense, all of its military district commanders, 13 of its 15 army commanders, 57 of its 85 corps commanders, 111 of 195 division commanders, 220 of its 406 brigade commanders, and half of its regimental commanders—all executed. The Officers' Corps had only just begun to recover from Stalin's rash and drastic actions, and the Soviet armed forces would continue to be handicapped by a lack of competent officers throughout the war.

It suffered from no such handicaps in the realm of equipment. "[I]n strictly numerical terms, the Soviet forces may actually have been the best equipped in the world at that time," the U.S. Official History records.[11] According to Stalin, the Soviet Union had 24,000 tanks when the war broke out. Military aircraft production totaled 17,745 airplanes between January 1, 1939 and June 1941, a figure which far exceeded the German total. In addition, the army had 67,335 artillery pieces and mortars (larger than 50mm) when Barbarossa began. Unfortunately for Stalin, many of his tanks and airplanes were obsolete by German standards.

The newest Soviet tanks, the T-34, KV-1, and KV-2, however, were far superior to anything the Germans had or had even designed. The T-34 was a medium tank of 28 tons (three tons heavier than the heaviest PzKw IV) and had a top speed of 32 miles per hour (eight miles per hour faster than the PzKw IV). The German short-barreled 75mm gun was inferior to the T-34's long-barreled 76mm gun in both range and power. The heavy KV-2 (Kliment Voroshilov-2) weighed 52 tons and, at 20 m.p.h., was slower than the PzKw IV, but much more heavily armored. Its 76mm gun outgunned the PzKw III and IV. In addition, despite their greater weights, the T-34 and KV had such wide treads that they had as much as 25 percent lower ground pressure per square inch than the German tanks, and thus had much better traction and maneuverability in mud and snow. They also featured welded, sloping hulls and turret armor, which made them invulnerable to all but the heaviest German anti-tank weapons.

The new Soviet light tank, the T-60, weighed 6.5 tons, mounted a 20mm main battle gun, and was roughly equal to the PzKw II. It was inferior to both the PzKw III and IV, but it could be built rapidly in ordinary automobile plants, using standard automotive components. In 1940, the Soviets built 2,421 T-60s, 117 T-34s, and 256 KVs. By June 1941, they had constructed 1,225 T-34s and 639 KVs.

The equipment deficiencies of the Soviets' armored forces would not have been so serious had not their armored doctrine been so badly flawed. General Dmitrii G. Pavlov, the Soviet armor "expert," returned from Spain in the late 1930s, convinced that the tank had little place on the modern battlefield. In 1939, as a result of his recommendations, the tank branch ceased to exist as an independent arm and its forces were distributed as brigades throughout the infantry armies, much like those of the French Army. Following the victories of the panzer divisions in Poland, France, and the Balkans, the Soviets in 1941 fanatically tried to reestablish the tank corps, but this process was still in its early stages in the summer of 1941. As a result, the Red Army would not be able to duplicate or match the combined arms tactics of the Wehrmacht on the battlefields of 1941.

Like the rest of the Red Army, the Soviet air forces were also in transition in June 1941. The vast majority of Soviet aircraft were technologically inferior to their German counterparts at that time. The most modern Soviet airplanes with the squadrons were the MiG-3, YAK-1, and LAGG fighters, and the IL-2 dive-bomber, a ground attack aircraft that was slow but heavily armored and difficult to shoot down. Only the MiG-3 exceeded the Me-109 in speed (it could fly at more than 370 miles per hour), but the Soviet pilots were badly trained compared to their opponents, and their tactics were distinctly inferior. The Soviet air units had 2,739 aircraft of these modern designs with their squadrons in 1941. Most of its more than 15,000 airplanes were much older, and many were biplanes. Some of their fighters actually featured gunsights *painted* on their cockpit windshields.

The might of a military force, of course, cannot be measured in its weapons alone. Soviet military preparations were also flawed by an over-concentration on weapons at the expense of the auxiliary and supplementary equipment needed to make the weapons effective. Much of the artillery, for example, depended upon ordinary farm tractors as prime movers, and the motorized units had less than half of their authorized allocation of trucks. They also lacked radios and trained signals personnel. Most Soviet tanks, including the newer models, did not have radios, and some of the infantry units even lacked rifles. During the first German offensive, many Soviet troops tried to dig foxholes with their helmets, because they had no shovels or entrenching tools. In short, the Red Army would prove to be a vast, primitive, and cumbersome opponent in the summer of 1941.

Barbarossa
22 June–15 November, 1941

FINLAND

GULF of FINLAND

BALTIC SEA

Leningrad • Schluesselburg
Tallinn • Tikhvin •

18th ARMY

Luga •

Staraya Russa •

Pskov •

Riga •

0   200 miles
0   200 km

- - - GERMAN LINE OF 22 JUNE
······ GERMAN LINE OF 10 JULY
——— GERMAN LINE OF 15 NOVEMBER

ARMY GROUP NORTH

16th ARMY

XXXXX

9th ARMY

Kalinin •

3rd Pz Grp

4th Pz Grp

● Moscow

Koenigsberg •

POLAND

Vitebsk •

Vyazma •

Orsha •

Smolensk •

4th ARMY

Grodno •

Minsk •

Mogilev •

Tula •

Bialystok •

2nd Pz ARMY

Warsaw •

Bryansk •

Orel •

Brest-Litovsk •

PRIPYAT MARSHES

ARMY GROUP CENTER

Lublin •

2nd ARMY

XXXXX

Rovno •

Kiev •

6th ARMY

Lvov •

Dnieper R.

Kharkov •

CARPATHIAN MOUNTAINS

Bug R.

17th ARMY

Donetz R.

HUNGARY

Uman •

Kremenchug •

1st Pz ARMY

Pervomaysk •

ARMY GROUP SOUTH

Stalino •

Rostov •

Taganrog •

RUMANIA

Odessa •

Perkop •

Melitopol •

SEA of AZOV

11th CRIMEA ARMY

BLACK SEA

Bucharest •

Sevastapol •

Dvina R.

Don R.

CHAPTER IV

THE FRONTIER BATTLES

THE OPENING GUNS

"The first salvo!" Sergeant Pabst recalled. "At the same moment everything sprang to life. Firing along the whole front—infantry guns, mortars. The Russian watchtowers vanished in a flash. Shells crashed down on all the enemy batteries, which had been located long before. In file and in line, the infantry swarmed forward. Bog, ditches; boots full of water and mud. Ahead of us the barrage crept forward from line to line. Flamethrowers advanced against the strongpoints. The fire of machine guns and the high-pitched whip of rifle bullets. . . . Then, at Kanopky Barracks, came the first serious resistance. . . . 'Assault guns, forward!'"[1]

Operation Barbarossa took the Soviet defenders in the frontier zones completely by surprise.

After Field Marshal von Leeb redeployed his forces to Memelland and East Prussia, the Masurian 291st Infantry Division was on his far left (Baltic Sea) flank. It was commanded by Lieutenant General Herzog.

Kurt Herzog was born in Quedlinburg, in the Harz Mountains (now in Saxony-Anhalt in eastern Germany) on March 27, 1889. He was educated in cadet schools and joined the army of the Kingdom of Saxony as a senior officer cadet on November 1, 1907. He attended the War School at Glogau and was commissioned in the 78th Field Artillery Regiment in Leipzig in 1908. He was on detached duty with the Military Riding Schools at Dresden and Hanover from 1909 to 1913, and was assigned to the Saxon 53rd Reserve Artillery Regiment as a battalion adjutant when World War I began. He commanded a battery from May 1915 to January 1917, and fought in Flanders, and at Ypres, La Bassé, the Somme, and Loos. He served on the Eastern Front (1916–17) and fought in Galicia and in the drive to the Dnestr. He was attached to the 54th Field Howitzer Regiment of the Austro-Hungarian Army as part of an officer exchange program from January to May 1917. Herzog was promoted to first lieutenant in September 1914, and to captain on October 5, 1916.

Captain Herzog returned to the 53rd Reserve Artillery Regiment (now back on the Western Front) in the spring of 1917 and twice temporarily commanded the II Battalion in Belgium from April to July 1917. He also briefly commanded a battery and served as an instructor at an artillery course at Truskawiec, Poland (now Truskavets, western Ukraine) until November 1917, when he became adjutant of the 152nd Artillery Command (Arko 152). He began his General Staff training in September 1918, and completed the course in January 1919, after the Armistice. He was detached to the Saxon Military Affairs Ministry from then until September 1919, when he was transferred to the League of Nations Department of the Reich War Ministry in Berlin. He remained there until the summer of 1921.

After temporarily serving with the 7th Signal Battalion and 19th Infantry Regiment in Bavaria, where he broadened his military background, he served as battery commander in the Prussian-Saxon 4th Artillery Regiment at Dresden (1921–23) and in the Prussian 3rd Artillery Regiment at Frankfurt on the Oder (1923–27). He then spent five years as an instructor at the Infantry School at Dresden (1927–1929) and the Artillery School at Jueterbog, south of Berlin (1929–32). Promoted to major in 1929, he was commander of the III Battalion/3rd Artillery Regiment when the Nazis came to power on January 30, 1933.

Herzog led the III Battalion of the 3rd Artillery Regiment from April 1932 to October 1934. Promoted to lieutenant colonel on September 1, 1933, he assumed command of Artillery Regiment Halberstadt on October 1, 1934. He was promoted to colonel on July 1, 1935, and assumed command of the Prussian 13th Artillery Regiment (also at Halberstadt) on October 15. He became commander of the 31st Artillery Regiment (formerly Artillery Regiment Halberstadt) on October 6, 1936. He led it until March 1, 1938, when he became commander of Arko I in Koenigsberg, East Prussia. He was promoted to major general on March 1, 1939.

Germany mobilized for war on August 26, 1939. That same day, Herzog became commander of replacement troops in Wehrkreis I. On October 1, as resistance in Poland collapsed, he was transferred to Potsdam, where he assumed command of the newly created 108th Artillery Command. He became the leader of the 291st Infantry Division, which was then forming in the Arys Maneuver Area (in the Masurian Lakes region of southern East Prussia), on February 6, 1940. His new command was nicknamed "the Elk Division," and its unit emblem was an Elk's head, which was certainly appropriate for a Masurian unit. Herzog's task was to convert his green recruits and draftees into a first-class combat force. The division had excellent human material, but it had not completed its unit training and was considered too inexperienced to be placed in the first wave of attacking divisions during the invasion of France and the Low Countries in May 1940, although it did participate in the final stages of the campaign. Little worse for the wear, the 291st returned to East Prussia in July and resumed training. Herzog was promoted to lieutenant general on February 1, 1941.

The 291st Infantry Division deployed on the Baltic Sea coast, on the far northern wing of Army Group North, in the spring of 1941. On June 22, it attacked from the Memel area and quickly overwhelmed the surprised Soviet frontier troops. It then advanced 44 miles in 34 hours, an incredible pace for a non-motorized division. It pushed on to Liepaja, a major Soviet naval base, which it captured after a bitter struggle on June 29. The Elk division continued its rapid advance and soon loosely surrounded Riga, the capital and major port of Latvia, and repulsed several desperate attempts by the Soviet garrison to break out of the city. Although casualties were heavy, the division held its line, and contained and eventually helped destroy the Russian garrison. Remaining with Army Group North, the 291st took part in the conquest of the Baltic States and pushed on to the outskirts of Leningrad, where one of its regiments (the 505th Infantry) knocked out 155 concrete pillboxes (including several with built-in guns) in a single day. It then helped trap 12 Soviet divisions in the Oraneinbaum pocket.

Meanwhile, on June 22, Kurt von Tippelskirch's Schleswig-Holstein 30th Infantry Division assembled south of Memel and attacked the

Soviets in the zone just south of Herzog's 291st Infantry.

Kurt Oskar Heinrich Ludwig Wilhelm von Tippelskirch was born in Berlin-Charlottenburg on October 9, 1891, the son of a major general. He was educated in cadet schools and entered the Imperial Army as a senior officer cadet on June 24, 1909.

Tippelskirch was commissioned second lieutenant on March 20, 1911, as a member of the 3rd Guards Grenadier Regiment. He took part in the invasion of France in August 1914, but was captured in the drive on the Marne the following month and was a prisoner of war (POW) until 1920. He was nonetheless accepted into the Reichswehr and commanded a company in the 9th Infantry Regiment at Postdam from 1920 to 1924. He married Elly Gallencamp, the sister of future General of Artillery Curt Gallencamp,[2] and their son, Adolf-Hilmar von Tippelskirch, became a member of the General Staff and earned the Knight's Cross commanding a battery with the 3rd Artillery Regiment on the northern sector of the Eastern Front.

Kurt von Tippelskirch became a General Staff officer in the 1920s and served in several staff positions. He was promoted to major in 1928 and to lieutenant colonel two days after Hitler came to power on January 30, 1933. Later, he commanded the 27th Infantry Regiment at Rostock (1934–36), served in the Defense Ministry, and became chief of *Oberquartiermeister IV* (the intelligence branch) of the OKH on November 10, 1938. He did little to improve German military intelligence, which was tactically excellent but strategically poor. He was nevertheless promoted to colonel on March 1, 1935, major general on April 1, 1938, and lieutenant general on June 1, 1940. He assumed command of the 30th Infantry Division on January 5, 1941.

Despite the fact that it had no water obstacles to its front, the 30th Infantry Division had a difficult time on June 22. Initially, the advance was rapid and several of the newly constructed Soviet bunkers were not even manned. Soon, however, they ran into at least a battalion of Mongolian construction workers, who fought bravely and well. They hid in the crops and ambushed German columns all day long. Long before it dawned on most of the Wehrmacht, the men from Schleswig and Holstein realized that the upcoming war with Russia was going to be much tougher than almost anyone in the Nazi leadership had ever dreamed.

Operation Barbarossa took the Soviet defenders in the frontier zone completely by surprise. Only in General Mikhail Petrovick Kirponos's Kiev Military District was there a degree of readiness.[3] Many of the trucks and tractors used to tow the Soviet guns were away at construction sites or in the fields. The Red Air Force had just completed a series of night training exercises, and its pilots were in bed and their machines short of fuel. Many men were on leave, and several important border fortress units were away from their positions, on field training exercises to the east. Those who were on the border were taken completely by surprise. At one post on the Bug River, German frontier guards called out the Soviet guards, as if an emergency were taking place. When the unsuspecting Reds came out, the Germans shot them down. All along the border, Soviet positions and installations were then rocked by the roar of 6,000 guns—all German. Barracks, supply depots, communications centers, outposts, forward headquarters, and military and civilian targets of every description went up in flames. On the western bank of the Bug River, engineers began putting down pontoon bridges, while infantrymen and motorcycle troops moved quickly across the river in rubber dinghies and assault boats. At one point, an entire battalion of underwater tanks, originally designed for Operation Sea Lion, crossed the Bug, led by Colonel Count Manfred Strachwitz.[4] South of the important fortress of Brest (the Polish fort Guderian had captured in 1939), Baron Geyr von Schweppenburg's XXIV Panzer Corps bolted across the river, capturing every important bridge in its sector, overrunning Soviet border guards and the rearguards of retreating troops, and smashing Soviet anti-tank positions.

One of the key positions for the Germans lay north of Brest, in the zone of General of Infantry Hermann Geyer's IX Corps, where they had to launch a difficult assault across the Bug River.

Hermann Geyer was born in Stuttgart, the capital of Wuerttemberg, on July 7, 1882. He joined the Imperial Army as a *Fahnenjunker* in the 119th Grenadier Regiment on July 4, 1900, and was commissioned on October 18, 1901. He was officially with his regiment until 1913, when he entered the War Academy to begin General Staff training, although he was detached to the 13th Engineer Battalion (1904-05) and the I Sea Battalion (1906–09). He was promoted to first lieutenant in 1910.

On August 2, 1914, the day World War I began, Geyer was promoted to captain and assigned to the General Staff of the Military Governor of Cologne. He remained here until May 1916, when he was transferred to the 33rd Fusilier Regiment on the Eastern Front, where he briefly commanded a company and a battalion. He was then transferred to the staff of the chief of the General Staff of the Field Army on July 3, 1916. Except for a month in the autumn of 1916, when he was on the General Staff of the 199th Infantry Division (then in combat in Galicia), he spent the rest of the war in this position. After the Kaiser abdicated, he was assigned to the Armistice Commission in Spa (1918–19) and was a member of the German Peace Delegation (1919). He then served in the Defense Ministry (1919–22).

Geyer was promoted to major in March 1922 and spent two months on the staff of the commander of the Infantry School at Doeberitz. Although he was already earmarked for greater things, Geyer lacked command experience at this stage of his career. As they occasionally did, the Army Command remedied this situation by giving him a company, despite the fact that he was a major and thus a grade above company commander. He nevertheless commanded a company in the 13th Infantry Regiment at Ludwigsburg from May 1, 1922 to October 1, 1923. He then returned to staff duties with the 5th Infantry Division at Stuttgart (1923–27). Promoted to lieutenant colonel in 1927, he returned to Ludwigsburg as commander of the II Battalion (February 1, 1927–October 1, 1928). He then headed a department in the Defense Ministry (1928–31) and was promoted to colonel in 1930.

On February 1, 1931, Hermann Geyer assumed command of the Prussian-Brunswickian 17th Infantry Regiment at Brunswick and Goslar. He was succeeded by Hermann Hoth on October 1, 1932, the day he assumed leadership of the Infantry Command V. In this capacity, Geyer was also deputy commander of the 5th Infantry Division. He was promoted to major general on December 1, 1932.

On February 1, 1933, the day after Hitler became chancellor of Germany, Hermann Geyer became chief of staff of Group Command Two in Kassel. This was one of Germany's two army-level headquarters. He was promoted to lieutenant general on January 1, 1934, and on

August 1, returned to Stuttgart as commander of Wehrkreis V and the 5th Infantry Division. As the Wehrmacht expanded, Geyer gave up command of the 5th Infantry but remained Wehrkreis commander until April 30, 1939. He was promoted to general of infantry on August 1, 1936.

Hermann Geyer retired from the army on April 30, 1939, and was named honorary colonel of the 119th Infantry Regiment. After the fall of Poland, however, he was recalled to active duty and was named commander of the IX Corps on October 25, 1939. He led his corps with considerable success in Belgium and France the following year. He redeployed it to Poland in September 1940.

Like most of General Geyer's operations, everything also went according to plan on June 22. Dinghies and assault boats were used in the initial assault, and the bridgehead was quickly established. By 9 a.m., a heavy equipment bridge had been completed, and trucks, artillery, and assault guns poured across the river. Less than six hours after the campaign began, the IX Corps was in full pursuit mode.

Along the entire 500-mile length of the Bug, not a single German attack miscarried. Simultaneous with the ground attack, the Luftwaffe pounded on targets further to the rear and on the Red Air Force. By noon, they had knocked out dozens of Soviet airfields, blasted their fuel dumps, cut their supply lines, pulverized troop units as they attempted to assemble, and destroyed 1,200 Soviet airplanes, 800 of them on the ground. They ranged as far east as Sevastopol, where they bombed one of the most important Soviet naval bases. The Germans lost only ten planes themselves. At the Officers' Club in Minsk, General Dmitry Pavlov, the commander of the Western Military District, was watching a comedy when his intelligence chief arrived and whispered in his ear that the Germans were attacking. Pavlov turned to his deputy, General Ivan V. Boldin, and said that the message was some "nonsense" about Germans firing along the border. He continued watching the play.[5]

When the Soviet generals were finally jolted into reality, they found themselves hamstrung by orders from Moscow. Timoshenko told General Bolden: "No actions must be taken against the Germans without our consent. Comrade Stalin has forbidden our artillery to open fire."

"It's not possible," Boldin shouted into the receiver. "Our troops are retreating. Whole towns are in flames. Everywhere people are being killed." But the order stood.[6] At 7:15 a.m., Stalin finally issued a directive authorizing the Red Army to fire on the invaders. They were forbidden, however, to cross the border into German territory.

That morning, Moscow ordered Lieutenant General Ivan Ivanovich Kopets, the commander of Air Forces, West Front, to bomb the enemy. He knew that his slow Ilyushin and Tupolev bombers, unescorted by fighters, would have little chance against the Messerschmitts, but he did as he was told. Almost every Soviet general tried to carry out his orders, many of which were ridiculous: The memory of Stalin's Great Purge was still fresh on everyone's mind, and there was a suspicious commissar looking over every general's shoulder.

Kopets was right: his aircraft were shot down so easily that Field Marshal Kesselring called it "infanticide." By June 23, Kopets had lost all of his bombers—more than 500 aircraft. Then he killed himself.[7] Lieutenant General Pavel Rychagov, the commander of aviation units in the northwest, also did as he was told, with equally disastrous results. Within a week he was sentenced to death for treason (i.e., for having failed) and was executed without benefit of a trial.

Russian bomber squadrons also tried to destroy Constanta, Romania's Black Sea port, and the Ploesti oilfields. They were met by the Me-109s of III Group, 52nd Fighter Wing (III/JG 52), which shot down 45 to 50 Soviet airplanes in five days, and brought the attacks to an abrupt halt.

Meanwhile, back in Moscow, Defense Commissar Timoshenko had no idea what was happening at the front. Generals, who knew that Stalin equated failure with treason, were afraid to report the truth to the Kremlin, and even Zhukov thought that the situation was developing favorably. Timoshenko therefore ordered a general counterattack.

At the front, Colonel General Kirponos's armies were ordered to surround and destroy the German forces that had attacked them, and to push on to Lublin, a Polish city well behind German lines, within two days. Kirponos knew that this order was crazy: some of his divisions had disappeared entirely, communications were down, the Red Army was in complete disarray, and the Germans had broken through in several places. His political commissar, however, was Nikolai N. Vashugin, who had played a major role in the Great Purge. Vashugin told him to carry out his order. Noting the commissar's threatening tone,

Kirponos nodded and attempted to do so. Naturally, the counterattack was unsuccessful, robbed Kirponos of much of his reserve, and was very costly in terms of Russian lives.

During the first two months of Operation Barbarossa, the Luftwaffe was successful everywhere it struck. German bomber units flew up to six missions a day in the first few days of the campaign, while dive-bombers and fighters flew up to eight missions, depending upon the distance from their forward airfields to their targets. The German pilots were amazingly successful in their attempts at establishing aerial supremacy from the outset. "It was like shooting ducks," Colonel Johannes Steinhoff recalled.[8] This sense of individual superiority over the Russian pilot remained with the German aviator throughout the war. "The German pilot gained and retained the ascendancy over his Russian counterpart mainly because of his superior ego factor," Constable and Toliver wrote. They stated further:

> All the qualities of individual intelligence, independence initiative, and enterprise which fitted him temperamentally for the highly individualized art of aerial combat were encouraged and developed in his training. The Soviet system with its leveling tendencies and opposition to individualism was less than an ideal environment in which to breed fighter pilots.
>
> Even as the Russians got steadily better with the passage of time, the individual German fighter pilot never lost the inner conviction that he was a better man than his foes . . . . The capacity of the German fighter pilots to sustain themselves in the air under such adverse conditions show that what a fighter pilot thinks of himself will manifest itself in what he achieves.[9]

In the tactical sphere, the Luftwaffe commanders such as Helmuth Foerster were also performing extremely well.

Helmuth Foerster was born in Gross-Strehlitz, Upper Silesia (now Strezelce Opolskie, Poland) on April 19, 1889. He entered the army as a *Fahnenjunker* in the 1st Railway Regiment on September 23, 1907, and was commissioned in early 1909. He became an aviator in 1910 and was a member of Test Flying Command Doeberitz from then until 1913, when he became adjutant to the inspector of flying troops. He was an officer and pilot with the 31st Air Battalion from the outbreak of World War I to 1915, when he joined the staff of the chief of aviation affairs. He was promoted to first lieutenant in 1914 and to captain in 1915. In 1916, he underwent General Staff training and was on the staff of the commander of air forces from 1917 until 1919, when he was separated from the army. Despite a solid record, he was not one of the 180 air officers Colonel General Hans von Seeckt selected for his 4,000 man officer corps in the 100,000-man "Treaty Army." He was discharged with the honorary rank of major.

After 15 years in the private sector of the economy, Foerster secretly rejoined the service as a lieutenant colonel in the Luftwaffe on March 1, 1934. Goering's air force needed General Staff officers and, after 30 days with the Reich Air Ministry, he was sent to East Prussia as chief of staff of Higher Air Office Koenigsberg. Shortly after Hitler renounced the clause of the Treaty of Versailles which forbade Germany to have an air force, this command was renamed *Luftkreis I* (I Air District).

Foerster was promoted to colonel on August 1, 1935, the same day he assumed command of the 253rd Bomber Wing "General Wever." He commanded KG 253 until 1937, when he became commander of the Luftwaffe's instruction troops, which became the Instruction Division on February 1, 1938. He was promoted to major general that same day. Meanwhile, in the Luftwaffe's internal politics, he allied himself with Goering's deputy and enemy, State Secretary for Aviation and Inspector General of the Luftwaffe, Eduard Milch. This led to his promotion to lieutenant general on January 1, 1940. Foerster, a special duties officer to Colonel General Milch, was named his chief of staff when Germany invaded Denmark and Norway, and Milch was placed in charge of the 5th Air Fleet. Milch, however, was reluctant even to go to Norway, so Foerster did a disproportionate amount of the work, a fact not lost on Goering.

After the fall of France, Foerster was the leader of the Luftwaffe's contingent to the Franco-German Armistice Commission, a post he held until April 18, 1941, when he was named Military Commander Serbia. He was promoted to general of fliers the next day. Meanwhile, the air units in France planned to redeploy to the east for the invasion of the Soviet Union. The plan was to attack the United Kingdom with such force as to deceive the Allies into thinking that Hitler intended to resume the Battle of Britain; then they would quickly move to airfields in the east. As part of this operation, Colonel General Ulrich Grauert took off with elements of his I Air Corps on May 15, 1941. He never returned. He was jumped by British fighters and was shot down over St. Omer, near Pas de Calais, France. Helmuth Foerster, selected to replace him, assumed command on May 31, 1941, only three weeks before the invasion began.

Despite his lack of familiarity with his new command, General Foerster excelled on "Null Day," the day the attack was launched, and thereafter. In the zone of I Air Corps alone, German pilots attacked 77 Soviet airfields in 1,600 sorties during the first three days of the campaign. It shot down 400 enemy airplanes and destroyed another 1,100 on the ground. By August 23, it had shot down 920 enemy airplanes and destroyed 1,594 more on the ground, a total of 2,514 Soviet airplanes destroyed—more than three times the number of aircraft in the entire 1st Air Fleet!

To the north, also in support of Army Group North, lay Colonel Wolfgang von Wild's Air Command Baltic, which also distinguished itself.

Wolfgang von Wild was born at Frankfurt/Main on April 26, 1901. Shortly after his 17th birthday, he joined the Imperial Navy as an officer cadet on July 1, 1918. He was assigned to the battleship *Silesia* (*Schlesien*) on October 1, only a month before the Kiel Naval Revolt led to the abdication of the Kaiser. Officer cadet Wild joined the right-wing Freikorps in order to fight Communist and other insurrectionists and was seriously wounded in February 1919. In late July, he returned to duty, this time with the infamous Ehrhardt Naval Brigade, which attempted to overthrow the government in the Kapp Putsch of 1920. After the coup was defeated, Wild was given the opportunity to join the Reichswehr, which he promptly did. He spent the period September 1920-September 1923 in a variety of training courses. He was finally commissioned ensign (*Leutnant zur See*) on April 1, 1923.

Wolfgang von Wild served as a watch officer on a torpedo boat (1923-24) and as a platoon leader with a coastal defense battalion (1924-26). Promoted to lieutenant (j.g.) in 1925, he attended an artillery officer observers' course at the Ship Artillery School in Kiel (1926), before becoming adjutant of the 1st Torpedo Boat Half-Flotilla. After a year as a watch officer on a torpedo boat, he became an aerial observer with the Radio Test Command at Warnemuende on October 1, 1930. He attended a number of special courses as part of his General Staff training, before being sent to Italy in 1932, where he underwent secret flight training. He returned to Germany the next year as a group leader with the Radio Test Command. Promoted to lieutenant in April 1933, he became the liaison officer between the Naval Station North Sea and the Air Office Kiel, the cover name for Luftkreis VI. He transferred to the secret Luftwaffe on October 1, 1934, and was officially designated a captain in the air force in 1935.

Wild was chief of operations on the staff of the Fuehrer of Naval Air Forces from 1934 to 1936. Promoted to major on March 1, 1936, he was a company commander in the 16th Air Replacement Battalion from 1936 to 1937. He went on to become chief of operations to the commander of flying schools (sea) and (sea) replacement battalions. In December 1938, he became commander of the 506th Coastal Air Group. His title was changed to commander of 806th Coastal Air Group and commandant of air base Dievenow in October 1939. Meanwhile, he operated against the Poles, with considerable success. He was named Flight Leader Baltic Sea on April 21, 1941. He had been promoted to lieutenant colonel on January 1, 1939

Wild's Air Command Baltic sank 66,000 tons of Soviet shipping, as well as five destroyers. It also destroyed 58 Russian airplanes, while losing only 20 itself. Most importantly, however, it forced the Soviet Baltic Fleet back towards the Gulf of Finland and Leningrad, where it could not hinder the advance of the left flank of the 18th Army. With its mission accomplished, it was redesignated Luftwaffe Command South and transferred to the Crimea in October. Wild, meanwhile, was promoted to colonel on August 1.

The success of 1st Air Fleet was matched all along the front. No one, however, was more successful than Field Marshal Kesselring.

Albert Kesselring, who was known as "Smiling Al," was born in Markstedt, in the Lower Franconia district of Bavaria, on November 30, 1885. His father, a school teacher, saw to it that his son received an excellent education at the Classical School in Bayreuth. Albert would, in fact, be known as a sophisticated, diplomatic and urbane officer throughout his life.

Perhaps influenced by the military bases in nearby Kitzingen, young Albert decided on a military career and joined the Bavarian Army as a *Fahnenjunker* in the 2nd Bavarian Foot Artillery Regiment at Metz on July 20, 1904. He attended the War School at Munich and was commissioned second lieutenant on March 8, 1906. He underwent training as a balloon observer with the Bavarian Airship Battalion in 1912.

In 1910, Kesselring became the victim of an arranged marriage. As part of the bargain, his wife's mother received the right to live with the couple until her death, which occurred after World War II. Because of his strongly Catholic beliefs concerning divorce, Kesselring never left this loveless and unhappy marriage; instead, he devoted himself to his career. The marriage produced no children, although the couple did adopt Rainer Kesselring, the son of Albert's second cousin.

Albert became adjutant of the I/2nd Bavarian Foot Artillery Regiment in 1912 and fought in Lorraine, on the Somme and in Flanders in 1914 and 1915. In September, he became a special duties officer with the 1st Bavarian Foot Artillery Brigade, also on the Western Front, and remained in this post until May 1917, when he was named adjutant of the 3rd Bavarian Artillery Command (Bavarian Arko 3). From late November 1917 until January 3, 1918, he was attached to the 2nd Bavarian Landwehr Division, where he underwent on-the-job General Staff training. He was then admitted to the General Staff without any further training and was not even required to attend the abbreviated three-month course at Sedan. Kesselring served on the General Staff of the 6th Army and the III Bavarian Corps (also on the Western Front) during the last year of the war. He was, meanwhile, promoted to first lieutenant (1913) and to captain (May 19, 1916).

Very depressed by the loss of the war, Kesselring considered leaving the army, but did not. He joined the 24th Artillery Regiment (1919-20), commanded a battery in the Bavarian 7th Artillery Regiment at Nuremberg (1921-22), served in the defense ministry (1922-25), on the staff of the Army Command (1925-30), and in the Army Personnel Office (1930-32). He commanded the III Battalion of the 4th Artillery Regiment in Dresden (February 1932-September 1933), and was promoted to major (1925), lieutenant colonel (early 1930) and colonel (1932). Then, somewhat against his will, he was transferred to the secret Luftwaffe on October 1, 1933.

Because of the air force's shortage of experienced General Staff officers, and because of his high reputation for competence within the army, Kesselring was named chief of the Luftwaffe's administrative office. Here he was involved in the reestablishment of the German aviation industry, the construction of several secret factories, and in research and development with aviation engineers. He also underwent pilot training and would often fly three or four times a week. He would be shot down five times during World War II but was always able to bail out or crash-land his airplane.

On June 3, 1936, Kesselring replaced General Walter Wever as chief of the General Staff of the Luftwaffe after the latter was killed in a flight accident. As chief, Kesselring was deeply involved in the acquisition of the Me-109 fighter, the Ju-87 dive-bomber and other airplanes, as well as in research and development, the establishment of Luftwaffe bases, and the formation and development of the parachute branch. On the negative side, he (with the full approval of Erhard Milch and Hermann Goering) scrapped Wever's four-engine, long-range bomber projects. As a result, Germany never developed an effective strategic bomber, a fact that would have severe repercussions in Russia from 1942 onwards.

Kesselring soon tired of the continuous political in-fighting with Milch, the state secretary for aviation and the inspector general of the Luftwaffe. In 1937, he submitted his retirement papers. Not wishing to lose Kesselring, Goering gave him command of the III Air District (Luftgau III) in Berlin instead. The general held this post from June 1, 1937 until February 4, 1938, when he assumed command of the 1st Air Fleet.

After brilliantly supporting Bock's Army Group North during the Polish campaign, he was given command of the 2nd Air Fleet in the West on January 12, 1940. During the French campaign, he again performed brilliantly, which led to his promotion to field marshal on July 19, 1940. He had previously been promoted to major general (October 1, 1934), lieutenant general (April 1, 1936) and general of fliers (June 1, 1937). The rank of colonel general he bypassed altogether.

Many Americans consider Kesselring a military genius because of his conduct of operations in Italy from 1943 to 1945. He was not a genius, although he certainly showed flashes of brilliance. He certainly failed to show genius during the Battle of Britain, however, when he supported the idea of launching terror attacks against London instead of continuing the attacks on the bases of the RAF's Fighter Command, as advocated by Field Marshal Hugo Sperrle. We know now that Sperrle was right: Hitler's shift to terror bombing saved the United Kingdom.

Kesselring's air fleet continued the terror attacks, with varying degrees of intensity, until May 1941, when it redeployed to Poland for Operation Barbarossa. Kesselring's 2nd Air Fleet virtually wiped out the Red Air Force in the central combat zone within 48 hours of the beginning of the war. Kesselring claimed to have destroyed 2,500 Soviet airplanes during the first week of the campaign. Hermann Goering did not believe this claim, so he ordered an investigation to determine if Kesselring had inflated the size of his victory. The investigators reported that Kesselring had underestimated the number of airplanes his pilots had destroyed by 200 to 300.

One of the major reasons for the success of 2nd Air Fleet and of Army Group Center during the first days of Operation Barbarossa was Martin Fiebig, a close air support expert whom Kesselring assigned to II Air Corps three weeks before the invasion began.

Martin Fiebig was born on May 7, 1891, in Roesnitz, Upper Silesia. A product of the cadet school system, he entered the army as a Faehnrich in the 18th Infantry Regiment on March 3, 1910, and was commissioned second lieutenant on March 20, 1911. A battalion adjutant when the war broke out, he fought in East Prussia, Poland and Russia in 1914 and early 1915, before he underwent flight training. He became a squadron leader in the 3rd Bomber Wing and was the commander of the 9th Bomber Wing in the East when the war ended. He was discharged as a captain, apparently at his own request, in February 1919.

Fiebig worked for Lufthansa, the German national airline, from 1919 to 1934, before joining the Luftwaffe as a major on May 1, 1934.

Initially the commandant of the air base at Greifswald, Vorpommern, he was promoted to lieutenant colonel and assumed command of the Bomber Flight School at Fassberg, Lower Saxony, in 1936. He was advanced to the rank of colonel on June 1, 1938, and became commander of the 253rd (later 4th) Bomber Wing "General Wever" at Gotha, Thuringia, a month later. By now a close air support expert, he flew in support of the 18th Army when the invasion of France, Belgium and the Netherlands began on May 10, 1940. Before the day was over, Fiebig was shot down and captured by the Dutch. Freed when The Hague surrendered on May 16, he became commander of a close air support battle group supporting Panzer Group Guderian. On August 1, he was named chief of flight security at the air ministry.

Colonel Fiebig was appointed close air support leader of the IV Air Corps in the West on April 2, 1941, the day after he was promoted to major general. He was named close air support leader of the II Air Corps on June 1, and played a major role in 2nd Air Fleet's victories in Operation Barbarossa. He held the same job with Richthofen's VIII Air Corps from November 15, 1941 to April 11, 1942.

To the south, Loehr's 4th Air Fleet was experiencing similar success rates. Ritter Robert von Greim's V Air Corps was particularly successful.

Alexander Loehr was born on May 20, 1885 in Turnu-Severin, Romania. Originally a citizen of the Austro-Hungarian Empire, he attended cadet schools and was commissioned directly into the Austrian Army as a second lieutenant on August 18, 1906. Initially he was a platoon leader in the engineer battalion of the 85th Infantry Regiment, although he later served in the regiment's machine gun battalion.[(10)] He attended the Austrian War Academy in Vienna (1910-13), graduated as a General Staff officer, and underwent aerial observer training. During World War I, he was made a staff officer with the 58th Infantry Division (1914-15) and served in the aviation department of the War Ministry (1915-18). He also spent three months as an acting battalion commander in the 74th Infantry Regiment (January-March 1918) and was wounded twice in the Great War. He remained at the War Ministry (which was now called the Ministry for Army Affairs) until 1927, working primary in aviation. He spent six months (1927-28) on the staff of the 2nd Bicycle Battalion, before becoming director of the air force department in the ministry in 1928. He officially became commander of the Austrian Air Force in 1934. Meanwhile, he was promoted to captain (1915), major (1920), lieutenant colonel (1921), colonel (1928) and major general (1934).

The Third Reich annexed Austria on March 12, 1938. Twelve days later, Loehr was promoted to lieutenant general and was named commander of Luftwaffe forces in Austria. His title was changed to Luftwaffe Commander Ostmark (the new name for Austria) in 1938. He was promoted to general of fliers on March 25, 1939, seven days after he was named commander-in-chief of the 4th Air Fleet. Loehr commanded the 4th in Poland, the Balkans campaign, the Battle of Crete, and on the Eastern Front (1941-42). He was awarded the Wounded Badge in Silver after the Polish campaign, which indicates that he was wounded in action, although the details of his injury have not come down to us. He was promoted to colonel general on May 3, 1941.

Robert von Greim was born in Bayreuth, Bavaria, the son of Ludwig von Greim, who retired as an army lieutenant colonel and later became a captain in the Bavarian police. Robert entered the army as a *Fahenjunker* in the Bavarian Railroad Battalion on July 14, 1911. He attended the War School at Munich in 1912 and was commissioned *Leutnant* in the Bavarian 8th Field Artillery Regiment on October 25, 1913. He initially served as a battery officer and became a battalion adjutant in 1914. Between August 1914 and the fall of 1915, he fought in Lorraine, including the battles of Cotes de Meuse and St. Mihiel. From August to November 1915, he underwent aerial observer training. On October 10, he shot down his first enemy airplane while flying in a two-seat aircraft, even though he was still an observer and still in training. (He was spotting for the artillery at the time.) He served as an observer with Field Flying Battalion A until October 1916, when he transferred to the Bavarian 1st Flying Replacement Battalion at Schleis-sheim to undergo pilot training. He then served six weeks with the 46th Flying Battalion (February-early April 1917) and spent the rest of the war commanding the 34th Fighter Squadron (Jasta 34) and the 10th Fighter Group, except for the period July 2 to August 1, 1918, when he was recovering from a wound. He and a sergeant also launched what was arguably the first successful aerial attack against enemy tanks on August 23, 1918.

Greim (a first lieutenant since January 1917) shot down 28 enemy airplanes during the war and was awarded the *Pour le Merite* on October 14, 1918. Nine days later, he was awarded the Bavarian Military Max Joseph Order, which carried with it a non-hereditary knighthood and the title *Ritter*.

After the armistice, Greim returned to Munich and rejoined his regiment (the 8th Bavarian Artillery). For 10 months, he was chief of air postal station Munich, and in 1920 he flew an aspiring Austrian politician named Adolf Hitler to Berlin during the Kapp Putsch. The weather was bad and Hitler became so airsick that he swore he would never fly again. (He later changed his mind.) The Putsch, meanwhile, collapsed about the time Hitler and Greim arrived.

Ritter von Greim, a man of right-wing political views, was unhappy with the Weimar Republic. He made no attempt to remain in the Reichswehr and was discharged on March 31, 1920, with an honorary promotion to captain. He enrolled in the University of Munich in 1920 and passed the Junior Law Exam in 1922. He was employed by a bank from 1922 to 1924, but found this job boring, so he removed himself to Canton, China, where he was the chief organizer and trainer of military flying for the Chinese National government of Chiang Kai-Shek from 1924 to early 1927. He had a low opinion of Chinese students, whom he felt had no fine touch at the stick.

Greim returned to Germany in the spring of 1927, where he was the chief of the German Air Sport Foundation's flying school at Wuerzburg. He entered the secret Luftwaffe as a major on April 1, 1934, when he assumed command of the Doeberitz Flying Group of Fighter Wing Richthofen. He commanded the 132nd Fighter Wing "Richthofen" and Air Base Doeberitz from July 1, 1934 to March 31, 1935. After Hitler renounced the military clauses of the Treaty of Versailles on March 9 and 16, 1935, Greim was named inspector of Air Inspectorate 3–fighter and ground attack units. He was promoted to lieutenant colonel on September 1, 1935.

On February 10, 1936, Greim became inspector of flight security and equipment. He was promoted to colonel on April 20, 1936. Then, on June 1, 1937, he was named chief of the powerful Luftwaffe

Personnel Office in the Reich Defense Ministry. He was promoted to major general on February 1, 1938, and assumed command of the 5th Air Division on February 6, 1939. After the Polish campaign, the division upgraded to V Air Corps on October 25, 1939, and Greim was promoted to lieutenant general January 1, 1940. He led his corps with great success during the French campaign, which led to his promotion to general of fliers on July 19, 1940. He was, of course, less successful during the Battle of Britain.

During the first four days of Operation Barbarossa, Ritter von Greim's relatively weak V Air Corps flew 1,600 sorties, destroyed 774 Soviet aircraft on the ground, and another 136 in the air. By July 3, Greim was able to report that his men had destroyed their 1,000th Soviet airplane on the ground.[11] By June 24, wrote Goralski, the German Air Force had destroyed about 2,000 Soviet planes. "In just seventy-two hours the largest air force in the world had been reduced to an ineffectual remnant."[12] On June 29, at the end of the first week of the campaign, OKW reported the destruction of 4,017 enemy aircraft, at a cost of 150 German airplanes destroyed or heavily damaged, a ratio of 27 to 1.12.

By June 24, with most of the Red air forces smashed, the Luftwaffe turned almost all of its attention to direct and indirect support missions for the army. In these types of operations, Wolfram von Richthofen excelled.

Baron Wolfram von Richthofen was born on his family's Barzdorf estate, near Striegau, Lower Silesia, on October 10, 1895. He was educated in the cadet school system and graduated from Gross Lichterfelde in 1913. He entered the service as a Faehnrich in the 4th Hussar Regiment on March 22, 1913, was commissioned second lieutenant on June 19, 1914, and served primarily on the Eastern Front as a squadron officer and platoon leader. He began pilot training in the fall of 1917 and joined the 1st Fighter Wing in March 1918. This unit was commanded by the Red Baron, Manfred von Richthofen, who was Wolfram's cousin. After Manfred was killed in action on April 21, 1918, the wing was commanded by Hermann Goering. Wolfram's cousin Lothar was also in the unit, and he ended the war with 40 kills. [13]

Wolfram became an ace in his own right and ended the war with eight confirmed kills. Not wishing to remain in the Reichswehr, he was discharged in 1920 with an honorary promotion to first lieutenant. Less affected by defeat than most of his contemporaries, Richthofen married Jutta von Selchow (1896-1991) that same year. The couple would eventually have three children. Meanwhile, Wolfram enrolled in the Hanover Technical School, where he earned his engineering diploma in 1924 and an advanced degree in 1929. Meanwhile, he rejoined the army on November 1, 1923, as a second lieutenant in the Prussian 11th Cavalry Regiment in Berlin. He soon began his secret General Staff training and was promoted to first lieutenant (permanent rank) in 1925. He was given command of a company in the 5th Motorized Transport Battalion in 1928, and was promoted to captain in 1929. Later that year, he was attached to the Army's Statistical Department (T 3) in the defense ministry and was then sent to Italy to study the Italian Air Force (1929-32). He commanded a company in the 6th Motorized Transport Battalion (1932-33), before transferring to the secret Luftwaffe on October 1, 1933.

Richthofen rose rapidly in the new air force. He was promoted to major (June 1, 1934), lieutenant colonel (April 20, 1936), colonel (January 23, 1938), major general (November 1, 1938), and general of fliers (July 19, 1940). The rank of lieutenant general he skipped altogether. He started out an advisor in the Air Ministry (1933-34), but was soon promoted to chief of testing and development (1934-37), at a time when Germany was just producing the Me-109 fighter, the He-111 and Do-17 bombers and the Hs-123 dive-bomber.

Richthofen was the most competent and influential assistant to Ernst Udet, the incompetent chief of the Technical and Air Armaments Office. The baron went to Spain and watched the new airplanes in actual combat in the Spanish Civil War in 1936. He returned to Iberia in January 1937 as the chief of staff of the Condor Legion, the German force supporting Generalissimo Francisco Franco's Nationalists. Franco especially respected the Red Baron's nephew, who became the spokesman for the Legion with the Spanish government. It was here that Wolfram von Richthofen became impressed with the dive-bomber—especially the Ju-87 Stuka.[14] Because of Richthofen's influence with Udet, the Luftwaffe became too enamored with the concept of dive bombing. It evolved into an unbalanced service that essentially became "flying artillery" for the army, but it lacked an effective long-range bomber; in fact, it never did develop one.

Richthofen returned to Germany in October 1937, as a special duties officer in the Air Ministry. He assumed command of the 257th Bomber Wing (KG 257) on April 1, 1938, but returned to Spain on November 1, as the last commander of the Condor Legion. Thanks in significant measure to the Condor Legion, the Loyalist government in Madrid surrendered on March 29, 1939. The Spanish Civil War was over.

Baron von Richthofen returned to Berlin in July 1939 and became commander of the Special Purpose Air Division, which consisted mainly of dive-bomber and close air support squadrons. He led in Poland with great success. On October 3, his command was redesignated the VIII Air Corps. Richthofen led it in the French campaign, again with great success. The Stuka, however, was no match for the Spitfire, so Richthofen's command was decisively defeated in the Battle of Britain and was, in fact, withdrawn fairly early in the campaign. Richthofen resumed his successful ways in 1941, when his corps played a major role in the conquests of Greece and Yugoslavia, and was a decisive factor in the Battle of Crete. It also did tremendous damage to the Royal Navy in the eastern Mediterranean. In June 1941, however, it flew north, in order to support Army Group Center in Operation Barbarossa.

On June 24, the Army's VIII and XX Corps of Strauss's 9th Army came under heavy tank and cavalry attack near Bialystok and Lunna. Richthofen committed his entire corps to their aid and destroyed 105 tanks by nightfall. Throughout the campaign of 1941, the Luftwaffe—and especially the Stukas of VIII Air Corps—continued to support the army in an outstanding manner. The flying artillery destroyed command posts, tanks and bunkers, smashed troop concentrations, and caused all manner of destruction to the Red armies and the Soviet war machine.

Unfortunately for the Germans, the Luftwaffe bombers had neither the numbers nor the range to disrupt rail traffic east of the Dnieper. Because the Third Reich had no strategic air forces, Soviet engineers were able to hastily dismantle every possible piece of industrial machinery and send it east, where it would be reassembled in the Urals or beyond. In all, nearly 300 industrial complexes were evacuated from the Ukraine alone, along with nearly 150 smaller factories. Almost 500 factories were transferred from the Moscow area to the east. In all, some 1,300 large plants were shipped east, a move requiring 6,500,000 railroad cars. Although dislocated and badly hurt, the industrial potential of the Soviet Union had not been destroyed; if the blitzkrieg did not conquer the U.S.S.R. before the onset of winter, Russia, with a population almost three times that of the Third Reich, would be able to recover.

For the Germans, the first unpleasant surprise of the campaign came on the night of June 23, in the zone of Georg-Hans Reinhardt's XXXXI Motorized Corps, on the left wing of the 4th Panzer Group, in the zone of Army Group North.

Georg-Hans Reinhardt was born at Bautzen, Saxony, on March 1, 1887, and joined the army as a *Fahnenjunker* in the 107th (8th Saxon) Infantry Regiment "Prince Johann Georg" at Leipzig on March 25, 1907. He was commissioned second lieutenant on August 14, 1908, and became adjutant of the III Battalion in January 1910. He spent several months in 1912 attached to the 18th Ulan Regiment to learn more about the cavalry branch. He went to war with his regiment and fought in Luxembourg (1914), on the Marne (1914) and in Flanders (1914–16). He was promoted to captain on May 22, 1916 and began his General Staff training shortly thereafter. In January 1917, Reinhardt was a General Staff officer with the 8th Cavalry Division on the Eastern Front and, at the end of the war, was chief of operations of the 192nd Infantry Division on the Western Front. He joined the Reichswehr and was a General Staff officer with the 4th Infantry Division in Dresden, Saxony, in 1925, when he was promoted to major. In the fall of 1925, he was given command of a cavalry squadron in the 12th (Saxon) Cavalry Regiment at Dresden. After three years of command, he was transferred to the defense ministry, where he labored for four years (1928–31) in the T 4 department of the Truppenamt, the secret General Staff. He was promoted to lieutenant colonel on October 10, 1931.

Colonel Reinhardt assumed command of the III Battalion of the Saxon 10th Infantry Regiment at Dresden in the fall of 1932. He was promoted to colonel on April 1, 1934 and was appointed chief of the

Army Training Office in Zossen (1934–37). He was promoted to major general on April 1, 1937.

Georg-Hans Reinhardt saw that the future lay in the motorized branch, so he secured for himself an appointment as commander of the 1st Rifle Brigade of the 1st Panzer Division at Weimar on October 12, 1937. When Hitler created the 4th Panzer Division at Wuerzburg on November 10, 1938, Reinhardt was its commander. He led it in Poland, where it suffered heavy casualties in the initial (and unsuccessful) assault on Warsaw. Reinhardt was nevertheless promoted to lieutenant general on October 1. On February 15, 1940, he was named commander of the XXXXI Motorized (later Panzer) Corps, which he led in Belgium and France. He was promoted to general of panzer troops on June 1, 1940, and was placed in charge of the 3rd Panzer Group (later Army) on October 5, which he led into the Soviet Union on June 22, 1941.

East of the Lithuanian village of Rossizny (Raseiniai), the 1st and 6th Panzer Divisions of Reinhardt's XXXXI Motorized Corps came under heavy attack from the Soviet III Armored Corps, which was equipped mainly with the Klim Voroshilov series tanks, the KV-l and KV-2, which weighed 43 and 52 tons, respectively. The KV-2, in fact, weighed twice as much as the heaviest German tank: "all armored-piercing shells simply bounced off them," the 1st Panzer reported. One KV-2 was hit more than 70 times by German anti-tank fire, but not a single round pierced the armor. The anti-tank gunners soon took to aiming at their tracks, hoping to immobilize them, and then to finish them off with artillery or anti-aircraft guns, or blow them up at close range with high explosives. Fortunately, the Soviets showed no tactical skill or under-standing of combined-arms methods, and merely launched repeated frontal attacks.

Meanwhile, Reinhardt was reinforced by Lt. Gen. Otto-Ernst Ottenbacher's 36th Motorized Division and Major General Ernst von Leyser's 269th Infantry Division. It was good for the Germans that they rushed to the scene, for Reinhardt needed all of the help he could get.

Ernst Ulrich Hans von Leyser was born in the village of Steglitz (which is now Berlin-Steglitz) on November 18, 1889. He was educated in the cadet schools and entered the army as a *Leutnant* in the 5th Foot Guards

Regiment on March 24, 1909. When Germany mobilized in August 1914, he was transferred to the 1st Guards Reserve Infantry Regiment. He spent the entire war with this regiment, fighting in Belgium (1914), Poland (1914-15), and the Western Front (1916-18), including the battles for Flanders, and Somme, La Bassee and Cambrai. At various times, he was a platoon leader, battalion adjutant, company commander, brigade adjutant and battalion commander. Meanwhile, he was promoted to first lieutenant (1915) and captain (July 1918). Despite a solid record of accomplishment, he was not selected for the Reichsheer. He joined the police and remained with them until March 1935, when Hitler renounced the Treaty of Versailles.

Leyser immediately rejoined the army as a major, but was quickly promoted to lieutenant colonel (1936) and colonel (March 1, 1937). He was initially acting commander of the 77th Infantry Regiment, which was then forming in Bonn and Cologne, but was transferred to the command of the 2nd Anti-tank Battalion on August 1, 1935. He later directed XIV Anti-tank Command. When Germany mobilized on August 26, 1939, Leyser took charge of the 6th Infantry Replacement Regiment at Bielefeld, just behind the Western Front. On October 25, after Warsaw surrendered, he assumed command of the 169th Infantry Regiment, which he led with success in Belgium and France. As a result, he was promoted to major general on February 1, 1941 and was placed in command of the Schleswig-Holstein 269th Infantry Division in East Prussia on April 1. Although part of the I Corps of the 18th Army, as soon as he learned that General Reinhardt was in trouble, he rushed to the battlefield with his division.[15]

Otto-Ernst Ottenbacher was born in Esslingen, in the Baden-Wuert-temberg area of southwestern Germany, on November 18, 1888. He joined the army as a *Fahnenjunker* on June 29, 1907 and was commissioned on November 19, 1908. He was a member of the 121st Infantry Regiment, which fought in France (1914), Russia (1914), Serbia (1915) and the Western Front (1915-18). He remained in the Reichswehr and was a major when Hitler came to power in 1933. He was promoted to lieutenant colonel on October 1, 1933, to colonel on August 1, 1935, to major general on April 1, 1939 and to lieutenant general on March 1, 1941. In the meanwhile, he commanded the 54th Infantry Regiment at

Glogau (now Glogow, Poland) from 1934 to 1938. He became commandant of Fortress Loetzen in Silesia (now Gizycko, Poland) in 1938. On July 1, 1940, he became commander of the 177th Replacement Division in Vienna.

Up until this point, Otto Ottenbacher had not seen action in World War II and was apparently not considered a "rising star" in the Wehrmacht. Then, for reasons not made clear by the records, he was given command of the 36th Infantry, which was converting into a motorized division in Kaiserslautern. Sent to the east in the spring of 1941, Ottenbacher (like Leyser) rushed to Rossizny when Reinhardt came under attack. The Battle of Rossizny was not decided until June 26, when the more experienced Germans launched a flank attack, drove the Soviets into a swamp, and smashed the III Armored. The Reds lost 200 tanks in this battle.[16]

On Reinhardt's right flank lay the LVI Motorized Corps, which was commanded by the man most of the German senior officers and many other people (including this author) considered the best general Germany produced during World War II: General of Panzer Troops (later *Generalfeldmarschall*, Field Marshal) Erich von Manstein. As B. H. Liddell Hart later recalled: "The general verdict among the German generals I interrogated in 1945 was that Field Marshal von Manstein had proved the ablest commander in their army, and the man they had most desired to become Commander-in-Chief."[17] This was the opinion of Field Marshal Rommel, Gerd von Rundstedt, the senior German field marshal, and even Heinz Guderian, the "Father of the Blitzkrieg" and a man not easily impressed by anyone other than himself, and many others agreed with him. Even Hitler said: "Manstein is perhaps the best brain that the General Staff Corps has produced."[18] He was universally respected and even held somewhat in awe by the German generals, a class not exactly known for its lack of personal ego. This is precisely why Hitler feared him.

Manstein was born to be a general. When he first saw the light of day, in Berlin on November 24, 1887, his name was Fritz Erich von Lewinski. His father was General of Artillery Eduard von Lewinski, the product of a distinguished Prussian military family that dated back to the Teutonic knights. Field Marshal Paul von Hindenburg was his uncle. Erich, however, was the tenth child born to the Lewinski family, and Frau von Lewinski's sister (Frau Hedwig von Manstein, nee von Sperling) was childless, so the Lewinskis gave him to her. (This was typical of they way uncontested adoptions were handled in the 19th century.) His adopted father was General of Infantry Georg von Manstein and young Erich eventually took his name, becoming Fritz Erich von Lewinski gennant von Manstein, or Erich von Manstein for short.

Manstein was educated in the cadet schools at Strasbourg, Ploen and Gross Lichterfeld (also called Berlin-Lichterfeld), and also served in the Corps of Pages of Kaiser Wilhelm II. He entered the Imperial Army as a Faehnrich in the elite 3rd Prussian Foot Guard Regiment in 1906 and was commissioned second lieutenant on January 27, 1907. He became a battalion adjutant in the 3rd Foot Guards in 1911 and began his General Staff training at the War Academy in 1913. He was promoted to first lieutenant on June 19, 1914.

He left the War Academy when Germany mobilized on August 2, 1914, and became regimental adjutant of the 2nd Guards Reserve. He fought in Belgium and France in the fall of 1914, before his regiment was transferred to the Eastern Front. Here he participated in his uncle's victory at Tannenburg and in the subsequent pursuit. He was, however, seriously wounded in November 1914, and did not return to duty until June 1915, as a General Staff officer in Army Group Gallwitz in Poland and Serbia. He was promoted to captain on July 24, 1915, and became adjutant of the 12th Army on the Eastern Front on August 19. He was transferred to the Western Front in January 1916 and was adjutant of the 11th Army in the Battle of Verdun. Here was transferred to the General Staff of the 1st Army in July 1916 and fought on the Somme, before being sent back to the Eastern Front, as chief of operations of the 4th Cavalry Division in Courland. Sent back to France in May 1918, he ended the war as Ia of the 213th Reserve Assault Division on the Western Front.

In the "war after the war," Manstein served on the General Staff of Frontier Guard Command East at Breslau, operating against the Poles. Here, in 1920, he married Jutta von Loesch, who gave him two sons and a daughter. Manstein did his initial command time as a company commander in the 5th Infantry Regiment at Angermunde, Brandenburg (about 40 miles east of Berlin) from 1920 to 1923. He then served as a

General Staff officer in Wehrkreis I (Koenigsberg), II (Stettin) and IV (Dresden). Promoted to major on February 1, 1927, he was assigned to the Operations Branch of the Truppenamt in 1929. On April 1, 1932, Manstein was promoted to lieutenant colonel, and on October 1 he assumed command of the Jaeger Battalion of the 4th Infantry Regiment at Kolberg. He became a colonel on December 1, 1933.

Manstein continued his advancement on February 1, 1934, when he became chief of staff to Erwin von Witzleben, the commander of Wehrkreis III. He was appointed chief of the Operations Branch of the General Staff of the Army on July 1, 1935, and was promoted to major general on October 1, 1936. Six days later, he became deputy chief of the General Staff (*Oberquartermeister I*) under Ludwig Beck. In this position he tried to shield Jewish servicemen from discriminatory Nazi regulations.

He lost his job because of his anti-Nazi attitude on February 4, 1938, during the Blomberg-Fritsch crisis, but was considered too competent to be sent into retirement, so he was given command of the 18th Infantry Division at Liegnitz. During the Sudetenland crisis of 1938, he was appointed chief of staff of Ritter von Leeb's 12th Army. He was promoted to lieutenant general on April 1, 1939, and was named chief of staff of Gerd von Rundstedt's Army Group South (later A) during the Polish campaign.

As chief of staff of Army Group A in late 1939, he devised the plan that led to the conquest of France in six weeks. He was named commander of the XXXVIII Corps on February 15, 1940, and was promoted to general of infantry on June 1. In late February 1941, he became commander of the LVI Motorized (later Panzer) Corps.

The LVI Motorized Corps did not face the same determined opposition the XXXXI Motorized faced further north. Even resistance from Soviet tank units was ineffective because, as was the case along most of the front, the Germans had been supplied with high explosive (HE) ammunition (good for close support missions against infantry), and not armored-piercing (AP) anti-tank shells. Manstein's spearhead, moreover, was led by an extremely capable officer at the head of an excellent division: Major General Erich Brandenberger, commanding the 8th Panzer.

Erich Brandenberger was born in Augsburg, Swabia, on July 15, 1892. He entered the army as an officer cadet in the 6th Bavarian Field Artillery Regiment on August 1, 1911, and was commissioned on October 25, 1913. He fought on the Western Front in World War I, spending the entire war with his regiment except for the period of March 10, 1915 to May 1, 1916, when he was orderly officer to the Duke of Calabria. He served as a battalion adjutant, regimental adjutant, battery commander and battalion commander in Lorraine, Woevre, the Somme and other campaigns. After the war, he served in the Freikorps Denk while simultaneously acting as adjutant of the Special Purpose Security Staff of the III Bavarian Corps.

Accepted into the Reichsheer, he underwent secret General Staff training and served on the General Staff and in the Defense Ministry in Berlin from 1920 to 1928. He was a battery commander in the 7th Artillery Regiment at Nuremberg from 1928 to 1930, when he returned to the General Staff with Group Command 1 in Berlin. He was on the staff of the 3rd Infantry Division from 1931 to 1932, when he became a course director for General Staff trainees at the secret War Academy. He remained in Berlin as a group director of the training department of the army, initially in the Reich Defense Ministry (1933-36).

On October 6, 1936, he assumed command of the 74th Motorized Artillery Regiment at Meiningen. This unit was part of the 2nd Panzer Division and was Brandenberger's first significant introduction into the blitzkrieg concept. He returned to static units in January 1939, when he became chief of staff of Border Command *Eifel* (the German Ardennes). This unit became the XXIII Corps after the Polish campaign began. He was chief of staff of the XXIII Corps until February 15, 1941, serving in the Eifel, in the conquest of France, and on occupation duty in the Netherlands.

Brandenberger was a cool and controlled commander who radiated calm everywhere he went. Although he was totally without charisma, and looked like a slightly stuffy university professor, he was, in fact, tactically brilliant. He almost never made a mistake and took advance of every opportunity. The senior German officers came to recognize this, even at Fuehrer Headquarters. When Hitler decided to double the number of tank divisions by cutting the number of panzers in each division in half, Brandenberger was selected to command one of them.

He took a one-week familiarization course at the Panzer Troops School and assumed command of the 8th Panzer Division on February 20, 1941. He was promoted to first lieutenant in 1917, captain in 1923, major in 1932, lieutenant colonel in 1934, colonel on August 1, 1936, and major general on August 1, 1940.

Brandenberger's 8th Panzer Division quickly broke through the Soviet frontier defenses and drove toward Daugavpils, scattering the Russians as it went. In four days it covered more than 200 miles, and on the morning of June 26 was only a few miles from its first important objectives of the campaign: the road and railroad bridges crossing the 250-yard-wide river at Daugavpils. Four miles from the city the panzers stopped and General Brandenberger called up a strange convoy, which featured four captured Soviet trucks with drivers in Russian uniforms. They were led by 1st Lieutenant Wolfram Knaak, and were members of the Brandenburg Regiment, a special unit under Admiral Canaris, the head of the Abwehr. Manstein feared that an assault on the city by regular German troops would cause the Russians to blow the bridges, so he was going to try to take them by a ruse.

Shortly before 7 a.m., Knaak and his men drove past the Soviet rearguard, threaded their way through local traffic, and seized the bridge. At almost the same moment, a Soviet outpost brought the truck under machine gun fire. Knaak and his 30 men killed the bridge guards and began pulling explosives from the bridge, while the vanguard of the 8th Panzer immediately raced toward the bridge. Back in Daugavpils, more Russians arrived, and these had machine guns. They attacked both ends of the bridge and were held back only with difficulty. By the time the vanguard of the 8th Panzer arrived 20 minutes later, Lieutenant Knaak and four of his men were dead, and 20 others had been wounded. But the traffic bridge was secure, and the Dvina River had been breached.

A short distance away, the fourth truck had taken the railroad bridge after a sharp little battle. The Russians had managed to set off one charge, but it caused little damage. Before the day was out, the 8th Panzer and Major General Curt Jahn's 3rd Motorized Divisions were across the river.

Manstein wanted to continue the pursuit while the Soviets were still off balance. "The safety of an armored formation in the enemy's rear depends on its continued movement," was an adage he had coined.[19] Hitler, however, was getting jittery again, and was afraid of his own success. He ordered LVI Corps to halt and await the arrival of the left wing of the 16th Army, which was more than 60 miles farther back. Manstein, whose corps already posed a threat to Leningrad, was quite displeased with this order. He realized that speed was of the essence, and the entire concept of Barbarossa demanded that a breakthrough and rapid advance must be maintained. But orders were orders, and he obeyed them.

The LVI Motorized Corps, which had gained 200 miles in four days and was only 300 miles from Leningrad, sat still for six days. It was some time before the shattered Soviet communications system informed General Kuznetsov about what had happened, but as soon as he did learn, he drew all of his reserves and surviving combat forces back to the old Stalin Line, on the former Russian-Estonian frontier between Lake Peipus and Sebezh, and threw the XXI Mechanized Corps into a counterattack, in an effort to retake Daugavpils. Manstein quickly defeated the Soviet attack but, when he at last received permission to advance again on July 2, he found that his opponent was no longer a beaten mass of men on the run; he was organized, prepared, and much more difficult to deal with. And Leningrad was much farther away than it had been on June 26.

This battle and the subsequent delay highlight one of the principle features of the Soviet soldiers and High Command during the entire war. Whenever they were surprised by a swift and powerful blow, even if it was delivered by a numerically inferior force, the cumbersome and inflexible Soviet command would be seized with paralysis. However, when they were given time to organize and prepare they would resist fiercely, even if they knew that they were deliberately being sacrificed. This was evident at the Baltic Sea naval fortress of Liepaja, which held out against the reinforced 291st Infantry Division of the 18th Army from June 24 to June 29, and was only taken after bitter street fighting. Most of the Soviet positions had to be reduced by the infantry gun companies or by field howitzers. The fortress of Brest-Litovsk, attacked unsuccessfully by Major General Fritz Schlieper's 45th Infantry Division on June 22, is another example of this characteristic.

Fritz Schlieper was born in Berlin-Friedenau on August 4, 1892, and joined the army as a *Fahnenjunker* in the 17th Foot Artillery Regiment on February 24, 1911. He was commissioned *Leutnant* on August 18, 1912, and fought on the Western Front in World War I. He was selected for the Reichswehr and was a major when Hitler came to power in 1933. He was promoted to lieutenant colonel in 1934 and took command of the 17th Artillery Regiment at Nuremberg on October 15, 1935. He was promoted to colonel on March 1, 1936, and moved up to the command of Arko 24 at Chemnitz, Saxony, on May 1, 1938. When Germany mobilized on August 26, 1939, Schlieper became chief of staff of Wehrkreis XIII at Nuremberg. He was sent to Poland on October 23 as chief of staff of Guard Sector Center. Promoted to major general on November 1, 1939, Schlieper became chief of operations of Kuechler's 18th Army that same day. After serving in the Netherlands, Belgium and France, he apparently fell ill and was without an assignment from November 25, 1940 until May 1, 1941, when he assumed command of the Austrian 45th Infantry Division.

The Soviet defenders at Brest-Litovsk put up a heroic resistance and held up the 45th Infantry Division for an entire week. Finally, on June 29, its citadel was smashed by the attacks of an entire wing of Stukas carrying 4,000-pound bombs. Several groups of fanatics held out in the fortress's subterranean passages for at least a week longer before they were all killed. In all, the 45th Infantry took 7,000 prisoners, but lost 482 killed and more than 1,000 wounded. This amounted to five percent of the total German casualties on the Eastern Front, up to that time.

On the ground, the German Army in Russia was outnumbered from the beginning. On June 22, it struck the Soviet Union with 146 divisions: 3,000,000 men, 600,000 vehicles, 750,000 horses and 3,580 armored vehicles. They were met in the frontier zones by 139 Soviet divisions and 29 independent brigades, a total of 4,700,000 men.[20] Yet the Germans seized and maintained the initiative in every sector. Unlike the Russian officers, the German commanders and non-commissioned officers had been trained to exercise personal initiative and to think for themselves when orders from above were lacking: "the German higher commander rarely or never reproached their subordinate unless they made a terrible blunder," General of Panzer Troops Hermann Balck recalled. "They left him room for initiative and did not reprimand him unless he did something very wrong. This went down to the individual soldier, who was praised for developing initiative. Of course there were exceptions, but generally independent action along the line of the general concept was praised and was accepted as something good."[21] The Germans called this mission-oriented tactical doctrine *Auftragstaktik*, and it was superior in every respect both to the tactical doctrine of the Soviets and to the order-oriented doctrine that the Fuehrer later forced on the Wehrmacht.

Another reason for the initial German victories, and specially those of the *panzertruppen*, was superior communications. German tanks communicated by radio, while Soviet tankers were generally forced to use hand-and-arm signals. Even when they had radios, the Russian communications usually failed. The German radios were much more robust and could withstand the constant jarring and bouncing of the panzer. The lion's share of the credit for the superiority of the German radio belongs to one man: General of Signal Troops Fellgiebel.

Erich Fellgiebel was born in Poepelwitz, Silesia, near Breslau, on October 4, 1886, and spent virtually his entire 39-year military career in communications. He joined the army as an officer cadet in 1905 and was commissioned in the 2nd Telegraph Battalion on January 27, 1907. He was detached to the 128th Infantry Regiment as a signals officer (1909-12) and became an instructor at the Cavalry Telegraph School in Spandau, while simultaneously pursuing studies at the Charlottenburg Technical College (1913-14). When World War I began, he became commander of the Light Radio Station of the 4th Cavalry Division. He was later on the staff of the General Government of Belgium (late 1914-1915); Radio Commander 9 in Lodz, Poland, on the Eastern Front (1915); and commander of the 20th Heavy Radio Station (February-December 1915). He became adjutant to the commander of Telegraph Troops with Field Marshal August von Mackensen's 9th Army (February 1916) and commander of the Telegraph Troops with that same army (November 6, 1917). He was Radio Commander of the 7th Army from March to September 1917, when he was detached to the 398th Infantry Regiment and then to the Posen 56th Field Artillery Regiment on the Western Front.

He was on the General Staff of the Brandenburg 6th Infantry Division on the Western Front from January until August 1918. Without an assignment at the end of the war, Fellgiebel joined the Guards Corps in early 1919 and was then assigned to the Prussian War Ministry, where he remained until October 1919, when he became a signals advisor to the Troop Office (the secret General Staff) in the Reich Defense Ministry (1919-23). He was promoted to first lieutenant in 1914 and to captain the following year.

Despite his relatively low rank, Fellgiebel was already considered a communications genius, which was indeed the case. He did his troop time from 1923 to 1926, commanding a company in the Prussian 2nd Signal Battalion in Stettin, before becoming chief of operations of the Saxon 4th Infantry Division in Dresden (1926-28). Promoted to major in 1928, he was named director of the Coding Office in the defense ministry in October. He held this post until February 1, 1931, when he returned to Stettin as commander of the 2nd Signal Battalion. The major was named chief of staff to the Inspector of Signals Troops on October 1, 1932, and was promoted to lieutenant colonel on February 1, 1933, two days after Hitler became chancellor.

Fellgiebel was named Inspector of Signals Troops on October 1, 1934, and held this post until the beginning of World War II. It was during this period that he invented the radio that (with various modifications) was placed in every panzer, and enabled the German tank troops to communicate with one another and with their leaders. This seems like a simple matter today, but it was considered a tall order in the 1930s, and Fellgiebel was hailed as a genius for solving this daunting problem. Thereafter, the German generals, and especially the panzer leaders, had boundless confidence in him. Even the Nazis respected his technological abilities, despite the fact that he made it no secret that he had no use for them. On October 12, 1937, he was named inspector of Wehrmacht Communications at OKW, while retaining his previous post with the army. He was promoted to colonel on February 1, 1935 and to major general on March 1, 1938.

Germany mobilized on August 26, 1939, and Fellgiebel was named chief of Army Signals Affairs and chief of Wehrmacht Communications the same day. As a result, he spent the first five years of the war at Fuehrer Headquarters. He retained these positions until July 1944, and added the position of General Plenipotentiary for Technical Matters of Communication in 1940, despite the fact that he was openly defeatist and practically chain-smoked cigars, a habit Hitler detested. Fellgiebel was promoted to lieutenant general on February 1, 1940 and to general of signal troops August 1, 1940, in recognition of his contribution to the victory over France.

The Gestapo soon became suspicious of Fellgiebel and even attempted to tape his telephone. Fellgiebel considered their efforts to spy on him as a bit of a joke—they were certainly no match for the senior communications expert in the Wehrmacht! They did not learn that he was a member of the anti-Hitler resistance until July 20, 1944, when Colonel Claus von Stauffenberg detonated a bomb under Hitler's table and Fellgiebel shut down most of the communications between Fuehrer Headquarters and the outside world. Meanwhile, however, through his radios, he played a major (although indirect) role in all of the German victories on the Eastern Front in 1941.

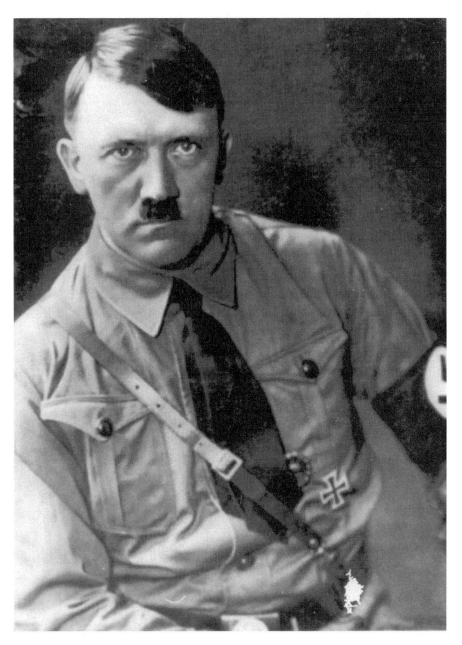

Adolf Hitler, the Fuehrer of Nazi Germany, seen here in a Brownshirt uniform. He is wearing his Iron Cross, 1st Class, and the Wounded Badge in Silver. (USNA)

Field Marshall Ritter Wilhelm von Leeb, commander-in-chief of Army Group North during Operation "Barbarossa." Somewhat anti-Nazi, he would not cooperate with the Einsatzgruppen and treated Soviet prisoners and civilians humanely. Frustrated because Hitler would not allow him to take Leningrad in September 1941, he resigned in January 1942, and was never re-employed. (Photo compliments of Colonel John Angolia.)

Colonel General Walter von Reichenau and Luftwaffe Colonel General Erhard Milch, the secretary of state for aviation and inspector general of the Luftwaffe, Spring 1940. Both men were promoted to field marshal on July 19, 1940. Reichenau commanded the 6th Army during Operation Barbarossa and succeeded Rundstedt as commander-in-chief of Army Group South on November 30, 1941. He died in January 1942. (USNA)

German infantrymen in action on the Eastern Front, June 22, 1941.
(USMHI)

Admiral Wilhelm Canaris (right), the chief of the Abwehr, speaking with
an army general and his aide. Canaris' failure as chief of German military
intelligence materially contributed to the defeat of the Third Reich. He
was executed by the Nazis in April 1945.

Colonel Bodewin Keitel, 1936. Then chief of staff of Wehrkreis IX, he later became chief of the army personnel office, due mainly to the influence of his older brother Wilhelm, the chief of the High Command of the Armed Forces (OKW). Eventually promoted to general of artillery, Bodewin lost his powerful position due to a dispute between the OKW staff and Hitler. Bodewin Keitel later commanded Wehrkreis XX in Poland. (USMHI)

Colonel General Alexander Loehr, commander of the 4th Air Fleet, Poland, 1939. Commander of the small Austrian Air Force in 1938, Loehr was never promoted to field marshal, largely because of his Austrian origins. He nevertheless was the only German officer to command an air fleet and army group throughout the war, leading 4th Air until 1942. He then commanded Army Group E in the Balkans from 1942 until the end of the war. He was executed by Communists in Yugoslavia after a mock trial in 1947. (USNA)

The German commanders-in-chief inspect the troops, circa 1940. Left to right are Grand Admiral Erich Raeder, Field Marshal Walter von Brauchitsch, and Reichsmarschall Hermann Goering. Brauchitsch was determined to capture Moscow in late 1941 but failed, and Hitler relieved him of his command. (Photo courtesy Colonel John Angolia.)

Joachim Lemelsen, shown here as commander of the 29th Motorized Division 1940. He later commanded XXXXVII Motorized (later Panzer) Corps in Operation Barbarossa. (USNA)

Field Marshal Ritter Robert von Greim, the last commander-in-chief of the Luftwaffe. A World War I flying ace, Greim commanded V Air Corps, Luftwaffe Command Center, and 6th Air Fleet on the Eastern Front. Severely wounded during the Battle of Berlin, he committed suicide in an American prison hospital in May 1945. (USNA)

German mortar crew digs in at the base of a disabled Soviet T-34 tank, circa 1941. The quality of Soviet tanks proved to be a nasty surprise for the Germans during Operation Barbarossa. (USNA)

A typical German artillery unit. Unlike the popular image, the Wehrmacht was not a heavily motorized force. Most artillery units were horse-drawn and the vast majority of its divisions were marching infantry.

A Panzer Mark III (PzKwIII) which, along with the Mark IV, was the main German battle tank during Operation Barbarossa. In many ways, it was inferior to the Soviet T-34, KV-1, and KV-2 in 1941, but was nevertheless used until the end of the war. (Both photos USNA)

Hitler with Italian Air Marshal Italo Balbo, center, August 14, 1938.
General Ritter Eugen von Schobert is on the far right. The pro-Nazi
Schobert commanded the 11th Army during Operation Barbarossa until
September 12, 1941, when the engine of his Fieseler "Storch" airplane
failed. His pilot made an emergency landing into what turned out to be a
minefield, and he and Schobert were killed instantly. The large Luftwaffe
General (3rd from left) is Hugo Sperrle, a future field marshal and com-
mander of the 3rd Air Fleet on the Western Front. (USNA)

Finnish Field
Marshall Karl
Gustav Manner-
heim (right), the
ruler of Finland,
with General of
Infantry Waldemar
Erfurth (1879–
1971), the Ger-
man general
attached to the
Finnish Army,
1941 to 1944.
(USNA)

Colonel General Heinz Guderian, the "Father of the Blitzkrieg." Guderian commanded 2nd Panzer Army during Operation Barbarossa. He was sacked by his old enemy, Field Marshal Guenther von Kluge, in late December 1941. Later he became chief of the panzer inspectorate (1943–44) and acting chief of the General Staff (1944–45). (USNA)

Reichsmarschall Hermann Goering (left), the supreme commander of the Luftwaffe, speaking with Field Marshal Albert Kesselring, the commander in chief of OB South in Italy. During Operation Barbarossa, Kesselring commanded the 2nd Air Fleet on the central sector of the Eastern Front with great success. (USNA)

Colonel General Hans-Juergen von Arnim, shortly after he surrendered Army Group Afrika in Tunisia, May 1943. Arnim commanded the 17th Panzer Division during Operation Barbarossa and was severely wounded in the process. (USNA)

Colonel General Eduard Dietl, commander of the 20th Mountain Army, giving orders to General of Infantry Franz Boehme, commander of the XVIII Mountain Corps, 1944. After Dietl was killed in an airplane crash in June 1944, Boehme rose to the command of the 20th. He committed suicide in Nuremberg prison in 1947. During Operation Barbarossa, Dietl led Mountain Corps Norway against the Soviet Arctic ocean port of Murmansk but was unable to capture the city. (USNA)

Junkers Ju-87 "Stuka" dive bombers, which served as "flying artillery" for the army. Although the Luftwaffe won some spectacular tactical victories, its failure to develop a long range strategic bomber was a major contributing factor to the eventual defeat of the Third Reich. (USNA)

Field Marshal Albert Kesselring, the commander-in-chief of the 2nd Air Fleet, talks with his men during the Battle of Britain, 1940. Kesselring led 2nd Air Fleet during Operation Barbarossa. (USNA)

Field Marshal Gerd von Rundstedt, who commanded Army Group South during Operation Barbarossa. He later commanded OB West in France. Hitler sacked him four times, the last on March 15, 1945, after the Americans captured the Rhine River railroad bridge at Remegen. This photograph was taken on May 2, 1945, shortly after Rundstedt was captured by members of the U.S. 36th Infantry Division. He was in the hospital at Bad Tölz, undergoing treatment for arthritis at the time. (USNA)

General of Waffen SS Theodor Eicke, who commanded the SS motorized division"Totenkopf" (Death's Head) during Operation Barbarossa. At various times. Eicke was commandant of Dachau, inspector general of concentration camps, and commander of the 3rd SS Division "Totenkopf." A violent man noted for his anti-Semitism and anti-Christian bigotry, he was killed in action on the Eastern Front in February 1943. (USNA)

General (later Field Marshal) Friedrich Paulus. As deputy chief of the General Staff, he was deeply involved in planning Operation Barbarossa. He later succeeded Field Marshal Walter von Reichenau as commander of the Sixth Army and was forced to surrender in Stalingrad at the end of January 1943. (USNA)

Colonel General Franz Halder, the Chief of the General Staff 1938–1942. Halder was the primary planning officer for Operation Barbarossa. So sure was he of a German victory, he did not provide the German Army with winter clothing for the winter of 1941–42, which constituted one of the worst failures of the campaign. Hitler relieved him in September 1942, and he ended up in a concentration camp. (USNA)

Karl von Rothenburg (second from left), commander of the 25th Panzer Regiment, 7th Panzer Division. An "up and coming" Panzer officer, he was killed during the first week of Operation Barbarossa. The general in the photo (3rd from right) is Erwin Rommel, the future "Desert Fox." The panzers in the background are captured Czech tanks, which were used extensively during Barbarossa, especially by the 6th, 7th, 8th and 9th Panzer Divisions. This photograph was taken in France, 1940.

A German signals unit laying wire (Both photos USNA)

A dirty German infantry private shows the strain of Operation Barbarossa, 1941. (USNA)

CHAPTER V

BATTLES OF ENCIRCLEMENT

The first major ground battle of the campaign, the Battle of Bialystok-Minsk, fought in the zone of Fedor von Bock's Army Group Center, is a good example of Auftragstaktik. It consisted of two double envelopments. The deeper envelopment was directed against Minsk, the capital of Belorussia, 170 miles to the Soviet rear. Bock planned for Hoth's 3rd Panzer Group to attack it from the north, while Guderian's 2nd Panzer Group enveloped it from the south. Simultaneously, the shorter envelopment would take place to the west. It focused on the Bialystok salient, with the infantry of Strauss's 9th Army attacking from the north, and von Kluge's 4th Army advancing from the south. When the encircled Soviet forces were destroyed, Bock planned yet another battle of encirclement, this time against Smolensk, using the 3rd and 2nd Panzer Groups. This envelopment would advance the German front yet another 150 miles to the east, across the Dnieper River and well over half the way to Moscow.

Guderian and Hoth both thought that the initial target should be Smolensk, which should be taken in a huge envelopment. Bock felt that this was beyond the capabilities of his army group, which consisted mainly of non-motorized infantry. An envelopment of this magnitude, he believed, would leave too many holes, through which the encircled Soviets could escape. Brauchitsch was indecisive and Hitler made the final decision, in favor of von Bock. With the benefit of hindsight, it seems clear that von Bock was correct.

Army Group Center provides a prime example of the tremendous rivalry and ill-feeling that existed between senior members of the German armed forces. The most prominent characteristic that distinguished the arrogant Bock, for instance, was his overwhelming ambition. He did not like Brauchitsch, largely because he felt that he himself should have been named commander-in-chief of the army rather than Brauchitsch, who had been junior to him at the time. Still carrying a grudge, Bock very much resented having to take orders from Brauchitsch. Stubborn and intolerant, he had also developed bad relations with Kluge, Strauss, and especially Guderian, who was equally intolerant and had a running feud with most of the senior generals in the army.

Guderian found von Kluge especially distasteful and, at one point, the two had almost met on a dueling field. Bock, Halder, and Brauchitsch all disliked Jodl, whom they considered an interloper, and the C-in-C of OKH and his chief of staff (Brauchitsch and Halder) deliberately excluded Jodl from army planning. Of course, everyone considered Keitel a blockhead, including Hitler himself. In addition, Halder considered Brauchitsch a gutless wonder, and his relationship with him was quite cool. Of the senior generals of Army Group Center, only the calm, level-headed and highly professional General Hoth seemed to maintain a correct relationship with everybody—which is a tremendous compliment to his diplomatic balm. In view of all of these personality disputes, the successes that Field Marshal von Bock achieved during the opening stages of the Russian campaign are nothing short of remarkable, and were achieved only because he did not interfere in the tactical affairs of his subordinates—and did not let anyone else interfere with them either.

The task of completing the northern half of the shorter encirclement fell to Colonel General Adolf Strauss.

Adolf Strauss was born on July 6, 1879 in Schermke, Saxony/Anhalt, in central Germany. He attended cadet schools (including Gross Lichterfelde) and entered the Kaiser's army as a senior officer cadet in the 132nd (1st Lower Alsace) Infantry Regiment on March 3, 1898. He attended the War School at Bad Hersfeld later that year and was promoted to second lieutenant on October 17, 1899. In 1904, he transferred to the 71st (3rd Thuringian) Infantry Regiment and, in 1905, to the 162nd (3rd Hanseatic) Infantry Regiment at Luebeck, where he became a battalion adjutant. He was promoted to first lieutenant in 1910 and was admitted to the War Academy in Berlin in 1911, but rejoined his regiment when World War I broke out. He spent the entire war on the

Western Front. Given command of a company, he was severely wounded early in the campaign and was in the hospital when he was promoted to captain on October 8. When he returned to duty in late 1914, he was assigned to the General Staff of the 17th Reserve Division, which was also serving on the Western Front. He ended the war commanding a battalion in the 99th (2nd Upper Rhineland) Infantry Regiment.

After the war, Strauss was selected for the Reichswehr and served as a company commander in the 6th Infantry Regiment in Luebeck, Schleswig-Holstein in 1920. He commanded the regiment's training battalion from 1920 to 1924, when he was transferred to the staff of the Troop Maneuver Area Hammerstein. He later served at Infantry School at Doeberitz as an instructor (1926-27), before returning to Luebeck as a staff officer with the 6th Infantry. Here he commanded the III Battalion (1929-32) and was briefly given command of the regiment in 1932. He was then named commander of the Prussian 4th Infantry Regiment at Kolberg (1932-34). In the meantime, he was promoted to major (1924), lieutenant colonel (1929) and colonel (April 1, 1932).

Adolf Strauss was posted to the defense ministry in Berlin as inspector of infantry on September 1, 1934. Promoted to major general on December 1, he became Infantry Leader VI at Bremen on October 1, 1935. Fifteen days later, this command was upgraded and redesignated 22nd Infantry Division, with Strauss as its first commander. He was promoted to lieutenant general on April 1, 1937.

Strauss assumed command of Wehrkreis II at Stettin on November 10, 1938, ten days after he was promoted to general of infantry. When Germany mobilized on August 26, 1939, this corps-level headquarters was divided into territorial and field components. The territorial staff remained behind as Wehrkreis II, while Strauss led the field headquarters—designated II Corps—in the invasion of Poland. It was sent to western Germany that winter.

General Stauss gave up command of the II Corps on April 30, 1940 and was placed in OKH reserve. One month later, he assumed command of the 9th Army, replacing Colonel General Walter Blaskowitz. (The army itself had only been officially activated on May 14.) The 9th Army was in OKH reserve during the first phase of the French campaign, which ended in the fall of Dunkirk. The 9th Army then took charge of a sector north of Soissons and covered the left flank of Fedor von Bock's

Army Group B during the second phase of the French campaign. It advanced east of Paris and ended the campaign deep in Burgundy. For his part in the victory of France, Adolf Strauss was promoted to colonel general on July 19, 1940.

The 9th Army was selected to take part in the first wave of the invasion of the United Kingdom, but the Luftwaffe's defeat during the Battle of Britain made this impossible. Strauss's army was sent to the east in the spring of 1941 and was involved in Operation Barbarossa from the first day.

The 6' 1", 175-pound Strauss was completely bald and had an impressive military bearing. He was highly thought of by the Nazis and was certainly professionally competent, although pro-Nazi in attitude. He cooperated with the *Einsatzgruppen* (murder squads), mistreated Russian prisoners and implemented the Commissar Order.

Meanwhile, the Germans began to lose highly skilled officers. One of the most notable deaths among them was that of Colonel Karl Rothenburg, one of the first of Rommel's old "Ghost Division" to suffer the fate that awaited many others.

Karl Rothenburg was born in Fuerstenwalde, near the river Spree in Brandenburg, on June 8, 1894 and entered the Imperial Army as a private in the 5th Foot Guards Regiment on April 1, 1914. Four months later, World War I broke out. Rothenburg first saw action near Namur, Belgium, but was soon on his way to Silesia with his regiment. The 5th Foot Guards fought against the Czar's armies in Poland, Galicia, and in the Carpathians. After serving on the Eastern Front, Rothenburg was involved in the trench warfare on the Western Front. He distinguished himself in combat, both as an enlisted man and as an officer. On November 8, 1915, he was awarded a direct battlefield commission as a second lieutenant of reserves. Later he was awarded the *Pour le Merite*, which was the equivalent of the Congressional Medal of Honor when awarded to someone of such junior rank. By the time the Armistice was declared, however, Karl Rothenburg had had enough of war and the army. He was discharged at this own request on December 18, 1918.

Rothenburg spent the next 14 years in the police. On July 26, 1935, however, he rejoined the army as a major. He foresaw that the future lay in mobile warfare and, as the holder of the "Blue Max," he was in a much better position to influence his own assignments than the average field grade officer. In 1936, he was named commander of the II Battalion of the 6th Panzer Regiment, despite the fact that he had no experience in tanks and was a grade junior to his appointment.

The 6th Panzer took part in the *Anschluss* (the occupation of Austria, 1938) and the occupation of the Sudetenland (1938). Meanwhile, Rothenburg was promoted to lieutenant colonel on April 1, 1938; on March 1, 1939, he was promoted to the command of the 6th Panzer Regiment, which he led in the Polish campaign. As part of Heinz Guderian's XIX Motorized Corps, it attacked from Pomerania to Thorn in northern Poland and cut the Polish Corridor, uniting East Prussia with the rest of the Reich. It then redeployed to the east and attacked to the southeast, ending campaign with the capture of the Polish fortress of Brest-Litovsk.

During the conquest of Poland, the German light divisions (numbered 1st through 4th) proved too cumbersome in combat. Hitler and OKH therefore decided to convert them into panzer divisions. Each division, which already had a tank battalion, was given two more panzer battalions and a panzer regiment headquarters. Rothenburg was named commander of the newly formed 25th Panzer Regiment of Lieutenant General Georg Stumme's 7th Panzer Division, nicknamed "the Ghost Division." A poorly equipped unit by German standards, it had no Panzer Mark IIIs (PzKw IIIs), the best tank in the German Army until 1942.

Despite some serious maintenance problems, Rothenburg's regiment performed brilliantly in the French campaign. It broke through the Allies' Meuse River defenses, smashed through Belgium and France, and overran the French 1st Armored Division, destroying more than 100 French tanks and some 30 armored cars in the process. It helped check the British counterattack at Arras, overran the French 31st Motorized Division, and helped destroy the 1st French Army at Lille. It then turned south, captured Cherbourg, and pushed almost to the Spanish border by the time the French surrendered. Rothenburg was decorated with the Knight's Cross on June 3, 1940 and was promoted to full colonel on August 1, 1940.

Rothenburg's attitude in battle was entirely fatalistic: he simply did not fear death. Perhaps because Rommel had similar view, he often rode with Rothenburg in the colonel's command tank. They were, in fact, kindred spirits. Like Rommel and many other German panzer commanders, Rothenburg habitually placed himself at the forefront of each advance. This fearless attitude cost Rothenburg his life; three years later, it led to Rommel's death, after he joined the anti-Hitler conspiracy.

The 25th Panzer Regiment was engaged in occupation duties in the Bordeaux region until February 1941, when it was sent to East Prussia. It crossed into Russia on June 22, 1941, and was immediately involved in the Battle of the Minsk Pocket. In the early stages of this huge battle, Colonel Karl Rothenburg was critically wounded near Grodeck-Ostrochichy (south of Minsk) on June 27, and died two days later, one of the first in a long line of officers.[1] By April 1944, the division, which in 1940 boasted a strength of more than 15,000 men and 218 panzers, was down to a total fighting strength of 1,872 men, nine guns, 11 anti-tank guns and nine tanks, one of which was a captured Russian T-34. By early 1945, it did not have a single tank left.

A hero of two wars, Karl Rothenburg was buried with full honors. He was posthumously promoted to major general, effective June 1, 1941. For the rest of the war, the 25th Panzer was semi-officially referred to as "the Rothenburg regiment."

Another noted officer to fall was Hans-Juergen "Dieter" von Arnim, the commander of the 17th Panzer Division. Although he was not killed (see below), he was seriously wounded on June 28 and temporarily was replaced by Major General Ritter Karl von Weber, who was mortally wounded on July 18 during the Smolensk encirclement. (He died in the hospital at Krasny on July 20.) He was temporarily replaced by Colonel Rudolf-Eduard Licht (July 18-21, 1941), until Lieutenant General Ritter Wilhelm von Thomas arrived to take command. Arnim returned to duty on October 5, but was promoted to corps command and was succeeded by Licht on November 11, 1941. Thus four different men commanded the 17th Panzer in six different tenures during Operation Barbarossa. The situation was not this bad in most divisions, but command turnover was a common phenomenon on the Eastern Front in 1941.

As the infantry of Strauss's 9th Army and Kluge's 4th Army converged on Bialystok from the north and south, General Pavlov, the commander of the Soviet West Front, made the serious mistake of moving his remaining reserves from the Minsk area west, to attack the German infantry. Apparently he was unaware that an even greater danger existed in the rapidly moving panzer columns north and south of Minsk. The Soviet reserves were quickly engaged in heavy fighting against the infantry of Strauss and Kluge, while Hoth and Guderian pushed well east of Bialystok with their tanks and motorized formations. At this point, Hitler panicked. On June 25, only three days into the war, he began to interfere in the business of his generals; bypassing Brauchitsch, he ordered von Bock to abandon the Minsk encirclement in favor of a much shorter one. Bock fiercely objected to this change with every argument he could muster, and this time Hitler (who respected Bock) gave way. The result was a tremendous victory for the Germans, primarily due to the efforts of Heinz Guderian and Hermann Hoth.

Heinz Wilhelm Guderian was born in Kulm, West Prussia (now Chelmno, Poland) on June 17, 1888. Both his father and son became German generals. Heinz attended cadet schools and entered the army as a Faehnrich in early 1907. He attended the War School at Metz in 1907 and was commissioned in the 10th Jaeger Battalion at Metz on January 27, 1908. From October 1912 to October 1913, he was on detached duty with the 3rd Telegraph Battalion in Kolbenz. In 1913, he moved to Berlin, when he began his General Staff training. His class, however, never graduated, due to the outbreak of World War I. Guderian served as a signals officer with the 5th Cavalry Division, the 4th Army and the Army High Command, all on the Western Front. He also served as Ib (chief supply officer) of the 4th Infantry Division, chief supply officer of the 1st Army, and on the staff of the 52nd Reserve Division during Battle of the Aisne (1917). Later, he served as Ic (chief intelligence officer) of the X Reserve Corps and chief of operations (Ia) of Army Detachment C, all as a provisional General Staff officer. He attended the abbreviated General Staff course at Sedan from January 10 to February 8, 1918, and was admitted to the General Staff, with the right to wear the red strips on his trousers. He later declared this the happiest day of his life. He returned briefly to his previous position at Army Detachment C (February-May 1918), before becoming Ib of the XXXVIII Reserve Corps. On September 20, 1918, Guderian was named chief of operations of the German forces in occupied Italy. He was here when the war ended. Meanwhile, he had been promoted to first lieutenant (1914) and captain (1915).

After the war, Guderian was involved in protecting Germany's eastern borders against the Poles. From May 30 to August 24, 1919, he served as Ib (and, for a brief period, acting Ia) of the Iron Division in Estonia, where he saw action against the Bolsheviks. He never forgave General von Seeckt for recalling him to Germany, even though Seeckt was only shielding him from leftist German politicians. In any case, he was assigned to his old battalion, the 10th Jaeger, which became the III/17th Infantry Regiment in 1920. Guderian commanded a company in this unit from 1920 to 1922, when he was detached to the 7th Motor Transport Battalion in Munich, his first experience in motorized units. From 1922 to 1924, he was with the Department of Motor Transport Troops (In 6) in the Defense Ministry. He was then posted to the General Staff of the 2nd Infantry Division in Stettin, where he was allowed to pursue his studies in motorized warfare. Because of his forceful and dynamic personality, he soon became the leading advocate of the blitzkrieg concept of operations. He has, in fact, gone down in history as the "Father of the Blitzkrieg."

Guderian returned to the defense ministry in 1927 as a member of the operations department of the Truppenamt. He also served as a tactics instructor with the Motor Transport Instruction Staff, where he converted other disciples to the idea of the blitzkrieg. Working under his comrade and protector, General Oswald Lutz, Guderian successively served as chief of staff of the Inspectorate of Motor Transport Troops (1931-34), chief of staff of the Inspectorate of Motorized Troops (1934-35) and chief of staff of the Panzer Troops Inspectorate. Meanwhile, he was promoted to major (1927), lieutenant colonel (1931) and colonel (October 1, 1933). Among those converted to the idea of the blitzkrieg was none other than Adolf Hitler himself. This led to the creation of the first three panzer divisions on October 15, 1935. Heinz Guderian himself was given command of the 2nd Panzer Division at Wuerzburg. He was promoted to major general on August 1, 1936.

On February 4, 1938, as part of his deal with Adolf Hitler, General von Brauchitsch purged the army of senior officers who were anti-Nazi or who had run afoul of the Nazis. One of those to go was Guderian's mentor, Oswald Lutz, history's first general of mobile troops. Guderian did not lift a finger to try to help his former protector and, in fact, seemed delighted to assume his mantle. He became chief of the Panzer Troops Inspectorate on February 4 and was promoted to lieutenant general on February 10. During the Sudetenland crisis, he commanded the XVI Motorized (later Panzer) Corps (April-November 1938), was promoted to general of panzer troops on November 23, and became general of *Schnelle* (fast or mobile) troops the next day.

The day Germany mobilized for World War II, Guderian was named commander of the XIX Motorized Corps. He led it with brilliant success in Poland, Belgium and France. During the mopping up phase of the French campaign, his command was enlarged to three corps and was designated Panzer Group Guderian. As a reward for his victories, he was promoted to colonel general on July 19, 1940. His headquarters was upgraded to 2nd Panzer Group on November 16, 1940. It would become 2nd Panzer Army on October 5, 1941.

Hermann Hoth, the son of an army medical officer, was born in Neuruppin, Prussia, on April 12, 1885. He was educated in the cadet schools at Potsdam and Gross-Lichterfelde (1896-1904) and joined the army as a Faehnrich in the 72nd (4th Thuringian) Infantry Regiment on February 27, 1904. He attended the War School at Danzig (1904-05) and was commissioned second lieutenant on January 27, 1905. He served as adjutant in the II Battalion from 1907 to 1910, when he was selected for General Staff training. Promoted to first lieutenant in 1912, Hoth graduated from the War Academy in 1913 and (after a short tour with the 3rd Foot Artillery Regiment) returned to the 72nd Infantry as regimental adjutant.

He was assigned to the General Staff of the 8th Army (Eastern Front) when World War II began and was promoted to captain on November 8, 1914. He was signals officer with 10th Army from February to September 1915, when he joined the General Staff of the XVII Reserve Corps. He spent four weeks in the spring of 1916 commanding a battalion in the 342nd Infantry Regiment (also on the Eastern Front) and became acting commander of the 49th Flight Training Battalion in June.

After briefly being attached to the staff of the Second Army on the

Western Front, Hoth was transferred to the staff of the commanding general of German air forces (October 1916–August 1918). He was chief of operations of the 30th Infantry Division on the Western Front at the end of the war and held this position until August 1919, when he joined General Maercker's Freikorps. In 1920, he commanded a company in the 32nd Reichswehr Infantry Regiment and then another company in the 18th Reichswehr Infantry Regiment at Padenborn. In December, he was transferred to the Defense Ministry and served in the important Organizations Department until October 1923. He became Ia to the Infantry Leader II at Stettin (October 1923–May 1925), when he returned to the Defense Ministry. He worked in the Training Department until the beginning of 1929, when he assumed command of the I Battalion/4th Infantry Regiment at Stargard, Pomerania (now Stargard Szczecinski, Poland) (January 1929–November 1930). He then was on the operations staff of Group Command One (1930–32), commanded the 17th Infantry Regiment at Brunswick (1932–33), and was commandant of Luebeck (1934).

Hoth became Infantry Commander III at Liegnitz on October 1, 1934. On October 15, 1935, this command was upgraded to the 18th Infantry Division, which Hoth led until April 1, 1938. After spending several months without an assignment, he became the first commander of the XV Motorized Corps on November 10, 1938. This corps played a major role in the conquests of Poland and France, and was upgraded to Third Panzer Group on November 16, 1940. Hoth, meanwhile, was promoted to major (1924), lieutenant colonel (1929), colonel (1932), major general (October 1, 1934), lieutenant general (October 1, 1936), general of infantry (November 1, 1938), and colonel general (July 19, 1940).

By 1941, General Hoth was considered one of the best commanders in the German Army. He was certainly highly respected by his men, who called him "Papa" Hoth.

During the first week of the invasion, Hoth's Third Panzer Group and Guderian's Second Panzer Group continued to push east, often through primeval forests of oak and beech, interlaced with vast potato fields, and past dilapidated hamlets and villages, where they met scattered resistance. Then, suddenly, Hoth's columns turned abruptly south, while Guderian's broke to the north; both converged on Minsk, a city of a million people, which was now virtually undefended. The Belorussian capital fell to the 20th Panzer Division of Hoth's group on June 28, the same day that Strauss and Kluge closed the jaws on Bialystok.

The next day, Hoth's vanguard linked up with Guderian's spearhead, forming a giant double pocket trapping three Russian armies and parts of two others—40 divisions in all. It became the job of the 29th Motorized, 18th Motorized, and 19th Panzer Divisions to keep the Minsk pocket sealed until Bock could replace them with infantry units from the 4th and 9th Armies. These three divisions were commanded by Major General Walter von Boltenstern, Major General Friedrich Herrlein, and Lt. Gen. Otto von Knobelsdorff, respectively.

Walter von Boltenstern was born in Breslau, Silesia (now Wroclow, Poland) on November 26, 1889, and joined the army as a *Fahnenjunker* in the 4th (Queen Augusta) Guards Grenadier Regiment on November 16, 1910. Commissioned second lieutenant in 1911, he transferred to the 5th Guards in 1913. In December 1914, he became a company commander in the 262nd Infantry Regiment and fought in the Masurian Lakes battles in East Prussia (1914) and in Poland and Russia. He was promoted to first lieutenant in 1915. His company was transferred to France in 1916 and to Flanders in 1917. In February, Boltenstern became an orderly officer with the staff of the 79th Reserve Division, where he remained until the end of the war. He became a General Staff officer with the 79th Reserve in February 1918, and was promoted to captain on September 20. He rejoined the 5th Guards Grenadier Regiment in Germany in early 1919.

After the war, Boltenstern was a General Staff officer with the Freikorps (1919). He was an auxiliary officer or an advisor with the Defense Ministry, Wehrkreis III, and the 3rd Infantry Division until 1923, when he became a company commander in the 7th Infantry Regiment at Schweidnitz, Lower Silesia (now Swidnica, Poland), and remained in this position until 1928, when he became adjutant to the Infantry Commander VI at Bielefeld, Westphalia, in the Teutoburg Forest (1928–33). He was promoted to major in early 1932 and was named commander of the Training Battalion of the Prussian 4th Infantry Regiment on October 1, 1933. On October 1, 1934, he was promoted to lieutenant colonel and appointed adjutant of Wehrkreis III in Berlin.

A promotion to colonel followed on April 1, 1937.

Colonel von Boltenstern assumed command of the 71st Infantry Regiment of the 29th Infantry Division on October 12, 1937. He commanded it in its garrison at Erfurt (Thuringia) and in the campaigns in Poland, Luxembourg, Belgium, and France. He assumed command of the 29th Infantry Division itself on July 1, 1940, and oversaw its conversion to a motorized division in the fall of 1940, despite his lack of any significant background or experience in mobile warfare as practiced by Guderian, Hoth, et al. He was promoted to major general on August 14, 1940.

Friedrich Herrlein was born in Ehrenbreitstein, near Koblenz, on April 27, 1889, the son of an active duty officer. Educated in the cadet schools, he graduated from Gross Lichterfelde and joined the army as a *Faehnrich* in the 3rd Foot Guards Regiment on March 3, 1910. He attended the War School at Danzig (1910–11) and received his commission on March 20, 1911. When World War I began on August 2, 1914, he was a battalion adjutant in the 2nd Guards Reserve Regiment. He became adjutant of the regiment in late 1914 and held the post until August 2, 1916, when he was severely wounded on the Western Front. Earlier he had fought in Belgium (1914), the Eastern Front (1914–15), France, and Flanders (1915–16), and had been promoted to first lieutenant in 1915. He returned to duty as a company commander in the Guards Reserve Division's Replacement Depot in Germany in October 1916. Lieutenant Herrlein returned to the field as a company commander in the 1st Guards Reserve Regiment in December 1917, and became acting commander of the II Battalion in January 1918. He became adjutant of the 1st Guards Reserve Infantry Brigade on February 1, and took the abbreviated General Staff course at Sedan from May to August 1918. Meanwhile, he was promoted to captain on June 20, 1918. After recovering from an illness, he was transferred to the General Staff of the rather poor quality 242nd Infantry Division in the Ukraine on September 30, 1918, where he was when the war ended.

Herrlein rejoined the Guards in 1919 and commanded the I Battalion of the 2nd Reserve Regiment from January to August. Selected for the Reichswehr, he commanded a company in the Transitional Army and was transferred to Luebeck, where he was given a company in the 6th Infantry Regiment in the fall of 1920. He was detached to the Staff, 2nd Infantry Division at Stettin, in October 1921, to undergo subsidiary leadership training. A year later, he returned to the command of his company, which he led until the summer of 1924. He became adjutant of the 6th Infantry on October 1, 1924, after which he was sent to Potsdam, as a company commander in the elite 9th Infantry Regiment (1927–31). Finally promoted to major on April 1, 1931, he was assigned to the staff of the II/9th Infantry the same day. He became the adjutant of Infantry Command III on October 1, 1932, and a staff officer with the Potsdam Recruiting Area exactly a year later. In April 1934, he was transferred to Oldenburg, Lower Saxony, as a battalion commander in the 16th Infantry Regiment. Promoted to lieutenant colonel on August 1, 1934, he was given command of the I Battalion/65th Infantry Regiment at Delmenhorst, Wehrkreis X, on October 15, 1935.

Herrlein continued his upward career progression on October 6, 1936, when he assumed command of the 116th Infantry Regiment at Giessen, Hesse. Promoted to colonel on January 1, 1937, he commanded the 116th in the Saar (1939–40), and the battles in Luxembourg, Belgium and France (1940). He was on occupation duty with the Seventh Army in northern France until February 15, 1941, when he was transferred to the Koenigsbrueck Maneuver Area in Germany, where he assumed command of the 71st Infantry Division. For reasons not made clear by the records, he was given command of the 18th Motorized Division on March 28, 1941, despite his lack of training in motorized warfare. He would nevertheless turn out to be a good motorized divisional commander. He was meanwhile promoted to major general on January 1, 1941.

Otto von Knobelsdorff was born in Berlin on March 31, 1886. He was educated in the cadet schools at Bensberg and Gross Lichterfelde, and joined the Imperial Army as a *Fahnenjunker* in the 94th Infantry Regiment on April 25, 1905. Commissioned second lieutenant on August 18, 1906, he was a platoon leader from 1906 to 1911, when he became adjutant of the III Battalion. He was advanced to regimental adjutant in early 1914, and held this post in the early battles in Belgium, East Prussia, and Poland. He was promoted to first lieutenant in late

1914. Knobelsdorff was severely wounded on the Eastern Front on August 29, 1915, and did not return to duty until November, when he became a company commander. He also briefly commanded a battalion in the 94th Infantry.

He returned to Germany in the spring of 1916, where he commanded one of the 38th ID's replacement companies. He was promoted to captain in March. That summer he was back in action on the Western Front, commanding a composite battalion of the 94th and 95th Infantry Regiments during the Battle of Verdun. In October he served two weeks as adjutant of the 83rd Infantry Brigade, before being detached to the General Staff of the VII Corps in November. He was named Ib of the 200th Infantry Division in March 1917 and served in Romania, before being named chief supply officer of the 1st Guards Infantry Division in June 1917. After fighting in the Argonne and Russia, he was attached to the army on the Bug River until October, when he was sent to Sedan, France, to attend the abbreviated General Staff course. Knobelsdorff was attached to the cadre of the course from October 1917 to September 1918, when he became Ib of the Wuert-temberger 242nd Infantry Division. He was seriously wounded on October 21 and ended the war in the hospital.

After he recovered, Captain von Knobelsdorff commanded a company in the 94th Infantry Regiment in the Weimar area, before being accepted into the Reichswehr. He commanded a company in the Bavarian 21st Infantry Regiment at Nuremberg from July 1919 until the end of 1920, and then a company in the 15th Infantry Regiment at Eisenach, Thuringia, from January to August 1921. Then followed tours of duty with the staffs of the 6th Infantry Division at Muenster, where he was Id, or chief training officer (1921–23), with Artillery Command II at Stettin (1923–26), and with the 2nd Infantry Division, also at Stettin (1926–28).

He attended a special course at the University of Berlin in 1928 and 1929, was promoted to major (1929) and was named chief of operations of Artillery Command III at Frankfurt/Oder on October 19, 1929. Promoted to colonel on June 1, 1935, he became a lieutenant colonel on June 1 1933, and was chief of staff to the commandant of Berlin from 1933 to 1935. He assumed command of the 102nd Infantry Regiment at Chemnitz, Saxony, on October 1, 1935, and held the post until

February 1, 1939, when he took charge of the fortifications around Oppeln, on the Polish border. When Germany mobilized on August 26, 1939, he became chief of staff of Wehrkreis III. He had, meanwhile, been promoted to major general on January 1, 1939.

Otto von Knobelsdorff assumed command of the 19th Infantry Division on February 1, 1940, which he led in the Netherlands, Belgium, and France. He then took it back to Germany, where it reorganized as a tank division. It was officially redesignated 19th Panzer Division on November 1, 1940. He was promoted to lieutenant general December 1, 1940. Despite his lack of armored training, Knobelsdorff would excel as a panzer leader on the Eastern Front for the next three years. His first challenge was to help crush the Bialystok-Minsk Pocket, while simultaneously keeping as many Soviets from escaping as possible.

The Russians made several uncoordinated attempts to break out of the pockets, and a few units did manage to escape through the deep forests of Belorussia, but most were halted by Boltenstern, Herrlein, and Knobelsdorff. The pockets were finally cleared on July 3. Bock's forces took 290,000 prisoners, including several corps and divisional commanders, and destroyed or captured 3,332 Soviet tanks and 1,809 pieces of artillery. The Soviet Third and Tenth Armies had been totally destroyed, along with most of the Thirteenth Army and much of the Fourth and Eleventh Armies. Stalin had lost 22 infantry divisions and the equivalent of seven tank divisions and six mechanized brigades, as well as a province containing almost 10,000,000 citizens (of which nearly 3,000,000 were Jewish).

On June 29, even before this battle was over, Guderian ordered another bold move: he instructed his men to drive south of Minsk and then head east, toward Borisov on the Berezina River, to form a bridgehead there. The division he selected to spearhead this move was the 18th Panzer, commanded by an old friend: Major General Walter Nehring.

Walter Kurt Josef Nehring (pronounced *NAIR-ring*) was one of the founders of the theory of the blitzkrieg and, in the opinion of this author, was the best panzer commander of World War II.

Born in the Stretzin district of West Prussia, Nehring was the descendant of a Dutch family that had fled the Netherlands to escape religious persecution three centuries before. His father was a schoolteacher and reserve officer who moved the family to Danzig while Walter was still a child. Early in life, Nehring decided to become a soldier. He entered his father's regiment, the 152nd Infantry, as a *Fahnenjunker* on September 16, 1911. Commissioned prior to the outbreak of World War I, Nehring endured the harsh Prussian training without complaint. He did complain about the low pay, however, and once remarked that Prussian officers served their king and country pretty much at their own expense.[2]

Early in the Great War, Nehring was a platoon leader on the Eastern Front until he was shot in the head and the throat. After he recovered, he was attached to the 141st Infantry Regiment and was named adjutant of its II Battalion in late 1914. He returned to action on the Eastern Front (now in Poland) but was almost immediately shot again, this time in the leg. He recovered quickly and rejoined his parent regiment, the 152nd, in early 1915. He was given command of a rifle company shortly thereafter.

In 1915, the Eastern Front bogged down in trench warfare, which Nehring found distasteful. He therefore volunteered for flight training, which he began on June 6, 1916, the day he was promoted to first lieutenant. His career as an aviator was destined to be brief. On June 20, he was flying as an observer when his airplane crashed and he suffered a broken jaw. By the time he was discharged from the hospital, his passion for aviation had cooled considerably, and he returned to the infantry. In December 1916, he was named commander of a machine gun company in the 22nd Infantry Regiment on the Western Front.

During the Battle of Mount Kemmel in Flanders, Nehring was shot through the stomach—his third wound of the war. Months in the hospital followed. (Nehring spent more time in the hospital than he did on the Eastern Front.) He was released from the medical facilities in late September 1918 and assigned to the replacement machine gun company in East Prussia, where he served until the end of the war.

During "the war after the war," Nehring was a member of a Freikorps force that checked the incursions of Polish irregulars and the Polish Army against Prussia. He was in combat as early as December 1918. Later, in the spring of 1919, Nehring again became a machine gun company commander and a reconnaissance officer. Later, he was accepted into the Reichsheer and was named adjutant of the 20th Infantry Brigade, where he served as one of the liaison officers between the Reichswehr and the Freikorps.

In 1923, young Nehring married the daughter of an East Prussian *junker*, was promoted to captain, became adjutant of the 2nd Infantry Regiment, took his Wehrkreis exam, and scored so high that he was selected to attend the War Academy in Berlin. As part of the course, he was temporarily attached to the Mobilization and Planning Department in the Reichs Defense Ministry. In accordance with General Seeckt's directive that all Reichsheer officers must have an area of concentration, Nehring chose to specialize in the organization and employment of motorized units. (He was influenced in this decision by Major Heinz Guderian, a member of the department who rapidly became a close personal friend.) This was a pregnant moment in the history of the German Army.

Nehring successfully completed General Staff training and returned to the field army as a training officer with the 6th Motorized Battalion. This gave him a chance to put into practice some of the theories he had been developing. His ideas concerning tank and armored reconnaissance tactics proved to be so successful in the autumn maneuvers of 1929 that the Army Command ordered all other motorized battalions to be trained along the same lines.

In 1931, General Oswald Lutz was named inspector of motorized units.[3] With Guderian as chief of staff of the inspectorate and Nehring as chief of operations, a triumvirate was formed which not only revolutionized the German Wehrmacht, but the very nature of warfare in general. Both Guderian and Nehring wrote extensively and were tireless advocates of armored and motorized warfare.

In 1933, Nehring went to Italy and studied Mussolini's tank forces. He then came home and worked on the blitzkrieg theories that would shake the world just a few years later. Many senior German commanders opposed these ideas, including General Ludwig Beck, the chief of the General Staff. Nehring was more diplomatic in advancing his theories than his friend Guderian, who tended to believe that all opposition to his theories was inspired solely by pure malicious intent. Nehring's theories included the use of dive-bombers as flying artillery for the panzer units, because they could launch pinpoint attacks, as opposed to standard bombers, which could be used effectively only against area targets.

By now considered an international expert on armored warfare, he studied the Soviet Army. Via extensive research and interviews with officers returning from the secret German tank training facility in Russia, he was able to calculate the output of Soviet tractor factories, which would no doubt be converted to tank production if there were a Russo-German war. He determined that the Soviet military-industrial complex had the capacity to produce more than 1,000 armored fighting vehicles per month. Guderian presented this information to Hitler and was met with scorn and disbelief, but Nehring's predictions were accurate.[4]

Walter Nehring, together with Lutz and Guderian, was responsible for inventing blitzkrieg warfare. Guderian has received the lion's share of the credit and deservedly so, but he neither invented nor advanced the concept all by himself. The less forceful Lutz and the less visible Nehring also deserve credit, as do several lesser lights.

In 1936, Nehring was selected to organize the shipment and resupply of men and equipment (including tanks) to the Condor Legion, and the German military mission in Spain. After he returned to Germany, he was named commander of the 5th Panzer Regiment at Wuensdorf (October 1, 1937).

In 1939, as war clouds gathered over Europe, Heinz Guderian, who was now commander of the XIX Motorized (later Panzer) Corps, arranged for his number one assistant to be posted to the XIX Motorized as chief of staff. The transfer took place on July 1. The corps crossed into Poland on September 1.

Guderian's panzer tactics shocked the world in both Poland and France, which were conquered in campaigns of five and six weeks, respectively. At one point in France, Nehring took his theoretical operations plans, changed the dates, and sent them to the units without further modification. They worked perfectly. The best units of the French Army were destroyed in Belgium and northern France, and the British Expeditionary Force escaped via Dunkirk after abandoning its remaining vehicles, guns, tanks, and other heavy equipment.

On June 1, 1940, Nehring became chief of staff of Panzer Group Guderian, which controlled three motorized corps. France surrendered three weeks later. Nehring, meanwhile, was promoted to major general and, on October 25, was given command of the 18th Panzer Division, which was officially activated in Leisnig, Wehrkreis IV, the next day.

Nehring spent the next few months bringing the 18th Panzer up to speed. In March 1941, it redeployed to Prague, and on June 22, crossed into the Soviet Union, with Walter Nehring in the lead vehicle.

The 18th Panzer Division would be alone, 60 miles behind enemy lines. It jumped off on June 30. At noon on July 1, Major Willi Teege's II Battalion of the 18th Panzer Regiment reached Borisov, where it met a stiff counterattack from crack troops (officer cadets and NCOs) of the armored training school, as well as the 1st Motorized Rifle Division, which was equipped with the new T-34 tanks. Soon, however, the rest of Nehring's division came up and took the bridge at Borisov, which the defenders had not been authorized to blow up. The road to the Dnieper was clear.

Meanwhile, Walter Model and Baron Willibald von Langermann und Erlenkamp, the commanders of the 3rd and 4th Panzer Divisions, respectively, were also heading for the Berezina.

Walter Model was born in Genthin, Saxony-Anhalt, on January 24, 1891, the son of a music teacher of very modest means. He joined the army in 1909 as a *Fahnenjunker* in the 52nd Infantry Regiment and almost quit, due to the harshness of the training, but was persuaded to continue by his uncle. When World War I began, he was sent to the Western Front, where he became a battalion adjutant. He was severely wounded near Arras in May 1915, the first of three wounds he suffered during the war. Promoted to first lieutenant in 1915, he took part in the early stages of the Battle of Verdun before being sent to an abbreviated General Staff course in 1916. He served on the General Staff of the 5th Infantry Division, where he fought at Verdun again (late 1916), and in the Vosges and Champagne sectors. Model was promoted to captain in November 1917 and served on the staff of the Guards Ersatz Division during the summer offensive of 1918. The end of the war found him on the staff of the 36th Reserve Division in the Somme sector.

Model served in "the war after the war," where he was engaged in putting down Communist insurrections in the Ruhr. It was here that he met Herta Huyssen, his future wife, who would give him three children:

Christa, Hella, and Hansgeorg, a future West German general.

Captain Model was selected for the Reichsheer and first established a reputation for himself by writing a small book about Field Marshal August Gneisenau (1760–1831). Later he became known as an expert on technical and training matters. Physically he was tough, incredibly energetic, extremely courageous, shorter than average and somewhat thickset. He wore a close-cropped "whitewall" haircut and constantly sported a monocle.

Model was assigned to the 2nd Infantry Regiment as a company commander (1920–25) and the 3rd Infantry Division (1925-28). He was progressively made a General Staff tactics instructor (1928), chief of the training branch at the Truppenamt, a battalion commander at Allenstein, East Prussia (1932), and chief of the army's technical office (late 1933). A pro-Nazi, he annoyed General Beck during the Sudetenland Crisis of 1938 by constructing duplicates of Czech fortifications and then proving that German forces could successfully attack them. He was nevertheless promoted to major (1929), lieutenant colonel (1932), colonel (1934), and major general (March 1, 1938). Humorless and with few friends, he was blunt, often rude, and outspoken. An uncomfortable subordinate, he was also a very difficult superior, especially to his officers, whom he hounded mercilessly.

Model served as chief of staff of the IV Corps during the Polish campaign and was chief of staff of the Sixteenth Army during the French campaign of 1940. Promoted to lieutenant general on April 1, 1940, he was named commander of the 3rd Panzer Division (the "Berlin Bear" Division) on November 13, 1940.

Fifty miles south of Borisov, Model's 3rd Panzer Division crossed the Berezina at Bobruysk, barreling through scattered opposition. Still further south, Baron von Langerman und Erlenkamp's 4th Panzer Division of Geyr's XXIV Panzer Corps also crossed the river and headed for Mogilev.

General Pavlov himself escaped the Minsk encirclement and set up a command post at Mogilev, 100 miles east of the pocket. On June 30, Moscow learned from a German propaganda broadcast the extent of the disaster. Zhukov telephoned Pavlov and asked if there was any truth to the German claims. Pavlov replied that there was a great deal of truth to them. He was immediately replaced as commander of the West Front by Andrey Ivanovich Yeremenko and summoned to Moscow, where he was promptly arrested, court-martialed, and shot, along with his chief of staff and several of his key advisors. His political commissar was not punished.

Defense Commissar Timoshenko personally assumed command of the West Front and Budenny's Reserve Front (the 19th, 20th, 21st, and 22nd Armies) on July 2, but could do nothing to halt the panzers on the Berezina, which had already been penetrated in a number of places. He dug in on the line of the upper Dvina and upper Dnieper and awaited the panzer onslaught. Guderian's spearheads reached the Dnieper the next day. They were 320 miles inside the Soviet Union, and had already covered about half of the distance to Moscow.

CHAPTER VI

STIFFENING RESISTANCE AND SLOWER PROGRESS

As the German spearheads drew nearer to Moscow, Leningrad, and Kiev, Soviet resistance stiffened. There were a number of reasons for this, and Hitler himself is to blame for much of the opposition. Thousands of men, including commissars, Jewish soldiers, officers, and others, knew that they had nothing to gain by surrendering. Stories of German atrocities spread rapidly throughout the Red Army from the first day of the invasion. Many of them were not true, but all too many of them were completely accurate. By the end of the first week of the war, SS Colonel Otto Ohlendorf's Einsatzgruppe D was already at work in Belorussia, which had a large Jewish population.

Even by Nazi standards, the murders here were indiscriminate. One day in Minsk, for example, the SS men hauled 280 prisoners out of the Minsk jail, lined them up in a ditch, and shot them all. Then, since the ditch was not yet full, they went back to the jail, brought out 30 more, and shot them too. It was discovered later that this second group included 23 skilled workers who had come from Poland as German employees. They had been billeted in the jail only because there was a housing shortage in war-torn Minsk. Naturally stories about atrocities of this nature, often embellished in the telling, spread like wildfire through the Soviet ranks. Commissars and others had little trouble convincing their often illiterate and unsophisticated enlisted men that a horrible fate awaited them if they allowed themselves to be captured by the Germans. Tales of unspeakable torture and unprovoked German cruelty and sadism also made the rounds throughout the Red Army in 1941.

Otto Ohlendorf was born in Hoheneggelsen, near Hildesheim, Lower Saxony, on February 7, 1907, the son of a small farmer. He joined the Nazi Party in 1925 and the SS in 1926. He decided early in life that a good education was the key to success, and in the 1920s and early 1930s studied law and economics at the universities of Leipzig and Goettigen. He graduated in 1933 and, by October of that year, was an assistant professor at the Institute of World Economics at the University of Kiel. Ohlendorf became a department head in the Institute in 1935.

The young SS man, who was considered smart, attractive, and intellectual, was a fanatical anti-Semite who looked upon himself as an honest civil servant. He hated corruption in all of its forms and even his Allied captors later described him as honest; however, he did not hesitate to murder those he considered subhuman, such as Jews and Slavs. (Describing Nazi ideas about morality is easy; explaining it, however, is sometimes impossible. I suppose one would have to describe Ohlendorf as an honest mass murderer.)

Ohlendorf joined the SD (Security Service) as an economic advisor in 1936 as an SS captain. He was promoted to SS major later that year, to SS colonel in 1939, and to SS major general in 1941. Meanwhile, he became head of Amt III (the Inland SD) in Reinhard Heydrich's RSHA (*Reichs-sicherheitshauptamt* or Reich Main Security Office) in 1939. His office dealt with ethnic Germans in the areas outside the Reich's prewar boundaries, and with matters of culture. (Amt IV was the Gestapo.) From June 1941 to June 1942, he was the commander of Einsatzgruppe D in the southern Ukraine and the Crimea.

Ohlendorf's Einsatzgruppe was one of four (A, B, C, and D) that murdered more than a million Jews, as well as tens of thousands of Soviet civilians, between 1941 and 1943. Einsatzgruppe D followed the Eleventh Army and, on a single day (December 13, 1941), murdered more than 14,000 people at Simferopol alone.

On the heels of the Einsatzgruppen came Hitler's Reichs-commissioners and civil administrators selected to rule the occupied lands, who were also major contributing factors to Soviet resistance at the front and to the proliferation of partisan bands behind it.

When the soldiers of the German Army entered the Ukraine, they were greeted as liberators. "In every village we're showered with bouquets of flowers, even more beautiful ones than we got when we entered Vienna," one soldier wrote in June 1941.[1] The Ukrainians (and the Poles living in the western Ukraine) disliked the Russians and hated the Communists, who had closed down their churches and murdered their priests and upper class. The villagers and peasants greeted the troops in their native costumes, carrying bread and salt (the traditional Ukrainian welcome for honored guests), serenaded them with balalaika music, offered them food and drink, and erected arches bearing such slogans as: "The Ukrainian peoples thank their liberators, the brave German Army. Heil Adolf Hitler!" This was before they met Erich Koch, the new *Reichskommissar* (Nazi-Govenor) for the Ukraine. (Map 5.1 shows the Eastern territories under German rule as they stood in September 1942, including the *Reichkommissariat* Ukraine and the districts under military rule.)

Erich Koch was born in Elberfeld, (which is now part of Wuppertal) in the Rhineland, the son of an industrial foreman, on June 19, 1896. He joined the army in 1915, fought in World War I, and was part of the notorious Freikorps Rossbach in Upper Silesia in 1919. He joined the Nazi Party in 1922 and was part of the resistance when the French occupied the Ruhr. He was imprisoned by the occupiers but, unlike some of his comrades, was not shot. After his release, he became a railroad clerk and a close friend of the insidious Martin Bormann, who later became chief of the Nazi Party and Hitler's private secretary. He was appointed Gauleiter of East Prussia in 1928, on the recommendation of the notorious Jew-bater, Julius Treicher. He was simultaneously named *Oberpraesident* (provincial president) of East Prussia in 1933.

Koch was already known for his ruthlessness, sadism, and corruption when Hermann Goering nominated him for the post to Reichskommissar prior to the invasion. Koch was theoretically subordinate to Alfred Rosenberg, the newly appointed Reich Minister for the Eastern Territories, but made it clear long before the invasion began that he intended to ignore Rosenberg completely.[2] Rosenberg had opposed his appointment with all of his might, but to no avail.

Koch's first official act upon taking charge of the Ukraine was to close the local schools, declaring that "Ukraine children need no schools. What they'll have to learn later will be taught to them by their German masters."[3] He quickly launched an anti-cultural campaign, and destroyed or plundered several Ukrainian museums and libraries, including every university library and the library of the prestigious Ukrainian Academy of Sciences at Kiev. The Gauleiter made it clear to everyone that he had nothing but contempt for Slavic *Untermenschen* (sub-humans), and, in his inaugural speech, told his subordinates: "Gentlemen: I am known as a brutal dog. Because of this reason I was appointed *Reichskommissar* of the Ukraine. Our task is to suck from the Ukraine all the goods we can get hold of, without consideration of the feeling or property of the Ukrainians. Gentlemen: I am expecting from you the utmost severity toward the native population."[4] Later he declared: "We are a master race; just remember that the lowliest German worker is racially and biologically a thousand times more valuable than the population here."[5]

The first crisis in the Ukraine occurred on June 30, when the OUN/B (the Organization of Ukrainian Nationalists/Bandera faction) staged an unexpected coup in Lvov, the capital of Eastern Galicia, which had just been captured by the Wehrmacht. It declared an independent Ukrainian state under the leadership of Yaroslav Stetsko, the loyal lieutenant of Stephen Bandera, a longtime leader of the Ukrainian nationalists, who was in exile in Paris. Presented with a *fait accompli*, the German Army considered the coup "premature and awkward," but not dangerous. It had been impressed that the OUN/B's "Nightingale Regiment" had staged a revolt shortly after Operation Barbarossa began (in places it had been savagely repressed by the NKVD and the retreating Red Army), and had conducted purges, pogroms and excesses against Communists, Russians, Poles, and Jews.

Koch and the Security Police, however, took a much dimmer view of the whole business. On July 2, the SD began arresting Bandera's supporters, and three days later the Stetsko government was dispersed. Stetsko was arrested on July 12, and Bandera was placed in a comfortable jail cell in Berlin. In mid-September, however, he and his principal lieutenants were tossed into the concentration camp at Sachsenhausen.[6] As if to emphasize the point that the Ukrainians would have no say in the governing of the Ukraine, Koch drove thousands of villagers out of the Zuman district, which he converted into a 175,000 acre private hunting estate for himself.

Koch agreed with Goering that "The best thing would be to kill all men in the Ukraine over fifteen years of age, and then to send in the SS stallions."[7] He soon made an informal deal with the Reichsmarschall and Himmler, whereby the SS would be given a free hand in its extermination program, in return for the allocation of economic resources and "general loot" to Goering.[8] Both, in turn, would support Koch against his archenemy, Rosenberg. They made a very effective unholy triumvirate. Koch's particular forte was to have prisoners whipped to death in public squares or parks, to encourage the Ukrainians to be obedient. Naturally, such acts had the reverse affect. Due to his policies of repression, "Germanization," murder, and exploitation, his region was soon infested with partisans. Koch's contempt extended to the German Army, which, in turn, refused to protect his hunting lodge from guerillas, who eventually burned it down; in fact, in September 1942, a gunman fired at Koch, but missed, and then made good his escape—in an army Mercedes. Koch was later charged with responsibility for murdering 400,000 Poles, as well as tens of thousands of Jews and Ukrainians.

Wilhelm Kube, the Landeskommissar of Belorussia, was another of the infamous Nazi administrators who wielded vast power in the newly conquered territories. Born on November 13, 1887, in Glogau, Silesia (now Glogow, Poland), he studied history, theology, and economics. Kube joined the NSDAP in the early 1920s and was elected to the Reichstag in 1924, one of the first Nazis to sit in the national parliament. He became Gauleiter of Brandenburg in 1928, and his area was extended to include Danzig-West Prussia and the Wartheland in 1939.

In Belorussia, Kube set up a large headquarters at Minsk and was soon assisting the SS in exterminating the large Jewish population of that city. (Many of those who escaped naturally joined the partisans.) He was delighted to find high-quality vodka, beer, and attractive, blonde-haired, blue-eyed female peasants, whom he called "blondies" and incorporated into his domestic service, which soon became a harem. His administrative staff, one author wrote, "consisted of woefully unprepared personnel . . . . Nazi waiters and diary men, yesterday's clerks and superintendents, graduates of quick training courses . . . dizzy with power, yet quite unfit for their jobs. In practice Kube's instructions were often disregarded by his subordinates . . . ."⁹

Kube's administration of Belorussia (White Russia) was, needless to say, a disaster. The partisan movement proliferated, but he continued to amuse himself with his harem and alcohol until September 22, 1943. That night, he went to bed only to find that one of his "blondies" had put an anti-personnel mine under his hot water bottle. It blew off both of his legs and he died within half an hour.

Kube was succeeded by SS Major General (later SS Lieutenant General) Kurt von Gottberg, whose rule was considerably harsher than Kube's. Naturally, neither were able to "win the hearts and minds" of the Belorussian people, and the policies of both caused the region to be heavily infested with partisans.

Heinrich Lohse, the Reich Commissioner of *Ostland*, as the Baltic States were called, was perhaps the best of a bad lot. Born in Muehlenbarbek, Schleswig-Holstein, on September 2, 1896, he worked as a salesman and from 1903 to 1912 was a teacher at the *Volksschule* in his hometown. He then worked in the shipyard in Hamburg until September 1915, when he was inducted into the German Army. He was discharged because of wounds in October 1916. After the war, he worked for farmers' associations and joined the Nazi Party in 1923. He soon became Gauleiter of Schleswig-Holstein and added the post of *Oberpraesident* in 1933. He became Reichs Commissioner of *Ostland* (the Baltic States, consisting of Latvia, Estonia, and Lithuania), the eastern part of Poland and the western districts of White Russia, Ukraine, and Russia).

Lohse enjoyed good food and bureaucratic procedure, and his capacity for administrative detail was amazing. He instructed his subordinates that people living in the Jewish ghettos were to receive no more food than was necessary to sustain life, but he was disturbed by the mass executions and was opposed to the "Final Solution," although he was careful not to voice his objections too strongly. Lohse was not the type of man to openly challenge Heinrich Himmler and Reinhard Heydrich, although he did what he could to mitigate the lot of the residents of the region. "So long as a people is peaceful, one should treat it decently," he instructed his staff. "To make political mistakes and to hit people over the head—anyone can do that."[10]

Because of Lohse's relatively benign policies, the industrial plants of Ostland contributed far more to Germany's war effort than those of other, richer districts, where the civil administrations were needlessly repressive. In addition, Estonia and Lithuania never became hotbeds of partisan activity, and the SS was even able to recruit a number of fairly good volunteer divisions to fight against the Communists in 1943 and 1944.

In addition to the blunders of the Nazis, patriotism also played a part in the increasingly stiff Russian resistance. Many Soviet peasants fought out of a simple love for Mother Russia. Communist propaganda played upon this theme very skillfully, which helped rally the troops at the front, increase industrial production in the rear, and begin partisan movements in the German communications zones. Finally, fear of their Communist masters was a major motivating factor in the increasingly fanatical Soviet resistance. Soviet soldiers who were captured were declared traitors for allowing themselves to be taken alive. Even a Russian prisoner who escaped and made it back to his own lines could expect nothing but a prison sentence, or worse. The fact that families of prisoners of war had their food rations taken away, which often meant they starved to death, further inspired the Russian soldier to fight to the end.

"There are no prisoners of war, there are only traitors," Stalin declared. When Stalin's eldest son, Yakov Djugashvili, was captured by the 14th Panzer Division in July 1941, the dictator had Yakov's wife, Yulia, thrown into prison for two years. Even when Hitler offered to trade Yakov for one of his nephews, who had been captured at the front, Stalin refused to make the swap. Yakov was later killed by the SS on April 14, 1943, when he deliberately crossed a "death line" at Sacksenhausen. According to the sentry who shot him, Yakov grabbed the perimeter wire and yelled at him: "Hey, you are a soldier, so don' t be a coward! Shoot me!" He died instantly.[11]

Such brutality from the top permeated the Soviet armed forces and citizenry with fear from top to bottom, thanks largely to the Commissars, the politruks, the NKVD, the KGB, and many other agencies that flourished in the ruthless totalitarian system that was the Soviet Union.

Russian patriotism, Nazi atrocities, and Stalin's brutal police state methods were not the only factors to slow down the German advance in early July 1941: the Soviet transportation system was a major drawback to the Wehrmacht. In 1941, the Soviet Union had 850,000 miles of "roads," but 700,000 of them were little more than cart tracks. Only 150,000 were classified as all-weather, and only 40,000 miles were paved.[12] Even the major roads were dirt, and the dust was tremendous. The infantry marched behind the panzers, often covering 30 miles a day, becoming harder and more physically fit each week. Their stamina rose as the brutal summer sun beat down upon them, hotter and hotter every day. Their uniforms became infested with dirt, vermin, and lice, yet the deeper they advanced into Soviet Russia, the more their morale actually improved. By July 1941, it was higher than it had ever been.

Panzer units were another matter. Unlike the infantry, with its horse-drawn supply wagons, they needed more than just rations and a few rounds of light ammunition. They required fuel, maintenance, oil, grease, and spare parts of every kind. The dirt roads of the Soviet Union soon turned to dust under the heavy treads of the tanks, clogging the engines and causing the moving parts of the panzers to wear more quickly. The supply units had a very difficult time keeping up, even in good weather. Manstein's LVI Motorized Corps, for example, had one marginal road over which to supply three panzer or motorized divisions. During the drive on Smolensk, Guderian only had two, for a panzer group that included 87,000 tanks and other motorized vehicles. In France, the typical infantry division had had one good road. Spare parts could not reach the maintenance units quickly enough or in sufficient quantities, and the German tanks and trucks were soon breaking down faster than their motor pools could repair them.

As a result, the combat strengths of the German motorized and panzer divisions began to fall dramatically. By early August, 30 percent of the German motor vehicles had broken down and were awaiting repair, and casualties and breakdowns had reduced the army's tank strength to less than 50 percent of its establishment. By the end of August, Fourth Panzer Group had only 70 percent of its authorized number of operational tanks—and it was in better condition than any other group in the East. Kleist's First Panzer Group was at 53 percent of its authorized strength, and Hoth's Third Panzer Group was at 41 percent. Only a quarter of Guderian's tanks were still operational.[13]

CHAPTER VII

THE BATTLE OF THE SMOLENSK POCKET

Despite their problems, Hitler's panzer spearheads continued to advance on the central sector of the Russian Front. By July 10, they had already covered half the distance to Moscow, but resistance was stiffening and progress was becoming more difficult. At Hitler's personal orders, and over the objections of Field Marshal von Bock, Army Group Center was reorganized. The Second and Third Panzer Groups were placed under the command of Kluge's Fourth Army, which was temporarily and unofficially dubbed Fourth Panzer Army, for the advance on Smolensk. Weichs's Second Army Headquarters, now up from Yugoslavia, took over the infantry divisions that had previously belonged to Fourth Army.

Guenther Hans von Kluge was born in Posen, Prussia (now Poznan, Poland) on October 30, 1882. He attended the cadet schools, including Gross Lichterfelde, joined the Imperial Army as a *Faehnrich* in 1900, and was commissioned in the 46th Field Artillery Regiment in 1901. A first lieutenant and battalion adjutant by 1910, he was sent to the War Academy for General Staff training. After he completed this course, he went to war in 1914 as adjutant of the XXI Corps. He later led a battalion on the Western Front (November 1915–April 1916), before joining the General Staff of the 89th Infantry Division. He served as an aerial observer in late 1916 and early 1917, and fought at Artois and in Flanders. He was on the General Staff of the Alpine Corps (1917–18), and was Ia of the 236th Infantry Division when he was seriously wounded at Verdun in October 1918. He did not return to active duty for a year.

After the Armistice, he served on the staff of the Peace Commission

(1919–21), on the staff of the 3rd Infantry Division in Berlin (1921–23), on the staff of the Defense Ministry (1923–26), as commander of the heavy artillery battalion of the 3rd Artillery Regiment at Sagan (1926–28) and as chief of staff of the 1st Cavalry Division at Frankfurt/Oder (1928–30). He succeeded Baron von Fritsch as commander of the 2nd Artillery Regiment in 1930, and the following year became Artillery Commander III *(Artilleriefuehrer III)* and deputy commander of the 3rd Infantry Division. In February 1933, he was promoted to major general and was named Inspector of Signal Troops. The following year he was promoted to lieutenant general and became commander of the 6th Infantry Division in Muenster.

Kluge continued his rapid advancement in the fall of 1934, when he was given command of Wehrkreis VI, also in Muenster. He was promoted to general of artillery in 1936. He was firmly on the side of his old friend, Werner von Fritsch, the commander-in-chief of the army, during the crisis of early 1938, but for once he had miscalculated politically. He was on Hitler's list to be retired when the dictator replaced Fritsch with Walter von Brauchitsch. He was, however, brought out of retirement in October 1938, when it appeared that Nazi Germany was about to go to war with Czechoslovakia and its allies over the Sudetenland. This time, Kluge commanded Army Group Six, which headquartered in Hanover and controlled three Wehrkreise in northern Germany.

In August 1939, just before the war began, Army Group Six became Fourth Army. Kluge was not high on Hitler's list to command this army, but for once the Nazi leader allowed himself to be overruled by the professionals, although the Fuehrer made it clear that Kluge was on probation. To Hitler's surprise, Kluge led his army very well in Poland, before he was severely injured in an airplane crash near the end of the campaign. Hitler nevertheless promoted him to colonel general, effective October 1, 1939. Kluge returned to the command of the Fourth Army and led it in the French campaign of 1940, and again did well. As a result, Hitler promoted him to field marshal on July 19, 1940. The following year, Kluge led the Fourth Army in Operation Barbarossa.

Kluge soon clashed with both Hoth and Guderian, because they were drawing panzer units off from the sides of the Minsk pocket and sending them east, toward the Dnieper, which was against Kluge's wishes. The new command arrangement was not a good one, partially because Kluge appeared to be in doubt as to what was his objective and did not seem to have much talent for leading panzer armies. He wanted, for example, to advance on a broad front, which merely pushed the Soviet armies east, instead of destroying them by encirclement. In fact, the plan for conducting the double envelopment against Smolensk was worked out by Hoth and Guderian, without consulting von Kluge, who made Guderian wait idly in Minsk for a week; then, at the last minute, Kluge tried to call off the Smolensk operation, only to reluctantly yield when Guderian convinced him that his preparations were already too far advanced to be cancelled. Guderian, of course, was harsh in his criticism of Kluge, whom he hated, but the more level-headed and objective Hoth also described Kluge's advance as a showpiece on how not to conduct armored warfare.[1]

Hoth was further handicapped in this operation because Hitler was meddling again. He became concerned over a Soviet buildup in the Nevel-Velikiye Luki sector (on the Army Group North-Army Group Center boundary), and instructed Hoth to detach Lieutenant General Kuntzen's LVII Motorized Corps to deal with this threat, leaving Hoth with only one corps (Schmidt's XXXIX Motorized).

Adolf-Friedrich Kuntzen was born in Magdeburg on July 26, 1889. He joined the army as a *Fahnenjunker* on March 10, 1909, and was commissioned in the 11th Hussar (light cavalry) Regiment on August 22, 1910. He transferred to the 1st Hussars when World War I began and served as an orderly officer on the regimental staff (1914–15) and as regimental adjutant (1915–17). From early 1917 until the spring of 1918, he was an orderly to the commander of the XXV Reserve Corps, after which he was admitted to the General Staff. He was on the staff of the military governor of Metz (1918) and of the 10th Replacement Division (1918–19). He served as a squadron commander in the 1st Hussars (January–May 1919) and on the General Staff of the 36th Infantry Division, before being detached to the Defense Ministry for supplemental (secret General Staff) training.

Accepted into the Reichswehr, he was a member of the staff of the 3rd Infantry Division in Berlin (1922–25) and a squadron commander with the 8th Cavalry Regiment at Brieg, Silesia (now Brzeg, Poland) (1925–28). He was then given a year off to study history and philosophy at the University of Berlin. From 1930 to 1933, he was a General Staff officer with the chief of the Army Command, and served in the HPA (Army Personnel Office) from July 1933 until February 1938. Meanwhile, he was promoted to first lieutenant (1915), captain of cavalry (1917), major (1929), lieutenant colonel (1932), and colonel (November 1, 1934).

When Brauchitsch purged the Personnel Office of its non-Nazi elements, Kuntzen was transferred to Fuehrer Reserve for several weeks. He was then posted to Cottbus (about 75 miles southeast of Berlin) and was "kicked upstairs" as commander of the 3rd Light (later 8th Panzer) Division. He assumed command on November 10, 1938, and led his division in Poland and France with considerable success. He was given command of the LVII Motorized Corps on March 15, 1941. He was promoted to major general on March 1, 1938, to lieutenant general on April 1, 1940, and to general of panzer troops on April 1, 1941.

Kuntzen smashed the Soviet troop concentration at Velikiye Luki, but his advance took him away from the critical sector at an important point in the battle. Hoth only had Rudolf Schmidt's XXXIX Motorized Corps to form the northern pincher against the Soviet concentration at Smolensk.

Rudolf Schmidt, known as "Panzer-Schmidt," was born in Berlin on May 12, 1886. Unlike the typical German tank leader, he spent most of his career in military communications. He joined the army as a *Fahnenjunker* in the 83rd (3rd Hessian) Infantry Regiment on September 25, 1906, and was commissioned second lieutenant on January 21, 1908. In 1911, he transferred to the 4th Telegraph Battalion and spent most of the next 23 years in communications units. He went to war in August 1914 with the 5th Telegraph Battalion and was promoted to first lieutenant on November 28. Later, he served on the Western Front with the telephone troops of the 1st Landwehr Division. In the fall of 1915, he became adjutant to the commander of Telegraph Troops of the Twelfth Army. Promoted to captain on December 18, he became the commander of the Guards Telephone Detachment on the Western Front in 1916. He was admitted to the General Staff that same year and was assigned to the staff of the Field Telegraph Leader. He ended the war on the General Staff of the Fourth Army in Flanders.

Schmidt was accepted into the Reichswehr in 1920 and remained in communications units. From 1924 to 1925, he commanded a company in the 3rd (Prussian) Signal Battalion at Potsdam. Promoted to major in 1927, he was a code (cipher) officer in the army's Abwehr (military intelligence) branch of the Truppenamt. In the fall of 1929, he was assigned to the training staff of the 6th Infantry Division at Muenster. A year later, he was transferred to the 3rd Infantry Division in the same capacity. In 1931, he became chief of staff of the Signal Inspectorate (In 7), was promoted to lieutenant colonel on April 1, and to colonel on October 1, 1933.

On August 15, 1934, he left the signals branch and assumed command of the 13th (Wuerttemberger) Infantry Regiment at Ludwigsburg. After a successful command, he was assigned to O Qu II, the training division of the general staff of the army. He was promoted to major general on October 1, 1936 and, despite no armored background whatsoever, was named commander of the 1st Panzer Division at Weimar on October 1, 1937. He took to tank warfare like a duck takes to water. He adapted extremely quickly and was soon accepted by the veteran panzer officers. He was promoted to lieutenant general on June 1, 1938. Even Hitler liked and admired Schmidt, without realizing that Schmidt had nothing but contempt for him and his party. Schmidt did an excellent job commanding the 1st Panzer during the Polish campaign. As a result, he was given command of the XXXIX Motorized Corps on February 1, 1940, and was promoted to general of panzer troops on June 1.

Smolensk was located at the head of navigation of the great Dnieper River, in an area of corn, flax, and dairy farms. The German advance toward it was slow, partially due to Kluge, partially due to Hitler, partially due to stiffening Soviet resistance, and partially because heavy summer rains turned the dirt roads into bogs. Schmidt's XXXIX Motorized Corps advanced on the city from the north, but was held up near Vitebsk on July 5 and 6 because of heavy flanking attacks by the Russian Twentieth Army and its 5th and 7th Mechanized Corps. Vitebsk finally fell to Stumpff's 20th Panzer Division on July 9, but the advance continued to be slow. Timoshenko had now been reinforced to a strength of seven armies, some of which were little more than corps, but his West Front still had almost 1,000 tanks. In places the Soviets fought like tigers; elsewhere, they ran like rabbits. On the whole, however, resistance was stiffening.

On the southern flank of the envelopment, Guderian advanced much more rapidly once he was allowed to begin. He crossed the Dnieper on July 10 and 11, secured two bridgeheads, and then quickly drove on Smolensk, shoving the Soviet Thirteenth Army before him. On the 12th he encircled four rifle divisions and part of the 20th Mechanized Corps near Mogilev. Hoth, meanwhile, captured Yartsevo, a cotton milling city, on July 15, at the same time Guderian's 29th Motorized Division took Smolensk. To the astonishment of General Halder, the two joined hands the following day, trapping the Soviet 20th and 16th Armies, and forming another large pocket. This did not end the battle, because the Soviets launched repeated breakout attempts, which were fierce but uncoordinated, and Timoshenko made several attacks designed to relieve the pocket from the east. Against Hoth's forces alone he threw the Thirtieth, Nineteenth, and Twenty-fourth Armies, but without success.

To the south, the Soviet Twenty-eighth Army struck from the important communications center of Roslavl against Second Panzer Group and made some progress, until it fell into a Guderian trap, executed by Geyr von Schweppenburg's XXIV Panzer and General of Artillery Wilhelm Fahrmbacher's VII Corps. (Map 4.1 shows the pockets at Smolensk and Roslavl, as well as the other battles of encirclement on the Eastern Front, where the Red Army of 1941 was devastated.)

The Battle of the Smolensk Pocket ended on August 5, when the last resistance was crushed. About 310,000 Soviet soldiers were captured, and 3,205 tanks and 3,120 guns captured or destroyed.[2] Three days later, the Battle of the Roslavl Pocket ended. Guderian took another 38,000 prisoners, along with 144 tanks and 848 guns, captured or destroyed.[3]

Meanwhile, General Kalmukoff, the commander of the 162nd Infantry Division, continued to push east, and launched a surprise attack across the Dnieper River.

Kurt Kalmukoff was born in Graudenz, West Prussia (now Grudziadz, Poland), on February 10, 1892. He joined the Imperial Army as a *Fah-*

nenjunker (officer cadet) in the 128th Infantry Regiment on March 15, 1910, and was commissioned second lieutenant on August 18, 1911. He went to war in 1914 as a platoon leader and fought in East Prussia (including the Battles of Tannenberg and Loetzen), Poland, and Russia. He later became a company commander in the 5th Reserve Infantry Regiment and fought in France and Belgium. He was promoted to first lieutenant on August 18, 1915 and to captain on August 18, 1918.

Kalmukoff joined the Reichswehr in the fall of 1919, was transferred to the Posen 4th Infantry Regiment at Deutsch Krone, where he commanded a company from 1920 until the end of 1927. He was an instructor at the Infantry School at Doeberitz near Berlin from early 1928 to August 1933, and was promoted to major in 1931. He became commander of the III/4th Infantry Regiment at Neustettin, Pomerania (now Szczecinek, Poland) on August 1, 1933, was promoted to lieutenant colonel the following year, and became a full colonel on April 1, 1937.[4]

Kurt Kalmukoff completed his successful troop command on October 1, 1936, and was transferred to Munich, where he was a course director at the War School until August 26, 1939, the day the Third Reich mobilized for war. Kalmukoff was named commander of the East Prussian 162nd Infantry Division, which he led in the conquest of northern Poland. In 1940, he led his regiment in Belgium, at Dunkirk, and in the subsequent occupation of France. He and his men were posted to Brittany, but returned to East Prussia in January 1941.

On June 22, 1941, the 162nd Infantry successfully forced the Bug River on both sides of Rzeczyca, using assault boats and rubber boats. It subsequently overran eastern Poland and Belorussia, and took part in the capture of Bialystok and in the battles of encirclement at Minsk and Smolensk.

The 162nd Infantry Division struck across the Dniepr River at Nowyi Bychoff at 4 a.m. on August 11, 1941. Two-thirds of the division was across the river by August 13, when General Kalmukoff's vehicle ran over a mine. The general and his adjutant, Major von Barnekow, were both killed. Colonel Gerhard Berthold, the commander of the 17th Infantry Regiment, assumed command of the division.[5]

Gerhard Berthold was born in Schneeberg, in the Schwarzenberg district of Saxony, in the Erzgebirge (Erz Mountains) east of Nuremberg, on March 12, 1891. He joined the Imperial Army as a one-year volunteer in the 106th Infantry Regiment of the Saxon 32nd Infantry Division in 1910, and was discharged into the reserves the following year. Recalled to active duty as a corporal in August 1914, he was assigned to the 102nd Infantry Regiment (also of the 32nd Infantry Division) and fought in Belgium and the Battle of the Marne. In early 1915, he volunteered for officer training and was promoted to *Faehnrich* in March. He attended Officer Training School and became a *Leutnant* on May 16, 1915. (Second lieutenants commissioned in this manner were called "60-day wonders" by the German enlisted men, but seldom to their faces. Sixty-day wonders had the same rights as any Prussian officer, including the right to administer an "ear boxing" to junior enlisted men. A Prussian ear boxing was a full blow to the side of the head, designed to burst an ear drum. Few 60-day wonders were retained in the Reichswehr, but Berthold would be an exception.)

Following his commissioning, Berthold rejoined his regiment and fought on the Aisne, on the Somme, in the Argonne (1916–17), in the Champagne region, in Flanders (where the division suffered heavy losses), on the Lys, and in Lorraine. During this time, he served as a platoon leader, company commander, and regimental adjutant, and was wounded at least once. He was promoted to first lieutenant in June 1918 and was accepted into the Reichsheer in late 1919. He was assigned to the 10th Infantry Regiment at Dresden in 1920, but was transferred to the 11th Infantry Regiment at Leipzig in the fall of 1921, where he remained until January 1927. Assigned to the staff of the 1st Infantry Division at Koenigsberg, he returned to the 10th Infantry as a company commander on March 1, 1929.

He apparently began his General Staff training while in Koenigsberg; in any case, he was officially assigned to the Armed Forces Office of the Defense Ministry in Berlin in April 1930. He was, in fact, undergoing secret General Staff training. He graduated in the spring of 1932 and returned to the 10th Infantry, where he remained as a company commander until the end of June 1935. He then spent two years on the General Staff of the Army (OKH) from July 1, 1935 to September 1937. From October 1, 1937 to November 10, 1938, he was Ia of Wehrkreis VIII in Breslau, where he worked for future Field Marshals von Kleist and Busch. He was attached to the staff of the 17th Infantry Regiment of the 31st Infantry Division at Brunswick from then until Germany mobilized. He assumed command of the 82nd Infantry Regiment (also of the 31st Infantry Division) on August 26, 1939.

Gerhard Berthold led the 82nd Infantry in the invasion of Poland and its subsequent redeployment to the lower Rhine. On December 1, 1939, he handed command of the 82nd to Colonel Friedrich Hossbach and took command of the 17th Infantry Regiment, which he led in Belgium and France. The 17th Infantry was on occupation duty in Normandy in August but, after the planned invasion of the United Kingdom was cancelled, Berthold and his regiment returned to Poland.

Berthold was in all of the battles of the 31st Infantry Division from June 22, 1941 to January 20, 1942. Succeeding Kalmukoff as commander of the division after the latter was killed in action on August 13, 1941, he fought in the battle of encirclement at Smolensk, in the battle of Vyasma, and in the battles of Bryansk, Tula, and Moscow, as part of the Second Panzer Army. Berthold was promoted to major general on September 1, 1941. He had previously been promoted to captain (1926), major (1933), lieutenant colonel (1935), and colonel (March 1, 1938).

In the meantime, southeast of Smolensk, Stalin had established a new army group, the Central Front, under F. I. Kuznetsov, from part of Timoshenko's command. As soon as the Battle of the Smolensk Pocket was over, Guderian hurled the XXIV Panzer Corps into its rear, west and north of Gomel, in coordination with von Weichs's Second Army, which attacked from the east. By the time the battle of the Gomel Pocket was over on August 24, the 13th and 21st Armies of Central Front were virtually destroyed, and another 84,000 prisoners had been captured, along with 144 tanks and 848 guns.[6]

By the first of September, Field Marshal von Bock's Army Group Center had carried out its initial mission brilliantly. From June 22 to the end of August, it had inflicted more than three-quarters of a million casualties on the Russians and had destroyed several Soviet armies, captured more than 600,000 men, and destroyed or captured some 7,000 Soviet tanks and more than 6,000 guns. It suffered fewer than 100,000 casualties itself; more importantly, it had advanced more than

500 miles, was well beyond the Dnieper, and was only about 185 miles from Moscow at its closest point.

In the meantime, Stavka had established a new Reserve Front under I. A. Bogdanov, who was given command of the 29th, 30th, 24th, 28th, and 31st Armies. He was ordered to dig in along a new line from Lake Ilmen to Bryansk. Behind this line, NKVD General Pavel A. Artemev, the commander of the Moscow District, dug in with his 32nd 33rd and 34th Armies. None of these was at full fighting strength because many of their men were raw recruits who were hurriedly drafted, handed a rifle, and sent into the line; the best Soviet formations in European Russia had already been destroyed. The Communists feverishly dug in and prepared to defend their capital, but Fedor von Bock was absolutely confident that he could brush these remnants aside and be in Moscow within a month. There is, in fact, little question that he could have done just that, had he been given permission to do so.

Hermann Hoth, Heinz Guderian, Franz Halder, and most of the other German commanders shared Bock's optimism. Hitler, however, was not much interested. On August 4, he gave his orders for the next phase of the campaign. Hoth's Third Panzer Group was to turn north, to join Army Group North in the capture of Leningrad; simultaneously, Guderian's Second Panzer Group was to turn south, to assist Rundstedt's Army Group South in the conquest of the Ukraine and the capture of Kiev. This order had the effect of stripping Bock's army group of four of its five motorized/panzer corps.[7] Richthofen's VIII Air Corps, which had provided Bock with excellent air cover, was also transferred to the north.

CHAPTER VIII

THE DRIVE TO LENINGRAD

While Bock was crushing his opponents in the massive double envelopments of Bialystok, Minsk, and Smolensk, Field Marshal Ritter von Leeb's Army Group North was having a more difficult time in the Baltic States. His problems in this campaign were mammoth. First, the terrain was flat, thickly forested, and sandy, with much marshland and many swamps. He had even fewer roads per corps than did von Bock, and his zone of operations was totally unsuited for mechanized operations. Like Bock's, Leeb's objectives were unclear. He had been ordered to capture the Baltic States and seize Leningrad, but no priority had been assigned to these missions. Was he supposed to clear the Baltic States first, or take Leningrad, and then mop up the Baltic States? He still had not received an answer when the campaign began.

Finally, Leeb himself was a problem. He was a defensive expert; he was neither trained nor suited for directing large mobile formations, which he handled here for the first time in his long career. His senior tank commander, Erich Hoepner, was a very capable panzer leader, but independent-minded and difficult to direct. Friction soon developed between them because Hoepner considered Leeb too slow, and Leeb became very nervous when the advances of the panzer generals, in keeping with their standard tactics, put them dozens of miles ahead of the infantry, with nothing in reserve to cover their rear.

Erich Hoepner was born on September 14, 1886, in Frankfurt/Oder. He entered the army as a *Fahnenjunker* in the Schleswig-Holstein 13th Dragoon Regiment on March 10, 1905. (A dragoon is the traditional name for a soldier who is trained to ride to battle on horseback but then to fight on foot.) He was commissioned on August 18, 1906, became regimental adjutant in 1911, was sent to the War Academy to begin his

General Staff training in 1913, and was promoted to first lieutenant in 1914. Hoepner was assigned to the staff of the XVI Corps as an orderly officer when World War I broke out. He served on the Western Front and was successively on the General Staff of the VI Corps, First Army, Seventh Army, and the 105th Infantry Division, where he served as Ia during the Battle of Picardy. He was promoted to captain of cavalry in 1915.

After the war, he was on the staffs of the 36th Infantry Division and 17th Reichswehr Brigade (1919–20), and was selected for retention by the Reichswehr in 1920. A commander of a squadron in the Prussian 2nd Cavalry Regiment at Allenstein (1920–21), Hoepner was later on the staff of the Cavalry Inspectorate in the Defense Ministry in Berlin (1921–23), on the staff of the 1st Cavalry Division in his hometown (1923–27), and on the staff of the 1st Infantry Division in Koenigsberg, East Prussia (1927–30). He was promoted to major in 1926 and to lieutenant colonel on April 1, 1930, the day he assumed command of the I Battalion of the 17th Infantry Regiment at Brunswick.

On October 1, 1932, he became commander of the 4th (Prussian) Cavalry Regiment at Potsdam, which led to his promotion to colonel on February 1, 1933, the day he became chief of staff of the 1st Infantry Division in Koenigsberg. He remained in the East Prussian capital for his next assignment, chief of staff of Wehrkreis I (October 1, 1934 to October 1, 1935). He was chief of staff of Group Command One (an army-level headquarters in Berlin) from then until October 12, 1937, when he assumed command of the 1st Light Brigade at Wuppertal, North Rhine-Westphalia. On October 19, 1938, his headquarters was upgraded to the 1st Light Division (which later became the 6th Panzer Division). Hoepner was meanwhile promoted to major general (January 1, 1936) and lieutenant general (January 30, 1938).

General Hoepner believed that Hitler's expansionistic policies would lead Germany to disaster. Unlike many officers, he did not feel bound by his oath of allegiance to the Fuehrer, and he was a member of the anti-Hitler conspiracy from the beginning. (Significantly, his Ib was Claus von Stauffenberg, who would lead the anti-Hitler coup attempt on July 20, 1944.) Hoepner was prepared to use his unit against Hitler during the Sudetenland Crisis of 1938, but the opportunity never arose, because Hitler seemed to be avoiding Berlin like the plague. He did not return to the capital until after the British and French signed the Munich Accords, and the opportunity to overthrow him was lost.

Called the "Old Cavalryman" by his men, Hoepner was named commander of the XVI Motorized Corps (headquartered in Berlin) on November 24, 1938, and was promoted to general of cavalry on April 20, 1939. He led the XVI with great success in Poland, the Netherlands, Belgium, and France, for which he was rewarded with a promotion to colonel general on July 19, 1940. His headquarters was upgraded to Fourth Panzer Group on February 17, 1941, and would become the Fourth Panzer Army on January 1, 1942. Meanwhile, the invasion of the Soviet Union began.

Leeb attacked at 3:15 a.m. on June 22, with Kuechler's Eighteenth Army on the left, Hoepner's panzer group in the center, and Busch's Sixteenth Army on the right. He was initially faced by General Fedor I. Kuznetsov's Northwest Front (Eighth and Eleventh Armies), which consisted of some 30 divisions, including two mechanized corps (four armored and two mechanized divisions), as well as a few independent tank brigades. To the Soviet rear lay General Markian M. Popov's Leningrad Military District (later North Front), which included the Twenty-third, Seventh, and Tenth Armies, and the 10th Mechanized Corps—another 20 divisions.

Leeb's forces initially advanced very rapidly, breached the Dvinsk River line, and won important victories at Daugavpils and Rossizny. By June 28, his units had won the battle of the frontier, had destroyed or captured more than 400 tanks and armored vehicles, 200 guns, several hundred aircraft, and several warships along the Baltic coast, but had only taken 6,000 prisoners. The Reds were in full retreat but had not been destroyed.

Ritter von Leeb did not object to Hitler's order paralyzing Manstein's LVI Motorized Corps at Daugavpils for almost a week. Since he protested far more frequently than the average German field marshal against orders that he did not like, it must be assumed that Leeb agreed with this timid decision. In any case, he met with General Hoepner on July 1 and proposed that the Sixteenth Army (on the southern flank of the army group) wheel north and seal off the Baltic States, while the Fourth Panzer Group protected its eastern flank. Hoepner vigorously objected; he wanted to advance between Lake Peipus and Ilmen, on the direct route to Leningrad, with his entire command. Leeb, therefore, proposed a compromise: Manstein would drive on Novorzhev (in the direction of Lake Ilmen), along with the Sixteenth Army, while Reinhardt's XXXXI Motorized—Hoepner's other corps—advanced on Ostrov, in the direction of Leningrad. Hoepner did not like this plan either, because it was a broad-front approach. The bold General Hoepner favored a narrow, quick-thrust advance on Leningrad, but Leeb overruled him.

For much of the campaign, Reinhardt's XXXXI Motorized Corps was spearheaded by the outstanding 1st Panzer Division, which was initially led by Lieutenant General Friedrich Kirchner, and then by Major General Walter Krueger.

Friedrich Kirchner was born in Zoebigker, near Leipzig, Saxony, on March 26, 1885. He attended cadet schools and joined the army as a senior officer cadet in the 107th Infantry Regiment on February 28, 1906. He spent five years with the 107th before transferring to the 17th Ulans. From 1914 to 1918, he served as a squadron leader, General Staff officer, and battalion commander; meanwhile, he was promoted to second lieutenant (January 27, 1907), first lieutenant (1913), and *Rittmeister* (1915).

Kirchner joined the 12th Cavalry Regiment in Dresden after the war and served as a squadron commander from 1920 to 1928. He was on the staff of the 2nd Cavalry Division (also in Dresden) from 1928 to 1932, before being transferred to the 10th Cavalry in Torgau (1932–33). From October 1, 1933, he commanded a battalion in the 11th Cavalry Regiment at Neustadt, Upper Silesia (now Prudnik, Poland) until October 1, 1935, when he left the cavalry after 24 years and assumed command of the 1st Rifle Regiment of the 1st Rifle Brigade of 1st Panzer Division. The 1st Rifle was based at Gera; Kirchner later took command of the brigade, which was stationed at Weimar (November 10, 1938) and, after the Polish campaign, the division itself (November 3, 1939). He was, in the meantime, promoted to major (1928), lieutenant colonel (1932), colonel (1934), and major general (March 1, 1938). He became a lieutenant general on April 1, 1940.

Commanding the 1st Panzer Division, General Kirchner fought in Luxembourg, Belgium, and France in 1940. His division did well and was redeployed back to East Prussia in September. It crossed into Russia as part of Hoepner's Fourth Panzer Group and fought in the Battle of Duenaburg. On July 17, 1941, Friedrich Kirchner was seriously wounded. He was replaced that same day by his senior brigade commander, Major General Walter Krueger.

Walter Krueger was born in Zeitz, Saxony, on March 23, 1892, and joined the army as an officer cadet in the 181st Infantry Regiment on March 17, 1910. He attended the War School at Metz and was commissioned *Leutnant* in the 19th Hussar Regiment in 1911. During World War I, he served on the Western Front and was a platoon leader in the Saxon Ulan Reserve Regiment, an orderly officer with the staff of the 24th Reserve Division, and a company commander and acting battalion commander in the 107th Infantry Regiment. He was promoted to first lieutenant in 1915.

After the war, Krueger returned to the 19th Hussars/19th Cavalry after the Armistice, but transferred to the 12th Cavalry Regiment at Dresden, where he was a squadron commander from 1923 to 1929. Promoted to captain in 1928, he remained in Dresden as a staff officer with the 2nd Cavalry Division (1929–31). On October 1, 1931, he was promoted to major and joined the staff of the Cavalry Inspectorate (In 1) in the Defense Ministry, where he remained until 1936. He was promoted to lieutenant colonel in 1934, became chief of the inspectorate on October 1, 1936, and was promoted to colonel on April 1, 1937. From October 1, 1937, until Germany mobilized on August 26, 1939, Krueger commanded the 10th Cavalry Regiment at Zuellichau, Brandenburg (now Sulechow, Poland). His regiment was then dissolved and used to form the 4th, 14th, and 24th Reconnaissance Battalions. Krueger himself was given command of a reserve regiment; however, seeing that the future lay in the armored branch, he arranged to be given command of the 1st Rifle Brigade of the 1st Panzer Division on November 3, 1939.

Krueger led his brigade with great success in Luxembourg, Belgium, and France. The 1st Panzer redeployed to East Prussia in September 1940. His promotion to major general occurred on April 1, 1941; he crossed into Russia on June 22, 1941. Krueger assumed command of the 1st Panzer Division on July 17, the day General Kirchner was wounded.

Krueger took Ostrov against weak opposition on July 4. Lieutenant General Petr Petrovich Sobennikov, who had replaced Kuznetsov as commander of the Northwest Front, desperately tried to establish a new front south of Lake Peipus, using the 1st Mechanized Corps and two reserve rifle corps. Reinhardt, however, was too fast for him and took Pskov on the southern shore of Lake Peipus, thus establishing a jump-off point for the drive on Leningrad despite heavy Soviet armored counterattacks. Meanwhile, Manstein ran straight into the 21st Mechanized Corps in the Novorzhev sector. He found that the dirt roads running through the swamps and thick forests were jammed with abandoned Soviet tanks, vehicles, and guns. For the first time in the campaign, Manstein was compelled to halt. Hoepner was forced to withdraw the LVI Motorized Corps and send it after Reinhardt. General Hoepner wanted to send both panzer corps north-northeast, directly toward Leningrad, but Leeb again insisted on the broad frontal approach and sent Manstein eastward, toward Novgorod and Lake Ilmen, despite the forested and swampy terrain.

On July 7, Brauchitsch appeared at Leeb's headquarters and approved Hoepner's plan for an advance on Leningrad: the XXXXI Motorized Corps would advance along the Pskov-Luga-Leningrad road, while Manstein's LVI Motorized drove on Novgorod, then on to Leningrad. These were the only two routes to the capital of the Czars, which meant that the element of surprise would be totally lacking, and the two panzer corps would be separated from each other by more than 100 miles of forests and swampland, and well out in front of the infantry.

Reinhardt began his advance on July 10, but faced stiff resistance and very difficult terrain. He was stopped on July 12, after a gain of only a few miles. Two days later, Manstein was attacked by the reinforced Russian Eleventh Army, and at one point was completely cut off from the rest of the German Wehrmacht. Hoepner, meanwhile, executed a bold move: he sent Manstein's entire command to the north, to turn the flank of the Russian units barring Reinhardt's way. The maneuver worked; by July 17 the Luga position had been overcome and Fourth Panzer Group was only 80 miles from Leningrad. Unfortunately for the Wehrmacht, Hitler and the OKH became nervous and ordered Hoepner to halt Manstein's corps until the infantry of the Sixteenth Army could come up and secure his right flank.

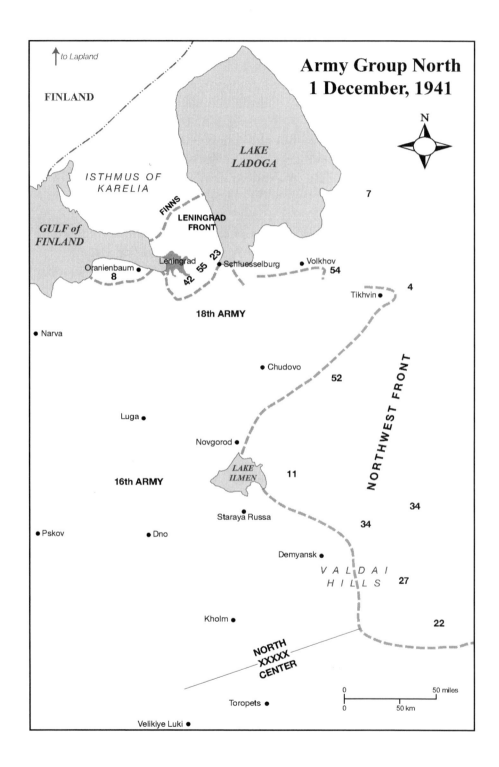

Army Group North
1 December, 1941

Leeb, who for once favored the bold solution, appealed to the OKW, but could not get the order rescinded. He considered letting Reinhardt proceed alone, but did not. The ensuing delay gave the Russians three weeks to rally their forces and prepare their defenses.

Leeb's army group had now advanced 430 miles into Soviet Russia and was only 80 miles from Leningrad. Leeb had cleared most of the Baltic States of Russian forces, but was at the end of a 430-mile supply line that was subject to attack by Russian partisans, bypassed units, and stragglers. Also, as one moves east, European Russia opens up like a funnel. Army Group North's frontage increased with every step Leeb's men advanced. Adding to the problems, Hitler had finally decided that Eighteenth Army must complete the conquest of the Baltic States before attempting to take Leningrad.

Finally, Hitler required Busch to cover the left flank of Army Group Center, to the extent that 60 percent of Sixteenth Army's infantry was engaged in this task by the middle of July. As a result, there were no foot soldiers to spare for Fourth Panzer Group, which was exposed to probing attacks by the Soviet Twenty-seventh Army and elements of the Eleventh Army, while yet another new Soviet army, the Twenty-second, was committed to the front, this one against Busch. Leeb's rate of advance, which had averaged 17 miles a day for the first three weeks of the campaign, slowed to barely one mile a day in August.

Hoepner resumed his drive on Leningrad on August 8, with Reinhardt on the left and Manstein on the right. The swampy, forested terrain was utterly unsuited for armor, and Soviet resistance was well prepared and fierce. Reinhardt's three divisions, the 1st Panzer, 6th Panzer, and 36th Motorized, were led by Krueger, Major General Franz Landgraf and Otto-Ernst Ottenbacher, respectively.

Franz Landgraf was born in Munich on July 16, 1888. He attended cadet schools and joined the army as a *Faehnrich* in the 5th Bavarian Infantry Regiment on July 7, 1909. Commissioned on October 26, 1911, he went to the field with his regiment in 1914 and fought in Lorraine and Flanders, while serving as a platoon leader, battalion adjutant, and company commander. In May 1915 he transferred to the 1st Bavarian Jaeger Regiment of the elite Alpine Corps. He was named adjutant of his regiment and remained in this position for the rest of the war, serving in

Italy, France (including the battles of Verdun and the Argonne in 1916), Romania (1916–17), Hungary, Italy (1917), Lorraine (1918) and the Balkans (1918). He was promoted to first lieutenant in 1915.

Landgraf rejoined the 5th Bavarian after the Armistice but joined the Freikorps Bamberg in April 1919 and served with it for almost a year. Promoted to captain in 1919, he joined the 46th Reichswehr Infantry Regiment in February 1920. This regiment became part of the 21st Infantry Regiment at Nuremberg on October 1, 1920, and Landgraf was given command of one of its companies. He held this position until 1928. Landgraf was named adjutant to the commander of the Grafenwoehr Troop Maneuver Area in the fall of 1928 and remained there until April 1, 1934, when he returned to the 21st Infantry as commander of its training battalion at Erlangen. He was promoted to major in 1931.

On October 1, 1934, Franz Landgraf became a lieutenant colonel. That same day, his battalion was used to form the 2nd Rifle Regiment at Meiningen. Landgraf was thus absorbed into the *Panzerwaffe* (armored force). He commanded a battalion in the 2nd Rifle until October 1, 1936, when he assumed command of the 7th Panzer Regiment, which was then forming in the Ohrdruf Troop Maneuver Area. He was promoted to colonel on June 1. Landgraf led his regiment in Poland and, on October 15, 1939, assumed command of the 4th Panzer Brigade of the 10th Panzer Division. This brigade included the 8th Panzer Regiment and his own 7th Panzer. He led it in Belgium and France in 1940 and was promoted to major general on September 1. Sent back to Germany, he assumed command of the 6th Panzer Division on January 6, 1941.

The three divisions of the XXXXI Motorized Corps suffered so many casualties that Hoepner considered abandoning the offensive. Finally, on August 14, he broke out at last, but Leeb had to take away half of his panzer group almost immediately, because a major crisis had developed to the south, in the zone of Christian Hansen's X Corps.

Christian Hansen was born in Schlesiwg on April 10, 1885, and joined the army as a *Fahnenjunker* in the Schleswig-Holstein 9th Foot Artillery Regiment in the fortress of Ehrenbreitstein (near Koblenz) on March 1,

1903. He was commissioned on August 18, 1904, and spent two years at the Military Technical Academy (1906–08). After serving a year as an instructor at the Foot Artillery Firing School, he returned to his regiment in October 1909. A year later, he was detached to the War Academy in Berlin to undergo General Staff training. He graduated in 1913 and was attached to the Greater General Staff until Germany mobilized in August 1914.

He was initially assigned to the chief of Field Railroad Matters of the Sixth Army and served behind the Western Front. Later, he was on the staffs of the Tenth Army, 33rd Reserve Division, and the 58th Special Purposes Command, before being transferred to the operations staff of the Grand Headquarters in March 1917. He remained here until 1919. Meanwhile, he was promoted to first lieutenant (1912) and captain (1914). He joined the General Staff of the Military Government at Thorn (1919–20) and was briefly on the staff of Infantry Commander 2 and the Defense Ministry, before being posted to the 6th Infantry Division at Muenster (1920–22). From 1922 to 1925, he commanded a battery in the Prussian 2nd Artillery Regiment at Stettin, followed by a tour of duty as chief of operations of the 1st Infantry Division at Koenigsberg (1925). In late 1925, he was assigned to the staff of Group Command Two at Kassel, and from 1926 to 1928 was at Muenster, on the staff of Wehrkreis VI. He was promoted to major in 1926.

Hansen joined the staff of the III Battalion/2nd Artillery Regiment at Itzehoe in 1928, before returning to Berlin and the General Staff of the Second Group Command in 1930. He was promoted to lieutenant colonel that same year. From 1930 to 1932, he was on the staff of the Hessian-Wuerttemberger 5th Artillery Regiment at Ulm, before becoming a course director at the Artillery School at Jueterbog. Promoted to colonel on April 1, 1933, he assumed command of the 1st Artillery Regiment at Koenigsberg (with battalions at Insterburg and Allenstein) on October 1. Promoted to major general on April 1, 1936, he assumed command of the 25th Infantry Division at Ludwigsburg on October 6. He became a lieutenant general on March 1, 1938. After leading his division in the Saar, he was given command of the X Corps on October 15, 1939, which he led in the conquest of the Low Countries. He was promoted to general of infantry June 1, 1940. He redeployed his command to Poland in early 1941, and crossed into the Soviet Union on June 22.

On August 1, on the left flank of the Sixteenth Army, Hansen began an advance on Staraya Russa, an important transportation center on the southern side of Lake Ilmen, in order to provide cover for the deep right flank of Army Group North for its final advance on Leningrad. The Soviets were fully ready for this onslaught and committed the entire Eleventh Army to the defense, behind deep minefields, in dug-in tanks, bunkers, and extensive field fortifications. General Hansen attacked with the 126th, 30th, and 290th Infantry Divisions, which were commanded by Lieutenant Generals Paul Laux, Kurt von Tippelskirch, and Baron Theodor von Wrede, respectively.

Paul Laux was born in Weimar on November 11, 1887. He joined the army as an officer cadet on February 20, 1907, and was commissioned in the 134th (10th Saxon) Infantry Regiment on August 14, 1908. When World War I began, he became adjutant of the I/134th Infantry Regiment and fought in Belgium, the Marne, and in France. He was promoted to first lieutenant in 1914 and to captain in 1916. He was appointed directly to the General Staff of the XXVII Reserve Corps (1916–18) and was a battalion commander in the Saxon 58th Infantry Division from 1918 to October 1919. He was selected for the Reichswehr, and in 1920 was transferred to the Saxon 11th Infantry Regiment at Leipzig. He became a company commander in 1922, and transferred to the staff of the III Battalion in 1923. Later he was sent to Dresden, where he served on the staff of the Artillery Commander IV (1923–25), the Infantry Commander IV (1925–27), and the 4th Infantry Division (1927–30). He joined the staff of Artillery Commander VI in Muenster, Westphalia, in 1930. This command was transferred to Hanover in October 1934, where it was redesignated 19th Infantry Division. Laux, meanwhile, was promoted to major in 1929, lieutenant colonel in 1933, and colonel on July 1, 1935. He assumed command of the 24th Infantry Regiment at Braunsberg, East Prussia (now Braniewo, Poland) on October 1, 1935.

Colonel Laux spent October 1937 to November 1938 attached to the commander of Air Region Weimar. He was then transferred to Passau, Lower Bavaria, as Infantry Commander 10. He was promoted to major general on April 1, 1938. When Germany mobilized on August 26, 1939, he became Ia of the First Army on the Western Front. On October 5, 1940, after the fall of France, Laux was named commander of the 126th Infantry Division, which was then forming in Sennelager, a camp near Paderborn in western Germany. Laux was promoted to lieutenant general on January 1, 1941, and moved his division to East Prussia in the spring of 1941.

Baron Theodor von Wrede was born in Wandsbeck, a suburb of Hamburg, on November 3, 1888. He entered the army as a *Fahnen-junker* in the 5th Ulan Regiment on March 7, 1907, and received his commission the following year. He fought in World War I, served in the Reichswehr, and was a major when Hitler came to power. Later, he was promoted to lieutenant colonel (October 1, 1933), colonel (August 1, 1935), major general (April 1, 1939), and lieutenant general (March 1, 1941). A member of the military attaché branch in the 1930s, he was appointed military attaché to Budapest in 1937, and held this post until after the Polish campaign. On October 26, 1939, he assumed command of the 393rd Infantry Division, which he led until May 7, 1940. This *Landesschuetzen* division, which was then in the process of forming, consisted mainly of men over the age of 45 and was used as an occupation/guard force in Poland. On June 6, he assumed command of the 290th Infantry Division, which he led in the final stages of the French campaign. It was posted on the Atlantic coast until January 1941, when it redeployed to East Prussia.

After a week of heavy fighting, Hansen, Wrede, Tippelskirch, and Laux penetrated the last nine miles to Staraya Russa, where they were soon engaged in house-to-house fighting. Despite the odds against them, the veteran German infantrymen slowly pushed the defenders back. But the Soviets were hatching a nasty surprise for them.

On August 12, Soviet Marshal Kliment E. Voroshilov, the latest commander of the Northwest Front, threw his newly activated Thirty-fourth Army (eight infantry divisions, a tank corps, and a cavalry corps) into an attack on Staraya Russa, with the objective of pinning the X Corps against the southern shore of Lake Ilmen and destroying it. On August 15, Leeb had to hurriedly transfer LVI Motorized from the Fourth Panzer Group to the Sixteenth Army in order to save Hansen and his men. On August 19, after a forced march of more than 100 miles, Manstein hurled his two divisions (Kurt Jahn's 3rd Motorized and the SS Motorized Division "Totenkopf," under the permanent command of Theodor Eicke and temporarily led by Georg Keppler) into the rear of the Thirty-fourth Army.

Kurt Jahn was born in Schmalkalden, Thuringia (central Germany) on February 16, 1892. He joined the army as a *Fahnenjunker* in the 30th (2nd Baden) Field Artillery Regiment on March 8, 1910 and attended the War School at Metz from October 1910 to June 1911. He was commissioned second lieutenant on August 18, 1911, and went to the field with his regiment when World War I began three years later. He fought in Alsace-Lorraine, Artois, Champagne, on the Somme, Verdun, on the Lys, and the Aisne, among other battles. Jahn, meanwhile, was promoted to first lieutenant on August 18, 1915, and to captain exactly three years later. Meanwhile, he served as battalion adjutant, regimental adjutant, adjutant to the commander of Arko 29 (1916–17), and on the staff of the 29th Infantry Division (1917–18), of which the 30th Artillery was a part. In the last year of the war, he was admitted directly to the General Staff and served on the staff of the V Corps and the 42nd Infantry Division on the Western Front. After the war, he was transferred to the Baltic area, where he was part of the Freikorps. In the fall of 1919, he joined the General Staff of Wehrkreis I in Koenigsberg, East Prussia.

In 1921, Captain Jahn joined the staff of Group Command One in Berlin (1921–23) and worked as an advisor to the training department (T 4) of the Reich Defense Ministry from 1923 to 1925. He was on the staff of the 2nd Infantry Division as an Abwehr (intelligence) officer from 1925 to 1928, when he became a battery commander in the 2nd Artillery Regiment (1928–31). (Although the regimental headquarters was at Stettin, Jahn's battery was stationed at Schwerin in Mecklenburg-Vorpommern.) He was promoted to major on November 1, 1930.

Jahn joined the staff of the 5th Infantry Division at Stuttgart in 1931 and remained there until 1934. He was promoted to lieutenant colonel on May 1, 1933, assumed command of Artillery Regiment Ulm in 1934, and was promoted to colonel on May 1, 1935. His regiment became the Hessian-Wuerttemberger 5th Artillery Regiment in 1936. On October 6, 1936, Kurt Jahn became the commander of the newly formed 35th Artillery Regiment at Karlsuhe, Baden, and the following October 1 assumed command of Arko 35, also at Karlsruhe. On March 1, 1938, he became commander of the Artillery School at Jueterbog, south of Berlin. This was Nazi Germany's largest artillery training facility and it led to Jahn's promotion to major general on January 1, 1939.

On October 5, 1940, General Jahn became the first commander of the 121st Infantry Division, which was then forming in Troop Maneuver Area Muensterlager in Hanover. Although he was promoted to lieutenant general on November 1, Jahn never led the 121st in combat. It remained at Muensterlager until the spring of 1941, when it redeployed to East Prussia for the invasion of the Soviet Union. Then, on May 25, Paul Bader, the commander of the 3rd Motorized Division, was given a corps-level command and Jahn was selected to succeed him. His appointment is a bit surprising, given the fact that he had never before been associated with the mobile branches and lacked experience and training in motorized warfare. He nevertheless adapted extremely quickly and distinguished himself throughout Operation Barbarossa.

Theodor Eicke, the permanent commander of the SS Motorized Division "Totenkopf," was a major figure in the history of the *Waffen-SS* (armed SS) and the SS in general, because he was largely responsible for building the concentration camp system.[1] The 11th child of a railroad station master, he was born in Huedingen, Alsace (now Hampont, France), on October 17, 1892. He grew up in relative poverty and was poorly educated. Dropping out of the German equivalent of high school in 1909, Eicke enlisted in the Rhineland-Palatinate 23rd Infantry Regiment of the Imperial Army, then stationed in Landau. He was transferred to the 3rd Bavarian Infantry Regiment in 1913 and to the 22nd Bavarian Infantry Regiment in 1914. He fought in the Lorraine campaign of 1914, in the Ypres battles (1914–15), and in the trench warfare in Flanders. In 1916, he was transferred again, this time to the 2nd Bavarian Foot Artillery Regiment of the 2nd Bavarian Infantry Division, which suffered 50 percent casualties in the Battle of Verdun. He was in the reserve machine gun company of the II Corps from 1917 until the end of the war, earning both grades of the Iron Cross—very high decorations for an enlisted man in World War I.

Eicke went on leave and married Bertha Schwebel in December 1914. She gave him two children: Irma (1916) and Hermann (1920). Married life and fatherhood had little influence on Eicke, however; when he returned to Germany after four years on the Western Front, he was a very embittered and violent man. The left-wing revolutionaries and radicals who were running wild in Germany filled him with hatred and disgust. Fully believing the "stabbed in the back" myth that the German Army had been betrayed by Communists, Jews and the "November criminals," and had never been beaten in the field, he soon became involved in extreme right-wing political and paramilitary groups.

As a result, Eicke had a hard time keeping jobs until 1923, when he went to work as a security officer for I. G. Farben in Ludwigsburg. At this corporation, right-wing extremism and hatred for the Weimar Republic were not considered problems, and he remained there until he became a full-time SS man in 1932. Meanwhile, he joined the Nazi Party in 1928 and the *Schutzstaffel* (SS) in 1930. He became an SS *Untersturmmfuehrer* (second lieutenant) and platoon leader later that year.

Eicke threw himself into the tasks that the SS gave him with the fanatical energy of a true believer. His first mission was recruiting, which he did so well that Himmler promoted him to SS *Sturmbannfuehrer* (major) within three months of his joining the SS. By late 1931, he was an SS *Standartenfuehrer* (colonel) and commander of the 10th Standarte. His advance was abruptly halted the following year, however, when he was arrested for conspiring to commit political assassination and for illegally possessing high explosives. Fortunately for him, the Bavarian minister of justice was a Nazi sympathizer. He granted Eicke a temporary parole for reasons of health, and the SS man promptly fled the country. Fascist Italy gave him sanctuary, and Himmler promoted him to *SS-Oberfuehrer* and gave him command of the SA and SS Refugee Camp at Bozen-Gries, Italy, but he did not return to Germany until Hitler became chancellor in 1933.

While Eicke was in exile, one of his enemies within the party, Joseph Buerckel, the Gauleiter of the Palatinate, tried to have him replaced as commander of the 10th Standarte. When he returned to Germany, Eicke and a group of armed followers stormed party headquarters in Ludwigshafen in March 1933 and locked Buerckel, who was roughly equal in rank to a U.S. governor, in a broom closet for two or three hours, before the local police rescued him.

Eicke once again had gone too far, and Buerckel extracted revenge quickly. He had Eicke arrested, declared mentally ill, and thrown into a psychiatric facility as a "dangerous lunatic."[2] Himmler (who was furious at the *Oberfuehrer*) let him languish in the mental institution for weeks while Eicke attempted to act normal and wrote him several letters, begging to be released. Finally, the former chicken farmer relented and gave Eicke a new assignment—commandant of the concentration camp at Dachau.

From the Nazi point of view, Dachau was a mess when Theodor Eicke arrived on June 26, 1934. He quickly rid the place of corrupt guards and/or those who talked about what they did in public, dismissed about half of the 120-man staff, and established the code of conduct that became a model for all concentration camps. Undisciplined brutality was replaced by well-organized brutality, based on the principle of unquestioned and absolute obedience. Whippings, for example, were administered by all officers and men on a rotating basis; SS men now tortured inmates impersonally, without anger, remorse or conscience. Under Eicke, Heinz Hoehne wrote, "anyone who still retained a shred of decency and humanity was very soon brutalized."[3] As far as the Nazis were concerned, Dachau had become a model concentration camp.

Himmler rewarded Eicke's "success" by promoting him to *SS-Brigadefuehrer* on January 30, 1934. During the "Night of the Long Knives" (the purge of the Brownshirts), Eicke personally shot Ernst Roehm, the chief of the Stormtroopers. This earned him a promotion to inspector of concentration camps and commander of all SS guard units on July 5, 1934. He was promoted to *SS-Gruppenfuehrer* (SS lieutenant general) six days later.

Eicke initially headquartered on the Friedrichstrasse in Berlin, but soon moved his staff to the Sachsenhausen concentration camp at Oranienburg, north of Berlin. The inspectorate remained here until the fall of Berlin in 1945. By 1938, he directed five large camps (Dachau; Sachsenhausen; Buchenwald, near Weimar; Lichtenburg; and Mauthausen, near Linz, Austria, as well as several smaller ones.) Vicious, brutal, humorless, cruel, ruthlessly ambitious, extremely racist and a fanatical Nazi, Eicke excelled as chief of the concentration camps, in the views of Himmler and his deputy, Reinhard Heydrich. He also developed his Death's Head guard units (the *Totenkopf-verbaende* or SSTV) into paramilitary units. Eventually they spent three weeks each month in military training, spending only one week a month on guarding prisoners. By the end of 1938, he had four SSTV regiments.

When World War II began, Eicke mobilized three of his regiments (about 7,000 men) and played a minor role in the Polish campaign, mainly using his Einsatzgruppe against Poles and Jews. By early 1940, Eicke had created the *Totenkopfdivision* (SSTK), a motorized infantry division of 15,000 men. It performed bravely in Belgium and France, but with a distinct lack of tactical skill. Lack of trained General Staff officers plagued the Waffen-SS throughout its existence. Eicke's entire division had only one such officer, until he collapsed due to exhaustion, overwork, and the stress of having to deal with Theodor Eicke on a daily basis.

Due to poor logistical management, the division's combat troops were without supplies for at least three days and had to rely on food taken from French civilians and on aid provided by the SSTK's neighbor, Erwin Rommel's 7th Panzer Division. The situation deteriorated to the point that, with Eicke's approval, Rommel's Ia and Ib, both trained General Staff officers, took over the rear area of the Totenkopf Division, and ran it as well as their own. The supply situation cleared up immediately.

Eicke also did a poor job as a divisional commander. His corps commander, Erich Hoepner, gave him a fierce dressing down and called him a butcher to his face. He could not fire him, however. The courage of the SS fanatics did much to mitigate Eicke's tactical ineptitude, however, and Eicke did, at least, learn from his mistakes. He did a much better job on the Eastern Front.

The SS Motorized Division "Totenkopf" invaded the Soviet Union on June 24, crossed the Dvina at Dvinsk, overcame bitter Soviet resistance in central Lithuania, broke though the Stalin Line, and earned the praise of Erich von Manstein. Meanwhile, on July 6, 1941, Theodor Eicke was returning to his command post after a day at the front with his men. His vehicle ran over a land mine and his right foot was shattered. He was flown back to Germany and underwent an emergency operation in Berlin. It would take him three months to recover. Even then, he did not recover completely: as late as mid-1942, he still limped and had to walk with a cane.

SS Colonel Matthias Kleinheisterkamp took command of the division on July 7, which he led until SS Major General Georg Keppler arrived to assume command.[4]

Georg Keppler was born in Mainz on May 7, 1884, the son of an army colonel.[5] Keppler followed in his father's footsteps and joined the army as a *Fahnenjunker* in 1913. Commissioned in the 73rd Fusilier Regiment in June 1914, he was wounded in action at St. Quentin on August 29. Following his recovery, he served on the staffs of the 39th Infantry Brigade and the 19th Reserve Division and was wounded twice more. Not selected for the Reichsheer, he joined the State Police in Hanover in 1920. Later he transferred to Thuringia and Jena. Keppler joined the NSDAP in 1930 and rejoined the army in briefly in 1935, before joining the SS *Verfuegungstrupe* (or SS-VT), the first SS combat division, as an SS major in the fall of 1935. He commanded a battalion in the Deutschland SS Regiment before becoming the first commander of the "Der Fuehrer" SS Regiment in Vienna in 1938, which he led in the Western campaign of 1940 and in the early stages of the Russian campaign before becoming acting commander of the "Totenkopf" SS Division on July 15, 1941. Unlike some of the other SS commanders (including Eicke), Keppler proved to be capable from the first day.

Led by Jahn and Keppler, Manstein's flanking attack took the Russian flankers by surprise, trapping them between himself and Hansen. By August 23 the Soviet army had been destroyed and 246 guns had been captured. Manstein could not return to the north, however, because Voroshilov threw three more armies into an offensive against the land neck between Lakes Peipus and Ilmen, pinning down both Sixteenth Army and the LVI Motorized Corps in the process.

Meanwhile, in accordance with Hitler's orders, Eighteenth Army was reinforced with Schmidt's XXXIX Motorized Corps (from Army Group Center) and Richthofen's VIII Air Corps. With this help, Kuechler was able to push back the Soviet Forty-eighth Army to the north of Lake Ilmen. He took Novgorod, and on August 25 seized Chudovo, on the main Moscow to Leningrad railroad line. The Soviets reinforced this Fifty-fourth and Fifty-second), but they were unable to prevent Leeb from taking Mga on August 30. By September 4, the German Eighteenth Army had cleared Estonia of Soviet troops, as well as the entire southern shore of the Gulf of Finland, except for a small bridgehead at Oranienbaum, opposite Kronstadt, where the Soviet Eighth Army was besieged by Albert Wodrig's XXVI Corps.

Albert Wodrig was born in Berlin on July 16, 1883. He entered the service on August 22, 1901, as a *Fahnenjunker* in the 26th Field Artillery Regiment and was commissioned second lieutenant on January 27, 1903. He served in World War I, joined the Reichswehr, and was a to lieutenant colonel on the staff of Artillery Commander III in 1931. He was promoted to colonel on October 1, 1931, to major general on April 1, 1934, and to lieutenant general on March 1, 1936. He was stationed in East Prussia in the 1930s as a special purposes (z.b.V.) general with Wehrkreis I in Koenigsberg. The OKH thought that another corps-level headquarters might be needed in case of war with Poland, and that is exactly what happened. Wodrig commanded the ad hoc Corps Wodrig (which was also known as the 1st Special Purposes Staff) and fought in northern Poland in September and October 1939. Corps Wodrig was upgraded to the XXVI Corps on October 1, and Wodrig was promoted to general of artillery the same day.

Wodrig commanded the XXVI in the Netherlands, Flanders, and France in 1940 and directed his corps' redeployment to East Prussia in July. He led it in the sweep through the Baltic States, the Battle of Riga, and the early stages of the Siege of Oranienbaum, which would last until January 1944.

In the center, Leeb's troops were nearing the suburbs of Leningrad. This city, the number two city in the Soviet Union, was formerly St. Petersburg, the capital of the Czars. It had a population of 3,000,000 in 1941, contained major munitions plants, tank factories, textile mills, shipyards, and was the home port of the Soviet Baltic Sea Fleet. It was of major importance to the Soviet war effort, and its fall might very well endanger the continued existence of the Soviet Union. It was defended by troops in two major rings of fortifications that had been constructed around the city mainly by the women and children of Leningrad. The inner ring focused on Duderhof Hills, the key point in the defensive line.

The first German artillery shells landed in the city on September 4. Two days later it was subjected to its first bombing attack. With the Germans clearly closing in, Stalin reinforced Leningrad with his newly formed 52nd, 54th, and 55th Armies. In the city itself, Marshal Voroshilov, Political Commissar Zhdanov, and General Zakhvarov, the commandant of the city, formed 300,000 factory workers into 20 Red

Militia divisions. The troops were so raw and untrained, however, that they did little to impede the progress of the Germans, and most of them never came home

During the first week of September, Field Marshal von Leeb received the loan of General Hoth's Third Panzer Group (LVII and XXXIX Motorized Corps) from Army Group Center, which he used to defeat the Soviet Second, Thirty-fourth, and Twenty-seventh Armies between Staraya Russa and Kholm. This enabled him to anchor his right flank and bring up the XXVIII Corps (General of Infantry Mauritz von Wiktorin) and the XXXIX Motorized Corps (under the Headquarters, Sixteenth Army), for the decisive attack on the city.

For the final attack, Leeb deployed the following forces (left to right): Lt. Gen. Friedrich-Wilhelm von Chappuis's XXXVIII Corps of the Eighteenth Army; Reinhardt's XXXXI Motorized Corps, supported by Lt. Gen. Georg Lindemann's L Corps, both of Fourth Panzer Group, in the center; and the XXVIII Corps and XXXIX Motorized Corps of Sixteenth Army on the right flank. Reinhardt's XXXXI (36th Motorized Division, supported by the 1st and 6th Panzer Divisions) launched the main attack, while, on the extreme eastern flank, Rudolf Schmidt's XXXIX Motorized Corps, spearheaded by Major General Hans Zorn's reinforced 20th Motorized Division, had the task of capturing Schluesselburg on the southern shore of Lake Ladoga, which would seal off the city from the rest of the Soviet Union, except by water. The attack was to be supported by Alfred Keller's 1st Air Fleet.

Alfred Keller was born in Bochum, Westphalia, on September 19, 1882. Physically he was a small man, standing 5 feet 7½ inches tall and weighing only 160 pounds in 1945. He joined the army as a *Fahnenjunker* in the 17th *Pioneer* (Engineer) Battalion at Thorn, West Prussia (now Torun, Poland) on April 12, 1902, and was commissioned the following year. He became interested in airplanes shortly after the Wright Brothers made their historic flight but did not begin his formal military training until 1912, when he attended an aerial observers' course at Metz. (By then he was stationed at Wilhelmshaven as a fortress engineer. He had been promoted to first lieutenant in 1911.) In 1913 and 1914, he did his pilot's training at Darmstadt, and was appointed commander of the 27th Field Aviation Battalion when World War I began in August 1914. He flew over the Western Front and was promoted to captain later that year.

Unlike the vast majority of other famous World War I aviators, Keller did not achieve fame as a fighter pilot. He specialized in aerial reconnaissance and bombing; in fact, he was known as "Bomber" Keller, a nickname which stayed with him all of his life. Keller was the first man to conduct an aerial reconnaissance over Paris in October 1914. He spent 1915 and part of 1916 commanding army flight parks; he then commanded the 40th Air Battalion on the Western Front. From April 1, 1917, until the end of the war, he led the 1st Bomber Wing with great success. He blasted Dunkirk in a night raid in 1917 and did a considerable amount of damage to the shipping there. In September 1917, he pounded a British ground unit and forced it to retreat to Calais—a first in military history. He was awarded the *Pour le Mérite* for this action. During the night of January 30/31, 1918, Keller launched the first successful bombing attack against Paris. He caused considerable damage and even more panic in the city, and all of his airplanes successfully returned to base. He continued to put pressure on the French capital until the French generals withdrew several antiaircraft units from the front to defend the city—which was his objective in the first place.

Keller left the service in January 1920 (with an honorary promotion to major) and went into civilian aviation, working for the German Air Shipping Company, for Junkers Air, and as the business director of Danzig Air. In 1925, he became the director of the civilian flight school at Staken, Brunswick. He rejoined the army as a colonel on January 1, 1934, and was almost immediately named commander of the flight school at Brunswick. He was transferred to the secret Luftwaffe on February 1.

Keller became commander of the 1st Air Division on May 1, 1934, while retaining command at Brunswick. On July 1, he assumed command of the 154th Bomber Wing (KG 154) and the air base at Fassberg. This was, theoretically at least, a demotion, but no one seemed to view it as such in 1934. In any case, Keller was commander of Luftkreis IV (the IV Air District) on April 1, 1935, just three weeks after Hitler declared that the Luftwaffe existed. He was promoted to major general a year later, on April 1, 1936; was named commander of Luftkreis I in East Prussia on November 1, 1937; and became commander of Luftkreis II in Pomerania on January 1, 1938. He was promoted to lieutenant general February 1, 1938, and was named the leader of Luftwaffe Command East Prussia on August 1. This command became the 4th Air Division on February 1, 1939, and the IV Air Corps on October 3. Keller, meanwhile, was promoted to general of fliers on April 1, 1939, and to colonel general on July 19, 1940.

Keller led his formations with a considerable amount of success in Poland and France, although he was badly beaten in the Battle of Britain. He was, in fact, much better at training and organization than he was as a tactical commander. He was nevertheless named commander of the 1st Air Fleet on August 20, 1940.

Hans Wilhelm Karl Zorn was born in Munich on October 27, 1891. He attended cadet schools in Bavaria and joined the army as a *Faehnrich* in the 2nd Bavarian Infantry Regiment on July 7, 1911. He was commissioned in 1913. During World War I, he served as adjutant of the 2nd Bavarian Infantry and fought on the Western Front, including the battles in Lorraine, on the Somme, and Verdun. He was promoted to first lieutenant and became a brigade adjutant in 1917. He was also wounded at least once. After the war, he was attached to the Bavarian War Ministry (1919–20), before being assigned to the 19th Infantry Regiment at Munich. He began his secret General Staff training in 1921, was promoted to captain in 1922, and earned the red stripes of a General Staff officer in 1924. After briefly rejoining the 19th Infantry, he was assigned to the staff of the Railroad Branch in the Reich Defense Ministry. He was posted to Munich again in 1929, where he commanded a machine gun company in the 19th Infantry Regiment from 1929 to 1932. Promoted to major around 1931, he was sent back to Berlin the next year as chief of the Railroad Branch. Promotions to lieutenant colonel (1934) and colonel (1936) followed.

On May 1, 1938, Hans Zorn assumed command of his parent regiment, the 19th Infantry, but when Germany mobilized on August 26, 1939, he became chief of staff of the XXII Corps, which fought in southern Poland. During the French campaign, this headquarters became Panzer Group von Kleist. After the fall of Paris, Zorn was promoted to major general on July 1, 1940, and on November 11, he took charge of the 20th Motorized Division, which was then in France. He took it to

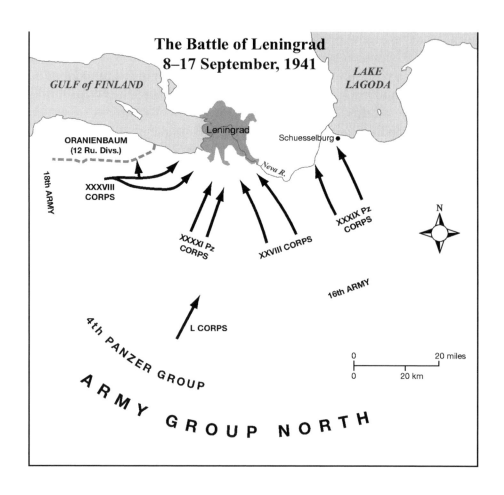

The Battle of Leningrad
8–17 September, 1941

GULF of FINLAND

LAKE LAGODA

Leningrad

ORANIENBAUM
(12 Ru. Divs.)

Schuesselburg

18th ARMY

XXXVIII CORPS

Neva R.

XXXXI Pz CORPS

XXVIII CORPS

XXXIX Pz CORPS

16th ARMY

N

L CORPS

4th PANZER GROUP

ARMY GROUP NORTH

0   20 miles

0   20 km

East Prussia in May 1941 and into Russia on June 22. Initially, the 20th Motorized was part of Hoth's Third Panzer Group and fought in the Battles of Bialystok and Minsk. It was then transferred to Army Group North.

On September 8, Leeb began his final assault on the city. Simultaneously, Keller's 1st Air Fleet subjected Leningrad to a massive bombing assault, during which it dropped tons of incendiaries. The bombs set fire to the Badayev warehouses, wooden buildings each separated from the next by only a few feet. Inside the warehouses lay Leningrad's entire reserve food supply—exactly the wrong way to store such critical provisions. The city's entire food reserve was burned, except for the sugar. It melted, all 2,500 tons of it, and flowed into the cellars, where it solidified into a substance that resembled hard candy. Later it was sold to the population "as is," when almost all the other types of food were gone.

Meanwhile, as if to underline the importance of the city, Stalin relieved Voroshilov and replaced him with Georgi Zhukov, his "troubleshooter" marshal, on September 9. Despite fierce resistance, Reinhardt's troops pushed slowly forward, until, at last, at 11:30 a.m. on September 11, Hill 167—the "General's Hill" of the Czars—fell, and 2nd Lieutenant Darius of the 6th Panzer Division signaled: "I can see St. Petersburg and the sea."[6] In the meantime, the men of the 291st Infantry Division knocked out 150 concrete pillboxes in a single day, while the 58th Infantry Division captured a Leningrad tram car in the suburb of Uritsk, only six miles from the center of the city.[7] Schleusselburg also fell, captured by Colonel Harry Hoppe's 424th Infantry Regiment of General Laux's 126th Infantry Division.[8] The capture of Schleusselburg also blocked the Neva, the waterway between the Baltic and Lake Ladoga, thus closing the system of rivers, lakes, and canals that linked Leningrad with the White Sea and the Arctic Ocean, and sealing off the city to the east.

By now, the forward tank crews could see the golden spires of the Admiralty building. Leningrad was doomed—or so it seemed. Then on September 12, Adolf Hitler ordered Ritter von Leeb not to take the city. He was merely to blockade it and starve it into submission. Simultaneously, Army Group North was ordered to give up the XXXXI Motorized Corps, LVII Motorized Corps, and the VIII Air Corps, as well as HQ, Third and Fourth Panzer Groups—a total of five panzer and two motorized divisions, and the bulk of its air support. In return, Hitler promised to send Leeb a German infantry division then in France, as well as the 250th (Spanish) "Blue" Infantry Division, and two parachute regiments.

Leeb immediately protested this strategically ridiculous order, but was overridden by Hitler, who had committed one of the greatest tactical blunders of the war. Thirty Soviet divisions were trapped in the city, but not destroyed. As winter descended on northern Russia, the Soviets were able to build a "road of life" across the ice of Lake Ladoga, and even constructed a railroad across it. Although thousands starved to death, just as Hitler had planned, Leningrad was nevertheless able to hold out for 28 months, tying down the vitally needed 18th and 16th Armies in the process. In the end, the Soviets managed to break the siege. Leningrad never was taken.

CHAPTER IX

THE BATTLE IN THE FAR NORTH

The commander of the German-Finnish forces in the Far North was Colonel General Nikolaus von Falkenhorst, the conqueror of Norway.

Nikolaus von Falkenhorst was born in Breslau, Silesia, on January 17, 1885. His name was Jastrzembski when he was born, but he changed it because it was too Slavic. He was educated in the cadet schools, entered the army as a *Faehnrich* in the 7th (2nd West Prussia) Grenadier Regiment, and attended the War Academy at Postdam, where he underwent officer training. He was promoted to second lieutenant on April 24, 1904, and became adjutant of the Fusilier Battalion of the 7th Grenadier in 1911. Promoted to first lieutenant in 1913, he was given command of a company when World War I began and fought on the Western Front. In December 1914, he was given an accelerated promotion to captain and became the adjutant of the 18th Infantry Brigade, a post which he held for two years. This unit was also on the Western Front. He was then transferred to the General Staff of Army Detachment Strantz (1916–17), the 2nd Infantry Division on the Eastern Front (1917), and the 12th Landwehr Division, which fought in Alsace and Galicia (1917–18). He also took a week-long General Staff course in Wahn in January 1918. Finally, on June 7, 1918, he became chief of operations for General Count Ruediger von der Goltz's *Ostseedivision* (Baltic Sea Division) in Finland, where he remained until late 1919.

Falkenhorst was admitted into the Reichswehr and served as a General Staff officer with the 29th and 6th Reichswehr Brigades (1919–20). He was on the staff of the II Battalion of the Prussian 8th Infantry Regiment at Liegnitz (1920–22), and on the staff of the operations branch of the Truppenamt (1922–28).[1] He was promoted to major in 1925.

Falkenhorst continued his professional climb in 1928, when he became commander of the I/1st Infantry Regiment at Koenigsberg (1928–30). This led to a promotion to lieutenant colonel on January 1, 1930. On October 1, he joined the staff of the 4th Infantry Division in Dresden, and on October 1, 1931, became the chief of staff of Wehrkreis IV (also in Dresden). He was promoted to colonel on October 1, 1932. From April 1, 1933 to April 1, 1935, he was military attaché to Czechoslovakia, Yugoslavia, and Romania, and was based in Prague. He then returned to his old post as chief of staff of Wehrkreis IV and was promoted to major general on August 1, 1935.

General Falkenhorst next served as chief of staff of Army Group Three (1935–36), commander of the 32nd Infantry Division at Koeslin, Pomerania (now Koszalin, Poland) (1936–39), and commander of the XXI Corps, which he led in Poland and on the Western Front (1939–40). He was promoted to lieutenant general on August 1, 1937, and to general of infantry on October 1, 1939.

When Hitler decided to invade Norway, either Keitel or Jodl remembered Falkenhorst's previous service in Finland (sources differ as to which). The Fuehrer summoned Falkenhorst to the Reichschancellery shortly before noon on February 21, 1940, and offered him command of the operation. Surprised, Falkenhorst nevertheless eagerly accepted. Hitler told him to return at 5 p.m. to present his invasion plan. Without maps or a staff of any kind, the general went to a bookstore, purchased a Baedeker travel guide, and repaired to his hotel room, where he mapped out his plan. It was revised only slightly. The invasion began on April 9. Within 48 hours, all of major cities of Norway were in German hands. Falkenhorst was promoted to colonel general on July 19, 1940.

While Leeb fumed outside Leningrad, Falkenhorst struggled forward against great obstacles, in an effort to take Murmunsk on the Arctic Ocean, another of the Soviet Union's vital ports. Despite its northerly location, Murmansk is an ice-free port, due to the warm ocean currents that loop north from Norway. Although Falkenhorst was ordered to take the port, his primary mission remained the protection of Norway, because Hitler was obsessed with the idea that the British might invade it. Falkenhorst's Group XXI was thus upgraded to the Army of Norway on December 19, 1940; Falkenhorst was named Armed Forces Commander, Norway; and Hitler reinforced him to a strength of more than 200,000 men. He also had 212 army and naval coastal defense batteries. These reinforcements proved to be a double-edged sword, however, because Hitler only allowed Falkenhorst to use 68,100 men for Operation Platinfuchs, as the advance to Murmansk was codenamed. He had firm orders not to disturb the 150,000 men (seven divisions) in Norway, an order that severely hamstrung Falkenhorst over the next several weeks.

Falkenhorst's main problem, however, was the terrain, which consisted mainly of bare, forbidding tundra characterized by boulders, gravel, rock outcroppings, and hundreds of small lakes left behind by the melting snow. There were no roads, railroads, or bridges; there was no food for the troops or forage for the horses; and there were no accurate maps. Everything had to be brought up by pack animal, and there were not enough pack animals. Mobile operations, the type of warfare at which the Germans excelled, were impossible here, and even the best mountain troops could only advance at speeds of a little more than a mile an hour. The Soviets, on the other hand, were fighting their kind of war. They were able to occupy well-prepared defensive positions, behind which they had stockpiled large quantities of ammunition, which enabled them to take advantage of the natural tenacity of their soldiers. In addition, the Reds had large artillery concentrations, command of the sea on and behind Falkenhorst's northern flank, and control of the air.

Falkenhorst divided his offensive into three widely separated sectors. On his northern flank lay Dietl's Mountain Corps Norway, while General of Infantry Hans Fiege's XXXVI Mountain Corps attacked in the center and Hjalmar Siilasvuo's III Finnish Corps (under German command) drove toward Belomorsk on the White Sea, through which the Murmansk-Leningrad railroad also passed. All three corps were opposed by elements of General Valerian A. Frolov's Fourth Soviet Army.

Eduard Dietl was an extreme German nationalist, a favorite of Adolf Hitler and a racist, but a good tactician and commander nevertheless. He was born in Bad Aibling, Upper Bavaria, on July 21, 1890, and entered the army as a private on October 1, 1909. He was promoted to *Fahnenjunker* on January 29, 1910, attended the War School in Munich for a year (1910–11), and was commissioned second lieutenant on October 26, 1911. Except for detached periods to attend army schools, he spent the first eight years of his career, including the first three years of World War I, with his regiment, the 5th Bavarian Infantry. Dietl habitually attended every school he could: prior to World War I, for example, he not only attended the officers' training course, but also the military firing school, the food supply course, the meat inspectors' course, and the searchlight school.

During World War I, which he spent almost entirely on the Western Front or in various hospitals, 2nd Lieutenant Dietl was a platoon leader for nine days before being promoted to battalion adjutant on August 11, 1914. He was wounded on October 11 and was not able to return to field duty until March 1915, when he again became adjutant of the I Battalion. Promoted to regimental adjutant in March 1915, to first lieutenant in July, and to 2nd adjutant of the 7th Bavarian Infantry Brigade in November 1916, he suffered his second serious wound in October 1917. When he returned to duty in December, he was promoted to brigade adjutant. He was seriously wounded in late October 1918, and was still in the hospital when the war ended. In the meantime, he had fought in Lorraine, Flanders (1914–15), Artois, the Somme, Flanders again (1916–17), Lorraine and northern France (1918). He suffered his last wound of the war in Flanders.

Dietl rejoined the 5th Bavarian Infantry in February 1919 but quickly transferred to Major General Ritter Franz von Epp's Freikorps, in order to fight Communists and left-wing insurrectionists in "the war after the war." He was promoted to captain in August and was selected for the Reichswehr a year later (August 1920). Freikorps von Epp, meanwhile, had become the 41st Reichswehr Infantry Regiment. It became the 19th Infantry Regiment in September 1920, and Dietl joined it as a company commander.

Like most of the Reichsheer regiments, the 19th did not concentrate in a single location, but had units scattered all over the map. The regimental headquarters, I Battalion, and 13th Company (the trench mortar company) were in Munich, while the II Battalion headquartered in Augsburg. The III (Jaeger) Battalion staff was at Kempten, along with the 11th and 12th companies, while the training battalion operated out of Landshut. The 9th and 10th Companies (of the III Battalion) garrisoned at Lindau. Except for periods of detachment, Dietl would be with various subdivisions of this regiment for the next 14 years.

Dietl commanded a company until 1924, when he was transferred to the training battalion. He was then detached to the Infantry School at Doeberitz as a tactics instructor (1924–28). This was a sure sign that "the powers that be" were satisfied with his progress, because the Reichswehr put a particularly heavy emphasis on training. He joined the III Battalion staff at Kempten in 1928 and was promoted to major in 1930. He became commander of the III Battalion on February 1, 1931, but was almost immediately sent to Norway, where he attended the Winter School of the Royal Norwegian Army at Akerhus. Here he met men whom he would one day fight. He returned to Germany in March and on April 1 was detached to the Army Mountaineer School in Stubai. Promoted to lieutenant colonel in early 1933, he was back on the Staff, 19th Infantry Regiment, in 1934.

After attending mountain maneuvers with the Italian Army, he was named acting commander of Infantry Regiment Amberg on October 1, 1934, which later became the 41st Motorized (later Panzer Grenadier) Regiment of the 10th Motorized Division. Dietl held this command for only a month; then he assumed command of Infantry Regiment Regensburg, which would later become (successively), the 20th Infantry, the 20th Motorized, and the 20th Panzer Grenadier Regiment. Promoted to colonel on January 1, 1935, Dietl assumed command of the 99th Mountain Regiment at Kempten on October 15, 1935. He was the unit's first commander and his headquarters personnel were from the former Staff, Training Battalion, 19th Infantry Regiment.

As part of the 1st Mountain Division, Dietl took part in the annexation of Austria, and was then promoted to major general on April 1, 1938. He assumed command of the 3rd Mountain Division, which was activated at Graz, Ostmark (formerly Austria) that same day. He led well during the Polish campaign and was promoted to lieutenant general on April 1, 1940. Eight days later, he landed in Narvik, Norway, where he distinguished himself in combat against the French and British, narrowly avoiding being pushed back in Sweden and internment. Hitler was delighted with his performance and named him commander of Mountain Corps Norway on June 14. Dietl organized his corps from elements of Headquarters, Group XXI and his own Staff, 3rd Mountain

Division. The Fuehrer further promoted him to general of infantry on July 19, 1940, and singled him out for praise in front of the world press corps. (Dietl later had the Army Personnel Office change his rank to general of mountain troops.) Hitler also earmarked Dietl to command the main thrust on Murmansk on June 22, 1941. The secondary thrust, far to the south, would be directed by General of Cavalry Hans Feige, chief of the XXXVI Corps Command.

Hans Feige was born in Koenigsberg, East Prussia (now Kaliningrad, Russia) on November 10, 1880. He was educated in cadet schools and entered the service as a second lieutenant in the 135th Infantry Regiment on March 22, 1900. He was a battalion adjutant from 1903 to 1907, when he became an instructor at the cadet school at Naumburg in Saxony-Anhalt. In 1909, he was transferred to the War Academy and began his General Staff training. He was promoted to first lieutenant at the same time.

Lieutenant Feige graduated from the War Academy in 1912 and was attached to the Greater General Staff in Berlin. He was promoted to captain in late 1913 and, when the Second Reich mobilized for World War I, was transferred to the General Staff of the IX Corps on the Eastern Front. He was later on the staff of the Eleventh Army, also in the East, and in September 1915, joined the staff of the 38th Infantry Division as a General Staff officer. He served on the Russian Front and then in the Oise sector in France, where he was severely wounded on March 18, 1916.

He returned to duty in early July on the General Staff of the Supreme Command of the Army, where he remained until the spring of 1917. Feige then became a General Staff officer with the 1st Naval Division, an infantry unit on the Western Front. In late January 1918, he was transferred to the Guards Replacement Division, which was then fighting in France, where he was promoted to major on July 15. After the war, he was part of Freikorps Goerlitz, until March 1920, when he joined the staff of Infantry Commander Schweidnitz. He was briefly attached to the Army Peace Commission, before joining the staff of the 1st Infantry Division in his hometown (late 1920). He had, in the meantime, been accepted into the Reichswehr.

Because he lacked command time, Feige was given command of the

III Battalion of the 6th Infantry Regiment at Flensburg in July 1923. (The regiment itself headquartered in Luebeck.) Already earmarked for greater things, he was promoted to lieutenant colonel on April 1925, and was named chief of staff of the 1st Infantry Division on February 1, 1926. Promoted to full colonel on April 1, 1928, he assumed command of the elite 9th Infantry Regiment at Potsdam on February 1, 1929. Exactly two years later, he became chief of the T 1 (operations) department of the Truppenamt, and was promoted to major general on October 1, 1931. He was attached to the staff of Group Command One in Berlin on October 1, 1932, and became group chief of staff on December 1. On October 1, 1933, Feige became a lieutenant general and assumed command of the 1st Cavalry Division at Frankfurt/Oder. He remained here until March 31, 1935, when he retired after 35 years of service.

Hans Feige was recalled to active duty when Germany mobilized on August 26, 1939. He was given command of Wehrkreis II (the II Military District) at Stettin, where he organized new divisions for the Wehrmacht, implemented the German draft in Pomerania and Mecklenburg, and provided existing divisions with trained replacements. He was promoted to general of cavalry (*charakter* or honorary) on September 1, 1940, and to general of cavalry (permanent rank) on December 1, 1940. On May 14, 1940, he was transferred to Norway as leader of the *Hoeheren Kommandos z.b.V. XXXVI* or the XXXVI Corps Command. (In the German Army, a corps command controlled divisions but with a reduced staff and fewer organic units, especially signal units; i.e., it was not a corps.) The XXXVI was later augmented and redesignated the XXXVI Mountain Corps on November 14, 1941.

Dietl's troops were in the Petsamo area, only 60 miles west of Murmansk, on June 22. Faced by two divisions of the Soviet Fourteenth Army, they pushed slowly forward, despite having to deal with Red naval landings in their rear. When the Communists reinforced the front with a third division, however, Dietl's offensive was brought to an abrupt halt, only 15 miles from its jump-off point.

Many miles south, in Falkenhorst's center, Feige's XXXVI Corps Command, with two German and one Finnish division, attacked from the Salla area toward Kandalasksha, in order to cut the Murmansk-

Leningrad railroad. This was heavily forested country: deep, dark, and depressing. The terrain definitely affected German morale, and the inexperienced SS Brigade "Nord" (later the 6th SS Mountain Division "Nord") was routed by the Soviets. For the first time in his career, General Feige was unsuccessful and his attacks produced practically nothing except long casualty lists. In the month of July alone, XXXVI gained only 13 miles, but lost 5,500 men.

Meanwhile, to the south, Siilasvuo's III Finnish Corps, which was acclimated to forest warfare, gained 40 miles and built a road behind itself. Unlike the Germans, the Finnish troops were impervious to the dark and depressing forests. Soviet General Frolov was nevertheless able to take advantage of the superior mobility provided by his railroad to shift troops back and forth, and the Finnish advance was also halted in heavy fighting.

Falkenhorst continued to try to get the offensive going again until mid-September, despite the fact that British submarines were sinking his supply ships at an alarming rate off of the northern coasts of Norway and Finland. By September 12, his supply situation was critical and his infantrymen had only 1.5 basic loads of ammunition left. By the 18th, the Soviets were attacking continuously, and Falkenhorst was forced to go over to the defensive in all sectors. The campaign in the Far North sector had been a failure.

The poor German performance had a definite impact on the Finns, who expected them to overwhelm the Soviets in a quick blitzkrieg war. They were very disillusioned by the German failure. Marshal Mannerheim made this clear when he returned Lt. Gen. Ewrin Engelbrecht's 163rd (Brandenburger) Infantry Division to German command, on the grounds that it was not up to the demands of this theater.[2]

South of the Army of Norway, Marshal von Mannerheim launched an offensive toward Leningrad with the main Finnish forces, which consisted primarily of the Karelian and South-East Armies. He was opposed by the 23rd and 7th Soviet Armies, which fought fiercely. Mannerheim pushed to within 30 miles of Leningrad and within 80 miles of Tikhvin, but because of his heavy losses and his disappointment with the German showing would go no further. German diplomatic pressure did no good; he would not advance again. On November 7, Hitler took the Murmansk forces away from Falkenhorst and gave them to Eduard Dietl, the commander of the newly created Army of Lapland, which was redesignated Twentieth Mountain Army in June 1942. Falkenhorst spent the rest of his active career keeping Dietl supplied as best he could, feuding with Joseph Terboven, the Reichskommissar of Norway, and preparing for an Allied invasion of Norway, which never came.[3] Feige was relieved of his command on November 30 and was replaced as commander of the XXXVI Mountain Corps by General of Infantry Karl Weisenberger, the former commander of the LIII Corps. Meanwhile, however, the Far North sector stagnated.

CHAPTER X

THE BATTLE OF KIEV

THE FINAL DECISION

During the first two weeks of August, while Falkenhorst and his men were battling it out on a secondary front and Stalin and Timoshenko were moving heaven and earth to scrape together every available formation for the defense of Moscow, the OKH and Army Group Center were virtually paralyzed with indecision. Bock and his subordinates were still almost unanimously in favor of resuming the offensive toward the Soviet capital, in spite of Hitler's decision; however, no one wanted to confront the wrath of the Fuehrer. Meanwhile, Guderian, once again on the edge of insubordination, was still planning for a drive against Moscow, despite Hitler's orders to the contrary. To prepare for this contingency, he ordered Geyr von Schweppenburg to attack Krichev.

Baron Leo Geyr von Schweppenburg, called "von Geyr," was born in Potsdam on February 2, 1886, the descendant of an old Wuerttemberger military family. He entered the service as a *Fahnenjunker* in 1904 and was commissioned in the family regiment, the 26th Light Dragoons (2nd Wuerttemberg Dragoons), in 1905. He was appointed to the War Academy in 1911, graduated in 1914, and went to war with his regiment in August. He was, however, soon transferred to the staff of the 9th Cavalry Division. Promoted to captain in 1915, he served on both the Eastern and Western Fronts and in the Balkans, where he was a liaison officer to the Bulgarian Army. He also served tours of duty as chief of operations of the 30th Infantry Division and 26th Landwehr Division on the Western Front, and was wounded at least once.

After the war, he helped the Freikorps suppress civil unrest in Stuttgart and the Ruhr. Selected for the Reichswehr, he spent the 1920s alternating between cavalry and General Staff assignments, and commanded the Prussian-Mecklenburger 14th Cavalry Regiment at Ludwigslust from 1931 to 1933. Meanwhile, he was promoted to first lieutenant (1913), captain of cavalry (1915), major (1925), lieutenant colonel (1930), and colonel (1932). Promotions to major general (September 1, 1935), lieutenant general (October 1, 1937), and general of cavalry (April 20, 1940) would follow. (Geyr would officially change his rank to general of panzer troops on June 4, 1941.)

A bright, well-educated, sophisticated and articulate person with great social skills, the multi-lingual Geyr represented Germany as military attaché in London, Brussels, and The Hague from 1933 to 1937, and proved to be an excellent military diplomat. Seeing that the future belonged to the panzer branch, he befriended Heinz Guderian and transferred to the tank army in 1937. He commanded the 3rd Panzer Division (October 12, 1937 to February 15, 1940) in Poland and the XXIV Motorized (later Panzer) Corps (February 15, 1940 to January 7, 1942) in the conquest of France and in Operation Barbarossa.

In accordance with Guderian's plan, Geyr's XXIV Panzer Corps fell on the three Russian divisions guarding the Sozh crossings in the vicinity of Krichev. The Soviet formations were quickly scattered by the 3rd Panzer, 4th Panzer, and 10th Motorized Divisions, and 16,000 more prisoners were taken. This was a strictly local victory, however; on August 11, Bock notified Guderian that his plan for an advance on Moscow had been rejected by the OKH as "completely unsatisfactory." [1]

On August 15, the Soviet offensive against Leeb's right flank at Staraya Russa began. As a result, Hoth was ordered to send another panzer corps (Schmidt's XXXIX, with the 12th Panzer, 18th Motorized, and 20th Motorized Divisions) to Army Group North, to help rescue Busch's Sixteenth Army. "We reckoned with 200 Russian divisions" when Barbarossa began, Halder noted in his diary that evening. "Now we have already counted 360. Our front on this broad expanse is too thin, it has no depth. In consequence the enemy attacks often meet with success." [2]

Bock's ability to continue the drive on Moscow was severely curtailed by the loss of the XXXIX Motorized, but still no final plans were made for the resumption of the offensive and vital time was wasted. On August 18, Brauchitsch finally mustered up enough courage to submit a memorandum to Hitler, calling for a drive against Moscow, but Hitler emphatically rejected it. In a handwritten answer, he informed the commander-in-chief of the army that the maximum effort was to be placed on the southern attack; furthermore, he criticized the OKH for allowing the panzer units to operate too independently and to push too far ahead of the infantry which, he said, had allowed too many enemy units to break through the loose encirclements and escape. Thus reprimanded and cowed, Brauchitsch meekly relayed Hitler's orders to Halder, and then to Army Group Center.

The final chapter in the crisis began on August 22, when Guderian was ordered to move his XXIV Panzer Corps to the Klintsy-Pochep area, on the left flank of Weichs's Second Army. Once again Guderian protested, stating that the idea of sending his panzer group to the south was "criminal folly." The next day, Halder arrived at von Bock's head-quarters at Novy Borisov. Here he met with Bock and Guderian, and on Bock's suggestion it was decided that the panzer leader should personally appeal to Hitler and talk him out of the drive to the south. Halder and Guderian boarded a Ju-52 and took off for Loetzen that very afternoon.

On landing at the airfield near Fuehrer Headquarters just before nightfall, they were met by Field Marshal von Brauchitsch, who was in a state of nervous agitation. " I forbid you to mention the question of Moscow to the Fuehrer," he told Guderian. "The operation to the south has been ordered. The problem now is simply how it is to be carried out. Discussion is pointless." Guderian replied that, in that case, he would fly back to his headquarters immediately, since any conversation he had with Hitler would be a waste of time. No, Brauchitsch answered, he must see the Fuehrer and report on the condition of the panzer group, "but without mentioning Moscow!" [3]

When the meeting took place, Guderian had a large audience, including Keitel, Jodl, and several OKW officers; neither Brauchitsch nor Halder was present. Hitler listened in silence to Guderian's report, and then asked: "In view of their past performance, do you consider that your troops are capable of making another great effort?"

"If the troops are given a major objective, the importance of which is apparent to every soldier, yes."

"You mean, of course, Moscow?" the Fuehrer asked.

"Yes," Guderian responded, and then gave him the reasons for his opinions. Hitler listened impassively until Guderian had finished. Then Hitler spoke in great detail about the economic reasons behind his decision, concluding: "My generals know nothing about the economic aspects of war." As the Leader spoke, Guderian noticed the attitude of the OKW officers in attendance. "I saw here for the first time a spectacle with which I was later to become very familiar: all those present nodded in agreement with every sentence that Hitler uttered, while I was left alone with my point of view."

Since he saw that the decision to attack into the Ukraine was not going to be reversed, Guderian recalled later, he begged Hitler not to split the panzer group as was intended, but to commit the entire 2nd Panzer to the operation. Hitler agreed to back Guderian on this point, and the appropriate order was issued the following day. As a result, Army Group Center was also deprived of General of Panzer Troops Joachim Lemelsen's XXXXVII Motorized Corps, leaving it with only von Vietinghoff's XXXXVI Motorized (7th Panzer, 11th Panzer, and 14th Motorized Divisions). Had the XXXXVII been allowed to remain with Army Group Center and rebuild its tank strength, instead of being committed to a long and resource-consuming drive to the south, the ensuing drive on Moscow might have been successful. This is doubtful, but, in any case, Halder felt betrayed. Guderian reported that, when he heard the news, the chief of the General Staff "suffered a complete nervous collapse, which led him to make accusations and imputations which were utterly unjustified."[4]

Unjustified or not, it is obvious that Halder believed that Guderian had allowed Hitler to bribe him. He telephoned Bock and told him that Guderian had let them down, and the relationship between the panzer group commander and the chief of the General Staff was never the same. Halder then urged Brauchitsch to join him in resigning in protest of the decision to forego Moscow. This Brauchitsch would not do, and Halder (who was no Beck) would not resign alone. So Hitler had his way; Army Group Center lost four of its five panzer corps, as well as three infantry corps and most of its air support, and Moscow was saved.

ARMY GROUP SOUTH

On June 22, it will be recalled, Rundstedt's Army Group South consisted of two wings. In the north, between the southern edge of the Pripyat

Marshes and the foothills of the Carpathians, lay Reichenau's Sixth Army, Kleist's First Panzer Group, and Stuelpnagel's Seventeenth Army. The other German army (Schobert's 11th) was intermixed the Romanian and Hungarian units and was not scheduled to go over to the offensive until July.

Facing Rundstedt was the bulk of the Red Army. Led initially by Colonel General Mikhail Petrovich Kirponos, the commander of the Kiev Military District, the forces defending west of the Ukraine included the 5th, 6th, 12th, and 26th Armies, with three mechanized corps (the 22nd, 4th, and 15th) in close support of the infantry. The 8th Mechanized Corps was about 250 miles east of the frontier, and the 19th and 9th Mechanized Corps were further back, at Zhitomir. The force Rundstedt struck on June 22 was thus much stronger than his own forces, but was too scattered; nevertheless, it gave a much better account of itself than did the Red units facing either Leeb or Bock.

The day the invasion began, Kirponos's main opponent was Colonel-General Ewald von Kleist, the commander of the First Panzer Group.

Paul Ludwig Ewald von Kleist was the descendant of a long line of Prussian generals and aristocrats who, like Field Marshal von Leeb, was very much aware of his ancestry. Three members of his family had been field marshals and 31 held the *Pour le Mérite*. The traditions of the Prussian officer and the Christian gentleman dominated his actions throughout his career. There was never any hint of scandal in his life or background. Certainly the thought of cooperating with the Einsatzgruppe never entered his mind. He looked upon the Nazi Party with a distaste he did not bother to hide. Unfortunately, he was not the stuff conspiracies are made of. Along with the rest of the army, he swore an oath to Adolf Hitler in August 1934, and he would never go back on it, even though several of his relatives did—and died for it. On the other hand, he was not blindly obedient either. This is why Hitler twice forced him into retirement and finally ended his military career.

Kleist was born in Braunfels an der Lahn, in the province of Hesse, on August 8, 1881. He entered the service as a *Fahnenjunker* on October 18, 1900, and was commissioned in the 3rd Field Artillery Regiment on August 18, 1901. He later became adjutant of the mounted battalion of the 3rd Field Artillery (stationed in Brandenburg) and transferred to the

14th Hussars in 1911. Meanwhile, he attended the War Academy (1911–14), was promoted to captain in 1914, and was assigned to the 1st Hussar Regiment when World War I broke out later that year. He spent most of the war on the Eastern Front, and led a cavalry squadron in the Battle of Tannenburg in October 1914. He returned to the General Staff in 1915 and did tours of duty with the 85th Landwehr and 86th Infantry Divisions (1915–16), and the XVII Reserve Corps (1916–17), all three on the Eastern Front. In the last two years of the war, he was successively chief of operations of the Guards Cavalry Division, the 225th Infantry Division, and the VII Corps (1917–19), all on the Western Front.

After the war, his career was typical for a Prussian general-elect: Ia of the 7th Reichswehr Brigade (1919–20), Ia of Infantry Commander VI in Hanover (1920–22), squadron commander in the 13th Cavalry at Hanover (1922–23), tactics instructor and General Staff officer at the Cavalry School at Hanover (1923–28), chief of staff of the 2nd Cavalry Division (1928–29), chief of staff of Wehrkreis III in Berlin (1929–31), commander of the elite 9th Infantry Regiment at Potsdam (1931–32), and commander of the 2nd Cavalry Division at Breslau (1932–36). Kleist made the Silesian capital his permanent home and purchased a nearby estate, which he called Weidebrueck. Photographs show that it was quite beautiful.

The 2nd Cavalry Division was disbanded in 1936 and its staff was used to form Headquarters, Wehrkreis VIII. Kleist remained in command and was responsible for the military administration of Silesia, as well as guarding the Polish and Czechoslovakian frontiers. He had three infantry divisions under his command, as well as the 3rd and 4th Frontier Zone Commands, and various paramilitary formations, including the Silesian Storm Troopers. He was promoted to general of cavalry on August 1, 1936. He had previously been advanced to major (1922), lieutenant colonel (1926), colonel (1929), major general (October 1, 1932), and lieutenant general (October 1, 1933). He would later be promoted to colonel general (July 19, 1940) and field marshal (February 1, 1943). Meanwhile, he married Gisela Wachtel in 1910. She gave him two children, both boys: Juergen Christoph Ewald von Kleist (1917) and Hugo Edmund Christoph Heinrich (1921). The oldest son, who was also called Ewald, served as a captain of cavalry on the Russian Front. Heinrich was medically unfit for military service due to a severe asthmatic condition. He also served in Russia, however, as an agricultural specialist. Like their father, both were devoted family men.

After Hitler named Walter von Brauchitsch commander-in-chief of the army on February 4, 1938, he purged the army of its potentially anti-Nazi elements, and the openly pro-Royalist Ewald von Kleist was one of the first to go. He departed, however, with a singular honor: he was authorized to wear the uniform of the colonel of the 8th Cavalry Regiment. Instead of the normal epaulettes of a general officer, Kleist wore cavalry epaulettes with the number "8" on them until he became a field marshal.

After a year and a half of retirement, Kleist was recalled to duty as commander of the XXII Corps, which he commanded during the invasion of Poland. Then he was sent to the Western Front, where he received a totally unexpected assignment: on February 29, 1940, his headquarters was temporarily redesignated "Panzer Group Kleist" and charged with the task of leading Germany's main panzer and motorized strike force during the Western campaign, which began on May 10, 1940. Kleist was indeed a surprise choice, since he had never been favorably disposed to the Panzerwaffe and disliked the fact that armored fighting vehicles were replacing his beloved horses with smelly engines. Why, then, did the High Command choose Kleist? Because they thought that the appointment of a competent conservative would be an effective counterweight to the perceived rashness of Heinz Guderian and his lieutenants.

Kleist did indeed clash with Guderian. During one argument, on May 16, Kleist ordered him to halt his headlong advance and reprimanded him fiercely for disobeying an order. The Father of the Blitzkrieg responded by demanding to be relieved of his command. Kleist was "momentarily taken aback," Guderian recorded later, but he accepted the challenge and sacked Guderian on the spot. [5]

General von Kleist has since been severely criticized by certain historians for taking this action. Kleist, however, was merely reprimanding Guderian for disobeying orders: he did not intend to relieve him until Guderian literally asked for it. Kleist was simply insisting that his orders be obeyed, all commanders must; otherwise, the entire military system will not work.

Later that day, on instructions from Rundstedt, Colonel General Wilhelm List (commander of the Twelfth Army) restored Guderian to command. He also informed Guderian that the halt order had come from Hitler, not from Kleist. (Kleist apparently did not feel it necessary to divulge the source of his orders to the corps commander.) He imposed a compromise on Guderian by which he would be allowed to continue his advance under the disguise of a "reconnaissance in force," but could not move his main headquarters. This compromise was acceptable to Kleist, who had only relieved Guderian because he had challenged him to his face, not out of personal animosity. Ewald von Kleist was not that kind of man.

Panzer Group Kleist was remarkably successful in France, which led to his promotion to colonel general. Later, in the spring of 1941, the headquarters became Staff, First Panzer Group, led by Kleist with equal success in the conquest of Yugoslavia. But more spectacular successes lay ahead.

On June 22, Soviet General Kirponos ordered up all three of his mechanized corps, with the intention of concentrating them northeast of Rovno (where the 22nd Mechanized Corps was already in position) and launching a massive counterattack from there against the First Panzer Group's left flank. General von Kleist, however, was too fast for him. The highly capable Prussian cavalryman broke through the Soviet frontier defenses and headed directly for Rovno, where he smashed the 22nd Mechanized Corps on the very first day of the invasion. The 15th Mechanized Corps tried to reach Rovno from the south, but was blocked by von Kleist and received a bloody check.

A series of uncoordinated counterattacks developed, in which Kleist defeated each Soviet unit piecemeal. The 8th Mechanized Corps (which was equipped with modern T-34 tanks) attacked alone and was severe-battered, while the 9th and 19th Mechanized Corps struggled for four days to reach the battlefield, under relentless bombardment from the Luftwaffe. They were already at about half strength when they went into action on June 23 and were promptly swamped by the veterans of the First Panzer Group. In all, Kleist's 600 panzers defeated 2,400 Soviet tanks, many of which were technologically superior to his PzKw IIIs and IVs, the best tanks the Third Reich had in 1941. Kirponos's counterat-tacks, however, had at least slowed down the German advance. "The enemy leadership in front of A. G. South is remarkably energetic,"

Halder recorded in his diary, "his endless flank and frontal attacks are causing us heavy losses." The next day he added: "One has to admit that the Russian leadership on this front is doing a pretty good job."[6]

Kirponos's tank losses in the frontier battles were extremely heavy; by June 28 he was in full retreat, covered by the survivors of his mechanized corps. Kleist took Lvov (Lwow) on June 30, reached the old Stalin Line on July 3, and broke through it on July 6, despite several strong Soviet counterattacks. On July 10, Kleist took Zhitomir (about 90 miles west of Kiev), after defeating heavy attacks from the 4th, 15th, and 16th Mechanized Corps. That same day the Soviet Fifth Army, reinforced with the surviving elements of the 9th, 19th, and 22nd Mechanized Corps, emerged from the southern edge of the Pripet Marshes and cut Kleist's main supply line. Field Marshal von Reichenau, following behind with his Sixth Army, had to commit much of his infantry to restore contact with von Kleist.

The terrain of Galicia and the western Ukraine was far from ideal for armored operations. It was heavily forested, much of it was swampy, and the roads were predominately made out of sand or dirt. Bypassed Red Army or partisan units operating in the German rear constantly disrupted German supply lines, to the point that, between June 22 and July 10, the First Panzer Group could only average an advance of ten miles a day, or even less than that—far from Hitler's hoped-for blitzkrieg.

Meanwhile, on July 10, Stalin reorganized his forces in the south. The South and Southwest Fronts, under F. V. Tyulenev and Kirponos, respectively, were merged to form the Southwest Theater, under Marshal Semon Budenny. His commissar was Nikita Khrushchev, who was a highly capable man. In July 1941, he had special orders to see to the "organization" (i.e., evacuation) of industry from the threatened sector. Along with his longtime friend, Anastas Mikoyan, who was in charge of industrial evacuation throughout the country, Khrushchev achieved miracles. In 1941, nearly one-fourth of the total industrial capacity of the Soviet Union was dismantled and shipped east, to the Urals and beyond, out of the reach of Goering's predominantly short-ranged Luftwaffe. Unfortunately for the Soviet Union, Khrushchev's talent was in no way matched by Budenny, the military commander of the theater.

Semen Budenny was a survivor. He had been a sergeant major in a cavalry division prior to the Revolution, but joined the Communists in 1917. A year later he turned up in Tsaritsyn (later Stalingrad), where he, Stalin, and Aleksei Yegorov (who died in the 1937 purge) formed the 1st Red Cavalry Army. Two years later he fought against the Poles, where he proved himself incapable of properly commanding even a division. After a humiliating defeat, he was sent to Georgia, where he led a punitive cavalry expedition against the local inhabitants in 1920. He held no further active commands until 1941.

Nevertheless, this jovial friend of Stalin was promoted to Marshal of the Soviet Union, and, except for Voroshilov, was the only man of his rank to survive the purges of 1937/38. By 1940, he was First Deputy Commissar of Defense, when he toured Bessarabia, which Stalin had just extorted from Romania. Typically, he decided to inspect a red wine distillery, and (along with his aides) ended up in one of the vats with a number of naked girls, bathing in about four feet of wine. The wet phase of the orgy ended when another guest, angry at not being able to climb into the vat, fired a machine gun burst into the vat and wounded three of the participants. The marshal, who was noted for his huge handlebar moustache, then adjourned to the rear of the building with several naked companions.

Budenny bore a superficial resemblance to the General George S. Patton, the legendary American tank expert, with his love of horses, the cavalry charge, his mahogany-handled revolvers, and his unorthodox manner. He had none of Patton's ability to lead men in battle, however; Stalin's appreciation of his reliability was the sole reason that he had advanced to this high rank. The dictator ordered Budenny to hold Kiev at all costs and gave the southern sector priority in the allocation of men and equipment. Aided by the rail system of the Ukraine (the most highly deployed in the Soviet Union), Budenny was soon able to marshal formidable forces in two areas (as dictated by the railroads): one in Kiev itself, and a second at Uman. By the second week in July, he had about 1,500,000 men—roughly half of the strength of the Red Army in Europe at that time.

Kleist, meanwhile, concentrated his three motorized corps (the III, XIV, and XXXXVIII) at Zhitomir, and on July 12 started an offensive aimed at separating Uman and Kiev. He made rapid progress against Budenny's predominately infantry ("infantry heavy") forces, and during the night of July 15/16 cut the vital Berdichev-Kazatin railroad, effectively splitting the Red forces in two. Meanwhile, Reichenau's Sixth

Army followed Kleist and applied pressure to the flanks of the Kiev concentration, while Karl-Heinrich von Stueplnagel's Seventeenth Army pinned down the Uman forces from the west and north. At the same time, the infantry of Colonel General Ritter Eugen von Schobert's Eleventh Army pushed across the Bug River at Gaivoron, 30 miles south of Uman, and headed toward Novo Ukrainka, deep in the Soviet rear.

Marshal Budenny reacted very slowly, and did not seem to appreciate the danger facing his Uman concentration. In any event, General of Infantry Wietersheim's XIV Motorized Corps of Kleist's group rapidly turned due south and linked up with Stueplnagel's vanguard at Pervomaysk, forming the first large encirclement on the southern sector of the Eastern Front. [7] By the time the Uman Pocket was cleared by the 11th and 17th Armies on August 8, the Reds had lost 103,000 men captured, including two army commanders, along with 317 tanks and 1,100 guns captured or destroyed. [8] By this time, Kleist's spearheads had advanced as far as Kirovgrod, more than 100 miles southeast of Kiev. By August 17, the III Motorized and XIV Panzer Corps had captured Krivoy Rog (the principal iron ore center of the Soviet Union) and had pushed into the great bend of the Dnieper.

In the meantime, Schobert, supported by Germany's Hungarian and Romanian allies, was threatening Odessa and advancing on the Dnieper estuary against light opposition. He crossed the mighty river above Kherson on August 21. General von Mackensen's III Motorized Corps crossed the river above the huge industrial city of Dnepropetrovsk the following day and entered the place on the 25th. Now nothing stood between Kleist's panzers and the occupation of the Donetz Basin except a few scattered militia units and local defense troops.

In the meantime, as we have seen, Guderian prepared to advance behind Kiev from the north. Elements of Reichenau's hard-marching army had already worked their way behind Kiev and were nearing Cherkassy, while the seven infantry divisions of Stuelpnagel's Seventeenth Army (freed by the fall of Uman) marched 30 to 40 miles a day and seized a bridgehead over the Dnieper at Kremenchug on August 22 and 23. The encirclement of Kiev was already taking shape.

While all of this was going on, Budenny sat in the capital of the Ukraine, doing nothing. His few surviving tanks were largely immobilized by lack of fuel, but, even so, he did very little to prevent the encirclement of Kiev. He assigned the task of defending the north bank of the Dnieper (southeast of Kiev) to the Forty-eighth Army, which was much too weak to hold a front of over 120 miles against the Seventeenth Army and the First Panzer Group. But Stalin had ordered Budenny to hold Kiev at all costs, and that is what he intended to do, oblivious to the encirclement that was developing behind him.

At Stavka, Marshal Boris M. Shaposhnikov, the chief of the General Staff of the Soviet Army, called for a timely retreat of Budenny's armies from Kiev to Kharkov, or perhaps even to the Donetz Basin.[9] Stalin, however, insisted upon fighting at Kiev. His reasons are obscure, but he was probably afraid that the Ukrainians (whom he had severely persecuted in the 1930s and who were already greeting the Germans as liberators) would join the Germans if he lost the city. He was right: had it not been for Hitler's foolish occupation policies, they no doubt would have done so.

THE BATTLE OF THE KIEV POCKET

General Guderian wheeled south and began his drive behind Kiev on September 9, taking the Russians completely by surprise. (Map 10.1 shows the Kiev encirclement.) The gap between Timoshenko's armies (facing Army Group Center) and Budenny's northern flank was over 120 miles, defended only by remnants of the Soviet Fifth Army, which could do little to even slow him down. The Second Panzer Group was delayed as much by the poor roads through the deep forests as by the Soviets.

Guderian's group was divided into two columns (one for each corps), which advanced about 30 miles apart. Baron Geyr von Schweppenburg's XXIV Panzer Corps was spearheaded by Lieutenant General Walter Model's 3rd Panzer Division, while the 17th Panzer Division (under the temporary command of Ritter von Thoma) led the advance of Lemelsen's XXXXVII Motorized.

Joachim Lemelsen was born in Berlin on September 26, 1888. He entered the service as a *Fahnenjunker* in the 40th Artillery Regiment at Burg (near Magdeburg) on July 1, 1907. Commissioned the following year, he served in World War I as a battalion adjutant (1914–15), regimental adjutant in the 104th Field Artillery, and an orderly officer with the 52nd Infantry Division (1916–17), all on the Western Front.

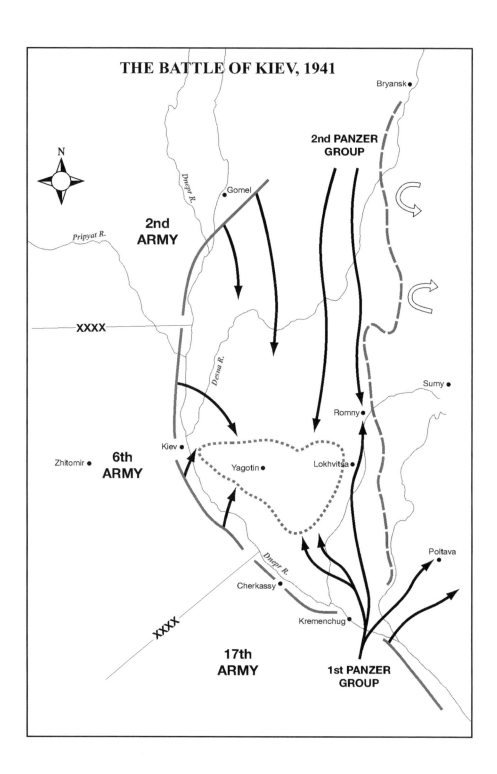

He was then a General Staff officer with the Coastal Defense Army at Hamburg (1917) and chief supply officer (Ib) of the 21st Infantry Division in France. After serving a month as a battalion commander in the 87th Infantry Regiment, he attended the abbreviated General Staff course at Sedan (October–November 1917), and was then named Ib of the VI Reserve Corps (1917–September 1918). He ended the war on the staff of the 58th Special Purposes Corps.

After the war, Lemelsen rejoined the 40th Artillery as a battery commander (1918–19). He later commanded a machine gun company in the 7th Reichswehr Regiment (1919) and an infantry gun battery (1919–20). In 1921, he commanded a battery in the Prussian-Saxon 4th Artillery Regiment at Dresden, and was on the regimental staff (1921–22) and the staff of the 1st Infantry Division at Koenigsberg (1922–23). He then commanded a battery in the 1st Artillery Regiment at Koenigsberg from 1923 to 1927. He was an instructor at the Artillery School at Jueterbog from 1927 to 1930 and, after attending the University of Berlin for a year, commanded the III Battalion of the 5th Artillery Regiment at Ludwigsburg (1931–33). He returned to the artillery school as a course director (1933–34) and was commander of the Artillery Lehr (Demonstration) Regiment at Jueterbog (1934–35). He then served as commandant of the War School at Dresden (1935–38), before becoming commander of the 29th Motorized Infantry Division (February 2, 1938–May 7, 1940). He was named commander of the 5th Panzer Division on May 29, which he led in the conclusion of the French campaign. He was promoted to first lieutenant (1914), captain (1916), major (1927), lieutenant colonel (1931), colonel (1934), major general (April 1, 1937), lieutenant general (April 1, 1939), and to general of artillery on August 1, 1940. (Later, on June 4, 1941, he changed his branch affiliation and became a general of panzer troops.) Lemelsen assumed command of the XXXXVII Motorized Corps on November 25, 1940, and led it throughout Operation Barbarossa.

By the third day of the offensive, Model had already covered 60 miles and captured the bridge over the Desna at Novgorod-Severski, thus overcoming the last natural barrier between the Second and First Panzer Groups. Kleist, meanwhile, took over the Seventeenth Army's footholds north of the Dnieper and attacked to the north on September 10. He was held up by the weak Thirty-eighth Soviet Army for two days, but on September 12 broke out from his bridgeheads at Cherkassy and Kremenchug and barreled into the Russian rear, spearheaded by Major General Hans Valentin Hube's 16th Panzer Division.

The one-armed Hube advanced with incredible speed, covering 43 miles in the first 12 hours. He made contact with Model near Romny, 130 miles east of Kiev, on September 14, closing the ring on the largest encirclement achieved during the Second World War. Inside the pocket, the confusion was total. Stalin relieved Budenny on September 13 and had him flown out of the pocket to command reserve forces in the interior. Although Stalin did not shoot his old friend (who lived until 1973), he never gave him another important command.

With Budenny's departure, the last semblance of central command also disappeared. On September 16, Stalin finally authorized the forces in the pocket to withdraw, but the breakouts were supervised by individual armies and corps, without central direction. As a result, they accomplished nothing and amounted to little more than human wave attacks. The third largest city in the Soviet Union fell on September 19, and by September 26, the battle was over. The final bag was 667,000 prisoners, with 3,718 guns and 884 tanks captured or destroyed. Among the dead was Colonel General Kirponos, one of Russia's most capable generals, who was killed by a German shell, presumably while attempting to find an escape route out of the pocket. His chief of staff was also killed, probably by the same shell. The Soviet Fifth, Twenty-first, Thirty-seventh, and Twenty-sixth Armies were largely destroyed, along with part of Thirty-eighth and Fortieth Armies, and the Ukraine, the breadbasket of the Soviet Union, was now lost to Stalin. As a reward for their part in this victory, the First and Second Panzer Groups were upgraded to panzer armies on October 6.

The task of finishing off the Kiev Pocket and overrunning much of the Ukraine and the Donetz Industrial Area beyond fell to Field Marshal Walter von Reichenau. He was more than up to the challenge, for he was an excellent commander, although not an excellent human being.

Walter von Reichenau was probably the most exceptional of Hitler's field marshals. Except for his pale blue eyes, he looked like a typical Prussian:

he had a stern, cold and forbidding appearance, augmented by an ever-present monocle. He was also brutally ambitious. Walter Goerlitz called him "a man devoid of all sentiment, at times, indeed, a cold-blooded, brutal man." [10] On the other hand, he was very innovative, independently minded, and accessible to the troops, with whom he was quite popular. He enjoyed automobile racing, swimming and boxing, and loved tennis; as a result, he was nicknamed "the Sports General."

The son of a Prussian lieutenant general and a Silesian mother, he was born in Karlsruhe on August 16, 1884. He joined the army as a *Fahnenjunker* in the 1st Prussian Guards Field Artillery Regiment in 1903 and received his commission on August 18, 1904. He went to Argentina with his father in 1908 and, as a member of the German Olympic Committee, visited the United States in 1913. His experiences in foreign countries would give him a sophisticated worldview and a more realistic understanding of international affairs than the vast majority of German officers. Throughout his career, he was an enthusiastic advocate of sending young officers overseas and requiring them to learn foreign languages. (Reichenau himself was fluent in English; later, he and his wife only spoke English at home.)

Reichenau was promoted to first lieutenant in 1912 and entered the War Academy for General Staff training in May 1914. His class never graduated, however, because Germany mobilized in August, when he was sent to the Western Front as regiment adjutant of the 1st Guards Reserve Field Artillery. He was promoted to captain on November 28, 1914, and served as a General Staff officer with the 47th Reserve Division, the VI Corps, and 7th Cavalry Division, fighting on both the Eastern and Western Fronts. He emerged from the conflict as a captain. During the "war after the war," he fought the Poles in Upper Silesia as Ia of the 7th Cavalry Division. Here he met and married Countess Alexandrine von Maltzan, the daughter of a landed, noble (and rich) Silesian family. Apparently Reichenau, who was a "lady's man" his whole life, never even considered being faithful to her.

Reichenau's marriage was a definite step up for him socially, although his own family was not without wealth. After retiring from the army, his father became one of the largest and most successful furniture manufacturers in Germany. His factory, which had been converted into a munitions plant, was destroyed by an Allied air attack in 1945.

Reichenau's rise in the Reichsheer was steady. He was a General Staff officer with Wehrkreis VI in Muenster (1920–22), after which he commanded the 8th (Machine Gun) Company of the 18th Infantry Regiment at Paderborn, Westphalia (1922–23). After finishing his troop duty, he was promoted to major (1923) and joined the staff of Wehrkreis III in Berlin (1923–26). He took his first trip to England in the summer of 1926. When he returned, he was assigned to the staff of Group Command One in Berlin, before being named commander of the 5th Signal Battalion at Stuttgart on November 1, 1927. He was promoted to lieutenant colonel on April 1, 1929.

Following his promotion, Reichenau spent several months in England, where he continued studying English and where he developed a high regard for the British. When he returned to Germany in the fall of 1929, he was named chief of staff in the Signals Inspectorate in the Defense Ministry, a position he held until February 1, 1931, when he was named chief of staff of Wehrkreis I in Koenigsberg, East Prussia. He was promoted to colonel on February 1, 1932. Reichenau's transfer to Koenigsberg was seen as professional exile within the army. He had been shipped here by General Kurt von Schleicher, a political soldier and a master intriguer who would maneuver himself into the chancellorship in late 1932, only to be replaced by Hitler Fifty-seven days later.

In 1932, Walter's uncle, Friedrich von Reichenau, a retired diplomat, president of the German Overseas League, and a fervent Nazi, introduced him to Adolf Hitler. They had a private meeting for an hour or more and Walter jumped on the Nazi bandwagon. Unlike Friedrich, however, his nephew's decision had little or nothing to do with his admiration of Hitler; rather, he looked upon Nazism as a tool to be used against Communism and to advance his own career and the interests of the army.

Reichenau introduced his commander, Werner von Blomberg, to Hitler. Blomberg, who was much more easily influenced and of a more romantic nature than Reichenau, was soon completely under Hitler's sway. Reichenau's gamble in linking himself with the Nazis paid off on January 30, 1933, the day Hitler took power and Blomberg was named minister of defense. Reichenau was promoted to major general on February 1, 1933, and was named head of the Ministerial Office in the Defense Ministry. Soon he was known as the chief liaison officer between the Nazis and the army.

Reichenau tried to arrange a sort of treaty of cooperation between the armed forces and the storm troopers (or SA). After Ernst Roehm, the chief of the SA, refused to cooperate, Reichenau played a major role in the "Night of the Long Knives," in which the Brownshirts were suppressed. Roehm and Reichenau's mortal enemy, Kurt von Schleicher, was among those murdered in late June and early July 1934. Reichenau then played an unsavory part in the cover-up of the murders of Schleicher and his wife. Shortly thereafter, in August 1934, Reichenau wrote the Oath of Allegiance that every soldier in the army had to take in 1934, when he swore allegiance to Adolf Hitler.

To date, Reichenau had advanced fairly rapidly, but, since he had never commanded anything larger than a battalion, he lacked command experience. With his influence with Hitler and Blomberg, he had no trouble getting a command. Typically, he skipped the divisional level altogether and asked for a corps-level assignment. On August 1, 1935, he was promoted to lieutenant general and on October 1, 1935, assumed command of Wehrkreis VII in Munich. Replaced as head of the Ministerial Office by Wilhelm Keitel, Reichenau was promoted to general of artillery on October 1, 1936.

During the Blomberg-Fritsch crisis of early 1938, Reichenau did not lift a finger to help his former mentor. "I had really expected different treatment from him," Blomberg later complained.[11] But Reichenau acted only in his own self-interest. Years later, when the Blombergs and Reichenaus happened to dine at the same restaurant at the same time, they ignored each other: in fact, Reichenau never spoke to Blomberg again, even though Blomberg had recommended him to succeed Fritsch as commander-in-chief of the army.

Becoming commander-in-chief was indeed Reichenau's next ambition and Hitler was leaning toward appointing him. His candidacy was only derailed when von Rundstedt and von Leeb interceded and informed Hitler that the army would "never" accept Reichenau, and Ludwig Beck (chief of the General Staff) and his deputy, Franz Halder, both announced that they would not serve under him. Even the usually spineless Wilhelm Keitel, the newly promoted commander-in-chief of the OKW, informed the Fuehrer that the army would not stand for Reichenau. Hitler vacillated a few days, but on February 4, 1938, he appointed Walter von Brauchitsch instead. As a consolation prize,

Reichenau succeeded Brauchitsch as commander-in-chief of Army Group Four, headquartered in Leipzig. This non-territorial command controlled all of the Reich's panzer, light and motorized divisions.

As early as the 1920s and throughout the 1930s, Reichenau was a powerful supporter of Heinz Guderian and the concept of the blitzkrieg. He translated several of B. H. Liddell Hart's works on armored warfare into German and ordered the Krupp Works to begin manufacturing panzers as early as 1933. He also shielded Guderian and the Panzerwaffe from Beck, Otto von Stuelpnagel, and other conservative generals, who wanted to break up the first panzer divisions and to use the tanks solely as infantry support vehicles. Reichenau, however, had an instinctive feeling as to how to use motorized forces, and he was very good at it.

Reichenau's headquarters was redesignated the Tenth Army in August 1939 and formed the main German strike force in the invasion of Poland. The general himself was the first German soldier to cross the Vistula. He swam it. Reichenau was promoted to colonel general on October 1, 1939. His command was redesignated the Sixth Army in late 1939 and he led it with great success in Belgium and France. He was promoted to field marshal on July 19, 1940.

In Russia, Reichenau cooperated with the Einsatzgruppe and only clashed with the SS once—not because they were committing mass murder, but because they were using too much ammunition. He then issued a murderous order, which the Nazis considered a model guide on how to deal with the Jews. He officially called upon them to limit their ammunition expenditure to two bullets per Jew.

By early October the Soviets had lost 2,500,000 men, 22,000 guns, 18,000 tanks, and 14,000 airplanes since the beginning of Operation Barbarossa. Hitler's strategic objectives had been largely achieved and the OKH was already discussing plans to withdraw and demobilize about 80 divisions from the Soviet Union after it surrendered. A wave of optimism swept through the General Staff at Zossen, where the general feeling was that one more major victory would finish off the Soviets.

At the front, however, the troops were not feeling nearly so optimistic. "The billet is full of lice," one German soldier wrote. "Socks which we put out to dry were white with lice eggs. We've caught fleas—

absolute prize specimens . . . . What a country, what a war, where there's no pleasure in success, no pride, no satisfaction; only a feeling of suppressed fury now and then . . . ." [12] The soldiers felt a deep sense of foreboding, as if they were advancing deeper into another world, a strange and dangerous world, from which many of them would not return. They were right.

CHAPTER XI

THE DOUBLE BATTLE OF VYAZMA-BRYANSK

When Hitler deprived Bock of 80 percent of his tank units in the second half of August, the road to Moscow was clear. By the end of the month, Stalin had rushed several new armies to the threatened sector, and Bock had no choice but to go over to the defensive with the Ninth and Fourth Armies. Because it was an obvious staging ground for an advance on Moscow, the most critical sector was in the Yelnya Bend, 47 miles east of Smolensk. On Stalin's orders, Timoshenko hurled all or part of four armies against this salient, which Bock defended with four divisions. Bock eventually committed a total of 12 divisions to the battle at different times, but after repulsing several heavy frontal attacks was nevertheless forced to abandon the salient. He fell back to positions near Smolensk, which he held despite repeated Russian attacks.

By the end of September, Stalin had concentrated 15 armies (1,500,000 to 2,000,000 men) against Army Group Center. These were, however, the weakest armies Moscow would ever put in the field. They were made up almost entirely of reservists who had little or no basic training. These armies also lacked mobility. They had few tanks or trucks, and even horses were in short supply. Their sole mission was to buy time until "General Winter" could arrive and save the Soviet Union.

After the fall of Kiev, the OKH thinned out Army Groups North and South, and reinforced Army Group Center to a strength of 70 divisions, including 14 panzer and eight motorized infantry divisions. In addition, it was supported by Kesselring's 2nd Air Fleet, which was reinforced until it controlled about 1,000 of the 2,400 aircraft operating on the Eastern Front. Field Marshal von Brauchitsch met with Bock and his principal subordinates on September 15 to discuss the next phase of operations: the destruction of Timoshenko's forces and the final drive to Moscow. Now that Soviet resistance in the Ukraine had been broken, Hitler no longer objected to seizing Stalin's capital before the onset of winter weather. Only Gerd von Rundstedt spoke emphatically against this course of action. He wanted to go into winter quarters at once, arguing that the Red Army could not be defeated before winter arrived, but his ideas were firmly opposed by Brauchitsch, Halder, Bock, Kluge, Hoth, Guderian, Kesselring, and others.

Specifically, Brauchitsch planned to commit three of Germany's five panzer groups/armies to the attack.[1] For this offensive, Hitler transferred Hoth's Third Panzer Group back to Army Group Center, along with five panzer and two motorized divisions, as well as Hoepner's Fourth Panzer Group and the Stukas of Richthofen's VIII Air Corps. He also returned Guderian's Second Panzer Army and Weichs's Second Army (nine divisions) to von Bock's control. Due to the lateness of the season and the poor mechanical condition of the tanks, the OKH decided not to return the Second Panzer, Third Panzer, and Second Army to Smolensk; they would attack from where they were.

This gave Army Group Center a total frontage of about 400 miles. From north to south, Bock deployed the Third Panzer Group (Hoth), the Ninth Army (Strauss), the Fourth Army (Kluge), the Fouth Panzer Group (Hoepner), the Second Army (Weichs), and the Second Panzer Army (Guderian). His plan was for Hoepner to break through the Soviet center and split the Red Army into two parts, which would then be destroyed in separate battles of encirclement. After he achieved his breakthrough, Hoepner was to wheel north and link up with Hoth (advancing to the south), to form a huge pocket around Vyazma. Meanwhile, Strauss and Kluge were to attack the Soviets frontally, penning them down north of the Smolensk-Yelnya line, while Hoth and Hoepner cut them off. Simultaneously, to the south, Weichs and Guderian were to converge on Bryansk and Zhizdra in a separate envelopment.

Bock began his offensive on the morning of September 30.

THE VYAZMA-BRYANSK ENCIRCLEMENT, 1941

Hans-Karl Schmidt (writing under the pseudonym Paul Carell) later called the double battle of Vyazma-Bryansk "the most perfect pincer operation."[2] The combined operation exceeded even Kiev in destruction to the Red

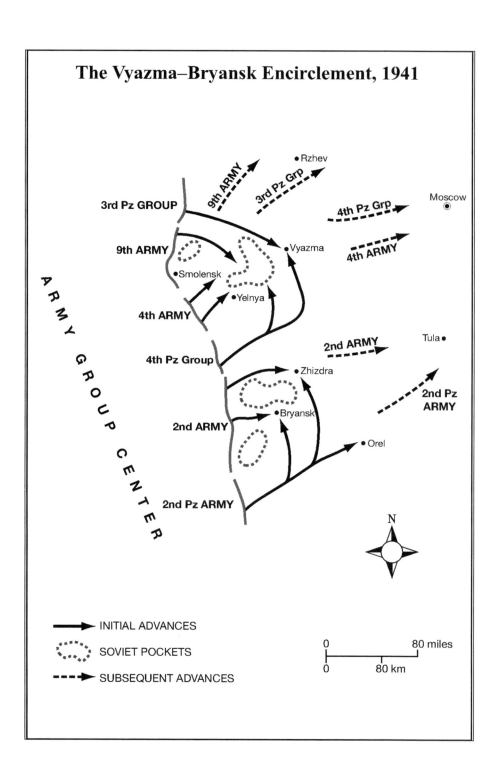

The Vyazma–Bryansk Encirclement, 1941

3rd Pz GROUP

9th ARMY

9th ARMY

3rd Pz Grp

• Rzhev

• Smolensk

4th Pz Grp

Moscow ⊙

4th ARMY

• Vyazma

• Yelnya

4th ARMY

4th Pz Group

A R M Y   G R O U P   C E N T E R

2nd ARMY

Tula •

• Zhizdra

2nd Pz ARMY

2nd ARMY

• Bryansk

• Orel

2nd Pz ARMY

N

INITIAL ADVANCES

SOVIET POCKETS

SUBSEQUENT ADVANCES

0   80 miles

0   80 km

Army. To spearhead this battle, Guderian chose Major General Baron Willibald von Langermann und Erlenkamp and his 4th Panzer Division.

Baron Willibald von Langermann und Erlenkamp was born in Karlsruhe on March 29, 1890. He was a cavalry officer who became a capable armored officer. Commissioned in the 5th Dragoon Regiment in 1910, he fought in World War I, where he was adjutant of the 7th Reserve Dragoons (1914–15) and a company commander in the 21st Reserve Division (1915) on the Western Front. He became a General Staff officer in 1916 (without even attending the abbreviated General Staff course at Sedan) and served with the X Reserve Corps and the 22nd Reserve Division (1916–18) on the Western Front. He joined the 15th Dragoons Regiment in the fall of 1918 and served with it until 1920.

Langermann spent the Reichswehr era in cavalry and school units, serving as a squadron commander in the 16th Cavalry at Erfurt (1921–27) and 13th Cavalry at Hanover (1927–30). He was an instructor at the Cavalry School (also at Hanover) from 1930 until 1935, and became commander of the 4th Cavalry Regiment at Potsdam in June 1935. The regiment was transferred to Allenstein, East Prussia, in October. After supervising this move, the Baron became inspector of cavalry and transport troops. He was, meanwhile, promoted to first lieutenant (1915), *Rittmeister* (1917), major (1930), lieutenant colonel (1934), and colonel (April 1, 1936). He was named commander of Special Administrative Division Staff 410 in late 1939, a real backwater post.

Three days before the invasion of France began, Langermann was given command of the elite 29th Motorized Infantry Division in France. This was a surprising appointment, given his background and the fact that he had been a major general for less than three months, the promotion dating from March 1, 1940. He nevertheless proved himself to be a skillful commander of mobile formations in the conquests of Belgium and France, and all of the senior generals who registered an opinion spoke highly of his performance. He was rewarded for his success by being given command of the 4th Panzer Division on September 8, 1940.

To everyone's surprise, Langermann easily broke through the Soviet Thirteenth Army and covered 80 miles on the first day of the battle. On

October 6, Hans-Juergen von Arnim's 17th Panzer Division took Bryansk in a surprise coup, and later that day Guderian linked up with Weichs's Second Army, encircling 26 divisions of the Soviet Third, Thirteenth, and Fifteenth Armies. The next day, Major General Wolfgang Fischer's 10th Panzer Division of Hoepner's Fourth Panzer Group took Vyazma and linked up with Third Panzer Group's vanguards, thus encircling six more Soviet armies and sealing the fate of 55 more enemy divisions. The fighting continued until October 17, and several Russian units did succeed in breaking out out to the east, but the Battle of Vyazma-Bryansk cost Stalin another 663,000 men, 1,242 tanks, and 5,412 guns.[3]

The Vyazma encirclement was an auspicious beginning for the Third Panzer Group's new commander, Georg-Hans Reinhardt. Meanwhile, Field Marshal von Brauchitsch, the C-in-C of the Army, had fallen out with General of Infantry Carl-Heinrich von Stuelpnagel, the commander of the Seventeenth Army, and relieved him of his command on October 5. Hoth was chosen to replace him, and Reinhardt succeeded Hoth. (At the OKH, this was looked upon as a promotion for Hoth.) Lieutenant General Otto Ottenbacher became acting commander of Reinhardt's XXXXI Motorized Corps until his permanent replacement, Lieutenant General Model, arrived on October 13. Major General Hermann Breith succeeded Model as commander of the 3rd Panzer Division.[4]

CHAPTER XII

THE OFFENSIVE ON THE FLANKS

Meanwhile, to the south, Rundstedt's armies continued to advance on a wide front, from the Donetz to the Black Sea, with the main thrusts aimed at the Crimean peninsula and Rostov, the gateway to the Caucasus. Under the command of Colonel General Ritter Eugen von Schobert, the Eleventh Army crossed the 750-yard-wide lower Dnieper on August 30, spearheaded by Hans von Sponeck's 22nd Air Landing Division, which was fighting as infantry.

Eugen Siegfried Erich von Schobert was born in Wuerzburg, Franconia, at the northern tip of Bavaria, on March 13, 1883, the son of Major Karl von Schobert. He entered the Royal Bavarian Army as a *Fahnenjunker* in 1902, and was commissioned second lieutenant in the 1st Bavarian Infantry Regiment on March 9, 1904. He underwent pilot training in 1911 but did not pursue aviation as a career option. He was promoted to first lieutenant in 1912.

Schobert spent the entire First World War with his regiment on the Western Front. He was promoted to captain in 1915, and by the spring of 1918 was commanding the III Battalion, which he personally led in a successful assault across a canal in the face of stiff British resistance. As a result, he was awarded the Military Order of Max Joseph, which carried with it the title *Ritter* and a non-hereditary knighthood.

After the war, Schobert was accepted into the Reichswehr and held a variety of staff and infantry command positions. He was promoted to major (1924), lieutenant colonel (1929), and colonel (1932). He was named chief of the Infantry Inspectorate in Berlin in late 1933 and was promoted to major general on October 1, 1934. He was named Infantry Commander VII at Nuremberg (and deputy commander of the 7th Infantry Division) in 1934. This unit became the 17th Infantry Division in 1935. Schobert held the post until 1936, when he became commander of the 33rd Infantry Division at Munich. He was promoted to lieutenant general on January 1, 1937.

When Hitler purged the army of its non-Nazi and anti-Nazi generals in order to advance Nazis and Nazi sympathizers, Schobert was one of those promoted. He became a general of infantry effective February 1, 1938, and took command of Wehrkreis VII in Munich on February 4. He took the non-territorial (corps) elements to the field in 1939 and fought in Poland, Belgium, and France. Continuing to enjoy the Fuehrer's favor, he was promoted to colonel general (July 19, 1940) and was given command of the Eleventh Army the day it was created (October 5, 1940). Schobert had married Alice Rieder-Gollwitzer in 1921. She gave him two sons and a daughter. His youngest son was killed in 1944 while serving as a fighter pilot in the Luftwaffe.

Count Hans Emil Otto von Sponeck was born on February 12, 1888, in Duesseldorf, the son of a captain of cavalry and a squadron leader in a Westphalian Ulan Regiment. He attended the Karlsruhe Cadet School (1989–1905) and the Cadet School at Gross Lichterfelde (1905–08). Commissioned second lieutenant, he joined the 5th Guards Regiment on March 19, 1908. He married a young woman named Anneliese Honrichs (1889–1961), who gave him two sons: Hans-Curt (1911) and Hans Wilhelm Otto (1913).

Sponeck became adjutant of the II Battalion of the 5th Guards in 1913 and served in this capacity until February 1915, when he was severely wounded. He returned to duty later that year as regimental adjutant. In the fall of 1915, he became a company commander. The following year, he became a General Staff officer and was assigned to Army Group Wuerttemberg. He was promoted to captain in 1917, and served on both the Eastern and Western Fronts during World War I.

After the war, Hans von Sponeck joined the Reichswehr and commanded a company in the 4th Infantry Regiment at Koblenz (1921–23) and in the elite 9th Infantry Regiment at Potsdam (1923–24). He was on the General Staff of the Artillery Commander III in Berlin (1924–27), a member of the army's Organizations Branch in Berlin (1927–30), Ia of the 3rd Infantry Division in Berlin (1930–34), and commander of the 48th Infantry Regiment at Neustrelitz (1934–37). He was, in the meantime, promoted to major (1928), lieutenant colonel (1934), and colonel (1934).

In 1937, Sponeck and his wife were divorced after 25 years of marriage. The following spring, he married Gertrud Konitzer, who was 15 years his junior. She gave him a son, Hans-Christoph, born on August 9, 1939. Meanwhile attached to the Luftwaffe, Sponeck commanded Luftgau III in Berlin (1937–38) and Luftgau VII in Munich (1938). He returned to the army on November 10, 1938, as commander of the 22nd Infantry Division. He was promoted to major general on February 1, 1938, and to lieutenant general on February 1, 1940. In the winter of 1939–40, the 22nd was converted into an air landing division, which Sponeck led in an unsuccessful air assault on The Hague, the capital of the Netherlands. Seriously wounded on May 10, he recovered to lead his division in Operation Barbarossa, where it fought as a regular infantry division.

Sponeck's men completed a pontoon bridge over the river on September 1, which was promptly brought under attack by the Red Air Force. The Soviets desperately tried to destroy the bridge, but were prevented from doing so by Colonel Moelders's 51st Fighter Wing.

Werner Moelders was born on March 18, 1913, in Gelsenkirchen, Westphalia, the son of a school teacher. His father, who was also a second lieutenant in the reserves, was called to the colors in 1914 and was killed in the Argonne Forest in March 1915. His son graduated from the Gymnasium (the German equivalent of high school) in early 1931. Moelders joined the army on April 1 as a *Fahnenjunker* in the infantry. He transferred to the secret Luftwaffe in 1935 but was declared unfit for flying because he could not pass the spin chair test. A devout young man with ambitions to become a pastor after completing his military service, Moelders approached the flight surgeon and asked for a key to the spin chair room. Impressed with the sincerity of this young man, the doctor complied. No doubt a mop and a pale were involved in this agreement, but Moelders practiced in the spin chair until he could complete the test without throwing up. On occasion, however, even after he finished fighter pilot training, he still suffered from nausea. Second Lieutenant Moelders was a squadron leader in JG 334 in March 1936. Later he became an instructor pilot at Wiesbaden.

In April 1938, he transferred to Spain, where he succeeded Adolf Galland as leader of the 3rd Squadron of the Condor Legion. Here he excelled, shooting down 14 enemy airplanes and invented new and revolutionary fighter tactics, including the "Finger Four" formation. Realizing that the pilot who sees his opponent first wins 80 percent to 90 percent of all dogfights, Moelders scrapped the wingtip to wingtip formations of World War I, and increased the distance between airplanes to several hundred feet, so his pilots spent the vast majority of their time looking for enemy aircraft, instead of avoiding midair collisions with each other. As a result, he returned to Germany with a reputation for possessing skill and maturity beyond his years.

Moelders remained a devout Christian who demanded that the rules of warfare be observed and that prisoners be treated decently. He frequently arranged for men whom he had shot down to dine with him and his officers before they were remanded to prisoner of war camps.

Lieutenant Moelders fought in Poland and in October 1939 was named commander of the III *Gruppe*, 53rd Fighter Wing (III/JG 53). In May 1940, he shot down his 20th airplane and was the first fighter pilot to be awarded the Knight's Cross. He was promoted to captain on May 27. On June 5, he was shot down by a French fighter and was captured, but was freed two weeks later after France surrendered.

Promoted to major shortly thereafter, Moelders was given command of JG 51 on July 27. He was wounded in a dogfight with a Spitfire the next day and did not fly again for a month. He nevertheless had 55 kills at the end of 1940—30 of them in the Battle of Britain. By the time the 51st Fighter Wing redeployed to the East in June 1941, he had 68 aerial victories. During the first 23 days of Operation Barbarossa, he shot down 27 Soviet airplanes, which meant that he passed Manfred von Richthofen's total of 80, making him the greatest fighter pilot in history up until that time. By mid-July, he had become the first man in history to shoot down 100 enemy airplanes. He scored his 101st victory, was promoted to colonel (at age 28!) and was ordered by Hermann Goering not to fly in combat anymore. He named Moelders "General of Fighter Pilots" (although he was only a colonel) and charged him with establishing tactical and operational doctrine within the *Jagdwaffe* (Fighter Branch).

Despite Goering's orders, Moelders returned to the Eastern Front, resumed *de facto* command of JG 51, and unofficially flew in combat, where he unofficially shot down about 30 Soviet airplanes. He flew back to Germany for a brief leave in September, married Luise Thurner Baldauf, and impregnated her immediately. They had a daughter, Verena Moelders, nine months later, although Werner Moelders never lived to see her.

During the battles of the Dnieper crossings, Moelders and his men shot down 77 Soviet bombers in two days, and Luftwaffe anti-aircraft gunners shot down 13 more. Soon the 1st and 4th Mountain Divisions were following the 22nd Air Landing Division across, and by September 12 the men of the Eleventh Army were advancing across the Nogay Steppe (a 12,000 square mile desert between the Dnieper and the Black Sea) toward the Perekop Isthmus, the western entrance to the Crimea. By now, however, they had to have a new commander.

On September 12, General von Schobert personally flew into the combat zone in a Fiesler Storch reconnaissance airplane. Near the front, his engine failed. The pilot brought the airplane down in an open area, unaware that it was a Soviet minefield. Pilot, general, and airplane were all blown to pieces. Erich von Manstein, the commander of the LVI Motorized Corps, was chosen to replace Schobert. Lieutenant General Ferdinand Schaal succeeded him as leader of the LVI Motorized.[1]

Manstein's first objective was the Crimea, a vast peninsula roughly the size of Belgium. At its southwestern tip lay the important Red naval base of Sevastopol, the home of the Soviet Black Sea Fleet. Whoever controlled Sevastopol and the Crimea also controlled the Black Sea and could exert tremendous diplomatic pressure on Turkey and Persia (now Iran). In Soviet hands, the peninsula also provided a dangerous air base for bombing raids against the Ploesti oilfields—always a source of worry for Hitler.

The Eleventh Army faced a difficult problem on the Crimea. It was separated from the mainland by the Putrid Sea, a saline marsh impassable to infantry or watercraft, including dinghies and assault boats. The only available land approach was over the Perekop Isthmus, which was a little more than four miles wide, and was protected by the "Tartar Ditch," a trench 40 to 50 feet wide that was built by the Turks in the 15th Century to protect the Crimea from the Russians on the mainland. Impassable for armor and impossible to bypass, it formed an ideal anti-tank ditch, and was well covered by Soviet fortified positions.

The first attempt to storm it was made on September 13 by General of Cavalry Erik Hansen's LIV Corps, spearheaded by the motorcycle battalion of the *Leibstandarte* Adolf Hitler and followed by Lieutenant General Bruno Bieler's 73rd Infantry Division.

Erik Hansen was born in Hamburg on May 27, 1889. He joined the army as a *Fahnenjunker* in the 9th Dragoon Regiment on October 1, 1907, and received his commission in 1909. He became regimental adjutant in 1912 and adjutant of the 45th Cavalry Brigade in 1916. Promoted to first lieutenant in late 1914 and to captain in 1916, he became a provisional member of the General Staff in early 1917 and was on the Staff of the Field Railroad Commander for four months. He transferred to the General Staff of the 45th Reserve Division (June–December 1917) and fought on the Aisne, at Chemin des Dames, at Verdun, and in Flanders. He attended the abbreviated General Staff course at Sedan from August 4 to September 3, 1917, and was quartermaster of the Guards Reserve Corps in France from January to September 1918. He was on the staff of Army Group Dallwitz from September 1918 until January 1919.

After the war he was with the Staff, VI Reserve Corps (1919), Staff, 2nd Naval Division (1919–20), and with the 3rd Cavalry Regiment at Rathenow and Stengal (1920–21). He was on the Staff of the 1st Cavalry Division at Frankfurt/Oder (1921–24), squadron commander in the 15th (Prussian) Cavalry Regiment at Paderborn (1924–27), on the staff of the Cavalry School at Hanover (1927–30), and on the Staff, Group Command One in Berlin (1930–31). He was chief of operations of the 1st Infantry Division in Koenigsberg (1931–33) when Hitler came to power.

Erik Hansen had been promoted to major (1929) and to lieutenant colonel (1932) before the Nazis came to power. Under the Hitler regime, he became a colonel (1934), major general (1937), lieutenant general (August 1, 1939), and general of cavalry (October 1, 1940). Meanwhile, he was chief of staff of the 3rd Cavalry Division at Breslau (1933–34), commander of Infantry Regiment Muenster (1934–35), commander of the 39th Infantry Regiment at Duesseldorf (1935–36), chief of the 1st Department of the Army General Staff (1936–38) and commander of the 4th Infantry Division at Dresden (1938–40). He led his division in Poland, Belgium, and France, and was named commander of the

Wehrmacht Mission to Romania on October 1, 1940. He held this post until June 1, 1941, when he was named commander of the LIV Corps, which he led in the drive to Odessa and in the Crimea.

Hansen's *coup de main* failed, and the SS men suffered heavy casualties. This was the situation when Manstein arrived to assume command of the Eleventh Army on September 17. The Perekop Isthmus was defended by Colonel General Fedor Isidorovich Kuznetsov's Fifty-first Independent Army, which established a deep fortified belt across it. Manstein attacked on September 24. He planned for the LIV Corps (73rd and 46th Infantry Divisions on line and the 50th Infantry Division in reserve) to break through the isthmus via frontal attack; then he would commit his pursuit force, General of Mountain Troops Ludwig Kuebler's XXXXIX Mountain Corps. Meanwhile, on the Nogay Steppe, General Hans von Salmuth's XXX Corps (72nd Infantry and 22nd Air Landing Divisions) and the Romanian Third Army would protect Manstein's rear against a Soviet counteroffensive from the east.

Initially, the plan worked just as Manstein hoped. Supported by heavy artillery fire, the LIV made slow but steady progress across the Perekop, despite bitter fighting and heavy casualties on both sides. The German infantrymen breached the Tartar Ditch and took the heavily fortified village of Armyansk, crushing the Soviet 276th and 156th Rifle Divisions in the process. Kuznetsov hurled his 40th and 42nd Cavalry Divisions, as well as parts of his 271st and 106th Rifle Divisions into counterattacks against Hansen's corps, but each one was turned back by the veteran infantry. Manstein's troops were on the verge of breaking through to the open country to the south when trouble broke out in his rear.

East of the Novag Steppe, the Stavka had stationed the South Front under the command of General Yakov T. Cherevichenko, which it reinforced with fresh formations. Suddenly, just as Manstein was about to achieve a decisive breakthrough on the Perekop, Cherevichenko struck Salmuth's XXX Corps and the Third Romanian Army with the Twelfth, Eighteenth, and Ninth Armies. Manstein was forced to abandon his offensive and turn to meet the threat. He reacted quickly, but even so, Cherevichenko's vastly superior forces threatened Eleventh Army with the possibility of encirclement and destruction until Ewald von Kleist came to the rescue.

Following its victory in the great battle of encirclement at Kiev, the First Panzer Army was available for commitment elsewhere. At the end of September, General of Cavalry Eberhard von Mackensen's III Motorized Corps had established a major bridgehead over the Dnieper at Dnepropetrovsk. When Cherevichenko launched his offensive, Kleist waited until he was fully engaged and then struck him in the rear with the entire First Panzer Army, while Manstein launched new attacks from the west. Between October 5 and 10, Kleist forced the Soviet assault divisions back against the Sea of Azov, and destroyed them in what became known as the Battle of the Mariupol (Osipenko) Pocket or the Battle on the Sea of Azov. By the time it was all over, most of the Soviet Eighteenth and Ninth Armies had been destroyed, and the Russians had lost 106,000 men captured, and 212 tanks and 672 guns captured or destroyed. General Andrei K. Smirnov, the commander of the Eighteenth Army, was among the dead.

As soon as the pocket was liquidated, Kleist turned east and advanced on Rostov. Simultaneously the German Seventeenth and Sixth Armies moved up on his left between Stalino and Kharkov, while Manstein's Eleventh Army returned to the Perekop, for another attack against the isthmus. As Seventeenth Army advanced eastward, it lost another fine commander.

Kurt Alfred Otto Erimar von Briesen was born in Anklam, Pomerania on March 3, 1886, the son of future General of Infantry Alfred von Briesen and his wife Olga, née von Kleist. His father would command the 35th Infantry and 49th Reserve Divisions in the Great War. Kurt's only brother would be killed in action in 1915; Kurt, meanwhile, joined the family business, so to speak, when he became a *Fahnenjunker* in the 2nd Guards Grenadier Regiment on September 16, 1904. Commissioned in early 1906, he became a battalion adjutant in 1910 and was detached to the War Academy to undergo General Staff training in the fall of 1913. His class never graduated, however, and von Briesen was named adjutant of the 15th Reserve Infantry Regiment on August 1, 1914, as World War I began.

Sent to the Western Front, he was severely wounded on August 23. When he returned to field duty on October 28, he was adjutant of the 26th Infantry Brigade. In September 1916, he was admitted directly to the General Staff and was transferred to the staff of the IV Corps; he became chief of operations of the 239th Infantry Division (also on the Western Front) in the spring of 1918. After briefly commanding the 52nd Volunteer Battalion, he became chief of operations of Wehrkreis II in 1919. Meanwhile, he was promoted to first lieutenant in 1913 and to captain in 1915. He married Charlotte von Gynz-Rekowski in May 1915. In early 1920, Briesen was retired from the army with the honorary rank of major. From 1922 to 1934, however, he worked for the army as a civilian employee and served as the organizer of the Pomeranian Border Guard units, which headquartered in Stettin under the command of Wehrkreis II.

Kurt von Briesen rejoined the army as a lieutenant colonel on April 1, 1934, and served as commandant of Neustettin from then until October 15, 1935, when he became commander of the 69th Infantry Regiment at Hamburg-Wandsbek. He assumed command of the 30th Infantry Division at Luebeck on February 4, 1938, the day Hitler and his lieutenants retired or transferred many anti-Nazi officers. (Briesen was a non-Nazi, as opposed to being an anti-Nazi.) He was promoted to colonel (1934), major general (August 1, 1937), and to lieutenant general (August 27, 1939).

General von Briesen led the 30th during the invasion of Poland, where his isolated division faced the major Polish counterattack of the campaign. On September 10, 1939, he was so badly wounded that his left forearm had to be amputated. He nevertheless remained in command and checked the Polish offensive with his last battalion. Hitler was so impressed by Briesen's performance that he personally decorated him with the Knight's Cross—the first received by a German general during World War II. Hitler later commented that when he was a boy, he always imagined that a Prussian general would look like the tall, bald, bullet-headed Briesen.

After the fall of Warsaw, Briesen returned to Germany, where he led his division on the Lower Rhine and in the Belgian and French campaigns. He briefly commanded occupied Paris and was promoted to general of infantry on August 1, 1940. He was named commander of the LII Corps, which was forming in Cologne, on October 25, and led it with considerable success at Uman, Kiev, and in the conquest of the Donetz.

On November 20, 1944, Briesen went forward to visit one of his regiments at the front, where he habitually spent a lot of his time. Shortly after noon, a pair of Soviet fighter-bombers jumped his staff car about ten miles west of Isjum. Struck by a dozen bullets, he died instantly. Shortly thereafter, the 30th Infantry Division was officially nicknamed *"Die Briesen Division."*

In the meantime, the Red Navy evacuated Odessa (which had been besieged by the Romanians) on October 16, and transported 80,000 troops and 350,000 civilians to the Crimea to reinforce Kuznetsov. Most of the civilians were used to construct fortified positions and anti-tank ditches. Manstein attacked the Perekop again on October 18, once again spearheaded by the LIV Corps, while von Salmuth's XXX Corps was posted in close reserve, ready to exploit a breakthrough. The fighting was no less bitter than the previous attempts, but after ten days, on October 28, Hansen broke through and the pursuit began.

By November 15, Manstein's six divisions had largely destroyed 12 Soviet divisions, had taken more than 100,000 prisoners, and had captured or destroyed more than 700 guns and 160 tanks. They were not, however, able to storm the naval fortress of Sevastopol, which Manstein brought under siege. They were also unable to eliminate the Soviet bridgehead on the Kerch Peninsula (on the far eastern side of the Crimea), which Manstein screened with Count von Sponeck's newly arrived XXXXII Corps. As winter approached, the Eleventh Army was therefore stalemated and stuck in the Crimea, facing an enemy on two sides. Meanwhile, Ewald von Kleist swept through the Donetz industrial region and drove on Rostov.

In 1941, the Donetz Basin produced 60 percent of the Soviet Union's coal and 75 percent of its coke, as well as 30 percent of its iron and 20 percent of its steel. After the destruction of Budenny's armies at Kiev and the partial destruction of Cherevichenko's South Front on the Sea of Azov, there was little Timoshenko could do to save it. Using the Fortieth, Twenty-first, Thirty-eighth, Thirty-seventh, and Sixth Armies, as well as the remnants of South Front, and taking advantage of the weather, he was nevertheless able to delay its capture long enough for Soviet industrial experts to evacuate much of its industry to the east. The fall of

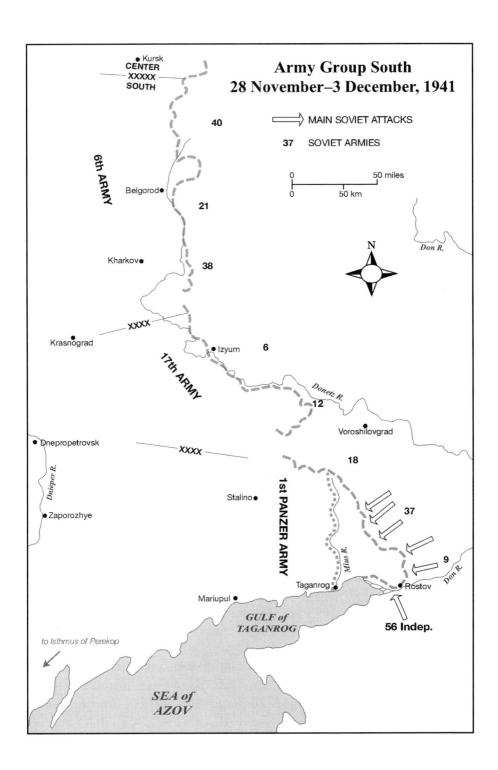

Army Group South
28 November–3 December, 1941

MAIN SOVIET ATTACKS

37   SOVIET ARMIES

the Donetz, however, was just a matter of time. Kleist took Taganrog on October 17, and Reichenau's Sixth Army occupied Kharkov, the most important industrial city in the region, by the end of the month. Rundstedt's army group was now in a position to advance on Rostov, on the Don River at the northeast tip of the Sea of Azov.

Field Marshal von Rundstedt, who consistently advocated halting and going into winter quarters, did not favor this operation. The old field marshal expressed the view that he could take Rostov, but would not be able to hold it. Hitler, however, ignored the marshal, because he badly wanted to capture Rostov, the gateway to the Caucasus and rich oilfields of the Caspian Sea region. The Fuehrer constantly interfered with this operation, ordering that both the Seventeenth Army (now under Hoth) and the Sixth Army (under Reichenau) keep in close contact with Kleist's left flank, despite Halder's warnings that this would leave Army Group Center's right flank exposed and create a gap between the Sixth and Second Armies.

Army Groups Center and South were, in fact, now advancing in divergent directions, and Weichs's Second Army was continually drawn to the east and southeast. It was soon too far away to be able to support Guderian's 2nd Panzer Army, which was moving toward the northeast against Moscow.

In accordance with Hitler's orders, Kleist began his advance toward Rostov on November 5, against the Ninth and Fifty-sixth Soviet Armies. He was hampered by rain and monumental supply difficulties, but by November 16, he was in position to attack the city. Winter had now arrived and the temperature was already –20 degrees Centigrade (–4 degrees Fahrenheit.). The German advance nevertheless continued, and Rostov fell to the 60th Motorized Division and the SS Motorized Brigade "Leibstandarte Adolf Hitler" on November 20. The Germans took another 10,000 prisoners when the city fell, but as Rundstedt had feared, the battle for Rostov was just beginning.

Karl Rudolf Gerd von Rundstedt was born at Aschersleben in the Harz Mountains on December 12, 1875. The descendant of an old Prussian *junker* family, he could trace his lineage back eight centuries. His father (also called Gerd) was a *hussar* (light cavalry) officer who became a major general. Young Gerd was educated at the cadet school at Oranienstein and at Gross Lichterfelde. He entered the army in 1892 at age 16 as a senior officer cadet and was commissioned second lieutenant in the Prussian 83rd Infantry Regiment at Kassel on June 17, 1893. (He would have preferred a cavalry unit, but his father, who had three other sons, could not afford it, although he did provide his boys with an English nanny and an excellent home school education.) Adolf Hitler was three years old at the time, and most of the men young Gerd would lead in World War II had not yet been born.

Early in life, Gerd adopted the sophisticated manners of an Old World gentleman. His tact and finesse in dealing with both individuals and problems, his consideration for the feelings of others, his diplomatic skills, and his overall bearing certainly impressed his superiors, who looked upon him as more mature and intelligent than his peers. His good breeding and family background did nothing to impede his advancement, nor did the fact that he was rarely unpleasant, never disagreed with his superiors and obeyed all orders without question. He did have a temper, but he usually managed to keep it tightly under control.

Second Lieutenant von Rundstedt served as a battalion and regimental adjutant until 1902, when (after ten years of service) he was promoted to first lieutenant. That same year, he married Luise "Bila" von Goetz, the daughter of a retired major. They had one child, a son named Hans who was born in 1903. He broke with family tradition and became a historian, but Lieutenant Dr. Hans Gerd von Rundstedt later served as his father's aide, starting in 1943.

Rundstedt also took his required Wehrkreis exam in 1902. Those officers who scored in the top 15 percent or so were sent to the War Academy in Berlin to undergo General Staff training. Only about a third of the 150 men selected to attend each year ever graduated and got to wear the red stripes of a General Staff officer. Rundstedt did well, however, and became a member of the General Staff on April 1, 1907. He had been promoted to captain six days before.

Rundstedt was attached to the Greater General Staff in Berlin from 1907 to 1910, followed by two years on the staff of the XI Corps. He became a company commander in the 171st Infantry Regiment in 1912. When World War I broke out in August 1914, he was named operations officer of the 22nd Reserve Division and served on the Western Front (including the Battle of the Marne) until November 1914; he was then promoted to major and was assigned to the staff of the General Government of Belgium.

Despite the fact that he was fluent in English and French (his mother was a Huguenot and his nanny was British), Rundstedt spent most of World War I on the Eastern Front. In the spring of 1915, he became chief of operations of a division serving in the Baltic States and fought against the Russians. At the end of the year, he was assigned to the staff of the General Government in Warsaw. In 1916, he was sent to Hungary as a corps chief of staff, and apparently did a brief tour of duty with the Turkish General Staff in 1917 before returning to northern Russia that fall, where he served as chief of staff of the LIII Corps in the Lake Peipus battles. After the Bolsheviks sued for peace, Gerd von Rundstedt returned to France as chief of staff of the XV Corps, a post he held when the war ended in November 1918.

When the Reichswehr was formed in 1920, Rundstedt was promoted to lieutenant colonel and was appointed Ia of the 3rd Cavalry Division at Weimar in Thuringia. Promoted to colonel on February 1, 1923, he became chief of staff of Wehrkreis II and the 2nd Infantry Division in Stettin, Pomerania (now Szczecin, Poland) in October. He was transferred to Paderborn, Westphalia, in early 1925, where he commanded the 18th Infantry Regiment until September 1926.

Rundstedt continued his rapid interwar advancement on October 1, 1926, when he became chief of staff of the Group Command Two at Kassel. He was promoted to major general on November 1, 1927, and assumed command of the 2nd Cavalry Division at Breslau in November 1928. His promotion to lieutenant general occurred on March 1, 1929, and he briefly commanded Wehrkreis III and the 3rd Infantry Division in Berlin (1932) before assuming command of Army Group One (also in Berlin) (1933–38). He was promoted to general of infantry on October 1, 1932, and to colonel general on March 1, 1938.

Rundstedt was a non-political general whom the Nazis found very useful. Hitler was impressed with his aristocratic manners (although he had little use for aristocrats in general) and apparently felt inferior to Rundstedt socially (which he was). Erich von Manstein, his chief of staff in 1939 and early 1940, later recalled that Rundstedt "had a charm about him to which even Hitler succumbed. The latter seems to have taken a genuine liking to him. . . . What probably attracted Hitler was the indefinable impression the general gave of a man from a past which he did not understand and to the atmosphere of which he never had access."[2]

In January 1938, when Defense Minister Werner von Blomberg and Colonel General Werner von Fritsch, the commander-in-chief of the army, were forced to retire, Hitler seriously considered giving Fritsch's old job to Walter von Reichenau, the most qualified Nazi officer available. It was Rundstedt (along with Ritter von Leeb) who blocked the appointment, telling Hitler that the army would simply not accept Reichenau. The position went to Walter von Brauchitsch instead.

Command Group One temporarily became Second Army during the Sudetenland crisis of 1938. Rundstedt opposed war with Czechoslovakia because he feared that Germany could not defeat Prague's allies, Great Britain and France. He did, however, advise Brauchitsch not to object too strenuously to Hitler's aggression, because he was afraid the Fuehrer would fire Brauchitsch and replace him with Reichenau. At this time, Rundstedt was first asked to join the anti-Hitler conspiracy. His reaction was distinctly negative—as it would continue to be for the next seven years. He did not, however, inform Hitler and the Nazis about the plot. His attitude was basically that he would join it if it succeeded. When Erwin Rommel approached him in 1944, his reaction was: "You, too?!" He then told the Swabian field marshal: "You are young. You know and love the people. *You* do it!" The Desert Fox tried. Rundstedt never lifted a finger to help him.

Rundstedt, meanwhile, retired in November 1938, and was simultaneously named honorary colonel of the 18th Infantry Regiment, a distinction he cherished above all others. From then on, he wore his regimental commander's uniform exclusively and was often mistaken for a colonel by the lower ranks. Whenever this happened, Rundstedt laughed.

Gerd von Rundstedt was recalled to active duty in May 1939 and was placed in charge of Working Staff Rundstedt, which played a major role in planning the invasion of Poland. However, his chief of staff, Lieutenant General Erich von Manstein, and Guenther Blumentritt, his chief of operations, did most of the actual work. Rundstedt remained at his home in Kassel, where the 18th Infantry was based, until just before the invasion began. This was typical of Rundstedt's leadership style. He never concerned himself with the "nuts and bolts" of an operation, which he left to his subordinates. Fortunately for him, most of these men were extremely talented, especially until the end of 1941. He remained aloof, unseen and almost invisible, rarely visited the troops, and spent virtually all of his time at his headquarters, which General Geyr von Schweppenburg said was characterized by "incredible idleness."[3] He also loved cheap detective novels, which he frequently read on duty. Because this habit embarrassed him, he always read them with a desk drawer open, so that he could quickly hide them when a visitor entered his office.

Working Staff Rundstedt was upgraded to Headquarters, Army Group South, in August 1939, and Rundstedt commanded it in the Polish campaign the following month. After Warsaw fell, he was briefly Commander-in-Chief, East, but was soon transferred to the Western Front, where his headquarters was redesignated Army Group A. Here Manstein came up with the plan that led to the conquest of France in a brilliant six-week campaign. Rundstedt approved the concept of operations, but when Brauchitsch and Franz Halder rejected it, he refused to "go over their heads" and submit the idea directly to Hitler. In the end, Manstein personally submitted the plan to Hitler, with the help of Hitler's army adjutant, Colonel Rudolf Schmundt.[4] The dictator approved it on February 18. The Manstein Plan worked exactly as its originator said it would. Between them, Army Groups A and B (under Fedor von Bock) destroyed the best French and British divisions in Belgium in three weeks. Rundstedt did nothing to help Manstein when Brauchitsch punished the uncomfortably brilliant general by transferring him to Pomerania, away from the center of action.

Although he later denied it, Rundstedt also made a major mistake in May 1940, when he advised the Fuehrer to halt his panzers in front of Dunkirk, rather than capture it by massed armored assault. As a result, the Royal Navy was able to evacuate more than 300,000 British and French troops. The magnitude of this mistake was not recognized at the time, however, and Hitler and most of the Wehrmacht thought that the war was won.

After France surrendered, Rundstedt was promoted to field marshal on July 19, 1940. Rundstedt's command was renamed Army Group South for Operation Barbarossa. Here, Rundstedt played a part in winning some of Nazi Germany's greatest tactical and operational victories. The strain of the campaign resulted in his first heart attack (a mild one) in November 1941, but Rundstedt nevertheless remained in command.

In November 1941, Hitler ordered Rundstedt to capture Rostov. The field marshal opposed the idea and signaled Fuehrer Headquarters that he could take the objective, but did not have the strength to hold it. Events proved him 100 percent correct. On November 28, in the bitter cold of a Russian winter, his depleted 1st Panzer and 17th Armies, under heavy Soviet counterattack, were at their breaking point. To avoid a complete disaster, Rundstedt ordered a general retrograde to the Mius. Two days later, the dictator signaled the field marshal to halt the retreat and to hold his positions at all costs. Rundstedt, who had a temper, signaled back to Fuehrer Headquarters that Hitler's order was "madness," and that he should find someone else to carry out the order, if he insisted it be obeyed. Rundstedt was relieved of his command that very evening. His successor, Field Marshal von Reichenau, initially tried to obey Hitler's command but reversed himself within 24 hours. He continued the retreat to the Mius on December 1.

On the other flank of the German invasion, the Leningrad sector, Hitler was not content merely to let Field Marshal von Leeb's Army Group North besiege the city. Turning down the marshal's request to allow him to extend his hold on the southern bank of Lake Ladoga, Hitler ordered him to seize the bauxite-producing region of Tikhvin, and then link up with the Finns on the Svir River on the eastern shore of Lake Ladoga—a move that would effectively encircle Leningrad. To accomplish this, Leeb would have to advance 250 miles in heavy winter weather.

Leeb's assault force, Rudolf Schmidt's XXXIX Motorized Corps, moved out of the Volkhov bridgehead on October 15 and headed for Tikhvin. This force included the 12th Panzer, 8th Panzer, 18th Motorized, and 20th Motorized Divisions, all of which were under strength. Schmidt nevertheless smashed the Fourth Soviet Army and threatened the rear of the Seventh Independent Soviet Army, which was facing the Finns on the Svir. In early November, Colonel General Baron von Weichs fell ill, and Rudolf Schmidt succeeded him as acting commander of the Second Army. Lieutenant General Juergen von Arnim replaced him as commander of the XXXIX Motorized Corps, now the spearhead of Army Group North's efforts to capture the bauxite mines and encircle Leningrad.

Hans-Juergen Bernhard Theodor "Dieter" von Arnim was born in Ernsdorf, in the Reichenbach district of Silesia, on April 4, 1889, the son of General Hans von Arnim (1861–1931) and his wife Martha Honrichs von Arnim (1865–1953). An old school aristocrat, he could trace his family tree back to 1388; his grandfather had been a lieutenant general and a member of the General Staff in the 1860s. Dieter entered the army as a *Fahnenjunker* in 1908, attended the War School in Danzig (1908–09), and was commissioned second lieutenant in the 4th Foot Guards Regiment on August 19, 1909. He was a battalion adjutant by 1913. When Germany mobilized on August 2, 1914, he was transferred to the 93rd Reserve Infantry Regiment of the 1st Guards Reserve Division, and served as a battalion adjutant in Belgium. He was severely wounded on September 17, which was the first of at least three wounds he suffered during World War I.

He rejoined the 93rd Infantry on the Eastern Front in November and was named acting regimental adjutant. He was posted to first lieutenant in January 1915, and held this post until June, when he was wounded again. Arnim returned to field duty in November and was given command of a company, which he led on the Eastern Front and in France until July 20, 1916. Wounded again, he returned to field duty in January 1917, and was promoted to captain and transferred to the Staff of the 4th Guards Infantry Division as an orderly. (The 93rd Infantry Regiment had, in the meantime, been transferred from the 1st Guards Reserve to the 4th Guards Division.) He secured leave in March 1917 and returned home, where he married Annemarie von Dechend, the 22-year-old daughter of a lieutenant colonel. Due to the pressing military situation, there was no honeymoon.

Dieter von Arnim served briefly on the staff of the Guards Reserve Corps in the spring of 1917 before being named adjutant of the 4th Guards Division, a post he held until after the war. Meanwhile, he fought on the Somme, at Ypres (1916), at Lens, in Flanders, at Ypres again (1917), on the Somme (1918), in the Battle of Picardy, on the Oise, in Lorraine, on the Marne, on the Aisne, and in the Ardennes. In June and July 1918, he served as an acting battalion commander in the 93rd Reserve Infantry Regiment. He was accepted into the Reichswehr as a matter of course.

Arnim commanded a company in the 29th Reichswehr Regiment at Charlottenburg, a suburb of Berlin, in 1919 and 1920. Here his only child, a daughter named Elisabeth, was born on January 21, 1920. Shortly thereafter, he was given a company in the 5th Infantry Regiment at Stettin (1920–21). He spent a year undergoing secret General Staff training with the 2nd Infantry Division (1921–22), before joining the staff of Group Command Two at Kassel (1922–24).

This appointment was arranged by his father-in-law, who was now a member of the General Staff. It was a fortunate assignment for von Arnim, who developed a reputation as an energetic and capable staff officer. He served in the Defense Ministry (1924–25), on the staff of the 7th Infantry Division in Munich (1926–29), and on the staff of Artillery Command VII in Munich (1929–32), at the request of the Wehrkreis commander, General Ritter von Leeb. Then followed a period of troop duty as commander of the I Battalion/2nd Infantry Regiment in Allenstein, East Prussia (1932–34), before he became Ia of Artillery Command VI in Westphalia and the Rhineland (1934–35), and commander of the 68th Infantry Regiment in Brandenburg (1935–38).

The 68th Infantry was part of the 23rd Infantry Division, whose pro-Nazi commander, Ernst Busch, was promoted during the Blomberg-Fritsch crisis of early 1938. General of Infantry Erwin von Witzleben, the commander of Wehrkreis III in Berlin, arranged for his own man, Major General Walter von Brockdorff-Ahlefeldt, to assume the vacant post.[5] Brockdorff-Ahlefeldt, a strong anti-Nazi and anti-Hitler conspirator like Witzleben, wanted his regimental commanders to be men of his own political views, and this Arnim was not. (Politically neutral, Arnim was no Nazi, but he was not an anti-Nazi either.)

On February 4, 1938, Arnim was named commander of the 4th Service Depot at Schweidnitz, Silesia, which represented a definite demotion. Arnim, however, refused to protest or even complain about his treatment, although his friends at the OKH knew that he had been subjected to an injustice. In May 1939, he was transferred back to Zossen as a *Sonstigesoffizier* (extra officer), where he basically cooled his heels until after World War II began.

On September 12, 1939, he assumed command of the 52nd Infantry Division, then in the process of forming in the Gross-Born Troop Maneuver Area. He led his division in the Saar and in France (where elements of the division were lightly engaged), before being named commander of the 17th Panzer Division, then forming in the Augsburg area of Bavaria. He had no experience or previous connection with the armored branch, and his appointment can only be explained because of his general efficiency and the fact that he had friends in Berlin and Zossen. He nevertheless satisfied Baron Maximilian von Weichs, the commander of the Second Army, who noted in February 1941 that the 17th Panzer was not fully formed, but was nevertheless a fundamentally good division, due to the "sure, confident hand" of General von Arnim. That same month, General Hermann Geyer, the commander of the IX Corps, reported that Arnim was a "well-balanced, calm man," and a "prudent, judicious organizer and trainer."[6]

Arnim commanded the new division from November 1, 1940 until June 28, 1941, when he was seriously wounded on the Eastern Front. He returned to duty on November 11, 1941, replacing Rudolf Schmidt as commander of the XXXIX Motorized Corps. He had in the meantime been promoted to major (1928), lieutenant colonel (1932), colonel (1934), major general (January 1, 1938), and lieutenant general (December 1, 1939). He would be promoted to general of panzer troops on December 17, 1941.

General von Arnim's XXXIX Motorized Corps took Tikhvin on November 8 but could advance no further, and was soon facing some of Stalin's best Siberian divisions, which the dictator committed to prevent his northern front from collapsing. Stalin's move placed Arnim in an extremely critical position. Facing vastly superior Soviet forces, the XXXIX Motorized Corps and its supporting I Corps occupied a salient 230 miles long, and were dangerously overextended as the winter of 1941/42 approached.

Field Marshal Erich von Manstein, who commanded LVI Panzer Corps and Eleventh Army during Operation Barbarossa. A military genius of the first order, Manstein is generally considered the best German general of World War II. (USNA)

Baron Wolfram von Richthofen and Hans Jeschonnek, the Chief of General Staff of the Luftwaffe. The relatively junior Jeschonnek was overly influenced by the baron, who had a powerful personality and who was a strong advocate of dive-bombing. (USNA)

General of Panzer Troops (later Colonel General) Hans-Valentin Hube, who commanded the 16th Panzer Division during Operation Barbarossa. The one-armed Hube later commanded the XIV Panzer Corps and the First Panzer Army. He was killed in an airplane crash on April 21, 1944. (IWM)

A Russian armored train, captured by the 29th Motorized Division in the early days of Operation Barbarossa. These trains, which were extremely effective during the Russian Civil War, proved to be virtually useless against Hitler's Panzers. (USNA)

General of Panzertruppen Baron Leo Geyr von Schweppenberg, who commanded the XXIV Panzer Corps during Operation Barbarossa. He had previously commanded the 3rd Panzer Division, and later led the XXXX Panzer Corps, the LVIII Reserve Panzer (later Panzer) Corps and Panzer Group West. He ended the war as chief of the Panzer Inspectorate. (USNA)

General Ritter von Greim congratulating two of his most successful fighter pilots. He is shaking hands with Guenther Lützow, who became a colonel and Fighter Commander Upper Italy. He was flying a Me-262 jet fighter when he was reported missing in action April 1945. He had 110 aerial victories at the time. The officer in the center is Walter "Gulle" Oesau, who Adolf Galland called the toughest man in the Luftwaffe. Colonel Oesau was commander of the 1st Fighter Wing when he was shot down over the Ardennes on May 11, 1944. He had 127 kills. (Air University Archives)

Alfred Rosenburg, the chief of Eastern Ministry, on trial for his life at Nuremberg, 1946. Known as the party's philosopher, he was a leading advocate of Lebensraum and the persecution of the Jews. He also advocated the rejection of Christianity. He was hanged on October 16, 1946. (USMHI)

General of Infantry Georg Thomas, chief of the economic office of the High Command of the Armed Forces. His estimates of Soviet economic potential were very low and constitute part of the failure of German military intelligence in 1941. General Thomas was an anti-Hitler conspirator and ended the war in a concentration camp. (USMHI)

Colonel General Fritz Fromm, the commander of the Home (Replacement) Army. He dabbled in the anti-Hitler conspiracy but had no idea his chief of staff, Colonel Count Claus von Stauffenberg, intended to personally assassinate the Fuehrer. He attempted to arrest Stauffenberg on July 20, 1944, but was arrested himself. Freed later that night by forces loyal to the dictator, he used a squad of troops to dispose of several inconvenient witnesses, including Stauffenberg. Since Hitler now lacked the witnesses to hang Fromm for treason, he had him shot for cowardice instead. (USMHI)

A forward observer and his radio operator on the Eastern Front, 1942. The radio man is wearing the Iron Cross, 1st Class, and the ribbon of the Iron Cross, 2nd Class. These men belong to the 29th Motorized Division, which was all but wiped out in the Battle of Stalingrad, 1942–43. (USNA)

Hitler(right) conferring with Colonel General Baron Werner von Fritsch, the Commander-in-Chief of the Army (left) and Colonel General (later field marshal) Werner von Blomberg, the minister of defense, 1935. Both men were forced to retire in early 1938. (Nazi Party Scrapbook, courtesy of Dr. Waldo Dalstead.)

Smolensk in flames, July 1941. Like many Soviet cities, much of Smolensk was burned to the ground during Operation Barbarossa. (USNA)

A German dispatch rider taking a nap during Operation Barbarossa, 1941. Troop exhaustion was a factor in slowing the German advance in September and October 1941. (Photo courtesy Colonel John Angolia)

German Infantry advancing through a burning Russian village, 1941. (Photo courtesy Colonel John Angolia)

General of Fighter Pilots Werner Mölders (third from left) speaking to some of his fighter pilots. This photo was autographed by his brother, Victor Mölders, who was also a fighter ace during WWII. Victor had seven kills when he got shot down over England during the Battle of Britain in 1940. He spent the next seven years in POW camps, but survived the war. (Author's personal collection)

Lieutenant Ritter Robert von Greim, World War I flying ace, circa 1917. An early Nazi, Greim took Hitler on his first airplane ride, during which the Fuehrer became violently ill. Greim became a field marshal and succeeded Hermann Goering as commander-in-chief of the Luftwaffe in the last days of WWII. Greim committed suicide in May 1945. (USMHI)

Colonel General Alfred "Bomber" Keller, the commander of the 1st Air Fleet during Operation Barbarossa, shown here as a World War I bomber captain. Keller held the Pour le Mérite for exceptional bravery. (USMHI)

Landenberg Prison during the Nazi era. Hitler was a prisoner here in 1924, and many generals and prominent Nazis were held here in the late 1940s. A number were executed here, including SS General Ohlendorf, the commander of Einsatzgruppe D. This photo was given to the author by U.S. Lt. Colonel Joe Williams, who served as post-war commandant of the fortress and who supervised the execution of dozens of war criminals.

Colonel General Erich Hoepner, former commander of the 4th Panzer Group during Operation Barbarossa, on trial for high treason, August 6, 1944. The general, who had been dismissed from the service for his part in the July 20, 1944 plot, is in civilian clothes, along with members of the Prussian police. Hoepner was earmarked to command the Replacement Army in a post-Hitler government. He was hanged a few hours after this photo was taken. (USNA)

Colonel General Hermann Hoth (center), who commanded 3rd Panzer Group and Seventeenth Army during Barbarossa. An extremely capable panzer commander, he later commanded 4th Panzer Army before Hitler sacked him as a defeatist on November 30, 1942. (USNA)

Luftwaffe Field Marshal Baron Woflram von Richthofen (left) speaks with the Fuehrer while Colonel Generals Kurt Student (chief of the parachute branch) and Hans Jeschonnek, Luftwaffe chief of staff (far right), look on. This photo was taken in 1943. (USNA)

Field Marshal Fedor von Bock, commander-in-chief of Army Group Center during Operation Barbarossa. Bock opposed the invasion and did not get along with any of his army or Panzer group commanders except Hoth, but he would not let Hitler interfere in their conduct of operations. The results were several major tactical victories for the Germans. (USNA)

An official portrait of Colonel General Eduard Dietl, who commanded Mountain Corps Norway during Operation Barbarossa.

Heinz Guderian the Father of the Blitzkrieg. He commanded 2nd Panzer Army until he was sacked by Kluge in December 1941. (USNA)

A formal portrait of Field Marshall Gerd von Rundstedt. (Courtesy of Col Ed Marino)

Field Marshal Günther von Kluge, commander of the Fourth Army during Operation Barbarossa. Kluge proved to be a poor handler of armor. He nevertheless succeeded Fedor von Bock as commander in chief of Army Group Center in late 1941. He later commanded Army Group B and OB West in Normandy. Marginally involved in the anti-Hitler plot, he committed suicide on August 17, 1944, rather than return to Berlin where the Gestapo was waiting for him. (USNA)

Field Marshal Ewald von Kleist, the commander of 1st Panzer Army during Operation Barbarossa. A veteran cavalryman, he did not distinguish himself as a commander of panzer troops in France (1940) but did well during the conquest of Yugoslavia and in Operation Barbarossa. (USNA)

A small FW or Arado plane at a makeshift airstrip in southern Russia. Along with the famous Fiesler "Storch," these nimble aircraft were a primary means for German commanders to visit their far-flung units.

Support vehicles for a Panzer unit somewhere in southern Russia, 1942. (Both photos courtesy of Wilhelm R. Gehlen)

A Soviet freighter under Luftwaffe air attack, Baltic Sea, 1941. (USNA)

Hitler shaking hands with Field Marshal Wilhelm Keitel , the commander-in-chief of the High Command of the Armed Forces (OKW). Hitler said that Keitel had the brains of a cinema usher, but retained the compliant Keitel in his post for seven years and promoted him to field marshal. Keitel was hanged at Nuremberg on October 16, 1946. (USNA)

CHAPTER XIII

TO THE GATES OF MOSCOW

THE BATTLE OF MOSCOW

As important as the fighting on the northern and southern flanks was, it was relatively insignificant compared to the operations in the central sector, where the decisive battles of the campaign were now being fought. Long before the infantry cleared the Vyazma-Bryansk pockets, Bock's panzer spearheads turned toward Moscow, the "grand prize" of Operation Barbarossa.

The going by now was very difficult, even though resistance was light, due to the fact that the Red Army had been crushed. The first snow fell on October 7. It melted quickly, but it began to rain incessantly on October 9, turning the Russian roads into rivers of mud. It was virtually impossible to bring up fuel, ammunition, food, replacements, or winter clothing to the front. There was very little winter clothing available in any case, because the OKH had accepted Hitler's conclusion that there would be no winter campaign, and had only ordered enough suitable clothing for about one-third of its divisions. There were also no replacements. When the campaign began, Colonel General Fromm, the commander-in-chief of the Home Army and an opponent of Operation Barbarossa, had warned that he could only furnish about 400,000 replacements in 1941, and these had been used up by September.

German successes had moreover brought about high casualties. As of the beginning of September, 14 divisions reported personnel deficiencies of greater than 4,000 men; 40 divisions were short between 3,000 and 4,000 men, while 30 divisions were 2,000 to 3,000 men below their authorized strengths.[1] Naturally, most of the shortages occurred in the combat units, especially the infantry. By September 26, the German Army had suffered 534,000 casualties on the Eastern Front, a figure that represented 15 percent of its total establishment in the East.

Bock nevertheless continued his offensive with a tenacity that bordered on stubbornness. On October 14, Reinhardt's panzers, closely followed by the infantry of the Ninth Army, took Kalinin, the northern hinge of Moscow's defenses, and rolled down the Volga as far as the Moscow Canal, only 70 miles north of the Kremlin. For the next three days there was panic in the capital of the Soviet Union, heightened by the news that government offices were being evacuated to Kuybyshev. There was widespread looting, the food distribution system broke down, and Communist Party members were assaulted on the streets. No one knew where Stalin was, and all sorts of rumors proliferated. Order was not restored until October 19, when the city was declared under a state of siege and special units of NKVD security troops took charge of the capital.

Since October 9, all of the forces defending Moscow had been under the command of Marshal Zhukov, whose primary objectives were to hold the city and keep his command "in being" until the winter arrived in earnest. The harsh and often brutal Zhukov organized "workers' battalions" from the Moscow factories and hurled them into battle, often with little or no basic training and armed only with Molotov cocktails. Meanwhile, more than 500,000 of the city's other inhabitants (most of them women) were drafted into construction battalions, and spent day and night digging anti-tank ditches and trenches and building bunkers.

Due to the broken, forested nature of the terrain north of the Soviet capital, Reinhardt never had the best chance of capturing Moscow. The real danger was to the south, where Heinz Guderian's Second Panzer Group had debouched in reasonably good tank country and was driving on Tula, a major industrial city south of Moscow. Consequently, Zhukov committed here the bulk of his best reserves, notably Colonel Mikhail E. Katukov's 4th Armored Brigade, an elite unit that consisted of former instructors and students of the Kharkov Tank School and was equipped with T-34 tanks.

On October 6, the 4th Armored launched a sudden attack on Guderian's spearhead, the 4th Panzer Division, and gave it a severe battering south of Mtsensk. General Geyr wanted to pull the 4th out of the line and replace it with the 3rd Panzer, but the poor condition of the roads made this impossible to do in less than two days; consequently, the

4th Panzer continued to struggle forward until the evening of October 11, when it finally reached the outskirts of Mtsensk. By now the mud was so thick that off-the-road movement was impossible: the vehicles on the road could only average a speed of six miles an hour, and the 4th Panzer was strung out for a distance of 15 miles. At that moment Katukov attacked again, and taking advantage of the superior maneuverability of his wide-tracked T-34s, virtually destroyed the elite 4th Panzer Division. Meanwhile, Stalin brought up his last strategic reserves: the Siberian divisions of General Iosif Apanasenko's Far Eastern Front, some of the toughest and best trained and equipped units in the entire Red Army.

By this point in the advance, the forward German units were in particularly bad shape. The infantry had received no new boots, socks, or shirts for weeks, and their footwear was literally falling apart. The supply difficulties were simply insurmountable: the German Army was now at the end of a 1,000-mile-long supply line, and the snow and the primitive road system severely limited the amount of food, fuel, and ammunition that the forward units could receive. The Third Panzer and the Ninth and Fourth Armies, for example, all used just two roads. Hoepner's Fourth Panzer Group had to share the only hard-surfaced road in his zone of operations with Weichs's Second Army, and Guderian had no hard-surfaced roads at all in his zone of operations.

Due to the cold, it was necessary to run the engines of the trucks and tanks every four hours, which further exacerbated the fuel crisis. In addition, the railroads were virtually useless. Most of the Soviet rolling stock had been evacuated or destroyed as the Red Army retreated (only 500 Soviet locomotives and 21,000 cars had been captured, amounting to about 10 percent of what was needed), and German trains were built for standard gauge rails, not for the wide gauge of the Soviet Union. The process of converting the broad-gauged Russian rail system to standard European gauge had just begun as 1941 neared its end.

Getting spare parts to the motor pools was also a major problem. At the end of October, for example, Walter Nehring's 18th Panzer Division had lost 59 tanks due to accidents and enemy action, but 103 tanks were inoperative due to a lack of spare parts.[2] The story was the same in all the panzer divisions, which were down to the strength of reinforced regiments as the Battle of Moscow began. Off of the roads, progress was virtually impossible except on foot. The mud was so bad that the 292nd Infantry Division reported that a team of 16 horses was not able to move a single howitzer of the 292nd Artillery Regiment. Motorized supply columns were averaging less than five miles a day, and more than 2,000 vehicles were stuck on the Moscow Highway alone. "The internal combustion engine is a dead loss in winter warfare," one German soldier wrote. "Everything has to go by sledge. Where all the sledges come from is a mystery. But how all the horses survive is a greater one still. . . . The native ponies live by water and straw and beating."[3] The Luftwaffe was grounded, but not the Red Air Force, which was operating on paved airfields in the Moscow area.

Due to all these difficulties, Field Marshal von Bock halted his offensive on October 30 to await freezing weather, when the ground would again be hard enough to bring up food and ammunition and he could resume the advance. Meanwhile, most of the infantry remained rationless; having consumed their Iron Rations (a concoction of chocolate laced with caffeine, to be eaten only in emergencies), they subsisted mainly on tea and potatoes looted from local farms. Some units lived on almost nothing but horsemeat for up to six weeks at a time. Soon sickness, the cold, dysentery, and malnutrition were causing more casualties than enemy bullets.

On November 12, General Halder arrived at Orsha and convened a conference for chiefs of staff aboard his special train. Among the invited was Colonel Baron Kurt von Liebenstein, Guderian's chief of staff. In spite of his junior rank, Liebenstein was one of the best and brightest officers in the German Army, and a man upon whom Guderian relied absolutely.

Baron Kurt von Liebenstein was born in Jebenhausen on February 28, 1899, and joined the 26th Dragoon Regiment as a *Fahnenjunker* on December 20, 1916. He fought on the Western Front in World War I, was commissioned on February 26, 1918, and was commanding his regiment's mortar unit when he was captured by the British on September 27. Released in early 1920, he joined the Reichswehr, and served in the 18th Cavalry from 1920 to 1931. He underwent General Staff training from 1931 to 1933, served in the Defense Ministry (1933–

36) and was a company commander in the 3rd Reconnaissance Battalion (1936–37). Promoted to captain in 1933 and to major in 1936, he was on the staff of the German military attaché to Paris from 1937 until World War II began.

Liebenstein benefited from his stay in Paris to develop an appreciation for French culture, good wines and women. British intelligence later noted that as a result of his travels, he was broader-minded than his contemporaries, and was fluent in French and fairly good in English. Liebenstein was also an anti-Nazi and detested all dictatorships.[4] He was promoted to lieutenant colonel on April 1, 1939, and was on the staff of the High Command of the Army until early 1940, when he became Ia of the 10th Panzer Division. In October 1940, he was named chief of staff of Guderian's XIX Motorized Corps, which later became Second Panzer Group on the Eastern Front.

At Orsha, General Halder announced the decision to continue the advance on Moscow rather than go into winter quarters, in spite of the lateness of the season. Orsha has been cited as an example of how Hitler forced his generals to take actions of which they disapproved, but in this case the example does not bare close scrutiny, because both Brauchitsch and Halder *wanted* to continue the offensive against the Soviet capital. In fact, after the fall of Kiev, Hitler had considered going into winter quarters, but Brauchitsch, Halder, Bock, and others persuaded him to concentrate his forces against Moscow.

The sole purpose of the Orsha conference, from the OKH's point of view, was to discuss how to take Moscow, not whether or not to try. In spite of the fact that the decision had already been made, however, General von Sodenstern, the chief of staff of Army Group South, emphatically expressed his objections to continuing the attack, as did Lieutenant General Kurt Brennecke, the chief of staff of Army Group North, and Colonel Baron von Liebenstein. Even Major General Hans von Greifenberg, the chief of staff of Army Group Center, pointed out the risks of continuing the advance, although he was not in a position to emphatically oppose it, because his commander, Field Marshal von Bock, was a leading advocate of pushing forward.

There was, in fact, a considerable amount of professional opposition to continuing the offensive within the German Army, which included two of the most respected members of the Officers' Corps, Field Marshals von Rundstedt and von Leeb. Unfortunately for the Wehrmacht, however, most of the opposition was concentrated at the middle and lower levels; it was not found at Fuehrer Headquarters, at the OKW or at the OKH.

The final effort to take Stalin's capital began on November 15. North to south, Bock attacked with the Ninth Army, the Third Panzer Group, the Fourth Panzer Group, Fourth Army, and the Second Panzer Army. Weichs's Second Army, while still part of Army Group Center, had to be moved far to the south to try to maintain contact with Army Group South, and played no further role in the Battle of Moscow. (Map 13.1 shows Bock's dispositions and his final thrusts toward the Soviet capital.)

By this time, the Germans in the Moscow sector were outnumbered. By November 20, the Germans had lost 750,000 men (230,000 of them killed) and General Fromm's 430,000 replacements had long been used up. The divisions in the East were short more than 300,000 men and the OKH was already recommending that 20 divisions be disbanded to provide for the others.[5]

Nor had German officer losses been light, and the senior officer casualties had been much heavier than in Poland, France, the Balkans, Crete, and North Africa combined. They included Colonel Guenther Weichhardt, the commander of the 551st Infantry Regiment, killed in action on June 28; Colonel Ernst-Richard Knecht, commander of the Nebelwerfer Lehr Regiment, killed on July 9; Colonel Fritz Hertzsch, commander of the 77th Infantry Regiment, killed on July 15; and Colonel (later General of Artillery) Walter Hartmann, leader of the 140th Artillery Command, who lost an arm and a leg on July 15.

The long list of other senior casualties included: Major General Karl Kalmukoff, the commander of the 31st Infantry Division, killed in action on August 13; Colonel Theodor Kretzschmer, commander of the 272nd Infantry Regiment, killed on August 18; Colonel Willi Daube, leader of the 371st Infantry Regiment, killed on August 20; Colonel Viktor Bartcky, commanding officer of the 513th Infantry Regiment, killed August 23; Colonel Gottfried Reis, commander of the 75th Artillery Regiment, killed on August 26; Lieutenant General Walter Keiner, commander of the 62nd Infantry Division, seriously wounded on

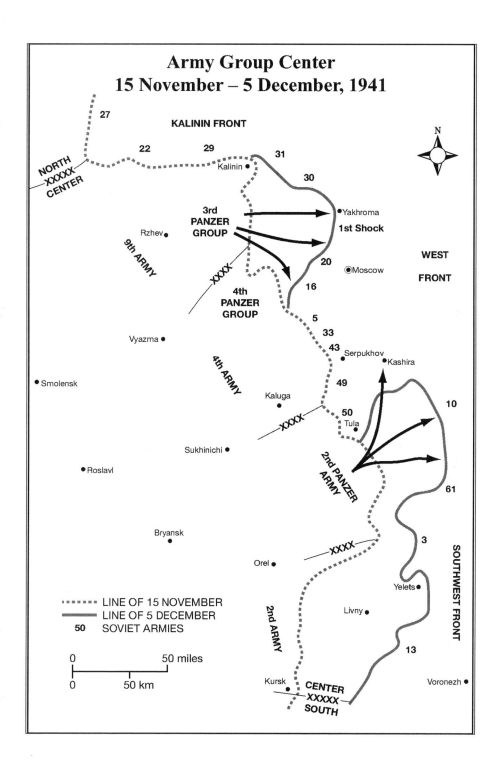

Army Group Center
15 November – 5 December, 1941

KALININ FRONT

27

22   29   31

NORTH
XXXXX
CENTER   Kalinin

30

3rd
PANZER   Yakhroma
GROUP
                1st Shock

Rzhev

9th ARMY   XXXX

                20

4th   ●Moscow
PANZER   WEST
GROUP   16   FRONT

Vyazma   5

                33

                43   Serpukhov
4th ARMY   Kashira

Smolensk   Kaluga   49
                              10
                 XXXX

                 50
                 Tula

Sukhinichi

                 2nd PANZER
Roslavl   ARMY   61

Bryansk   3

                 XXXX
Orel   SOUTHWEST FRONT
                         Yelets

········ LINE OF 15 NOVEMBER
──────── LINE OF 5 DECEMBER
2nd ARMY   Livny
50 SOVIET ARMIES

0   50 miles   13
0   50 km

Kursk   CENTER
         XXXXX   Voronezh
         SOUTH

September 17; Colonel Baron Hans-Heinrich von Seidlitz und Gohlau, chief of the 134th Artillery Command, killed in Kiev on September 20; Lieutenant Colonel Hans Liss, commander of the 71st Motorized Infantry Regiment, seriously wounded, October 3; Colonel Hans Daubert, commander of the 497th Infantry Regiment, killed on October 8; Colonel Horst von Wolff, commander of the 478th Infantry Regiment and a holder of both the *Pour le Mérite* and the Knight's Cross, killed on October 9; SS Lieutenant General Paul Hausser, commander of the SS Motorized Division "Das Reich," hit in the face by shell splitters, causing the loss of an eye, October 14; Lieutenant General Erich Bernecker, leader of the 124th Artillery Command, killed on October 28; Colonel Georg von Neufville, commander of the 195th Infantry Regiment, who died on November 4 from wounds received two days earlier; Major General Georg Braun, commander of the 68th Infantry Division, killed on November 14; and Colonel Harry von Arnim, commander of the 479th Infantry Regiment, and Colonel Dr. Bartsch, chief veterinary officer of the XXXVII Corps, both killed in October.[6] As for the senior German officers, the casualties were just beginning.

During the first two weeks of November alone, Stalin had brought up 100,000 men, 2,000 guns, and 300 tanks. By mid-November, Zhukov was able to deploy on three fronts: West Front (30th, 16th, 5th, 33rd, 49th, and 50th Armies); Kalinin Front (22nd, 29th, and 31st Armies); and South-West Front (3rd and 13th Armies). In all, he had 60 rifle divisions, 17 tank brigades, and 14 cavalry divisions, a total of 91 major combat formations. Even with all of this, Stalin was not yet through bringing up units from the East. By the end of the winter of 1941-42, he brought up 15 rifle divisions, three cavalry divisions, and eight tank brigades (1,700 tanks), as well as 1,500 airplanes, in addition to the units already at the front.[7] Bock, on the other hand, had only 38 infantry, 13 panzer, and seven motorized divisions, for a total of 58 major formations.[8]

Needless to say, many of the Soviet formations and all of the German units were well below their authorized strength. By now, large sections of the army were virtually immobilized. On November 19, Halder informed Hitler that 30 percent of the half-million trucks that had entered Russia had been destroyed or damaged beyond repair. Another

40 percent were nonoperational and awaiting overhaul or major repairs. Only 30 percent were still on the roads. Most of the army was now being supplied by two-wheeled wagons pulled by local Russian ponies, which were able to survive where the heavier European horses died, even though the ponies usually had nothing to eat except straw from the local thatched roofs.

Bock's progress toward Moscow was very slow. Hoth's Third Panzer Group captured Klin on November 23, and Baron Hans von Funck's 7th Panzer Division reached the Moscow-Volga Canal on November 28. The following day, the 7th Panzer pushed a battle group under the command of Colonel Baron Hasso von Manteuffel across the canal. The next day, he captured the bridge at Dmitrov before it could be blown up. Manteuffel, however, was soon under attack by the Siberians and could advance no further. Lieutenant General Rudolf Veiel's 2nd Panzer Division then made a superhuman effort, pushing into the outskirts of Moscow, and its reconnaissance battalion even managed to get Nazi Germany's only glimpse of the Kremlin, less than 15 miles away.

It was the high water mark of the Third Reich.

To the south, Guderian forced his way up toward Oka, but was unable to take Tula, which was defended by the entire Soviet Fiftieth Army reinforced by several workers' battalions. Guderian then bypassed it to the east, and continued his advance to the north, screening his long flanks with infantry formations. One of these was Lieutenant General Friedrich Mieth's 112th Infantry Division, which was posted on Guderian's right (eastern) flank. All three of Mieth's infantry regiments had suffered more than 50 percent casualties due to frostbite; his machine guns were so badly frozen that they could only fire single shots, and the packing grease on his anti-tank ammunition had frozen so solid that it had to be scraped with a knife before it would fit into the breech of the AT guns.

On November 18, the 112th was attacked by a fresh Siberian infantry division, outfitted in white quilted uniforms and armed with tommy guns, and supported by an entire brigade of T-34 tanks. It was too much for the weary, lice-infested survivors of the 112th, who broke and ran away. This was the first time such an incident had occurred on the Russian Front.

Zhukov wanted to hold his Siberians in reserve until the Germans had exhausted themselves; he then planned to commit them all in one devastating offensive. On the other hand, he was determined to halt Guderian's advance, which had already cut two important railroads leading to Moscow and was nearing a third. For this reason, he was forced to throw three Siberian infantry and cavalry divisions and two tank brigades into counterattacks against the Second Panzer Army earlier than he wished. These attacks halted the German advance and convinced Guderian that it would be impossible to take Moscow. On November 24, he turned up at Bock's headquarters and convinced the field marshal (who was ill and in bed) to telephone the OKH and ask permission to call off the offensive. Brauchitsch, however, made it clear that he was not allowed to make such a far-reaching decision. He ordered Guderian to continue to try to reach the Zaraisk-Mikhailov line and to cut the Ryazan railroad.

Meanwhile, Veiel's drive and Manteuffel's advance across the Moscow-Volga Canal had brought the wrath of the Siberian divisions down upon Reinhardt, whose Third Panzer Group was taken under heavy counterattack for five days. Conserving his strength while all of this was going on, Guenther von Kluge was personally commanded by Hitler that his Fourth Army should resume the offensive on December 2. The next day, Kluge broke the line of the Thirty-third Soviet Army north of Naro Fominsk and forced Zhukov to commit the reserves of his 33rd and 43rd Armies near the railroad town of Golizno. Kluge suffered heavy losses during this operation and on his own responsibility withdrew Lt. Gen. Karl Pflaum's 258th Infantry Division from the front on the grounds that it was no longer battle worthy.

The next day the temperature dropped to –4 degrees Fahrenheit, and Fourth Army was forced back in a heavy snowstorm. The following day, December 5, Field Marshal von Bock called off the offensive, with the acquiescence of the OKH. The nighttime temperatures by now had dropped to –25 degrees Fahrenheit, and many men had frozen to death. Dozens of tanks would not start because the oil in their engines had frozen, and artillery and machine guns would not fire because their lubricants had frozen. Hitler would not accept Bock's decision until December 8, but by then the Battle of Moscow was clearly over. The Soviet winter offensive had already been in progress in the central sector for two days, and Army Group Center was fighting for its very survival.

CHAPTER XIV

WHAT HAPPENED TO THE MEN OF BARBAROSSA

Hans-Juergen "Dieter" von Arnim led the XXXIX Motorized Corps on the Eastern Front until December 1, 1942. (It was, meanwhile, redesignated XXXIX Panzer Corps on July 9, 1942.) He was then hurriedly called to Fuehrer Headquarters, where he was named commander of the newly-formed Fifth Panzer Army, and was quickly flown to Tunis. He was promoted to colonel general on December 4, 1942.

Arnim led the Fifth Panzer Army against the Anglo-American and French forces in Tunisia until March 9, 1943. Here he again proved to be an excellent tactician, winning several local victories against the Allies, but turned out to be a poor strategic thinker. He also did not work well with Erwin Rommel, whom Arnim viewed as an upstart commoner. He succeeded Rommel as commander-in-chief of Army Group Afrika on March 9, but was forced to surrender on May 12. He spent most of the rest of the war in Clinton, Mississippi, on what is now part of the campus of Mississippi College. He was released from the POW camp on July 1, 1947. He died in a nursing home in Bad Wildungen, Hesse, on September 1, 1962.

Heinrich Aschenbrenner was expelled from the Soviet Union when Operation Barbarossa began and, on June 29, 1941, was named Higher Signals Leader with Luftkreis II. He was obviously an excellent signals officer and had the confidence of Hermann Goering, who named him Higher Signals Leader to the Commander-in-Chief of the Luftwaffe, a post he held from October 1, 1942 to April 10, 1945. From October to December 1943, he was simultaneously acting Higher Signals Leader for the 5th Air Fleet in Finland and Norway. He was promoted to major general on August 1, 1942, and to lieutenant general exactly two years later. At the end of the war, he was inspector for Foreign Personnel East. He surrendered on May 8, 1945, and was a POW until March 1948. He settled in Bielefeld, North-Rhine-Westphalia, where he died on December 11, 1960.

Gerhard Berthold fought against the Soviet winter offensive of 1941/42. He was named acting commander of the XXXXIII Corps in the Jucknov (Yucknov)/Spass-Demyansk sector on January 20, 1942, when Gotthard Heinrici became commander of the Fourth Army. Berthold received this command despite the fact he was only a major general—a very junior rank for even an acting corps commander. Kurt Brennecke was appointed permanent commander of the XXXXIII on February 1, but could not actually assume command until February 24. Berthold then returned to the 31st Infantry Division. On April 14, he led an assault on Saizewa-Gora, during which he was killed in action. He was posthumously promoted to lieutenant general on June 10, 1943.

Fedor von Bock's Army Group Center took the brunt of Stalin's winter offensive, beginning on December 6, 1941. By December 16, the army group was in desperate straits and Bock was nearly in despair. He poured his heart out to Colonel Rudolf Schmundt that day, along with a detailed description of the state of his own precarious health. He asked Hitler's chief adjutant to relay his comments to the Fuehrer and this Schmundt undoubtedly did. Two days later, Field Marshal Keitel telephoned Bock and informed him that Hitler suggested that he take an extended leave to restore his health. Bock did so immediately. He was replaced by Guenther von Kluge.

Bock was in the Fuehrer Reserve for less than a month. On January 16, he succeeded Field Marshal Walter von Reichenau as commander-in-chief of Army Group South. He led it in the initial phases of the German summer offensive of 1942, but his old confidence and decisiveness were notably absent. His slowness allowed several Soviet divisions to escape across the Don. As a result, when Army Group South was divided into Army Groups A and B, von Bock was given command of neither. He was placed in Fuehrer Reserve on July 15, and was never re-employed. He retired to his estate in Holstein-Schleswig.

After Hitler committed suicide on April 30, 1945, Bock received a telegram from Erich von Manstein, informing him that Grand Admiral Karl Doenitz was forming a new government at Flensburg. Even now angling for a new command, Bock left for that city at once, accompanied by his wife and daughter. Details of their deaths differ. Their car was attacked by British fighter-bombers on the Kiel Road near Lensahn, Holstein, on May 3 or 4, and all three were killed, although one report states that Bock was found alive on May 3. According to this story, he was carried to the Oldenburg Naval Hospital, where he died the next day. He was the only one of Hitler's 25 field marshals to die from enemy bullets.

Walter von Boltenstern led the 29th Motorized Division until September 20, 1941, when he was replaced by Max Fremerey. He remained in the Fuehrer Reserve until January 20, 1942, when he assumed command of the 179th Motorized Replacement Division at Weimar. His promotion to lieutenant general did not come until July 15, 1942, and he was never given another field command, suggesting someone in authority was not happy with his leadership of the 29th Motorized. He led the 179th Replacement until February 19, 1943, when he was assigned to the Reichs War Court. He was placed in Fuehrer Reserve in May 1944 and retired on January 31, 1945.

At the end of the war, Walter von Boltenstern was abducted by the Soviets. He died in a Communist prison on January 19, 1952.

Erich Brandenberger led the 8th Panzer until January 17, 1943, fighting on the northern and central sectors of the Eastern Front. (He was, however, struck with a piece of shrapnel on December 8, 1941, and had to hand command of the division over to Major General Werner Huebner. Brandenberger resumed command on March 20, 1942.) He was acting commander of the LIX Corps on the Russian Front from January 17 to March 15, 1943, when he went on leave. He assumed command of the XXIX Corps on May 21, 1943, and led it until July 2, 1944, fighting on the Mius, at Krivoy Rog, in the Dnieper retreats, at Uman, in the retreats to the Bug and the Dnestr, and into Romania. Meanwhile, he was promoted to lieutenant general on August 1, 1942, and to general of artillery on August 1, 1943. He changed his rank designation to general of panzer troops on November 8, 1943.

He led the Seventh Army on the Western Front from August 28,

1944 to February 20, 1945, and did an extremely good job with very limited resources, bogging the Americans down at Aachen and in the Huertgen Forest, and giving Hitler time to launch his Ardennes campaign. He was ordered to cover the left flank of the Fifth Panzer Army during the Battle of the Bulge. Prior to the offensive, he all but begged for a panzer division, but Hitler and the OKW refused to give him one. As a result, he was unable to prevent Patton's Third Army from relieving the fortress of Bastogne on December 26, 1944. (Had Hitler given Brandenberger a tank division, Manteuffel and the Fifth Panzer Army would probably have captured Bastogne.)

Field Marshal Model relieved him of his command on February 20, 1945. The two men had a personality conflict and "talked over each other's heads," as the Germans say. Model was a live-wire man of action and "son of the people," whereas Brandenberger was a thoughtful, methodical intellectual. Brandenberger handed command of the army over to General of Infantry Hans Felber on February 22 and left for home. An hour later, Allied bombers flattened the headquarters. Felber was wounded and several officers were killed.

Brandenberger, however, was now highly respected throughout the Wehrmacht and his performance during the Battle of the Bulge (where he had done everything possible with his limited forces) had only increased his reputation. On March 25, 1945, he was called out of retirement and given command of the Nineteenth Army, which was part of Army Group G, on the southern sector of the Western Front. He therefore did not have to deal with Walter Model. He led Nineteenth Army until "final victory" and surrendered to the Americans on May 6, 1945. He remained a prisoner of war until 1948. He retired to Bonn, where he died on June 21, 1955.

Brandenberger was a steady and dependable commander, but not a flashy one. A thorough study of the German and Allied records and the Stauffenberg papers have convinced me that he was one of the best army-level field commanders Germany had on the Western Front in the 1944–45 period. Despite tremendous pressure and often with a mediocre team, he always reacted with speed and an incredible calmness that transferred itself downward.

Walter von Brauchitsch submitted his resignation as commander-in-chief of the army on December 6, 1941, the day Stalin's winter offensive began on the central and northern sectors. (It had been in progress in the south since November 25.) Adolf Hitler, however, refused to accept it, on the grounds that he could not allow a change in command at that moment. Brauchitsch left the room without saying a word.

On December 16, Colonel Rudolf Schmundt informed Hitler that Brauchitsch had been secretly discussing withdrawals with Bock, von Kluge and Guderian, in contravention of Hitler's orders. Hitler immediately cancelled these plans and, three days later, dismissed the field marshal. Their final meeting, which lasted two hours, was acrimonious.

German radio announced the news of Brauchitsch's retirement without preface to the entire world. Hitler named himself commander-in-chief of the army, and Brauchitsch retired into obscurity. The Gestapo kept him under surveillance for a time, but this watch was soon dropped. The retired field marshal was now just a tired, sick and broken old man.

On August 3, 1944, two weeks after Colonel Count Claus von Stauffenberg's bomb narrowly missed killing the Fuehrer, Brauchitsch wrote a letter to the dictator disassociating himself from the conspirators of July 20 and offering his services once more. On August 19, the field marshal issued a public proclamation, welcoming Reichsfuehrer-SS Heinrich Himmler's appointment as commander-in-chief of the Replacement Army and condemning the conspirators in the strongest terms. By now Hitler's opinion of Brauchitsch had improved because of the effectiveness of the 88mm gun, which he had been very instrumental in developing, and because of his previous support of the V-2 rocket project, but the offer was not acted upon.

Field Marshal von Brauchitsch was arrested by the British at his estate in Rachut, Holstein, on August 26, 1945. Subsequently he was imprisoned in England before being transferred to Muenster, where he shared a cell with fellow field marshals Manstein and Rundstedt, and where his heart disease continued to progress. Despite the fact that he was practically blind, he was sent to "the Bunker" in Nuremberg, where he was forced to share a two-man cell with four other men. Finally transferred to Hamburg, he was scheduled to be tried by a British Military Tribunal in 1949, but his health continued to deteriorate and he died in the British Military Hospital at Hamburg-Barmbeck on October 18, 1948.

Kurt Brennecke, the chief of staff of Army Group North, gave up his post on January 18, 1942, and went on leave. He was promoted to general of infantry on February 1, 1942, and returned to active duty as commander of the XXXXIII Corps on February 19. He fought at Juchnow and Spass-Demjansk, but fell ill during the Stalingrad campaign and went into Fuehrer Reserve on January 27, 1943. He returned to duty in June as commander of the Division Commanders and Commanding Generals' Course in Berlin. Because of Allied bombers and troop advances, the course later moved to the Infantry School at Doeberitz, then to Hirschberg in the Sudetenland, and finally to Neustadt/Saale and Bad Wiessee, a resort town on Lake Tegernsee in the Bavarian Alps. He surrendered here to the Americans on May 8, 1945. Brennecke was a POW until March 31, 1948. He settled in Bonn, where he died on December 30, 1982. For a time, he worked on the Personnel Expert Committee of the West German Armed Forces (1955–56), which tried to ensure that no Nazi sympathizers were selected for the new *Bundeswehr* (West German Armed Forces).

Wilhelm Canaris held his post as chief of the Abwehr until February 1944, when he assured Field Marshal Kesselring that there was no possibility that the Allies would land in the rear of the German Tenth Army. They landed there with an entire corps the next day. Hitler fired Canaris on February 12, and he was sent into Fuehrer Reserve, while the SS absorbed the Abwehr. After Hitler's anger over the intelligence failure at Anzio abated, he placed Canaris in charge of a special naval transportation staff. He was arrested by the Gestapo on July 23, 1944, but the evidence connecting him with the July 20 plot was considered insufficient to bring him to trial. He probably would never have been tried had he not kept a diary at work that included accounts of his part in the anti-Hitler plot, and left it there after his dismissal as chief of the Abwehr. This diary was discovered by pro-Nazi General of Infantry Walter Buhle in early 1945.

When the admiral was tried, the main witness against him was Major General Hans Oster, one of his former department heads.[1] Canaris was executed at the Flossenbuerg concentration camp on April 9, 1945. Unlike most of the conspirators, Canaris does not seem to have been motivated by genuine anti-Nazi feelings; his participation in the plot seems instead to have been something of an insurance policy.

Adolf Hitler named Eduard Dietl commander-in-chief of the newly formed Army of Lapland on January 15, 1942, thus making him independent of General von Falkenhorst's Army of Norway, which was still responsible for supplying him. Dietl was promoted to colonel general June 1, 1942, and his command was redesignated Twentieth Mountain Army on June 20. It remained in action on the Far North sector of the Eastern Front until the fall of 1944. Meanwhile, in June 1944, Dietl visited Germany for a conference. On June 23, his airplane crashed near Harberg, Styria, in present-day Austria. All aboard were killed instantly. The dead included General of Infantry Thomas-Emil von Wickede, commander of the X Corps; General of Mountain Troops Karl Eglseer, commander of the XVIII Mountain Corps; and Lt. Gen. Franz Rossi, the commandant of Petsamo.

Theodor Eicke returned to Russia and resumed command of the SS Motorized Division, which successively became the 3rd SS Motorized Division, the 3rd SS Panzer Grenadier Division and the 3rd SS Panzer Division. Returning to the front against medical advice, he fought bravely in the battles of the Demyansk Pocket (later salient), but was suffering from combat fatigue by 1942. The loss of his son, who was killed in action on December 2, 1941, no doubt influenced his state of mind. He nevertheless remained in command and was promoted to *SS-Obergruppenfuehrer and General der Waffen-SS* (general of Waffen-SS) on April 20, 1942. By the time he was able to take the division back to France to rebuild in October, fewer than 2,000 men remained standing. It had started the campaign with 15,000 men.

After the fall of Stalingrad, the 3rd SS was rushed back to the Soviet Union. On the afternoon of February 26, 1943, Eicke became alarmed when radio communications with his panzer regiment failed. He jumped in a light reconnaissance airplane and at an altitude of 300 feet flew over a well-camouflaged Soviet position that included anti-aircraft guns. Eicke was probably killed before his bullet-riddled airplane crashed into the ground. Very few outside of the SS mourned his passing.

Nikolaus von Falkenhorst spent four years at his dual post as Wehrmacht Commander Norway and commander of the Army of Norway. Here he had two duties: guard against an invasion of Norway and supply the Twentieth Mountain Army, which was operating in Lapland. In the fall of 1944, Finland renounced its alliance with Germany and made peace with the Soviet Union. The Twentieth Mountain retreated from Russia and Finland to the Narvik sector, and the Third Reich did not need two army headquarters in Norway. Hitler, of course, chose to abolish the least Nazi of the two.

From his first day in command, Falkenhorst opposed repressive measures on civilians and tried to get along with and make life easier for the Norwegian people, and they appreciated his efforts. He even traveled through the countryside and along the streets of Oslo without an escort. He could have easily been assassinated, but no one tried, because everyone realized that Falkenhorst's replacement would be much worse than the benign Falkenhorst. On December 18, 1944, Hitler abolished Falkenhorst's Army of Norway and not the Twentieth Mountain Army. Falkenhorst was placed in the Fuehrer Reserve and never re-employed.

After the war, he was tried by a British court for obeying Hitler's Commando Order, which commanded that captured British commandos be handed over to the SS for execution. Falkenhorst was found guilty and was sentenced to death on August 2, 1946. His popularity with the Norwegians, however, saved him. Within a few weeks, his sentence was commuted to 20 years imprisonment and he was released on July 13, 1953. He retired to Holzminden, Lower Saxony, where he died on June 18, 1968, at the age of 82.[2]

Hans Feige returned to Germany after he was relieved of command of the XXXVI Mountain Corps. He was never re-employed and retired for the second and final time on June 30, 1942. He escaped to the west when the Red Army overran his native Prussia. General Feige settled in Schussenried, Wuerrtemberg, where he died on September 17, 1953.

Erich Fellgiebel, the chief signals officer of both the army and the Wehrmacht, was the first man arrested after the Stauffenberg assassination attempt failed on July 20, 1944. He was dishonorably discharged from the army by the "Court of Honor" on August 4, tried and condemned to death on August 10, and hanged in the Ploetzensee Prison in Berlin on September 4, 1944.

Gerhard Feyerabend, the General Staff officer who co-authored the Greiffenberg invasion plan, was a tactics instructor at the War Academy in Berlin from October 1940 to April 1941, when he became Ia of the Second Army. Here he served on the central sector of the Eastern Front prior to being attached to Army Group South as a special duties officer. On October 19, 1941, he was named chief of staff of the XXVII Corps, and fought at Vyazma, Rzhev, Spass-Demyansk, Nevel, and Orsha, among other battles. Promoted to colonel on December 1, 1941, he was sent to southwestern France and became chief of staff of the First Army on August 1, 1943. He was promoted to major general on February 1, 1944. He was sent back to the Eastern Front in August 1944 as acting commander of the 87th Infantry Division, which was being pushed back into the Courland (Kurland) Pocket, along with the rest of Army Group North. Feyerabend gave up command of the division on September 10 and apparently went on leave; however, he returned to the Courland Pocket on November 9, and assumed command of the outstanding 11th Infantry Division on November 18. He was promoted to lieutenant general on March 1, 1945.

The Courland Pocket was completely isolated from the rest of the German Wehrmacht, and Stalin made six separate major attempts to crush it and destroy the German Sixteenth and Eighteenth Armies. During the last battles in western Latvia, Feyerabend's division (along with the 14th Panzer) served as a "fire brigade," rushing from crisis to crisis, smashing Soviet spearheads, and restoring the German line in places it had buckled. As a reward for their performances, most of the 11th Infantry and 14th Panzer Divisions were selected for evacuation on the last ships.

The 11th Infantry embarked for Germany on April 30, 1945, the day Adolf Hitler shot himself. Feyerabend surrendered to the British on May 10. A POW until July 10, 1947, Feyerabend could not return home because East Prussia was behind Soviet lines and was eventually partitioned between Poland and Russia. He settled in Bavaria, where he died at Rottach-Egern, on Lake Tegernsee, on November 6, 1965.

Martin Fiebig, the close air support specialist, was promoted to lieutenant general on April 1, 1942, became acting commander of the 1st Air Division on the Eastern Front on April 12, and assumed command of the VIII Air Corps on July 1, 1942. He was transferred to Greece on May 22, 1943, where he was simultaneously commander of Luftwaffe Command Southeast and the X Air Corps. Here he led a variety of obsolete aircraft in action against partisans in Greece, Albania, and Yugoslavia. He was promoted to general of fliers March 1, 1943.

Fiebig fell ill and was in the Fuehrer Reserve from September 1, 1944 to February 1, 1945, when he took charge of the II Air Corps on the Eastern Front. He was transferred north on April 12, where he commanded Luftwaffe Command Northeast in support of Army Group Vistula. General Fiebig surrendered to the British in May 1945, but was turned over to the Yugoslavs on February 6, 1946. Like many others who fell into their hands, he was given a show trial and was hanged as a war criminal on October 24, 1947.

Helmuth Foerster commanded the I Air Corps until August 23, 1942, when he was named chief of air defense at the Reich Air Ministry. He held this post until August 1, 1944, when he was appointed chief of air transport, which was something of a demotion. He escaped Berlin just before the fall and surrendered to the Allies on May 9, 1945. A POW until June 30, 1947, he settled in Bavaria after the war and died at Lenggries, in the Bavarian Alps, on April 7, 1965.

Fritz Fromm, the commander of the Replacement Army, became somewhat anti-Hitler as the war began to turn against the Third Reich. He allowed General Olbricht, his deputy, and Colonel Count Claus von Stauffenberg, Olbricht's (and later Fromm's) chief of staff, to conspire against the Fuehrer, but Fromm made it clear that he would only join the conspiracy if it succeeded. He did, however, remind them to arrest his archenemy, Wilhelm Keitel, if the plot did succeed. The one-armed, one-eyed Colonel von Stauffenberg, however, was not about to trust the unreliable Fromm, and launched the coup on July 20, 1944, without Fromm's knowledge or permission.

When he saw that the putsch was falling apart, Fromm told Stauffenberg that he must commit suicide immediately. After Stauffenberg laughed out loud at the suggestion, Fromm attempted to place him under arrest; instead, Stauffenberg arrested Fromm and his lieutenants locked him up. About midnight, however, the general was set free by a Grossdeutschland Guard Battalion under Major Otto-Ernst Remer. To cover up his own ambivalent role in the affair, Fromm disposed of several inconvenient witnesses, including Colonel General Ludwig Beck, the former chief of the General Staff; General Olbricht; Colonel von Stauffenberg and his aide, Lieutenant Werner von Haeften; and Olbricht's chief of staff, Colonel Ritter Albrecht Mertz von Quirnheim. Meanwhile, Hitler personally ordered that Fromm be relieved of his command. He was arrested on July 21 and replaced by Reichsfuehrer-SS Heinrich Himmler.

The Gestapo was unable to conclusively prove Fromm's role in the conspiracy because he had murdered all of the important witnesses. He was nevertheless expelled from the army on September 19 and tried before the People's Court on March 7, 1945. The charges included cowardice and incompetence. He was sentenced to death by hanging.

Despite his lack of moral (or civil) courage, as an objective historian, I am forced to conclude that Fromm did an excellent job as commander of the Replacement Army. Hitler must have at least partially agreed, because he changed the sentence to the "more honorable" form of execution: death by firing squad. The sentence was carried out in the prison at Brandenburg an der Havel on March 12, 1945.

Hermann Geyer led the IX Corps with great success on the Eastern Front in 1941, fighting at Minsk, Smolensk, Vyazma, and Moscow, among other battles. He was older than the average German corps commander, and the physical strain of the Russian Front finally proved too much for him. He went into the Fuehrer Reserve on January 1, 1942, and was never re-employed. He was officially retired on December 31, 1943. At least one of his former men thought highly of him, however. Field Marshal Erwin Rommel used him as an advisor as he prepared his army group for the defense of Fortress Europe.

Geyer settled in Wildsee, near Bad Wildbad in the Black Forest. He committed suicide here on April 10, 1946.

Baron Leo Geyr von Schweppenburg commanded the XXIV Motorized

Corps until January 7, 1942. He later commanded the XXXX Panzer Corps (July 9 to October 1, 1942), LXXXVI Corps (February 21 to April 1, 1943) and LVIII Reserve Panzer Corps (August 5 to December 31,1943). He was assigned to OB West as commander-designate of Panzer Group West, which he led from January 24 to July 2, 1944. Hitler sacked him because the panzer general submitted a defeatist (but highly accurate) situation report concerning the Normandy front.

Geyr's forced retirement, however, only lasted a few weeks. On July 21, 1944, the day after the unsuccessful attempt on Hitler's life, his friend Heinz Guderian became the new chief of the General Staff of the Army. The following month, Guderian managed to get Geyr appointed as his successor as chief of the Panzer Troops Inspectorate (August 7, 1944 to May 8, 1945). Captured by the Americans at the end of the war, Geyr was released from the POW camps in July 1947, and became a prolific writer and commentator on military affairs. He died at Irschenhausen, Bavaria, on January 27, 1974.

Hans von Greiffenberg, who submitted an early plan for the invasion of the Soviet Union, was promoted to major general on August 1, 1940. He was named chief of staff of the Twelfth Army on January 1, 1941, and served in Yugoslavia and Greece during the Balkans campaign. He was appointed chief of staff of Army Group B on May 10, 1941. This HQ was redesignated Army Group South when Operation Barbarossa began on June 22. Greiffenberg was promoted to lieutenant general on April 1, 1942, the day he was made chief of staff of Army Group A, even though it was not officially activated until July 9. He took part in the drive to the Caucasus, the retreats to the Donetz, and the Battle of Kursk. He went into the Fuehrer Reserve on August 1 and, after an extended leave, became military attaché to Budapest on October 8, 1943. He was promoted to general of infantry and was simultaneously named Plenipotentiary General of the German Armed Forces in Hungary on April 1, 1944. He held this post until the end of the war and surrendered to the Americans on May 5, 1945. He was released from the POW camps on June 30, 1947, and died in Koenigstein, Taunus, in the Free State of Saxony in southeastern Germany, on June 30, 1951.

Ritter Robert von Greim led the V Air Corps until April 1, 1942, when he assumed command of Luftwaffe Command East. This headquarters became the 6th Air Fleet on May 5, 1943. Greim was promoted to colonel general on February 16, 1943.

On April 24, 1945, Greim was summoned to Fuehrer Headquarters in Berlin, which was all but surrounded by the Red Army. Flying a Fiesler Storch (a light reconnaissance aircraft), he was severely wounded in the foot by Russian shrapnel and his copilot, Hanna Reitsch (who was also reportedly his lover), landed the airplane on an improvised airstrip in the Tiergarten, near the Brandenburg Gate, the next day. Hitler visited him while he was undergoing medical treatment and told him that Hermann Goering had committed treason. He, the Fuehrer, had stripped the Reichsmarschall of all of his offices; he then promoted the astonished Greim to field marshal and named him supreme commander of the Luftwaffe.

On April 28, Hitler ordered Greim and Reitsch to fly out of Berlin and to arrest Heinrich Himmler. They got away at the last possible moment—it was later reported that some of the Soviet infantrymen actually saw them take off from the Tiergarten and feared that Hitler was escaping. Neither Greim nor Reitsch wanted to escape, however; they wanted to die with the Fuehrer.

Greim's tenure as commander-in-chief of the Luftwaffe only lasted a few days. Hitler committed suicide on April 30 and the Third Reich surrendered on May 8. That same day, the Americans captured Greim in Austria. He committed suicide in a U.S. Army hospital in Salzburg on May 24, 1945. He is buried in the *Kommunal Friedhof* (cemetery) in Salzburg.

Greim had one son, Hubert, who became a fighter pilot and was reported as missing in action in Tunisia. Later it was learned that he had been shot down by a British Spitfire, but had managed to bail out behind enemy lines. He was captured and spent the rest of the war in a prisoner of war camp.

Heinz Guderian was relieved of his command (the Second Panzer Army) by Adolf Hitler for ordering an unauthorized retreat before Moscow on December 25, 1941, and held no further field commands. He was, however, inspector general of panzer troops (1943–44) and acting chief of the General Staff of the Army (July 21, 1944–March 28, 1945), a job for which he was intellectually and temperamentally unsuited. The outspoken Guderian was again relieved by Hitler after a bitter argument on March 28, 1945, and surrendered to the Western Allies in northern Italy the next month.

Guderian later wrote a book, *Panzer Leader*, which has been translated into many languages. Although it is a highly valuable historic document, it should be read very carefully and not every word should be accepted at face value. Guderian's alleged opposition to Hitler and the Nazis is a case in point: as chief of the General Staff, for example, he did nothing to prevent the spread of Nazi doctrine within the army—in fact, quite the opposite is true. Guderian's first order as chief of the General Staff was to outlaw the traditional army salute and to order the adoption of the Nazi (Hitler) salute in its place. He also acted to expel anti-Hitler conspirators from the army, so that they could be tried (and usually hanged) by civilian authorities. Despite this, however, Guderian was an outstanding field commander and a brilliant tactician and innovator. He died in Schwangau, Bavaria, on May 14, 1954, and is buried in Goslar.

Franz Halder's tenure only exceeded Brauchitsch's by a year. On September 24, 1942, as his armies in the east drove on Stalingrad and the Caucasus oilfields, Hitler fired Halder and replaced him with General of Infantry Kurt Zeitzler. One officer commented that the Fuehrer disposed of Halder as if he were a poodle who defecated on the carpet. Heartbroken, Franz Halder retired to Aschau, Bavaria, where the Gestapo arrested him on July 23, 1944, three days after the Stauffenberg assassination attempt failed. He was dismissed from the army on January 31, 1945, and was imprisoned in the cellar of the infamous Gestapo headquarters on Prince Albrecht Street. Later he was held in the Flossenberg and Dachau Concentration Camps.

Fortunately for him, his early association with the German resistance could not be sufficiently proven to justify his execution. As the U.S. Army approached, he and a number of other prominent prisoners were marched south by the SS, but, unlike Dietrich Boenhofer, Halder was not murdered. He was liberated by American forces at Niederdorf, South Tyrol (Italy) on May 5, 1945, five days after Adolf Hitler committed suicide.

Halder was held as a prisoner of war by the Americans, the British, and the Americans again. Released on June 30, 1947, he was immediately named chief liaison officer to the U.S. Army Historical Division's Military History Program at Koenigstein and Karlsruhe. He worked for the Americans until 1961, and even received the U.S. Meritorious Civilian Service Award for his efforts.

As a student in Bavaria, Halder had learned the Gabelsberger method of shorthand. It had been replaced by other stenographic methods, so that few people and none of his associates could read it. Halder therefore kept a detailed daily personal diary from his Reichsheer days (i.e., from about 1934). The diary eventually filled 12 large notebooks. Unfortunately, the first five disappeared during the war. The surviving seven covered the period from August 14, 1939 to September 24, 1942. Halder successfully hid them from Gestapo searches and eventually got them published in a three-volume set (1962–64).[3]

After Halder finished editing his war diaries, he retired to Aschau, where he died on April 2, 1972.

General of Artillery Christian Hansen commanded the X Corps until October 23, 1943, when Field Marshal von Kluge, the commander of Army Group Center, was seriously injured in an automobile crash. He was succeeded by Field Marshal Ernst Busch, the commander of the Sixteenth Army of Army Group North. Busch, in turn was replaced by Hansen.

Hansen led his army during the retreat from Leningrad, the Narva battles, and in the retreat through eastern Latvia. On July 3, 1944, he reported himself ill and was placed in the Fuehrer Reserve. He retired from the army on December 31, 1944, and settled in Garmisch-Partenkirchen, where he died on August 7, 1972.

General of Cavalry Erik Hansen led the LIV Corps on the Eastern Front until January 20, 1943, taking part in the conquest of the Crimea, the siege and capture of Sevastopol, and the Siege of Leningrad. He then returned to his old job as chief of the German Military Mission to Romania. He was a better corps commander than a military diplomat, because the Romanians fooled him completely. When they defected to the Soviets in August 1944 (after Hansen assured Fuehrer Headquarters that they would not), most of the German Sixth Army and part of the

Eighth Army were captured and Hansen was trapped in Bucharest. He was taken prisoner by the Russians on August 26, 1944, and remained in Soviet prisons until October 1955. Finally released, he returned to his hometown, where he died on March 18, 1967.

Friedrich Herrlein led the 18th Motorized Division until December 15, 1941, when he was placed in the Fuehrer Reserve, apparently because of illness and exhaustion. He became the acting General of Infantry at the OKH on February 22, 1942, and was promoted to lieutenant general on September 1, 1942. From May 15 to 25, 1943, he was acting commander of the XXVIII Corps on the northern sector of the Eastern Front. He then returned to Zossen, but on October 5, 1943, he became commander of the LV Corps on the central sector of the Eastern Front.

Promoted to general of infantry on February 1, 1944, he led the LV during Operation Bagration (where most of Army Group Center was destroyed) and in the retreat across Poland and into East Prussia. He was relieved of his command on February 6, 1945, and was placed in the Fuehrer Reserve, but was attached to Army Group South as a special duties officer in March. He was captured by the Western Allies on April 18, and remained in captivity until May 1948. He returned to Giessen (where he had previously commanded the 116th Infantry Regiment) and died there on July 28, 1974, at the age of 85.

Kurt Herzog's 291st Infantry Division fought in the Battle of Volkhov (January to March 1942), during which Stalin's winter offensive was blunted. He had proven to be an excellent trainer and division commander. In recognition of his abilities, he was promoted to general of artillery on July 1, 1942, and was given command of the XXXVIII Corps the same day. General Herzog led the corps for the rest of the war and fought in all of the major battles on the northern sector of the Eastern Front. He was on leave from January 9, 1945, probably to get his family to safety and out of the path of the Soviet juggernaut that was threatening to engulf his homeland in East Germany. He met with Hitler in Berlin on January 12, where he was decorated with the Oak Leaves to his Knight's Cross. (He had received his Knight's Cross in October 1941.) He returned to command on March 15. Meanwhile, for reasons the records do not make clear, his corps was redesignated the XXXVIII

Motorized in January. As of the end of February, however, it did not have a single tank unit under its command. In any case, Herzog continued to do an excellent job as corps commander until the end of the war.

Since Army Group North (now Courland) was isolated in eastern Latvia, Herzog had no chance to escape Soviet captivity when the Third Reich capitulated. He surrendered the XXXVIII Corps to the Red Army on May 8, 1945.

General Herzog spent the rest of his life in Soviet prison camps. He died in Camp Vorkuta on May 8, 1948.

Erich Hoepner led the Fourth Panzer Army until January 8, 1942. Faced with bitter cold and overwhelming odds, he ordered an unauthorized retreat. Kluge informed Hitler, who relieved Hoepner of his command for "cowardice and disobedience." He revoked Hoepner's right to wear the uniform and his medals and stripped him of his pension. Hoepner demanded a court-martial. In early 1942, the military courts still worked, at least to a degree, so Hitler was faced with a choice: allow a court-martial or restore Hoepner's rights and pension. With typical bad grace, the Fuehrer chose the latter. He had, however, earned Hoepner's undying hatred.

On July 20, 1944, Erich Hoepner was named commander-in-chief of the Replacement Army by the conspirators who had seized the Bendlerstrasse (Nazi Germany's equivalent of the Pentagon). When he saw that the coup was falling apart, Hoepner dressed down Stauffenberg and his confederates and refused to have anything else to do with the conspiracy. It was too late, however. Hoepner was arrested that very night, expelled from the army, and sentenced to death by the People's Court on August 7. He was stripped naked and hanged with piano wire the next day.

Hermann Hoth commanded the Seventeenth Army on the Eastern Front until May 15, 1942, when he assumed command of the Fourth Panzer Army. In late 1942 and early 1943, the remnants of the Fourth Romanian Army were under his command as well. Hitler, however, grew angry at Hoth for taking too realistic a view of Germany's strategic situation in the East and sacked him on November 30, 1943. He was not re-employed until April 1945, when he was named commander of the

Harz Mountains sector. It was now too late to do anything significant, however, and Hoth surrendered to the Americans on May 8. A defendant in the High Command trial at Nuremberg in 1948, he was found guilty and sentenced to 15 years' imprisonment on October 27, 1948. He was incarcerated at Landsberg, where Hitler was confined in 1924.

Released on April 7, 1954, Hoth retired to Goslar, Lower Saxony, at the foot of the Harz Mountains. Here he wrote his memoirs, *Panzer-©operationen*, which were published in 1954. He died on January 25, 1971, after a lengthy illness. General Hoth is buried in Goslar, where Heinz Guderian is also buried.

Kurt Jahn commanded the 3rd Motorized Division on the Eastern Front until April 22, 1942, when he returned to Germany. On May 1, he assumed command of the 233rd Motorized Replacement Division at Frankfurt/Oder. After a brief detachment to the Reichs War Courts in February 1943, he was placed in the Fuehrer Reserve on March 1, but was recalled to active duty on March 15, as commander of the static 709th Infantry Division in Normandy. This would seem to be a serious demotion for a man who previously commanded a motorized division with such success, and indeed the 3rd Motorized Division would be the most important command he held during the war. All of this suggests that he ran afoul of someone in the High Command or in the powerful Army Personnel Office, although I have been unable to verify this opinion. In any case, on July 1, 1943, he was placed in charge of the 308th Higher Artillery Command (Harko 308), consisting mainly of horse-drawn artillery units, which supported the Second Army on the Eastern Front. He led Harko 308 until March 1, 1944.

Jahn was detached to the Headquarters, Army Group Center, on March 10, 1944, and served as acting commander of the 18th Panzer Grenadier Division (April 14 to May 24, 1944) and of the 12th Infantry Division (May 25–June 4, 1944) on the central sector of the Eastern Front. This was the seventh division-level command he had held during the war. He was then detached to the War Academy (now at Hirschberg in the Sudetenland), where he took a month-long Course for Commanding Generals, which, at this point in the war, was taken by prospective corps commanders.

Sent to Italy, he was acting commander of Army Detachment von Zangen (July 8 to 31, 1944). He was apparently without an assignment until September 1, when he became commander of the German-Italian Corps Lombardi, a rear-area command of third- and fourth-class units. Although it was one of the poorer corps available, it nevertheless qualified him for promotion. He became a general of artillery on October 1, 1944.

General Jahn surrendered to the British west of Mailand, Baden-Wuerrtemberg, on May 1, 1945, and was a prisoner of war until March 25, 1948. Following his release, he settled in Coburg, Upper Franconia, where he passed away on November 7, 1966.

Wilhelm Keitel remained at his post as commander-in-chief of the High Command of the Armed Forces until the end of the war. He was slightly wounded in the July 20, 1944 attempt on Hitler's life. He signed the instruments of surrender to the Soviets in Berlin on May 9, 1945. Four days later, he was relieved of his duties and arrested by U.S. Major General Lowell W. Rooks, Eisenhower's delegate to the Doenitz government. Keitel was initially confined on the *Patria* in Flensburg-Muerwik, but was moved to the Palace Hotel in Mondorf, Luxembourg, and eventually to Nuremberg, where he was tried as a war criminal. Here he wrote his memoirs, which are historically both interesting and valuable. He did not have time to complete them, however. He was hanged on October 16, 1946.

Alfred "Bomber" Keller led the 1st Air Fleet on the Eastern Front until June 25, 1943. He then went into the Fuehrer Reserve for the rest of the war. Unlike most officers with this status, however, he was not unemployed; rather, he took charge of the National Socialist Flying Corps (NSFK), which provided air cadets with basic ground and flight training. This was critical to the German Air Force because it had sent its training wings into battle from the first day of the war, and the training command was now on the verge of collapse. Keller did as well as he could, but was severely handicapped by a fuel shortage, which grew worse as the war progressed. He surrendered to the British at Luebeck on May 2, 1945. He was released in 1947 and died in Berlin on February 11, 1974.

Georg Keppler commanded the 3rd SS Motorized Division until September 29, when Theodor Eicke (who had partially recovered from his wounds) returned. Keppler was named temporary commander the "Nord" SS Division, but fell ill with a brain tumor. He was not able to return to duty until the spring of 1942, when he assumed command of the 2nd SS Panzer Grenadier Division "Das Reich," which was rebuilding in France. Keppler's tumor flared up again and he was hospitalized or on medical leave from February until the end of August 1943. When he returned to active duty, Keppler was named commander of the Waffen-SS District Bohemia and Movaria. From April to September 1944, he was commander of Waffen-SS in Hungary. Meanwhile, he was promoted to SS lieutenant general (April 1, 1942) and general of Waffen-SS (June 21, 1944).

Keppler temporarily replaced Sepp Dietrich as commander of the I SS Panzer Corps in France from August 16 to October 24, 1944. He then led the III (*germanisches*) SS Panzer Corps on the Eastern Front from October 30, 1944 to February 4, 1945. He assumed command of the XVIII SS Corps on February 12 and led it until the end of the war, surrendering to the Americans on May 22, 1945. A POW until April 1948, he settled in Hamburg, where he ran a chemist shop. He died in Hamburg on June 16, 1966.

Albert Kesselring's Headquarters, 2nd Air Fleet, redeployed to Italy in November and December 1941. Here Kesselring became Supreme Commander, South (OB South) and was charged with the tasks of supporting the Italians and resupplying Erwin Rommel's Panzer Army Afrika. An incurable optimist, he supported Hitler's "hold at all cost" policy, which led to the fall of Tunisia and the loss of 230,000 German and Italian soldiers in May 1943. He later forced the commander of the Italian Sixth Army to scatter his mobile (German) reserves all over Sicily, which resulted in another Axis defeat in July. His defense of Italy (1943–45), however, was often masterful.

Kesselring was seriously injured on October 23, 1944, when his automobile rear-ended a heavy artillery piece. He later laughed that the soldiers in Italy joked that the field marshal's head would heal, but the gun was a total write-off. He underwent emergency brain surgery and could not return to duty until January 14, 1945. On March 9, he replaced *Generalfeldmarschall* von Rundstedt as OB West. "I am the new V-3," he announced to his staff when he assumed command, but there was little he could do to restore the disastrous situation. He surrendered to an American major near Salzburg, Austria, on May 6, 1945.

Kesselring generally conducted the war in Italy as humanely as possible. He tried to preserve Rome, Florence, the Arno River bridges, Monte Cassino, and other cultural landmarks. On the other hand, although he was not a Nazi, Kesselring was definitely a Nazi sympathizer. After the war, he was tried for his part in the Ardeatine Massacre, in which 335 Italian civilians were shot in reprisal for a partisan attack that killed 42 German and Italian soldiers and policemen. He was found guilty on May 7, 1947, and was sentenced to death. Churchill, however, immediately declared the sentence too harsh and secretly interceded on his behalf. Two months later, Kesselring's sentence was commuted to life imprisonment and, after contracting throat cancer, he was released from prison on October 23, 1952. He had already been elected president of the *Stahlheim* (Steel Helmut), a neo-Nazi veterans' organization.

The last years of his life were marred by ill health. His relationship with his wife, however, improved after the death of his mother-in-law. Luise Anna Kesselring died in 1957. The field marshal passed away in Bad Nauheim, Hesse, on July 15, 1960. His tombstone records only his name, rank, and years of birth and death.

Eberhard Kinzel, the chief of Foreign Armies East, was fired by General Halder on May 1, 1942. Halder relieved him without prejudice, however, so Kinzel remained on the General Staff and was named chief of staff of the XXIX Corps at the end of the month. His corps was used to steady the unreliable Italian Eighth Army on the southern sector of the Eastern Front. He held this post until November 12, when he went into the Fuehrer Reserve, where he remained for more than two months. He was promoted to major general on January 1, 1943. On January 12, he was named chief of staff of Army Group North, thus bypassing several more senior officers. He held this post until July 18, 1944, and did very well. He even satisfied the extremely difficult Field Marshal Model. Kinzel was promoted to lieutenant general on September 1, 1943.

The Eastern Territories
under German Rule
September 1942

BALTIC SEA

Leningrad

N

Riga

REICHKOMMISSARIAT
OSTLAND

Moscow

Vyazma

REICH

Smolensk

Minsk

MILITARY AREA

Bialystok

Warsaw

Brest-Litovsk

Lublin

Rovno

REICHKOMMISSARIAT UKRAINE

Kiev

Lvov

Kharkov

HUNGARY

TRANSNISTRIA

Rostov

RUMANIA

Odessa

SEA of
AZOV

MILITARY

AREA

Bucharest

BLACK SEA

After a long rest, Eberhard Kinzel assumed command of the 570th Volksgrenadier Division, then forming in the Gross-Born Troop Maneuver Area, on September 1, 1944. This unit included the remnants of the 57th, 113th, and 337th Infantry Divisions, which had been partially destroyed on the Eastern Front. The 570th, which was redesignated the 337th Volksgrenadier Division on September 15, was sent to the Eastern Front. He fought in the battles around Warsaw, on the Vistula, and against the Red Army's breakout from the Baranov Bridgehead. The 337th Volksgrenadier was virtually destroyed near Danzig in February 1945. Kinzel was ordered to withdraw his division to West Prussia, where it was disbanded. Kinzel himself, however, received a new assignment: chief of staff of Army Group Vistula. He took up this post on March 3, 1945, and was promoted to general of infantry on April 20, Hitler's last birthday.

On April 22, as the Allies were on the verge of cutting Germany in two, Kinzel was named chief of staff of Operations Staff North under Grand Admiral Karl Doenitz. He was part of the German delegation to Montgomery's Twenty-first Army Group and was part of the surrender negotiations at Reims. The Allies dissolved the Doenitz government on May 23, 1945. Rather than go into captivity, General Kinzel committed suicide that same day.

Friedrich Kirchner was wounded on July 17 and did not return to active duty until October 14, 1941, when he became commander of the XXXXI Motorized Corps, temporarily replacing Walter Model. When Model returned to duty on November 15, Kirchner was given command of the LVII Motorized (later Panzer) Corps, which was then part of the Fourth Army on the central sector of the Eastern Front. He was promoted to general of panzer troops on February 1, 1942.

Kirchner was considered a good corps commander but not an army-level leader; therefore, the Army Personnel Office simply left him where he was for the rest of the war. His corps was transferred to the southern sector of the Eastern Front in the spring of 1942, and he fought in the Caucasus, at Rostov, Stalino and Kharkov, in the Donetz, in the Dnieper battles, at Pruth, and in Hungary and Silesia. He surrendered to the U.S. Army on May 8, 1945. Released from the POW camps in 1947, he retired to Fulda, in the province of Hesse, where he died on April 6, 1960.

Ewald von Kleist's First Panzer Group became First Panzer Army on January 1, 1942. Kleist continued to command it until November 22, 1942, when he was named commander-in-chief of Army Group A. Meanwhile, he tolerated no excesses from the SS or the Nazis in his area of command. Largely for that reason, he was very successful in recruiting anti-Soviet citizens into the German military; later, an entire Cossack cavalry corps was organized from his recruits. His campaigns in the Caucasus and the Kuban and the retreat to the Crimea show that he was a very gifted general and tactician. Hitler nevertheless sacked him on March 30, 1944, along with Field Marshal von Manstein. Hitler treated both men kindly, but neither was ever re-employed.

Kleist was investigated for anti-Nazi activities in 1944. It was determined that, although he did not take part in the July 20, 1944 assassination attempt, he knew about it and did not report it, as by law he should have done. The Nazis, however, decided that it would not be in their interests to put such a highly respected field marshal on trial, especially after the suicide of Ludwig Beck and the executions of Field Marshal Erwin von Witzleben and Erich Hoepner, so they let the matter drop.

Ewald von Kleist remained at Wiedebrueck until early 1945, when the Red Army invaded Silesia and neared Breslau. The field marshal and his wife emigrated to the tiny village of Mitterfels in Lower Bavaria, while Kleist's oldest son blew up Wiedebrueck, to prevent it falling into the hands of the Russians.

Field Marshal von Kleist was captured by the U.S. 26th Infantry Division on April 25, 1945. Extradited to Yugoslavia, where he was sentenced to 25 years' imprisonment after a very questionable trial, he was later handed over to the Soviets. He died of "general arteriosclerosis and hypertension" in Vladmir Prison on October 15, 1954. Two years later, his oldest son was released from prison in Silesia. He died in 1976. Gisela von Kleist died in West Germany in 1958, and Kleist's youngest son passed away in 1973. At last report, Kleist had 11 grandchildren, but he never saw one of them. He is buried in Russia in an unmarked grave.

When the German Army stalled before Moscow, Hans von Kluge was given command of Army Group Center on December 18, 1941, replacing Fedor von Bock. Here he demonstrated a talent for political survival, escaping blame for disasters, and finding scapegoats. Among others, he played a direct role in the removal of Colonel General Adolf Strauss, the commander of the Ninth Army, Colonel General Erich Hoepner, the commander of the Fourth Panzer Army, and General of Mountain Troops Ludwig Kuebler, who had succeeded him as commander of the Fourth Army. Most notably, he secured the dismissal of his old enemy, Colonel General Heinz Guderian, the "Father of the Blitzkrieg," who commanded the Second Panzer Army in Russia and who was relieved on December 25, 1941. (Guderian had once challenged Kluge to a duel.)

Largely thanks to General Model, the commander of the Ninth Army, Kluge managed to stabilize the German line in early 1942. Later that year, he conducted a brilliant deception campaign, and convinced the Soviets (including Stalin) that the German main offensive that summer would be directed at Moscow. It was, in fact, aimed at the Volga, Stalingrad and the Caucasus oil fields.

Kluge led the Fourth Army until October 28, 1943, when his car skidded on some ice and overturned, and he was seriously injured. He did not return to active duty for eight months. On July 2, 1944, he succeeded Gerd von Rundstedt as OB West, which included Army Group B, then fighting in Normandy. Kluge did not interfere with Rommel's conduct of operations in Normandy, but when Rommel was critically wounded on July 17, Kluge assumed the post of commander-in-chief of Army Group B himself, because he was afraid Hitler might appoint SS Colonel General Paul Hausser to the vacancy. (Hitler had named Hausser commander of the Seventh Army in Normandy over Rommel's objections.) Kluge knew Hausser from their days as cadets at Gross Lichterfelde and had little respect for his abilities. Subsequent events proved this to be a correct view.

Known throughout the Officers' Corps as "Clever Hans," Kluge was on both sides of the anti-Hitler conspiracy. After the July 20, 1944 as-sassination attempt failed, he was very frightened that Hitler and the Nazis would find out about him, and was desperate not to appear disloyal to the Fuehrer, who was indeed by now very suspicious of him. During the night of July 20, he sacked anti-Hitler conspirator General of Infantry Carl Heinrich von Stuelpnagel, the military governor of

France, and ordered him to release the SS and Gestapo agents he had arrested. Stuelpnagel was temporarily replaced by General Blumentritt, Kluge's OB West chief of staff.

On July 25, the Allies devastated the Panzer Lehr Division with a massive aerial bombardment. Kluge was slow to react and the Allies achieved their breakthrough. Kluge now blindly followed Hitler's orders, hoping to prove himself loyal to the Fuehrer. In accordance with Hitler's instructions, Kluge launched an unsuccessful series of counterattacks against the U.S. First Army near Mortain in the west, while Patton's U.S. Third Army and Montgomery's Twenty-first Army Group maneuvered to encircle Army Group B to the east. This encirclement was completed on August 19.

Meanwhile, on August 15, Kluge set out to visit Hausser's Seventh Army Command Post and disappeared. He was pinned down all day by Allied fighter-bombers and his communications truck was destroyed, but Hitler, who was now thoroughly paranoid, was convinced that Kluge was negotiating a secret surrender with the Allies. He ordered Field Marshal Model to assume command of OB West and Army Group B. Model arrived at Kluge's headquarters on the evening of August 17, with a letter relieving Kluge of his command and ordering him to report to Berlin. Kluge knew what that meant. On August 19, on his way back to Germany, he stopped at Metz, the scene of some of his World War I battles, spread out a blanket, and ordered his driver to leave him. He then took a cyanide capsule. Hitler ordered that he be buried quietly, with military pallbearers but without military honors. (His grave has since been destroyed.) Within three weeks, he forced Kluge's brother (a lieutenant general) and his son (a lieutenant colonel) into retirement. The Propaganda Ministry, meanwhile, officially attributed Kluge's death to a cerebral hemorrhage.

Otto von Knobelsdorff fell ill and, on January 4, 1942, gave up command of the 19th Panzer Division and was sent to the hospital in Bad Gastein. He returned to active duty on May 1, 1942, as commander of the X Corps on the northern sector of the Eastern Front. On June 1, he assumed temporary command of the II Corps at Demyansk, and on July 1 took charge of the ad hoc Corps von Knobelsdorff. He was promoted to general of panzer troops on August 1, 1942, and on October 10 became commander of the XXIV Panzer Corps, which was then heavily engaged in the Don sector, supporting the Hungarian Second Army and Army Group B. On November 30, Knobelsdorff assumed command of the XXXXVIII Motorized Corps, which he led until October 9, 1943, when he was reported as being severely ill. (He actually suffered a bit of a nervous breakdown and flew to Fuehrer Headquarters, where he told Hitler that he must make peace, or Germany would be overrun by the Russians.)

He did not return to active duty until February 1, 1944, when he took charge of the XXXX Panzer Corps on the southern sector of the Eastern Front. Here he fought in the retreat from the Dnieper and the fighting around Jassy, Romania, before he and his staff were sent to Lithuania. He fought on the East Prussian border but, on September 30, 1944, returned to France as the commander of the First Army. Hitler fired him on November 30 because he could not halt the Americans and because he objected to being stripped of his armor, which Hitler wanted for his Ardennes Offensive.

Otto von Knobelsdorff was captured by the U.S. Army on April 6, 1945, and was a POW until his release on December 21, 1947. He settled in Hanover, where he wrote a history of the 19th Infantry/Panzer Division. He died on October 21, 1966.

Erich Koch, the Reichskommissar of the Ukraine, escaped to East Prussia (where he was still Gauleiter) in 1944. He escaped East Prussia aboard his private yacht at the end of the war and went into hiding, but was finally captured by the British around May 1949. They extradited him to Poland, where he was sentenced to death in 1959. The Poles did not execute him, however, reportedly because he was seriously ill. (Rumors persist that Koch agreed to reveal the location of certain art treasures in exchange for his life, but this has never been proven.) Koch died in his cell 27 years later, on November 12, 1986, at the age of 90.

After the war with the Soviet Union began, Ernst-August Koestring, the military attaché to Moscow, returned to Germany via neutral states. He was promptly placed in Fuehrer Reserve, where he remained until August 1942. He was then attached to Army Group A (no doubt at the request of Colonel General Ewald von Kleist) as a special duties officer, where he dealt with Caucasus questions. Like Kleist, he was deeply involved in recruiting non-Russian peoples into the German Army and sometimes in forming them into units. This was somewhat against Hitler's policies, but they raised several Cossack cavalry formations and other "Eastern" battalions. He remained with Kleist until June 1943, when he became inspector for Turkish (*Turkvolk*) formations.

On January 1, 1944, he was named chief of volunteer formations with the Replacement Army and general of volunteer formations with the OKH. He gave up the former appointment in late November 1944 (after Himmler became commander of the Replacement Army) but was general of volunteer formations with the OKH until the end of the war. He surrendered to the Western Allies on May 4, 1945 and, somewhat remarkably, was not turned over to the Soviets. He was released from prison in 1947 and died in Unterwoessen, Upper Bavaria, on November 20, 1953.

Hans Krebs, the deputy military attache´ to Moscow, was temporarily interned on June 22, 1941, and returned to Germany via neutral states. He was on the staff of the OKH from July to January 1942. On January 14, he became chief of staff to Ninth Army and General Walter Model, which began a relationship which lasted almost until the end of the war. Krebs became chief of staff of Army Group Center on March 1, 1943, and followed Model to the Western Front on September 1, 1944, when he became chief of staff of Army Group B. He returned to Zossen as chief of the operations staff of the General Staff on February 17, 1945. He was severely wounded in an American bomber attack on Zossen, but when Hitler fired Guderian on March 15, he was appointed chief of the General Staff. He was meanwhile promoted to major general (February 1, 1942), lieutenant general (April 1, 1943), and general of infantry (August 1, 1944).

Krebs was the last chief of the General Staff. Hitler committed suicide on April 30, and Krebs played a role in the initial surrender negotiations with the Russians. Rather than fall into Soviet captivity, however, he shot himself in the head at 9:30 p.m. on May 1, 1945.

Walter Krueger commanded the 1st Panzer Division from July 17, 1941 to January 1, 1944, fighting in the Battle of Moscow and the Rzhev Salient, among other battles. He was promoted to lieutenant general on

October 1, 1942, and took the remnants of his command back to France to rebuild in December. He was then transferred back to the Balkans and then Greece, and finally to the Ukraine and the southern sector of the Eastern Front. On January 1, 1944, he was given command of the LVIII Panzer Corps, and was promoted to general of panzer troops on February 1. He led in southern France, Normandy, in the Luneville debacle, in the Eifel, the Ardennes offensive, and in the defense of the Roer.

Hitler held him partially responsible for the American breach of the Rhine, so Krueger was relieved of his command on March 25, 1945. On April 10, however, after Hitler had cooled down, he was named commander of Wehrkreis IV in Dresden. Krueger escaped the city before it fell to the Red Army and, with his staff and a few fourth-class units, surrendered to the Americans on May 10. He was released from the POW camps on June 26, 1947 and died in Baden-Baden on July 11, 1973.

General of Panzer Troops Adolf Kuntzen commanded the LVII Motorized Corps in Russia (1941) and the LXXXI Corps in France until September 4, 1944, when he was sacked for poor performance during the retreat to Germany. The charges were completely justified. Rather than trying to concentrate his forces, as he was ordered to do, Kuntzen threw his reinforcements into battle against General Patton's advance as soon as they arrived, and they were quickly destroyed. As a result of this piecemeal employment, his reinforcements were lost without even slowing up the famous American general. As a result, Kuntzen's career was ruined and he was never re-employed. He officially retired on December 31, 1944, and died at Hanover, Lower Saxony (*Niedersachsen*) on July 10, 1964.

Franz Landgraf led the 6th Panzer Division until November 23, 1941, when he fell ill due to stress and exhaustion. He returned to Germany and was in Fuehrer Reserve until May 1, 1942, when he assumed command of the Wuerttemberger-Baden 155th Motorized Replacement Division at Ludwigsburg. Landgraf was promoted to lieutenant general on September 1, 1942, and his command was upgraded to a panzer replacement division on August 1, 1943. He held his command until September 30, when he stepped down due to illness. His health continued to decline and he died in Stuttgart on April 19, 1944.[4]

Baron Willibald von Langermann und Erlenkamp was named commander of the XXIV Motorized (later Panzer) Corps on the Eastern Front on January 8, 1942, followed a week later by a promotion to lieutenant general. He became a general of panzer troops on June 1, 1942, fought in the Don campaign, and was killed in action during the Battle of Stalingrad on October 3, 1942.

Paul Laux commanded the 126th Infantry Division until November 28, 1942, when he assumed command of the II Corps on the northern sector of the Eastern Front. He was promoted to general of infantry December 1, 1942. He did a brilliant job evacuating the Demyansk Salient in 1943. He proved to be such an excellent corps commander that he was named commander of the Sixteenth Army of Army Group North on July 3, 1944. On August 29, he boarded a Friesler Storch and went out on a reconnaissance mission. He was shot down and critically wounded. The general was evacuated back to the military hospital at Riga, where doctors were unable to save his life. He succumbed on September 2, 1944.

The winter offensive in the sector of Wilhelm von Leeb's Army Group North began on January 7, 1942. It was ill-coordinated, but the weight of 11 Soviet armies against 31 exhausted German divisions, some of which were still in summer uniforms, brought the Soviets some success. By January 13, General Vlasov's elite Second Shock Army had broken through the Sixteenth Army on a 20-mile front between Novgorod and Chudovo and forced its way across the Volkhov. Temperatures in the northern sector now dropped as low as -49 degrees Fahrenheit. Leeb was losing thousands of men to frostbite and wounded soldiers were freezing to death by the score due to lack of blankets. The marshal committed his last reserves, but still the Reds continued to gain ground. Headquarters, 281st Security Division (under Lieutenant General Theodor Scherer) was on the verge of being surrounded at Kholm with 5,500 men, and the II Corps (General Count von Brockdorff-Ahlefeldt) and elements of the II Corps were threatened with encirclement at Demyansk.

On January 12, Leeb asked permission to pull the II Corps back and conduct a general retreat to the Lovat River. Hitler refused to abandon

Demyansk, because he believed that such salients tied down more Russians than Germans. Leeb, who by now was wondering aloud if Hitler and Stalin were not secretly allied against the German Army, refused to accept this reasoning. On January 16, he asked to be relieved of his command. He was replaced the next day by Colonel General von Kuechler. General of Cavalry Georg Lindemann assumed command of the Eighteenth Army.

Leeb retired to Hohenschwangau, Bavaria, where he was captured by American forces on May 2, 1945. He was the principal defendant in the OKW Trials at Nuremberg, which focused on German war crimes in Russia, especially the abuse of forced labor, the murder and mistreatment of Soviet POWs, and the Commissar Order, in which Hitler had ordered that Soviet political officers be executed without trial. The American court found little evidence against the morally upright Leeb, who had refused to cooperate with the SS murder squads (and had ordered his generals not to do so) or to mistreat prisoners. The court had to find him guilty for political reasons, but sentenced him to only three years imprisonment. Since he was given credit for time served, and had already served more than three years, he was released immediately. He returned to Hohenschwangau, where he died on April 29, 1956.

Joachim Lemelsen led the XXXXVII Motorized (later Panzer) Corps in Russia until October 1943, despite being wounded in the summer of 1942. He was acting commander of the Tenth Army in Italy (November 1 to December 31, 1943), commander of the Sixth Army in Russia (March 5 to May 1944), commander of the First Army in France (May 10 to June 5, 1944), Fourteenth Army in Italy (June 5 to October 15, 1944), Tenth Army again (October 24, 1944 to February 15, 1945), and Fourteenth Army in Italy (February 22 to May 2, 1945). A pro-Nazi, Lemelsen was an excellent motorized divisional commander and did well leading panzers in Russia. He was less successful as an army commander in Italy, although he did not perform badly. A British prisoner of war from May 6, 1945 until April 10, 1948, he died in Goettingen, Lower Saxony, on March 30, 1954.

Ernst von Leyser continued to lead the 269th Infantry Division on the Eastern Front, fighting in Courland, in the drive on and Siege of

Leningrad, and at Lake Ladoga. He gave up command of the division on August 31, 1942, and probably went on leave; he was promoted to lieutenant general on October 1. He assumed command of the XXVI Corps on November 1, 1942, and led it until November 1, 1943, spending the entire period engaged in the Siege of Leningrad, and receiving his promotion to general of infantry on December 1, 1942. He then was posted to the Balkans, where he commanded the XV Mountain Corps against partisans in Croatia. On July 20, 1944, he assumed command of the XXI Mountain Corps (also in Croatia), which he led until the end of the war. He surrendered to the Americans on May 8, 1945, but was accused of war crimes. He was tried at Nuremberg from May 1947 to February 19, 1948, in the Southeast Generals Case (also called Case VII). Found guilty, he was sentenced to ten years in prison, but was released on February 3, 1951. He died on September 23, 1962 in Garstedt, a town near Harburg in Lower Saxony.

Baron Kurt von Liebenstein was chief of staff of the Second Panzer Army until May 25, 1942. He assumed command of the 6th Panzer Regiment of the 3rd Panzer Division on June 20, and led it in the battles around Kharkov, and in the drive across the Don and into the Caucasus. He was named commander of the 3rd Panzer Grenadier Brigade of the 3rd Panzer Division in October 1942, but held the post only two weeks, as the brigade was dissolved on November 8.

Now an excess officer, Baron von Liebenstein went on leave for about five weeks and was then given command of the 164th Light Africa Division. He took charge on December 12, 1942, and led the division in the final retreats from Libya and in the Tunisian battles, mostly against the British Eighth Army. He was injured in an automobile accident on February 17, 1943, but was able to resume command of the division on March 13. He had been promoted to major general on March 1, 1943, while he was still on injured leave. He led the 164th Light, was awarded the Knight's Cross on May 10, 1943, and surrendered three days later.

In the POW camps, General von Liebenstein was noted for his sense of humor and his ability as an artist. His watercolors were said to be quite good. He was repatriated in 1947 and returned to Germany. When the West German Army (the *Bundesheer*) was created in 1956, he was appointed major general (equivalent to lieutenant general on the old World War II scale), and was named commander of Wehrkreis V, which was headquartered in Stuttgart. He retired on September 30, 1960, but remained in Stuttgart until his death on August 3, 1975.

Alexander Loehr commanded the 4th Air Fleet on the Eastern Front until July 1, 1942, when he was replaced by Wolfram von Richthofen. Loehr assumed command of the Twelfth Army in the Balkans the next day. In order to give him a promotion of sorts, this command was upgraded to Army Group E on January 1, 1943, and Loehr was commander-in-chief, Southeast (OB Southeast) until August 1943, when he was superceded by Field Marshal Rommel (for one day) and then by Field Marshal Baron Maximilian von Weichs. Loehr commanded Army Group E (which was really an army, not an army group, for most of his tenure) until the end of the war. Colonel General Loehr was handed over to the Yugoslavs on May 15, 1945, and was tried as a war criminal for the mass murders of Yugoslav civilians. After a show trial, he was sentenced to death by firing squad and was executed on February 26, 1947.

Heinrich Lohse, the Reichskommissar of Ostland, fled the area when the Red Army invaded it in 1944 and returned to Kiel, the capital of Schleswig-Holstein, where he was still Gauleiter. He was removed from office by Grand Admiral Karl Doenitz, the president of the Reich, on May 6, 1945, at the request of the British. He was arrested shortly thereafter and was tried as a minor war criminal in 1948. Found guilty, he was sentenced to ten years' imprisonment. He was released due to illness in 1951 and returned to his hometown of Muehlenbarbek, where he died on February 25, 1964.

Despite Bernhard von Lossberg's outstanding abilities as a military planner, Hitler never forgave Lossberg for correcting him vis-à∅-vis the evacuation of Narvik in April 1940. The fact that events proved Lossberg right and Hitler wrong aggravated the dictator even further. As a result, when Hitler sacked Brauchitsch, he got rid of the deputy chief of operations of the OKW at the same time. He sent Lossberg back to Norway, which was by now a distinctly backwater theater, as Ia (chief of operations) of the Army of Norway. Despite the fact that he was promoted to colonel on January 1, 1942, he spent the rest of his career in obscure, secondary theaters.

In Lossberg's periodic fitness reports, Falkenhorst and his chief of staff, Lt. Gen. Rudolf Bamber, praised Lossberg as having above average operational talents. Falkenhorst, however, had long since lost what influence he had ever had with Fuehrer Headquarters and the OKW, and his recommendation that Lossberg be employed at the front as a higher liaison officer to Germany's allied field forces was ignored.[5] Lossberg spent the rest of his career in obscure assignments.

He finally left Norway in April 1944 to assume the post of chief of staff to *Generaladmiral* Wilhelm Marschall's Special Staff Danube River, which led to his promotion to major general on September 1, 1944. In January 1945, he was named chief of staff of Wehrkreis VIII in Breslau. His commander was General of Cavalry Rudolf Koch-Erpach. When the Red Army overran Silesia later that month, the military district ceased operations and its headquarters was surrounded in Breslau. The general and his staff flew out of the pocket and, on February 26, 1945, Koch-Erpach was named commander of the LVI Motorized Corps, which had recently been decimated on the Eastern Front. Koch apparently intended to retain Lossberg as his chief of staff, but General of Infantry Wilhelm Burgdorf, the strongly Nazi chief of the powerful Army Personnel Office (HPA), had other ideas. Lossberg was replaced by Colonel Theoderich von Dufving on March 10, and Koch himself was succeeded by General of Artillery Helmuth Weidling on April 21.

Bernhard von Lossberg spent the rest of the war in the Fuehrer Reserve (i.e., he was unemployed). He was captured by British forces at Neustadt, Holstein, on May 5, 1945. Repatriated in July 1946, he wrote a memoir, *Im Wehrmachtfuehrungsstab: Bericht eines Generalstabsoffiziers* (In the Armed Forces Operations Staff: Report of a General Staff Officer). He retired to Wiesbaden, where he died on March 15, 1965.

Erich von Manstein led Eleventh Army (1941–42) and Army Groups Don (later South) (1942–44) on the Eastern Front with astonishing success, and was promoted to field marshal on July 1, 1942, after he overran the Soviet naval fortress at Sevastopol and completed the conquest of the Crimea. His eldest son, Lieutenant Gero von Manstein, who was born on New Year's Eve, 1922, was killed in action on the northern sector of the Eastern Front on October 29, 1942.

Field Marshal von Manstein and Field Marshal Ewald von Kleist were sacked by Hitler on March 31, 1944. Neither was ever re-employed. After the war, Manstein was tried by a British military court in Germany and in late 1948 was sentenced to 18 years imprisonment as a war criminal. Manstein may have been guilty, but his trial was hardly fair, since the prosecution was allowed to change the charges after the defense rested. He was released from prison in May 1953 and died in Irschenhausen, Bavaria, on June 12, 1973, at the age of 85.

Erich Marcks assumed command of the 101st Jaeger Division on December 10, 1940. He was promoted to lieutenant general on March 1, 1941, and led this division into Russia on June 22, 1941, but four days later was seriously wounded. His left leg had to be amputated and he spent the next nine months in hospitals or on convalescent leave. It was the fifth wound of his career.

Following the amputation of his leg, General Marcks did not return to active duty until March 25, 1942, when he became commander of the 337th Infantry Division in France. Later he assumed command of the LXVI Reserve Corps (September 20, 1942), LXXXVII Corps (October 1, 1942) and LXXXIV Corps (August 1, 1943), all in the west. He was promoted to general of artillery on October 1, 1942.

At midnight in Normandy on June 5/6, 1944, General Marcks' staff presented him with a cake and they celebrated his 53rd birthday. The party was brief, because Marcks already suspected that the D-Day invasion would land that day and in his sector. He was right, but Field Marshal Rommel was back home in Germany and Marcks could not get higher headquarters to believe that the Allies had come in such foul weather. He nevertheless fought a tremendous battle against the Allies; in fact, he was the only senior German general on June 6 who did not make a serious mistake.

Marcks fought the Anglo-Saxon advance through the hedgerow country of western Normandy. Here, west of Caen on June 12, his car was attacked by an American fighter-bomber. He reportedly was critically wounded but would not allow his aide to pull him from the car. Knowing that Germany was doomed, he cried: "No. It is better this way." He was killed when the airplane made a second pass and strafed the car again.

Gerhard Matzky held the post of *Oberquartiermeister IV* (O Qu IV) until November 1942, after which he went on leave. On January 10, 1943, he assumed command of the East and West Prussian 21st Infantry Division of the Eighteenth Army, which he led in the Siege of Leningrad and the subsequent retreat to the Narva. On March 28, 1944, he was named acting commander of the XXVIII Corps, replacing Herbert Loch, who had moved up to command of the Eighteenth Army. Matzky became commander of the XXVI Corps on July 6, 1944. He was promoted to general of infantry on September 4. He had been promoted to major general on April 20, 1941, and to lieutenant general on April 20, 1943.

General Matzky led the XXVI in the battles in Lithuania and the bitter fighting in East Prussia. He and his headquarters were evacuated back to northern Germany at the very end of the war and surrendered to the British. Matzky was a POW until February 1948. Released, he joined what became the Bundeswehr in 1951 and was named commander of the I Corps in Muenster in the spring of 1957. A lieutenant general (i.e., "three star" general under the new rank structure), he retired in early 1960. He died at Bad Godesberg (a Rhine River town on the southern outskirts of Bonn) on June 9, 1983, at the age of 89.

Walter Model led the 3rd Panzer Division in Russia until October 1, 1941, when he became commander of the XXXXI Motorized Corps. He was promoted to general of panzer troops on October 1, 1941 and, on January 12, 1942, was given command of the Ninth Army, which was nearly surrounded just west of Moscow. Model saved the Ninth Army and later, in the spring of 1943, conducted a skillful withdrawal from the Rzhev Salient in the spring of 1943. Meanwhile, he was seriously wounded on September 1, 1942, when a Soviet bullet cut his pulmonary artery. He returned to duty in January 1943 and led the Ninth Army in the Battle of Kursk, where his strategy was largely responsible for the German defeat. He nevertheless was given command of the Second Panzer Army (while simultaneously leading the 9th) and withdrew in good order, inflicting heavy losses on the Red Army in the process. He was promoted to field marshal on March 1, 1944, and on March 31, was given command of Army Group North. Later he commanded Army Groups South (later North Ukraine) and Center, before being sent to the Western Front. Known as "the Fuehrer's Fireman," he was given only the most difficult assignments, and he often mastered them. He was, in fact, possibly the best of the Nazi generals.

On August 15, 1944, Hitler ordered Model to report to la Roche Guyon to assume command of OB West and Army Group B. Model arrived on the evening of August 17 and discovered that he had inherited a disaster. He extricated as much of the 5th Panzer and 7th Armies as possible and evacuated German troops from most of France and of Belgium. In September, he gave up command of OB West to Field Marshal von Rundstedt but retained command of Army Group B. Later that month, he crushed a British airborne attack on Arnhem. He continued to command Army Group B in the Siegfried Line battles, the Battle of the Bulge, and the Battle of the Ruhr. As the war neared its conclusion, rather than surrender, he committed suicide in a woods outside Duesseldorf on April 21, 1945.[6]

Werner Moelders, the general of Fighter Pilots, continued to serve on the Eastern Front. On November 17, General Ernst Udet, the chief of the Air Armaments and Technical Office, committed suicide. Moelders flew back to Berlin to attend the funeral. After Udet was buried in the Invalidfriedhof, the German national cemetery, Moelders flew a Heinkel He-111 back toward the Eastern Front. An engine failed, and as he was making the final approach for an emergency landing at the airfield in Breslau, the second engine failed. The He-111 hit a power line and Moelders was killed. He was buried in the Invalidfriedhof, not far from where he stood at the funeral of Ernst Udet, less than a week before.

During the Cold War, the Communists ran the Berlin Wall through the Invalidfriedhof and destroyed about one-third of the cemetery, including the grave of Field Marshal von Reichenau. The grave of Werner Moelders still exists, along with those of Ernst Udet, Baron von Fritsch and Hans Valentin Hube. Reinhard Heydrich's gravestone was removed after the war, although one can still find his unmarked grave if one knows where to look. Curiously, the Communists preserved the grave of the Red Baron (although with a much smaller tombstone), even though all of the graves around him were destroyed.

Walter Nehring continued to lead the 18th Panzer Division on the Eastern Front, despite the fact that its combat strength had been reduced by 70 percent by November 23. In January 1942, he rescued the 216th Infantry Division, which had been surrounded at Ssuchinitshy, by literally cutting his way through the middle of the Red Army. Not only did he extricate the division, he even managed to bring off 1,000 wounded men.

On February 1, 1942, Nehring was promoted to lieutenant general and given command of the Afrika Korps. Here he did his usual brilliant job and played a major role in breaking the Gazala Line and capturing Tobruk. He was, however, seriously wounded during the 1st Battle of El Alamein, when a British fighter-bomber dropped a bomb right beside Nehring's vehicle. Several officers were killed in the blast. General Nehring was badly wounded in the head, the arm and the torso and had to be evacuated back to Europe.

Rommel was finally defeated at El Alamein and began to retreat to Libya on November 4. Four days later, the Anglo-American First British Army (General Kenneth A. N. Anderson) landed in French North Africa and drove for Tunisia, in order to take Rommel in the rear. Before they could do this, however, they had to capture the Tunisian capital of Tunis. Field Marshal Kesselring, the commander-in-chief South (OB South), summoned Walter Nehring from the hospital and ordered him to prevent this. Despite the fact that his arm was still not healing properly, Nehring accepted the challenge. He was given command of the XC Corps (which had not yet been formed) and flew to Tunis, where he managed to halt the Anglo-Americans until reinforcements could arrive. Nehring, however, openly questioned the wisdom of defending Tunisia at all. He foresaw that Anglo-Saxon air and naval power would one day cause the collapse of Axis supply lines, which would lead to the destruction of the XC and Panzer Army Afrika. No moral coward, Nehring frankly presented his view to the Nazis and the OKW. He was promptly branded a defeatist by Hitler and was denounced by Dr. Goebbels with special fervor.

After the Nazis ascended to power, Walter Nehring was rapidly promoted, receiving six promotions in eight years: lieutenant colonel

(September 1, 1934), colonel (March 1, 1937), major general (August 1, 1940), lieutenant general (February 1, 1942), and general of panzer troops (July 1, 1942). After Tunisia, there would be no more promotions. Walter Nehring left North Africa on December 9, never to return. His career was ruined.

In April and May 1943, Nehring's predictions came true. Axis supply lines collapsed and Army Group Afrika (5th Panzer and Panzer Army Afrika, which was now designated the First Italian-German Panzer Army) was destroyed. Nehring was unemployed for just over two months. Although he would never receive another advancement in rank, he was (like Erwin Rommel) simply too good a commander to leave on the shelf permanently. Meanwhile, on the Eastern Front, XXIV Panzer Corps had been smashed, and its last three commanding generals had been killed. Walter Nehring assumed command of the corps on February 10, 1943, and directed it on the Eastern Front until early 1945.

In January 1945, the Red Army crushed Army Group A, and the corps on Nehring's right and left collapsed. By January 17, Nehring was miles behind the Red Army's frontlines and was surrounded by a dozen Russian armies. Most other generals would have been finished at this point. Walter Nehring, however, called upon all his skill and experience to master a most desperate situation. He formed a "floating pocket" and maintained his perimeter as he retreated to the northwest, picking up stragglers, shattered divisions, intact units, and civilians as he went.

The civilians were justifiably terrified. The Reds were robbing, murdering, and raping at will. Often they would gang rape daughters in front of their horrified parents, then kill the daughters, and torture the parents to death. Rape victims included 12-year-olds and grandmothers in their 70s. Seeking to save themselves and their families from this fate, tens of thousands of panic-stricken civilians turned to Nehring to protect them. Not one was turned away. (Nehring understood what they were going through. His own home had been destroyed in an Allied air raid and members of his family were homeless refugees somewhere to the west.) Before long, there were more civilians within the floating pocket than there were soldiers on the perimeter. He linked up with Dietrich von Saucken's Grossdeutschland Panzer Corps (which was also surrounded) and continued pushing west.

The Communists had more armies attacking the floating pocket than

Nehring had divisions to defend it. Pounded by several armies every day, he turned back every attack. Stalin ordered the floating pocket destroyed. Despite odds of more than seven to one in their favor, this was something the Red Army could not do.

Without resupply and in the depths of winter, Nehring finally fought his way through to the Oder and reached German lines at the end of January—an incredible feat of military genius. He had covered 150 miles straight through the middle of the Red Army. "Generals Nehring and von Saucken performed feats of military virtuosity during these days that only the pen of a new Xenophon could adequately describe," Heinz Guderian wrote in admiration.[7] As Nehring himself recalled: "[L]ittle or no rest coupled with shortages of ammunition and fuel but with frost and snow in abundance, along frozen roads, against a stronger and more speedy enemy, traversing difficult country and crossing rivers which had no bridges . . . none of these could stop our determination to succeed and to defeat the enemy wherever he was met."[8]

Even Hitler was thrilled by Nehring's accomplishment. He personally decorated the panzer general with the Swords to his Knight's Cross, while Saucken (who already had the Swords) received the Diamonds. Hitler even let Nehring out of the professional doghouse, at least to a degree, and gave him command of the First Panzer Army in Upper Silesia. (He assumed command on March 20.) Nehring, however, did not receive (and never did receive) his promotion to colonel general.

General Nehring knew, of course, that the war was lost. When the final offensive began on April 16, he tried to reach the Anglo-Americans. Nehring's army headquarters and a handful of units escaped the final Soviet onslaught and managed to surrender to the U. S. Army. Released from the prisoner of war camps in 1947, he retired to a modest apartment in Duesseldorf and shunned publicity. He died in Duesseldorf on April 20, 1983.

Otto Ohlendorf gave up command of Einsatzgruppe D in June 1942 and returned to Germany. He was promoted to SS Gruppenfuehrer (SS lieutenant general) in November 1944, and became deputy secretary of state in the Reich Ministry of Economics, while retaining his post as chief of Amt III of the RSHA. He surrendered to the British on May 23, 1945, and was hanged in Landsberg prison in Bavaria in 1951.

Otto-Ernst Ottenbacher was named acting commander of the XXXXI Motorized Corps, replacing Georg-Hans Reinhardt (the new commander of Third Panzer Group) on October 6, 1941. He was succeeded by Walter Model on October 13. Unemployed for three months, he was given command of the XIII Corps on January 14, 1942. Part of the Fourth Army in the central sector of the Eastern Front, the XIII fought at Juchnov and Spass-Demensk in early 1942. Ottenbacher's performance, however, left something to be desired. He was relieved of his command on April 21 and was replaced by Lieutenant General Erich Straube. His career was effectively ruined, he was never promoted to general of infantry, and he was never given another important assignment. Unemployed until August 1942, he was sent to France (then a backwater area in the occupation zone), where he was attached to the headquarters of the military governor of France as an "extra" general. By 1944, he had been sent back to Germany and saw no further service. He retired to Stuttgart, where he died on January 7, 1975.

Friedrich Paulus served as deputy chief of the General Staff throughout 1941. Meanwhile, on November 30, Hitler sacked Field Marshal Gerd von Rundstedt as commander-in-chief of Army Group South and replaced him with his senior army commander, Walter von Reichenau. On December 3, while having a vegetarian dinner with the Fuehrer, Reichenau convinced Hitler that Friedrich Paulus should replace him as commander of the Sixth Army. Paulus was promoted to general of panzer troops on January 1, 1942, and took up his new post four days later.

Reichenau no doubt intended to guide his former chief of staff in his new duties, but he suffered a massive heart attack on January 12 and died on January 17. He was succeeded by the less capable Fedor von Bock. As desk soldier from his head to his toes, Paulus lacked decisiveness and convinced himself that Hitler was an infallible military genius. Although somewhat successful in the spring of 1942, Paulus allowed his army to get bogged down in street fighting in Stalingrad that fall. He was encircled by a massive Soviet counteroffensive on November 23. (Ironically, he was promoted to colonel general on November 20, the day after the Red offensive began.) Ignoring appeals from his corps commanders to break out while he still had a chance, Paulus obeyed

Hitler and presided over the destruction of the Sixth Army and the loss of 230,000 German and Romanian soldiers. Only 7,000 of the German soldiers ever saw the lights of home again.

On January 30, 1943, the tenth anniversary of the Nazi "Seizure of Power," Adolf Hitler promoted Paulus to field marshal. Since no German field marshal had ever been captured, this was a clear invitation for Paulus to commit suicide. He ignored the invitation and capitulated the next day. Hitler later declared that Paulus had done an about-face on the threshold of history.

Friedrich Paulus initially refused to cooperate with his captors but changed his mind in 1944. He joined the National Free Germany Committee and made anti-Nazi broadcasts, calling upon the soldiers to desert or to disobey Hitler's orders. This resulted in the arrest of his entire family. After the war, he appeared as a witness for the Soviet prosecution at Nuremberg; nevertheless, he was not released from prison until 1953. His wife had died in Baden-Baden four years before. Paulus settled in Dresden, East Germany, and became an inspector in the People's Police. He contracted motor neuron disease (amyelstrophic lateral sclerosis) in 1955 and possibly cancer as well. (He was a heavy smoker.) Field Marshal Paulus died on January 1, 1957.

Walter von Reichenau, the commander-in-chief of Army Group South, went on his usual six-mile cross-country run on January 15, 1942, in temperatures well below –20 degrees Fahrenheit. He looked ill later when he appeared in the headquarters mess for lunch. He ate a little, signed a few papers, and got up to leave. Before he reached the door, he collapsed with a severe heart attack. He never regained consciousness. When Hitler heard the news, he ordered that Reichenau be flown back to Germany for treatment by a famous heart surgeon. His airplane crashed en route, but Reichenau's biographer, Walter Goerlitz, states that he died of a cerebral hemorrhage, rather than injuries suffered in the crash. In any case, he was pronounced dead on arrival in Leipzig on the evening of January 17, 1942. He was buried in the Invalidhof, the German national cemetery in Berlin. His grave has since been destroyed.

Reichenau's daughter reportedly emigrated to the United States after the war. Her location and that of her family is a secret.

Georg-Hans Reinhardt was promoted to colonel general on January 1, 1942. He continued to lead the Third Panzer Army on the Eastern Front until August 16, 1944, when he succeeded Walter Model as commander-in-chief of Army Group Center. He led the remnants of the army group out of Russia and Poland and into East Prussia. Rather than to allow a large part of it to be needlessly cut off in East Prussia, he allowed the Fourth Army commander General of Infantry Friedrich Hossbach to conduct an unauthorized retreat in January 1945. When Hitler heard about it, he became furious and relieved Reinhardt and Hossbach of their commands on January 27. (Army Group Center had been renamed Army Group North two days before.)

Reinhardt would have had to be replaced in any case; he had been struck in the head by a bullet and was near death. He eventually recovered from his wound, only to be arrested by the Americans in June 1945. He was among the defendants in the High Command trial, where he was found guilty of war crimes and crimes against humanity, including abusing Soviet prisoners of war. He was sentenced to Fifteen years imprisonment but was released in June 1952. A holder of the Knight's Cross with Oak Leaves and Swords, General Reinhardt retired to Tegernsee, a resort town in the Bavarian Alps on Tegernsee lake, where he died on November 23, 1963.

Baron Wolfram von Richthofen continued to lead the VIII Air Corps, but with less success than previously. He was nevertheless promoted to colonel general on February 1, 1942. He did an outstanding job supporting Manstein's Eleventh Army in the Siege of Sevastopol, which fell on July 4. That same day, Richthofen was named commander-in-chief of the 4th Air Fleet. He supported Army Group A in the drive into the Caucasus and the Sixth Army in the Battle of Stalingrad. When the Sixth Army was surrounded, he called for it to break out immediately; Hitler, however, was guided by the advice of Hermann Goering, and ordered Richthofen to resupply it by air. The baron objected but tried, without success, to carry out the order. The Sixth Army surrendered on January 31, 1943.

Richthofen was not held responsible for the Stalingrad debacle and was promoted to field marshal on February 16, 1943. He continued to command the 4th Air Fleet until June 26, when he was named commander-in-chief of the 2nd Air Fleet in Italy. Here he concentrated his forces to oppose the first major Allied invasion of the European continent. Unfortunately, he concluded that they would land in Sardinia, but the landings occurred in Sicily, so the German airplanes were concentrated in the wrong place. He later succeeded in making life difficult for the Anglo-Americans at Salerno (September 1943), but this was his last hurrah. He continued to fight in this backwater theater with inadequate resources until his health deteriorated. On October 27, 1944, he went on indefinite leave with an inoperable brain tumor. He was placed in Fuehrer Reserve on November 27 and was captured by the Americans in an Austrian hospital in May 1945. He died in Bad Ischl, Austria, on July 12, 1945.

After Hitler sacked him as C-in-C of Army Group South, Gerd von Rundstedt returned to Germany, but his second retirement was destined to be brief. In early December 1941, SS General Sepp Dietrich convinced the Fuehrer that he had been wrong and had done Rundstedt an injustice. Hitler recalled Rundstedt to duty as OB West on March 10, 1942. (Rundstedt later referred to Dietrich as "decent, but stupid.") Rundstedt served two tours at OB West, from March 10, 1942 to July 2, 1944, and from September 4, 1944 to March 1945. Here he adopted a *laissez-faire* attitude. Unlike Rommel, he did not think that the Allies could be halted on the invasion beaches, and he did little to prepare the Atlantic Wall for defense. He believed instead that the decisive battle should be fought in the interior of France.

Rundstedt was, in fact, preparing for a 1941-style battle in 1944, having failed to realize that the Anglo-Saxon aerial superiority had rendered the great blitzkrieg victories of the past impossible. His strategy was to establish Panzer Group West under the command of his personal friend, General of Panzer Troops Baron Leo Geyr von Schweppenburg. He planned to allow the Allies to land and advance inland, out of the range of the big guns of the American and Royal navies, where von Geyr would attack and defeat them with his ten panzer and panzer grenadier divisions. Rundstedt took no interest in the details of Geyr's plan; instead, he retired to his headquarters with his brandy and cigarettes, and left the details of planning the battle to others.

The Allies landed in France on June 6, 1944. Despite a brilliant defense by Erwin Rommel and his men, the German line was stretched precariously thin by the end of the month. On July 1, Rundstedt received a telephone call from Field Marshal Keitel. In the course of the conversation, Keitel moaned: "What can we do, what can we do?"

"End the war, you fools," Rundstedt snapped. "What else can you do?" He then slammed the receiver down in Keitel's ear. Rundstedt was sacked again on July 2. As he left, he commented that he was glad that he would not be in command during the coming debacle.

Field Marshal von Rundstedt's third retirement was very short. He was outraged by the anti-Hitler conspirators' attempt to assassinate the Fuehrer and agreed to serve on the army's so-called Court of Honor, which expelled officers involved in the coup from the military so they could be arrested by the Gestapo and tried by the Nazi *Volksgerichtshof* (People's Court). Here most of them were physically tortured by the SS, verbally abused by the judge, and subsequently executed via slow strangulation.

Rundstedt became OB West for the second time on September 4, 1944. Almost simultaneously the Western Front stabilized, because the Allies had outrun their supply lines. General Dwight D. Eisenhower, the Allied supreme commander, diverted the bulk of his fuel and supplies to Montgomery, who launched an ambitious airborne-ground operation in Holland designed to breach the Rhine River, outflank the Siegfried Line, and capture the Ruhr industrial district, without which Germany could not wage war. This offensive was defeated by Field Marshal Walter Model at Arnhem.

Hitler, meanwhile, decided to launch a "last chance" offensive in the Ardennes. He built up while Rundstedt checked the Allies in the Siegfried Line battles from September to December. Rundstedt, however, opposed the offensive from the beginning. Frankly stating that the plan was "stupid," he simply handed the operation over to Model, who did not believe in it either. Once the order was given, however, Model did his best to carry it out. Rundstedt, on the other hand, would have nothing to do with it and was very annoyed when the Allied media dubbed the attack "the Rundstedt Offensive."

The Battle of the Bulge began on December 16, 1944. Although it raged into January 1945, Army Group B was effectively defeated by

December 26. Germany had lost at least 75,000 men and almost 600 tanks and assault guns. Worst still, the morale of the German *soldat* on the Western Front was broken. The war was lost.

Eisenhower began his final offensive on February 2, 1945. The Allies finally broke through the Siegfried Line on February 20 and Rundstedt, hampered as always by interference from Berlin, fell back across the Rhine. On March 7, the U.S. 9th Armored Division captured the Ludendorff Railroad Bridge at Remagen, breaching the Rhine River line. Bonn fell the next day, and on March 9 Hitler relieved Gerd von Rundstedt of his command. He was replaced by Field Marshal Albert Kesselring.

On May 2, 1945, Rundstedt was captured by the Americans at the resort of Bad Toelz, where he was undergoing treatment for arthritis. He was investigated as a war criminal and suffered his second heart attack during interrogation. It was determined that he had cooperated with the SS Einsatzgruppen during the Russian campaign, and he was scheduled to be tried by a British Military Tribunal; however, the Allied medical doctors concluded that his health had deteriorated to the point that he might not survive the stress of the trial. Meanwhile, his son died of throat cancer on January 12, 1948, and the old field marshal was temporarily released to attend the funeral. Gerd von Rundstedt was released from captivity in July 1948 and retired to Hanover, where he died on February 24, 1953. His wife had died the year before.

Hans von Salmuth commanded the XXX Corps until December 17, 1941, when he stepped down due to illness and exhaustion. Later he became a colonel general (January 1, 1943). Salmuth led the XXX Corps (1941–42), the Seventeenth Army (April to June 1942), the Fourth Army (June to July 1942), and the Second Army (July 1942 to February 1943), all on the Eastern Front. He was promoted to colonel general on January 1, 1943. A skillful tactical commander who was tough, rude, and somewhat brutal, Salmuth was unjustly relieved of the command of the Second Army in February 1943 for failing to obey one of Hitler's impossible "not one step back" orders. The Fuehrer and the Nazis thus earned Salmuth's undying hatred, for he was not a forgiving man.

The Nazis certainly thought more highly of Salmuth than he did of them. After briefly allowing him to command the Fourth Army in Russia for a second time, Hitler appointed Salmuth commander of the Fifteenth Army in northern France and Belgium. He assumed command on August 1, 1943. This was a position of great responsibility, for it was generally assumed that the Allies would land somewhere in Salmuth's area of operations, and probably in the Pas de Calais sector. The Allies, of course, instead landed in Normandy, in the zone of the German Seventh Army.

Salmuth was relieved of his command on August 25, 1944, after the Gestapo discovered that the general knew about the Stauffenberg anti-Hitler conspiracy, but did not tell anyone about it and made no effort to inform Hitler. Salmuth was captured by the U.S. Army at the end of the war. Put on trial for war crimes (he cooperated with the SS Einsatzgruppen, which murdered tens of thousands of Jews in Russia), he was found guilty and was sentenced to 20 years imprisonment. He was released in 1953 and retired to Wiesbaden, where he died during the night of December 31, 1961/January 1, 1962.

Fritz Schlieper, who finally captured Brest-Litovsk on June 29, 1941, continued to command the 45th Infantry Division until March 1, 1942. Promoted to lieutenant general on November 1, 1941, he was obviously not considered suitable to command a corps. He was made chief of the German Army Mission to Slovakia on May 1, 1942. He held this backwater post until August 1944 and never received another promotion. He became chief of a special staff at the OKH on August 17, but was not on active duty at the end of the war. He settled in Heidelberg, where he died on June 4, 1977.

Beppo Schmid was finally relieved as chief intelligence officer of the Luftwaffe in November 1942 and was assigned to the recently formed Hermann Goering Panzer Division. He commanded a battle group in Tunisia before returning to the Air Ministry as a special duties officer to Hermann Goering. He was given command of the XII Air Corps (of Air Fleet Reich) on September 15, 1943. He took command of the I Fighter Corps on April 1, 1944, and advanced to the leadership of Luftwaffe Command West (as the downgraded 3rd Air Fleet was called) on December 12, 1944. Meanwhile, he was promoted to major general on March 1, 1943, and to lieutenant general on July 1, 1944. Although he certainly did not distinguish himself in the defense of the Reich or on the Western Front, it is doubtful that even an extremely competent officer could have done much better, given the odds against him. Schmid—who owed his rank and position to his friendship with Hermann Goering—was certainly unable to check the combined might of the Royal and U.S. air forces. He was captured by the British on April 27, 1945, and held in POW camps for almost three years. He returned to Augsburg in the spring of 1948 and died there on August 30, 1956, at the age of 53.

Rudolf Schmidt became acting commander of the Second Army on November 15, 1941, when General von Weichs reported himself ill. When Hitler and Kluge sacked Heinz Guderian on December 25, he was given command of the Second Panzer Army. Schmidt was promoted to colonel general on January 1, 1942, despite his opposition to Hitler's "stand fast" orders, the fact that he agreed with Guderian and not Kluge on the issue of whether the army should retreat or not, and his willingness to use Soviet civilians as auxiliaries and even, on occasion, as combat troops.

Schmidt did a fine job commanding the Second Panzer Army. His career ended abruptly when the Gestapo, which was investigating his brother, accidentally discovered letters he had written which were highly critical of the Nazis in general and Adolf Hitler personally. The Fuehrer was shocked and apparently genuinely hurt and offended. He sacked Schmidt on July 10, 1943, despite the fact that his Second Panzer Army was covering the northern flank of Army Group Center's strike force during the Battle of Kursk, which was already in progress. Schmidt's brother was found guilty of espionage. Schmidt himself was hauled before the Reichs War Court, and Judge Advocate General Sack ordered that he be committed to a psychiatric facility. He was discharged from the army on Hitler's orders on September 30, 1943.

General Schmidt was captured by the Red Army at the end of the war. He remained in Soviet prison camps until 1955. He settled in Krefeld, North-Rhine-Westphalia (West Germany), but his health had been destroyed by years of imprisonment. He died on April 7, 1957.

Georg von Sodenstern remained on the Eastern Front as an army group chief of staff until August 13, 1943, when he was transferred to south-western France as commander of the Ninteenth Army. He did little to prepare the coast for defense and initially opposed Rommel's plan to defeat the invasion on the beaches, although he later came around to the idea. His anti-Nazi views were known, however, because he talked too much. (Sodernstern had a reputation for being gregarious and somewhat indiscreet.) On June 29, 1944, he was relieved of his command. He was replaced by General of Infantry Friedrich Wiese. His role in the anti-Hitler conspiracy of 1938 was never discovered. Never re-employed, he settled in Frankfurt/Main after the war and died on July 22, 1955.

Count Hans von Sponeck commanded the 22nd Air Landing Division in the Crimea until October 10, 1941, when Manstein gave up command of the XXXXII Corps of his Eleventh Army in the Crimea. He was posted on the Kerch Peninsula in eastern Crimea and ordered to guard the rear of the Eleventh Army forces besieging the Soviet fortress city and naval base at Sevastopol. In December, strong Soviet amphibious forces landed in his rear. Ignoring Hitler's order to stand fast, Sponeck conducted an unauthorized retreat, and it was a shambles. Many of his vehicles would not start and had to be abandoned; others broke down or skidded off the icy roads and were also lost along with several guns, howitzers, and other pieces of important equipment.

Because the XXXXII Corps suffered heavy material losses despite the fact that it had no contact with the enemy, Hitler ordered Sponeck relieved on December 26, 1941. He was arrested three days later and court-martialed in January 1942, with Hermann Goering presiding. Sponeck was found guilty and sentenced to death; however, Lt. Gen. Walter von Seydlitz-Kurzbach, a member of the court, fiercely objected to the sentence, and retired Colonel General Curt Haase personally protested to Hitler.

As a result, Sponeck's sentence was reduced to six years' imprison-ment. He began serving his sentence on March 6. After the Stauffenberg assassination attempt of July 20, 1944 failed, however, Heinrich Himmler (the Reichsfuehrer-SS and new commander-in-chief of the Replacement Army) ordered Sponeck executed. He was shot in the Germersheim prison on the morning of July 23. His wives asked for the body and (somewhat remarkably) got it. They buried Sponeck in the Dahner Ehrenfriedhof. His grave is still there.[9]

Adolf Strauss's depleted Ninth Army was mauled by Stalin's winter offensive. It was heavily attacked from the first day (December 6, 1941). By the second week in January 1942, it was nearly surrounded and Strauss could no longer handle the stress. He asked to be relieved of his command for reasons of health, and was retired on January 15, 1942. He was replaced by Walter Model, who saved the army in the Battle of the Rzhev Salient. Strauss retired to Luebeck and never held another major command. He was, however, recalled to active duty in August 1944, as chief of Fortress Command East, in which he essentially acted as an inspector and advisor. He surrendered to the British on May 3, 1945.

In the fall of 1948, the British announced that they intended to try Strauss as a war criminal. In the end, however, they decided that his health was too fragile to endure the ordeal. They ignored Soviet extradition demands and released the general on May 19, 1949. He returned to Luebeck, where he died on March 20, 1973.

General of Infantry Georg Thomas was forced out of his position as chief of the Defense Economy and Armaments Office at the OKW in November 1942, when that branch was absorbed by Alfred Speer, whose Ministry of Armaments was taking over virtually all responsibilities in the field of armaments. Without an assignment, Thomas was, in effect, retired from November 20, 1942 until October 11, 1944, when he was arrested. Roosevelt had publicly pronounced the "Unconditional Surrender" policy in 1943, and Thomas refused to participate further in the anti-Hitler conspiracy because he believed that Germany now had nothing to gain by leaving the war. The Gestapo, however, discovered that he had formerly been plotting to overthrow the Fuehrer as early as 1938.

Expelled from the army effective January 1, 1945, he was incarcerated at the Flossenburg and Dachau concentration camps. The SS moved Thomas and about 140 other prominent prisoners (including Franz Halder) to Tyrol in late April 1945. Here they murdered Dietrich Boenhoffer, the prominent anti-Hitler pastor, but simply abandoned most of the prisoners after Hitler committed suicide. Thomas was liberated by the Americans on May 5, 1945. Thomas's health, however, never recovered, and he died at Frankfurt/Main on December 29, 1946.

Kurt Tippelskirch led the 30th Infantry Division in the drive on Leningrad and defeated a major Soviet effort to turn the flank of the X Corps in a week-long battle. For this action he was awarded the Knight's Cross. He was with the division when it was encircled at Demyansk (along with the rest of II Corps) in January 1942, and remained in the pocket (which became a salient) for more than a year. Tippelskirch personally left Demyansk on August 27, 1942, when he was promoted to general of infantry and was named German general to the Eighth Italian Army on the southern sector of the Eastern Front. He was involved in the hard fighting in the winter of 1942/43. On February 18, 1943, he assumed command of the XII Corps of Army Group Center and fought at Spass-Demensk, Bryansk, Mogilev, and Minsk. He became acting commander of the 4th Army on June 4, 1944, and was in charge when it (along with the entire army group) was crushed by the Red Army. After some hesitation, Tippelskirch disobeyed his army group commander and retreated against orders. Had he not done so, the entire Fourth Army would have been destroyed. As it was, it lost 130,000 of its 165,000 men, and 10 of its 11 division commanders were killed or captured. One of the casualties was Tippelskirch's own son, now a major, who was killed at Mogilev on June 28.

Tippelskirch commanded Fourth Army until July 18, when he was seriously injured in an airplane crash. He returned to duty on October 31 as the deputy commander of the First Army on the Western Front. On December 12, he assumed command of the Fourteenth Army on the Italian Front, where he launched a surprise offensive that severely disrupted the Allies' preparations for their own offensive.

Kurt von Tippelskirch gave up command of the Fourteenth Army on February 22, 1945, and returned to Germany. He was given command of the Twenty-first Army (which was the former HQ, Fourth Army). He was named interim commander of Army Group Vistula on April 28 and held the post until the permanent commander, Colonel General Kurt Student, arrived on or about May 1. He surrendered to the Americans near Luebeck on May 2. Released from prison in 1947, he wrote an excellent book on World War II (*Geschichte des Zweiten Weltkrieges*), although it is now dated. He died at Lueneburg, Lower Saxony, on May 10, 1957.

Following his success in the early weeks of Barbarossa, Wolfgang von Wild was promoted to acting Flight Leader Atlantic, where he expected less success. He returned to the Eastern Front in February 1942, as Flight Leader South. Here he operated against Soviet forces in the Crimea and especially against the Red naval fortress of Sevastopol. After the fall of Sevastopol on July 2, he fell ill and was in the hospital until the fall of 1942. He was then posted to Athens as an air transport leader, and was Flight Leader Sardinia from December 1942 to June 1943, where he experienced no success in his efforts to help resupply Army Group Afrika in Tunisia. Colonel von Wild spent the rest of the war in backwater assignments, including tours as commander of Air Weapons School C (the combat observers' school at Parow and Stralsund) (October 1943 to September 1944), liaison officer between the Luftwaffe Defense Office and the 6th Air Fleet on the Eastern Front (November to December 1944) and Flight Leader 6 at Pillau, East Prussia (now Baltiysk, Russia) (December 1944).

As the Soviets overran East Prussia, Wild was recalled to Berlin, where he was designated as chief of a planned flight from Germany to Japan via the Norway-North Pole, Arctic Ocean-Bering Strait-Pacific Ocean route. Upon arrival, Wild would become a special air attaché to Tokyo. For his new post, Wild was promoted to major general on March 1, 1945. The flight, which was scheduled to begin on May 9, never happened. Hitler committed suicide on April 30 and Wild surrendered to the British on May 9. He was released from captivity on July 1, 1947. General von Wild died in Kassel on May 12, 1964.

Albert Wodrig continued to command the XXVI Corps on the northern sector of the Eastern Front until November 1, 1942, when he was succeeded by Ernst von Leyser. After an extended leave, he returned to Koenigsberg, where he assumed command of Wehrkreis I on January 31, 1943. He held this post until November 1, 1944, when the Red Army approached East Prussia and Hitler replaced him with General of Infantry Otto Lasch. (Hitler wanted to make sure that his "hold at all costs" orders were obeyed, so he appointed "fortress" commanders who had large families. Lasch, who commanded Fortress Koenigsberg, had a large family. When Lasch surrendered Koenigsberg too quickly to suit Hitler, he was sentenced to death *in absentia* and his family was thrown into a concentration camp.) Wodrig was never re-employed and had an opportunity to escape to the west, which he promptly did. He resided in Essen in the Ruhr after the war and died on October 31, 1972, at the age of 89.

Lt. Gen. Baron Theodor von Wrede led the 290th Infantry Division until May 1, 1942, when he was so badly wounded that he never returned to active duty. He was discharged from the service at the end of 1944. Wrede retired to Bonn, where he died on March 30, 1973.

Hans Zorn commanded the 20th Motorized Division until January 13, 1942. Two days later he was promoted to lieutenant general and was named acting commander of the XXXX Motorized Corps, which was defending a sector of the Fourth Army's front around Juchnov. When Georg Stumme, the permanent commander of the corps, returned to duty on February 15, Zorn was sent to Demyansk, where he served as an advisor to the commander of the II Corps. Promoted to general of infantry on June 1, 1942, Zorn was sent to northwestern France, and assumed leadership of the XXXII Corps Command (later LXXXI Corps) on June 10. He was sent back to the Eastern Front in September and assumed command of the XXXXVI Panzer Corps on October 1. He apparently became ill shortly thereafter; in any case, he turned command of the corps over to Baron Hans-Karl von Esebeck on November 22. He did not resume command until June 22, 1943, two weeks before the Battle of Kursk began. Zorn's task was to cover the northern flank of Army Group Center's attack force (Model's Ninth Army). In July and August, he was attacked by overwhelming forces; Zorn nevertheless was able to slow the Soviet progress and give Ninth Army a chance to extract itself, which it successfully did. On August 2, 1943, however, General Zorn's staff car was strafed by a Soviet fighter-bomber, and he was killed instantly.

APPENDIX 1

TABLE OF EQUIVALENT RANKS

U.S. Army	German Army
General of the Army	Field Marshal (*Generalfeldmarschall*)
General	Colonel General (*Generaloberst*)
Lieutenant General	General (*General*)
Major General	Lieutenant General (*Generalleutnant*)
Brigadier General	Major General (*Generalmajor*)
Colonel	Colonel (*Oberst*)
Lieutenant Colonel	Lieutenant Colonel (*Oberstleutnant*)
Major	Major (*Major*)
Captain	Captain (*Hauptmann*)
First Lieutenant	Lieutenant (*Oberleutnant*)
Second Lieutenant	Lieutenant (*Leutnant*)

SS Rank	German Army Equivalent
Reichsfuehrer SS (Himmler)	Commander in Chief of the Army*
None	Field Marshal
Oberstgruppenfuehrer	Colonel General
Obergruppenfuehrer	General
Gruppenfuehrer	Lieutenant General
Brigadefuehrer	Major General
Oberfuehrer	None
Standartenfuehrer	Colonel
Obersturmbannfuehrer	Lieutenant Colonel
Sturmbannfuehrer	Major
Hauptsturmfuehrer	Captain
Obersturmfuehrer	First Lieutenant
Untersturmfuehrer	Second Lieutenant

*Held by Field Marshal Werner von Blomberg (1933–38), Field Marshal Walter von Brauchitsch (February 4, 1938–December 1941), and Hitler (December 1941–April 1945).

APPENDIX 2

GERMAN STAFF POSITIONS

Chief of Staff (Not present below the corps level)

Ia	Chief of Operations
Ib	Quartermaster (Chief Supply Officer)
Ic	Staff Officer, Intelligence (subordinate to Ia)
Id	Director of Training (Not present below army level)
Iia	Chief Personnel Officer (Adjutant)
Iib	Second Personnel Officer (subordinate to IIa)
III	Chief Judge Advocate (subordinate to IIa)
Iva	Chief Administrative Officer (subordinate to Ib)
Ivb	Chief Medical Officer (subordinate to Ib)
Ivc	Chief Veterinary Officer (subordinate to Ib)
Ivd	Chaplain (subordinate to IIa)
V	Motor Transport Officer (subordinate to Ib)

National Socialist Guidance Officer (added 1944)
Special Staff Officers (Chief of Artillery, Chief of Projectors [Rocket Launchers], Chief Signal Officer, etc.)

NOTE: The Ia was referred to as the *Generalstabsoffizier* 1 (1st General Staff Officer or GSO 1); the Ib was the *Generalstabsoffizier* 2; the Ic was the *Generalstabsoffizier* 3; and the Id was the *Generalstabsoffizier* 4.

APPENDIX 3

GERMAN UNITS, RANKS AND STRENGTHS

Unit	Rank of Commander*	Strength
Army Group	Field Marshal	2 or more armies
Army	Colonel General	2 or more corps
Corps	General	2 or more divisions
Division	Lieutenant General/	10,000–18,000 men**
	Major General	200–350 tanks (if panzer)
Brigade***	Major General/	2 or more regiments
	Colonel	
Regiment	Colonel	2–7 battalions
Battalion	Lieutenant Colonel/	2 or more companies
	Major/Captain	(approximately 500 men per infantry battalion; usually 50–80 tanks per panzer battalion)
Company****	Captain/Lieutenant	3–5 platoons
Platoon	Lieutenant/	Infantry: 30–40 men
	Sergeant Major	Panzer: 4 or 5 tanks
Section	Warrant Officer/	2 squads (more or less)
	Sergeant Major	
Squad	Sergeant	Infantry: 7–10 men
		Armor: 1 tank

*Frequently, units were commanded by lower-ranking men as the war went on.
**As the war progressed, the number of men and tanks in most units declined accordingly. SS units usually had more men and tanks than army units.
***Brigade headquarters were rarely used in the German Army after 1942.
****Called batteries in the artillery (4 or 5 guns per battery).

APPENDIX 4

CHARACTERISTICS OF SELECTED GERMAN AND ALLIED TANKS OF WORLD WAR II

Model	Weight (in tons)	Speed (mph)	Range (miles)	Main Armament	Crew
BRITISH					
Mark IV "Churchill"	43.1	15	120	16-pounder	5
Mark VI "Crusader"	22.1	27	200	12-pounder	5
Mark VIII Cromwell	30.8	38	174	175mm	5
AMERICAN*					
M3A1 "Stuart"**	14.3	36	60	137mm	4
M4A3 "Sherman"	37.1	30	120	176mm	5
GERMAN					
PzKw II	9.3	25	118	120mm	3
PzKw III	24.5	25	160	150mm	5
PzKw IV	19.7	26	125	175mm	5
PzKw V "Panther"	49.3	25	125	175mm	5
PzKw VI "Tiger"	62.0	23	73	188mm	5
RUSSIAN					
T34/Model 76	29.7	32	250	176mm	4
T34/Model 85	34.4	32	250	185mm	5
KV 1	52	25	208	176.2mm	5
JSII "Joseph Stalin"	45.5	23	150	122mm	4

*Characteristics of each tank varied somewhat from model to model
**All American tanks were also in the British inventory. The British Shermans were sometimes outfitted with a heavier main battle gun. These Shermans were called "Fireflies."

NOTES

CHAPTER I: SETTING THE STAGE: THE WEHRMACHT, 1933–1941

1. Although Werner von Fritsch was cleared of these false charges, his career was over just the same. Named honorary colonel of the 12th Artillery, he accompanied his regiment to the field when Germany invaded Poland. On September 22, 1939, he committed suicide by deliberately exposing himself to Polish machine gun fire. Ironically, he is buried in the same cemetery as Heydrich, although Heydrich's headstone has since been removed.

2. Jodl, who was born in Bavaria in 1890, was also an artillery officer. He was chief of operations of OKW until October 1, 1938, when he assumed command of Arko 44 (the 44th Artillery Command) in Vienna. He returned to OKW when the war began and was again chief of operations from September 1, 1939 to May 9, 1945, when the Western Allies arrested Keitel. He was commander of OKW from then until May 23, when it was dissolved and he was arrested. Also like Keitel, he was hanged at Nuremberg on October 16, 1946.

3. David Irving, *War Path* (1979), p. 79.

4. Harold C. Deutsch, *Hitler and His Generals: The Hidden Crisis, January-June 1938* (1974), p. 121.

5. Telford Taylor, *Sword and Swastika: Generals and Nazis in the Third Reich* (1952; reprint ed., 1969), p. 167.

6. Viktor von Schwedler (1885–1954) was also a product of the German cadet schools system. He had been chief of personnel since 1933. When Wehrkreis IV was divided into its territorial and command components, Schwelder went to the field as commander of the IV Corps. He led it until October 18, 1942, when he was relieved of his command for criticizing Frederick Paulus's conduct of the Battle of Stalingrad. When he was proven right, he was taken out of retirement and again assumed command of Wehrkries IV on March 1, 1943. He held this post until January 31, 1945, when he was again placed in Fuehrer Reserve. As a result, he was able to escape Soviet captivity.

7. Bodewin Keitel (1888-1953) was born on the family farm in Hanover and joined the army as an officer cadet in 1909. He served as personnel officer until September 1942, when Hitler fired him in the same fit of rage in which he fired Franz Halder as chief of the General Staff and Field Marshal Wilhelm List as commander of Army Group A. Six months later, after Hitler cooled down, Bodewin was given command of Wehrkreis XX in West Prussia and Poland. He held this post until the Soviets overran the area in early 1945. A retired general of artillery, he resided in Goettingen, Lower Saxony (West

Germany) after the war. Among the senior German officers, he was considered much smarter than his brother, Wilhelm.

8. For a biography of Adolf Kuntzen, see below. Hans Behlendorff (1889-1961) was promoted to the leadership of the 31st Artillery Command (Arko 31) in Brunswick (Braunschweig). He rose to the rank general of artillery during World War II and commanded the 34th Infantry Division in Russia and LXXXIV Corps in France. He was placed in Fuehrer Reserve in the spring of 1943 and retired in late 1944. Wolf Keilig, *Die Generale des Heeres* (1983), p. 193; Dermot Bradley, Karl-Friedrich Hildebrand and Markus Roevekamp, *Die Generale des Heeres, 1921-1945* (1993-2006), Vol. 7, pp. 319-20 (hereafter cited as Bradley et. al.).

9. Oswald Lutz was briefly recalled to active duty in 1941 to head a special transportation staff headquartered in Frankfurt/Oder, but he never again held an important position. He retired again in the summer of 1942 and died in Munich on February 26, 1944, at the age of 67.

10. General Beck was born in the Rhineland in 1880. He was chief of the General Staff from 1933 to 1938, and was discharged with an honorary promotion to colonel general. He briefly commanded 1st Army in late 1938. He was deeply involved in the anti-Hitler conspiracy and committed suicide on July 20, 1944, after the Stauffenberg plot/assassination attempt failed. Wilhelm Adam (1877-1949) was known as the "Father of the Mountain Branch." He had been chief of the General Staff from 1930 to 1933. He later commanded Wehrkreis VII, the Armed Forces Academy and (briefly) Army Group 2. Like Beck, he was retired with an honorary promotion to colonel general.

11. Barry A. Leach, "Halder," in Correlli Barnett, ed., *Hitler's Generals* (1989), pp. 125-26.

CHAPTER II: THE PLANNERS

1. David Irving, *Hitler's War*, Volume I (1977), p. 110.

2. United States Department of the Army, "The German Campaign in Russia—Planning and Operations (1940-42)," *United States Department of the Army Pamphlet 20-261a* (1955) (hereafter cited as *DA PAM 20-261a*).

3. Matthew Cooper, *German Army* (1978), p. 263; *Halder Diaries*, December 5, 1940.

4. Cooper, *German Army*, p. 265.

5. Walter Warlimont, *Inside Hitler's Headquarters*, R. H. Barry, trans. (1964; reprint ed., n.d.), p. 139 (hereafter cited as Warlimont, *Inside Hitler's Headquarters*). Warlimont was born in Osnabrueck in 1894 and joined the army as a *Fahnenjunker* in 1913. He served in the artillery in World War I and became a brigade adjutant. After serving in the Freikorps, he was accepted into the Reichsheer and began his secret General Staff training in 1922. He visited the United States and England in the interwar years and served in the Spanish Civil War. After commanding the 26th Artillery Regiment in Duesseldorf (1937-38), he was assigned to the staff of OKW and eventually became deputy chief of operations. For future historians, he proved to be a valuable witness to events at Fuehrer Headquarters. Brilliant and arrogant, he was severely wounded during the July 20, 1944 attempt to assassinate Adolf Hitler and was not re-employed. He was sentenced to life imprisonment as a minor war criminal but was released in 1957. He retired to Kreuth, Upper Bavaria, where he died in 1976.

6. See Gene A. Mueller, *The Forgotten Field Marshal: Wilhelm Keitel* (1962) for the best biography of Keitel.

7. Heinz Hoehne, *Canaris*, J. Maxwell Brownjohn, trans. (1979), p. 6.

8. *Halder Diaries*, April 24, 1941.

9. Ibid., July 22, 1940.

10. Cooper, *German Army*, p. 261. Also see *DA Pam 20-261a*.

11. Paul Carell, *Hitler Moves East*, Ewald Osers, trans. (1965; reprint ed., 1966), p. 12. Paul Carell is the pseudonym for Paul Karl Schmidt (1911-1997), who served as press secretary for Joachim von Ribbentrop from 1940 to 1945. An honorary SS lieutenant colonel, he advised the SS on how to cover up the mass murder of the Hungarian Jews.

12. Albert Seaton, *The Battle for Moscow* (1971; reprint ed., 1980), p. 12.

13. Interrogation of Adolf Galland, 6 June 1945, Air University Archives, Maxwell Air Force Base, Montgomery, Alabama (hereafter cited as Interrogation of Adolf Galland).

14. Interrogation of Adolf Galland.

15. Adolf Galland, *The First and the Last* (1954; reprint ed., 1987), p. 142.

16. *DA Pam 20-261a*, p. 42. Also see Hermann Plocher, "The German Air Force Versus Russia, 1941," United States Air Force Historical Studies Number 153, manuscript on file at the Air University Archives, Maxwell Air Force Base, Montgomery, Alabama. Plocher served as chief of staff of the V Air Corps during Operation Barbarossa. Later he commanded the 6th Parachute Division on the Western Front and rose to the rank of lieutenant general.

17. Werner Baumbach, *The Life and Death of the Luftwaffe* (1960),136.

CHAPTER III: THE DEPLOYMENT

1. Taylor, *Sword and Swastikas*, pp. 240-41.

2. Henning von Tresckow was born in Magdeburg on January 10, 1901, and entered the service as a *Fahnenjunker* in the 1st Guards Regiment in 1917. He fought in World War I, joined the Reichsheer in 1926, and was Ia of the 221st Infantry Division when World War II began. He was chief of operations of Army Group A in 1940, and became Ia of Army Group B (later Center) in late 1940. He briefly commanded the 442nd Infantry Regiment (October-November 1943) and became chief of staff of 2nd Army on November 20, 1943. Promoted to lieutenant colonel (1940), colonel (1942) and major general (January 30, 1944), he was deeply involved in the plot to assassinate Adolf Hitler. He committed suicide on July 21, 1944, the day after the attempt failed.

3. Wilhelm von Leeb, *Defense*, Dr. Stefan T. Possony and Daniel Vilfroy, trans. (1943), p. ix.

4. John Toland, *Adolf Hitler* (1976; reprint ed., 1977), p. 403.

5. Leeb's younger brother, General of Artillery Emil von Leeb (1881-1969) commanded the XI Corps in Poland (1939) and was chief of the Army Munitions Office from April 16, 1940 until the end of the war.

6. Georg Tessin, *Verbaende und Truppen des deutschen Wehrmacht und Waffen-SS im Zweiten Weltkrieg, 1939-1945* (1979-1986), Vol. 1, pp. 52-53.

7. Seaton, *German Army*, p. 160.

8. H. Wolfgang Koch, ed., *Aspects of the Third Reich* (1985), pp. 328-29; Juergen E. Foerster, "The Dynamics of Volkegemeinschaft: The Effectiveness of the German Military Establishment in the Second World War" in Allan R. Millett and Williamson

Murray, eds. *Military Effectiveness*, Vol. III: *The Second World War* (1988), pp. 180-220 (hereafter cited as "Volkegemeinschaft").

9. Bernhard R. Kroener, "Squaring the Circle. Blitzkrieg Strategy and Manpower Shortage, 1939-1942," in Wilhelm Deist, ed., *The German Military in the Age of Total War* (1985), pp. 294.

10. Foerster, "Volkegemeinschaft," pp. 195-96.

11. Earl F. Ziemke and Magna Bauer, *Moscow to Stalingrad: Decision in the East* (1985), p. 11.

CHAPTER IV: THE FRONTIER BATTLES

1. Helmut Pabst, *The Outermost Frontier* (1957), p. 61.

2. Curt Gallencamp (1890-1958) commanded the 78th Infantry Division (1939-42) on the Eastern Front and the XXXI Corps Command and LXXXI Corps in the West (1942-44). He was sacked on August 10, 1944 and was never re-employed.

3. A native of the Ukraine, Kirponos was born in 1892. He fought in World War I and the Russian Civil War, and distinguished himself commanding the 70th Infantry Division against Finland in the Winter War (1939-40). Later he commanded II Corps (1940) and the Leningrad Military District (1940-41).

4. Count Manfred von Strachwitz (1893-1968) commanded the I/2nd Panzer Regiment in 1941.

5. Nicholas W. Bethell and the editors of Time-Life Books, *Russia Besieged* (1980), p. 30. Dmitrii (also spelled Dmitry) Pavlov was a veteran of World War I, the Russian Civil War and the Spanish Civil War, where he commanded a tank brigade. Proclaimed a Hero of the Soviet Union in 1937, he returned to Russia as head of the Tank and Armored Car Directorate. He escaped the Stalin purges, was promoted to colonel general in early 1941, and was named commander of the Western (Belorussian) Military District, which became the West Front after Operation Barbarossa began. He was executed on or about July 22, 1941. In 1956, three years after Stalin's death, he was officially exonerated.

6. Ibid., p. 31. Boldin (1892-1965) had previously commanded the 53rd and 18th Rifle Divisions (1931-38), the XVII Rifle Corps (1938), the Kalinin Military District (1938-39), a mechanized cavalry group during the Polish campaign (1939) and the 9th Army in Bessarabia (1940). Later he commanded the 19th Army (1941) and the 50th Army (1941-45).

7. Bethell, p. 65; Alfred Kesselring, *Kesselring: A Soldier's Record* (1954).

8. Trevor J. Constable and Raymond F. Toliver, *Horrido! Fighter Aces of the Luftwaffe* (1968), p. 64.

9. Ibid., p.14.

10. www.geocities.com/~orion47/WEHRMACHT/LUFTWAFFE/Generaloberst/Loehr. com. Accessed 2008.

11. Matthew Cooper, *The German Air Force, 1933-1945* (1981), p. 223; Plocher MS 1941.

12. Robert Goralski, *World War II Almanac, 1931-1945* (1981), p. 164.

13. Lothar von Richthofen was killed in an air accident on July 4, 1922.

14. The word "Stuka" was an abbreviation for *Stukampfflugzeug*, or dive-bomber.

15. See Helmut Roemhild, *Geschichte der 269. Infanterie-Division* (1967) for a more detailed history of this division.

16. Carell, *Hitler Moves East*, pp. 23-24.

17. B. H. Liddell Hart, "Foreword" in Erich von Manstein, *Lost Victories* (1982), p. 13.

18. Guderian, *Panzer Leader*, p. 241.

19. Carell, *Hitler Moves East*, p. 28.

20. Samuel J. Newland, *Cossacks in the German Army, 1941-1945* (1991), p. 7.

21. Hermann Balck and F. W. von Mellenthin, "Generals Balck and von Mellenthin on Tactics: Implications for NATO Military Doctrine, Dec. 19, 1980," United States Army Command and General Staff Publication *M 313-5* (1981), p. 21.

CHAPTER V: BATTLES OF ENCIRCLEMENT

1. The dates various authors give for Rothenburg's death differ slightly.

2. James Lucas, *Hitler's Enforcers* (1991), p. 104.

3. Oswald Lutz held only one insignificant assignment during World War II, as chief of a special transport staff at Frankfurt/Oder, and it only lasted a few months. He died in February 1944. Keilig, p. 213.

4. Lucas, *Hitler's Enforcers*, p. 108.

CHAPTER VI: STIFFENING RESISTANCE AND SLOWER PROGRESS

1. Bethell, p. 78

2. Rosenberg, the "party's philosopher," editor of the *Voelkischer Beobachter* and a leading anti-Christian bigot, had expected to be appointed foreign minister in 1933, but was disappointed. He had been named chief of the Office for Total Intellectual and Ideological Supervision of the NSDAP. He opposed the Hitler-Stalin pact of 1939 and was a long-time foe of Joachim von Ribbentrop. He was appointed head of the Reichs Ministry of Occupied Eastern Territories in 1941 but had little real power. He was nevertheless executed as a major war criminal at Nuremberg in 1946.

3. Robert Wistrich, *Who's Who in Nazi Germany* (1982), p. 175.

4. Juergen Thorwald, *Wen Sie Verderben Wollen* (1951), p. 74.

5. Wistrich, p. 175.

6. Alexander Dallin, *German Rule in Russia, 1941–1945* (2nd ed., 1981), pp. 199-200; Ihor Kamenetsky, *Hitler's Occupation of the Ukraine* (1956), p. 55.

7. Dallin, p. 123.

8. Alan Clark, *Barbarossa* (1965), p. 65.

9. Ibid., pp. 204-05.

10. Ibid., pp. 186-87.

11. Wayne M. Dzwonchya, "Armored Onslaught Frozen," *World War II*, Vol. 4 (May 1989), pp. 22-23. Yakow Djugshvili had been born in Baku in 1903 and was a lieutenant in a Soviet tank division at the time of his capture.

12. Ziemke and Bauer, p. 14.

13. Foerster, "Volkegemeinschaft," p. 202; Burkhart Mueller-Hillebrand, *Das Heer*, Vol. III (1954-69). Mueller-Hillebrand (1904-1987) was Halder's adjutant (1940-42) and chief of the Organizations Branch of the Army (1942). He ended up as a lieutenant general in the West German Army.

CHAPTER VII: THE BATTLE OF THE SMOLENSK POCKET

1. Hermann Hoth, *Panzeroperatioen* (1956). Page?
2. Seaton, *Russo-German War*, p. 130; Lucas, *Eastern Front*, p. 176.
3. Seaton, *Russo-German War*, pp. 126-30; Lucas, *Eastern Front*, p. 176.
4. The 4th Infantry Regiment was headquartered at Deutsch Krone, but elements of the regiment were stationed at Schneidemuehl, Neustettin and Stralsund.
5. See Rolf Hinze, *Geschichte der 31. Infanterie-Division* (1997); Friedrich Hossbach, *Infanterie im Ostfeldzug, 1941/42 (31. Infanterie-Division)* (1951). Also see *Kriegstagebuch des OKW*, Volume IV: 1898.
6. Seaton, *Russo-German War*, pp. 126-30; Lucas, *Eastern Front*, p. 176.
7. Although there were 11 motorized/armored corps fighting in Russia in 1941, they were not redesignated panzer corps until 1942. The LVI Motorized Corps was renamed the LVI Panzer Corps on March 1, 1942. The III, XIV, XXIV, XXXXVI, XXXXVII, XXXXVIII and LVII Motorized Corps became panzer corps on June 21, and the XXXIX, XXXX and XXXXI Motorized Corps were redesignated panzer corps on July 9.

CHAPTER VIII: THE DRIVE TO LENINGRAD

1. See Charles W. Sydnor, *Soldiers of Destruction: The SS Death's Head Division* (1990) for the best history of Eicke and his division.
2. Heinz Hoehne, *The Order of the Death's Head*, Richard Barry, trans. (1971), p. 228.
3. Ibid., p. 229. Among Eicke's guards at this time were Adolf Eichmann, who did much to implement the "Final Solution," and Rudolf Hoess, the future commandant of the Auschwitz extermination camp.
4. Matthais Kleinheisterkamp was the commander of the 3rd Totenkopf Infantry Regiment when Eicke was wounded. After Eicke returned, Kleinheisterkamp transferred to the Das Reich SS Division because he and Eicke did not get along. Kleinheisterkamp eventually rose to the rank of General of Waffen-SS (SS *Obergruppenfuehrer*) and was commander of the XI SS Corps during the Battle of the Halbe Pocket. He was captured by the Soviets on April 28, 1945 and committed suicide the next day.
5. See Mark Yerger, *Waffen-SS Commanders* (1997 and 1999), 2 volumes, the only history of the Waffen-SS division commanders.
6. Carell, *Hitler Moves East*, p. 270.
7. See Werner Conze, *Die Geschichte der 291. Infanterie-Division, 1940-1945* (1953), for the story of the 291st Infantry Division.
8. Harry Hoppe (1894-1969) was later promoted to lieutenant general and commanded the 278th Volksgrenadier Division in Italy (1943-45).

CHAPTER IX: THE BATTLE IN THE FAR NORTH

1. The 8th Infantry Regiment headquartered in Frankfurt/Oder, but the II Battalion was located in Liegnitz.
2. Karl Gustav Mannerheim, *The Memoirs of Marshal Mannerheim* (1959), pp. 429, 443, 448. The poor performance of the 163rd in Russia did not harm the career of General Engelbrecht (1891-1964), who later became a general of artillery and ended the war as High Commander Saarpfalz (Saar-Palatinate).
3. Joseph Terboven, an early Nazi, married Joseph Goebbels's former secretary and

mistress. He became Gauleiter of Essen in 1928 and *Oberpraesident* of the Rhineland in 1933. He soon developed a reputation as a petty and ruthless little demigod. He was named Reichskommissar of Norway on April 24, 1940 (over the objections of Keitel and Jodl) and moved into the crown prince's residence. His tyranny and bullying soon alienated the Norwegians. Terboven committed suicide on May 8, 1945, by blowing himself up in his bunker.

CHAPTER X: THE BATTLE OF KIEV

1. Clark, *Barbarossa*, p. 106.
2. Halder *Diaries*, August 15, 1941.
3. Guderian, p. 159.
4. Ibid., pp. 160-62.
5. Ibid., p. 87.
6. Clark, *Barbarossa*, p. 54; Halder Diaries. Date?
7. Gustav von Wietersheim (1884-1974) was another product of the cadet schools. He commanded the 29th Infantry (later Motorized) Division (1936-38) and the XIV Motorized (later Panzer) Corps (1938 to September 15, 1942) with considerable distinction. He was sacked because he opposed Paulus's orders during the Battle of Stalingrad. Even though events proved him right and Paulus wrong, he was never re-employed as a commander. Wietersheim ended the war as a private in the *Volkssturm* (home guard).
8. Plocher MS 1941. Seaton, *Russo-German War*, pp. 139-40. Also see James Lucas, *Alpine Elite* (1980) for the best English language description of the Battle of Uman.
9. Shaposhnikov was chief of staff of the Red Army from 1928 to 1931 and from 1937 to November 1942, when he retired due to ill health. He died in 1945.
10. Richard Brett-Smith, *Hitler's Generals* (1977), p. 186.
11. Taylor, *Sword and Swastika*, p. 104.
12. Pabst, *Outermost Frontier*, p. 35. Sergeant Pabst was killed in action in the fall of 1943.

CHAPTER XI: THE DOUBLE BATTLE OF VYAZMA-BRYANSK

1. The 3rd and 4th Panzer Groups were not upgraded to army status until January 1, 1942. The remaining panzer group, which was Rommel's force in North Africa, became Panzer Army Afrika on January 21, 1942.
2. Carell, *Hitler Moves East*, p. 141.
3. Guderian, p. 81.
4. A Rhinelander, Hermann Breith (1892-1964) previously commanded the 36th Panzer Regiment (1936-40) and the 5th Panzer Brigade from February 2, 1940 until May 22, when he was wounded in France. After he recovered, he was general of mobile troops at OKH before assuming command of the 3rd Panzer Division. He led the III Panzer Corps on the Eastern Front from January 3, 1943, until the end of the war. Promoted to general of panzer troops in 1945, he managed to surrender to the Western Allies.

CHAPTER XII: THE OFFENSIVE ON THE FLANKS

1. Ferdinand Schaal (1889-1962) had previously commanded the 10th Panzer Division

in Poland, France and Russia (1939-41) and had spent a few days as acting commander of the XXXIV Corps in September 1941. He led the LVI Motorized (later Panzer) Corps from September 13, 1941 to August 1, 1943. He was promoted to general of panzer troops on October 1, 1941. On September 1, 1943, he assumed command of Wehrkreis Boehmia-Moravia, which he directed until July 21, 1944, when he was arrested for obeying the orders of the conspirators of July 20. He spent the rest of the war in prison. He had been a cavalryman from 1908 to 1935 and had commanded the 16th Cavalry Regiment.

2. Manstein, p. 23.

3. Leo Geyr von Schweppenburg, "Panzer Group West (mid-1943-15 July 1944)," Foreign Military Studies MS # B 258, unpublished manuscript, United States Army, Office of the Chief of Military History (1947), and Leo Geyr von Schweppenburg, "Panzer Group West (mid-1943-15 July 1944)," Foreign Military Studies MS # B 466, unpublished manuscript, United States Army, Office of the Chief of Military History (1947).

4. Rudolf Schmundt was born in Metz in 1896, fought in World War I, served in the Reichswehr, and became Hitler's chief adjutant on January 28, 1938, the day Colonel Hossbach was fired. He succeeded Bodewin Keitel as chief of the Army Personnel Office on October 2, 1942 and held the position until his death. He was blinded and mortally wounded when Stauffenberg's bomb exploded on July 20, 1944, and died on October 1, 1944. Hitler promoted him to general of infantry on his deathbed. Although the German generals did not consider Schmundt particularly bright, the consensus was that he nevertheless did a very good job as chief personnel officer.

5. Witzleben was later hanged for his part in the conspiracy of July 20. Brockdorff-Ahlefeldt later led the II Corps on the Eastern Front and distinguished himself in the Battle of the Demyansk Salient. He had to return to Germany in 1942, however, due to illness. He died in early 1943.

6. Hans-Juergen von Arnim Personnel Record, United States National Archives.

CHAPTER XIII: TO THE GATES OF MOSCOW

1. Mueller-Hillebrand, *Das Heer*, Volume III, Chapter 10.

2. Foerster, "Volkegemeinschaft," p. 202.

3. Pabst, *Outermost Frontier*, p. 54.

4. Soenke Neitzel, *Tapping Hitler's Generals*, Geofrrey Brooks, trans. (2007), pp. 304-05.

5. Seaton, *German Army*, p. 186.

6. Mainly from Keilig, *Generale*, pp. 1ff.

7. Clark, *Barbarossa*, p. 170.

8. Seaton, *Russo-German War*, p. 203. These figures exclude the German 2nd Army.

9. Seaton, *Russo-German War*, p. 203; Halder, *Diaries*.

CHAPTER XIV: WHAT BECAME OF THE MEN OF BARBAROSSA?

1. Hans Oster was born in Dresden in 1887. He served in the artillery, fought in World War I and successfully applied for the Reichswehr. His career prior to 1933, however, was mediocre at best. A major in 1933, he was expelled from the sving an affair with the wife

of a fellow officer. He was allowed to return to active duty only after Hitler's military expansion was in full swing and even then only as an (E) or territorial officer. He nevertheless rose rapidly after he joined the Abwehr, being promoted to lieutenant colonel (1935), colonel (1939) and major general (December 1, 1942). Sacked in January 1944 for possible treasonable activities, he was discharged from the service and later arrested by the Gestapo. He probably would not have been caught had he not had treasonable documents on his desk that he tried to hide while the Secret Police were actually in the room. In addition, Oster talked too much when he had been drinking and thus earned the censure of Field Marshal von Witzleben. He did not try to defend himself at his trial. His sole objective seems to have been to take Admiral Canaris down with him—which he did. They were both executed at Flossenburg concentration camp on April 9, 1945.

2. Falkenhorst's daughter married Erich Dethleffsen, who became a major general and served as chief of staff of 4th Army and Army Group Vistula on the Eastern Front.

3. See Franz Halder, *Kriegstagebuch*, 1962-1964, 3 Volumes. For an abridged English version of these diaries, see Franz Halder, *The Halder War Diary, 1939-1942*, Charles Burdick and Hans-Adolf Jacobsen, eds, 1988.

4. Helmut Ritgen, *The 6th Panzer Division, 1937-1945* (1985): ff. 1; Peter Schmitz, Klaus-Juergen Thies, Guenter Wegmann and Christian Zweng, *Die deutschen Divisionen, 1939-1945*. (1993-1997), Vol. 2: 23-26.

5. Www.camp198.fsnet.co.uk, accessed 2008.

6. For the best biography of Model, see Steven H. Newton, *Hitler's Commander* (2005).

7. Guderian, p. 326.

8. Lucas, *Hitler's Enforcers*, pp. 116-17.

9. Sponeck's oldest son served in the Luftwaffe during World War II and died in 1999. His youngest son from his first marriage became a *Rittmeister* and was killed in action near the Don River in 1942. His youngest son became a West German diplomat. His first wife died in 1961. See http://www.historie.de/Militar/Personen/ Sponeck/Graf%29Sponeck.htm (the source for most of this book's information about Sponeck) for photographs of Sponeck, his grave, and related stories about the 22nd Air Landing Division.

BIBLIOGRAPHY

Balck, Hermann, and F. W. von Mellenthin. "Generals Balck and von Mellenthin on Tactics: Implications for NATO Military Doctrine, Dec. 19,1980," United States Army Command and General Staff Publication *M313-5*. McLean, Virginia: BDM Corporation, 1981.

Barnett, Correlli, ed. *Hitler's Generals*. London: Weidenfeld and Nicolson, 1989.

Baumbach, Werner. *The Life and Death of the Luftwaffe*. New York: Coward-McCann, 1960.

Bethell, Nicholas W., and the editors of Time-Life Books. *Russia Besieged*. Alexandria, Virginia: Time-Life Books, 1980.

Bradley, Dermot, Karl-Friedrich Hildebrand and Markus Roevekamp. *Die Generale des Heeres, 1921–1945*. 7 vols. Osnabrueck: Biblio Verlag, 1993-2006.

Brett-Smith, Richard. *Hitler's Generals. London: Osprey Publishing*, 1977.

Carell, Paul. *Hitler Moves East*. Ewald Osers, trans. 1965. Reprint, New York: Bantam Books, 1966.

Clark, Alan. *Barbarossa*. New York: William Morrow, 1965.

Constable, Trevor J., and Raymond F. Toliver. *Horrido! Fighter Aces of the Luftwaffe*. 1968. Reprint, Durrington, UK: Littlehampton Books, 1979.

Conze, Werner. *Die Geschichte der 291. Infanterie-Division, 1940–1945*. Bad Nauheim: H.H. Podzun, 1953.

Cooper, Matthew. *The German Air Force, 1933–1945*. London: Jane's Publishing Company, 1981.

———. *The German Army. Briarcliff Manor, NY: Stein and Day*, 1978.

Dallin, Alexander. *German Rule in Russia, 1941–1945*. 2nd ed. New York: Macmillan Company, 1981.

Davis, C. R. *Von Kleist: From Hussar to Panzer Marshal*. Mount Ida, AR: Lancer Militaria, 1979.

Deist, Wilhelm, ed. *The German Military in the Age of Total War*. Oxford, UK: Berg Publishing, Ltd., 1985

Deutsch, Harold C. *Hitler and His Generals: The Hidden Crisis, January–June*

1938. Minneapolis: University of Minnesota Press, 1974.

Dzwonchya, Wayne M. "Armored Onslaught Frozen." *World War II*. 4 (1989): 22–23.

Foerster, Juergen E. "The Dynamics of Volkegemeinschaft: The Effectiveness of the German Military Establishment in the Second World War." In Allan R. Millett and Williamson Murray, eds. *Military Effectiveness*. Vol. 3 of *The Second World War*. New York: Routledge,1988.

Galland, Adolf. Interrogation of. 6 June 1945. Air University Archives, Maxwell Air Force Base, Montgomery, Alabama.

———. *The First and the Last*. 1954. Reprint, New York: Bantam Books, 1987.

Geyr von Schweppenburg, Leo. "Panzer Group West (mid-1943–15 July 1944)." Foreign Military Studies MS # B 258. Unpublished manuscript, United States Army, Office of the Chief of Military History. 1947.

———. "Panzer Group West (mid-1943–15 July 1944)." Foreign Military Studies *MS # B 466*. Unpublished manuscript, United States Army, Office of the Chief of Military History. 1947.

Goralski, Robert. *World War II Almanac, 1931–1945*. New York: G.P. Putnam's Sons, 1981.

Guderian, Heinz. *Panzer Leader*. Translated by Constantine Fitzgibbon. 1957. Reprint, New York: E.P. Dutton, 1967.

Halder, Franz. *The Halder War Diary, 1939–1942*. Charles Burdick and Hans-Adolf Jacobsen, eds., Novato, California: Presidio Press, 1988.

Halder, Franz. "The Private War Journal of Generaloberst Franz Halder, Chief of Staff of the Supreme Command of the German Army, 14 Aug 39–24 Sep 42." Washington, DC: Department of the Army, Office of the Chief of Military History. 1950.

Hinze, Rolf. *Geschichte der 31. Infanterie-Division*. Meerbusch: Verlag Hinze, 1997.

Hoehne, Heinz. *Canaris*. J. Maxwell Brownjohn, trans. Garden City, NY: Doubleday, 1979.

———. *The Order of the Death's Head*. Richard Barry, trans. New York: Coward-McCann, 1971.

Hossbach, Friedrich. *Infanterie im Ostfeldzug, 1941/42 (31. Infanterie-Division)*. Osterode: Giebel und Oehlschlaegel, 1951.

Hoth, Hermann. *Panzeroperationen*. Heidelburg: Kurt Vowinckel Verlag, 1956.

Irving, David. *Hitler's War*. 2 vols. New York: Viking Press, 1977.

———. *The War Path*. New York: Viking Press, 1979.

Kamenetsky, Ihor. *Hitler's Occupation of the Ukraine*. Milwaukee, Wisconsin: Marquette University Press, 1956.

Keilig, Wolf. *Die Generale des Heeres*. Friedberg: Podzun-Pallas-Verlag, 1983.

Kesselring, Alfred. *Kesselring: A Soldier's Record*. Westport, Conn.: Greenwood

Press, 1954.

Koch, H. Wolfgang, ed. *Aspects of the Third Reich*. New York: Palgrave Macmillan, 1985.

Kroener, Bernhard R. "Squaring the Circle. Blitzkrieg Strategy and Manpower Shortage, 1939–1942." In *The German Military in the Age of Total War*, Wilhelm Deist, ed., 282-303. Oxford, UK: Berg Publishing, Ltd., 1985.

Leach, Barry A. "Halder." In *Hitler's Generals,* Correlli Barnett, ed., 101–126. London: Weidenfeld and Nicolson, 1989.

Leeb, Wilhelm von. *Defense*. Dr. Stefan T. Possony and Daniel Vilfroy, trans. Harrisonburg, PA: Military Service Publication Company, 1943.

Lossberg, Bernhard von. *Im Wehrmachtfuehrungsstab: Bericht eines Generalstabsoffiziers*. Hamburg: H.H. Noelke Verlag, 1949.

Lucas, James. *Alpine Elite*. New York: Jane's Publishing, 1980

———. *Hitler's Enforcers*. London: Cassell, 1991.

———. *War on the Eastern Front, 1941–1945: The German Soldier in Russia*. Briarcliff Manor, NY: Stein and Day, 1979.

Mannerheim, Karl Gustav. *The Memoirs of Marshal Mannerheim*. New York: E.P. Dutton, 1959.

Manstein, Erich von. *Lost Victories*. Anthony G. Powell, ed. and trans. Chicago: Regnery, 1982.

Milch, Erhard. Interrogation of. 6 June 1945. Air University Archives, Maxwell Air Force Base, Montgomery, Alabama.

Millett, Allan R., and Williamson Murray, eds. *Military Effectiveness*. Vol. 3, *The Second World War*. New York: Routledge, 1988.

Mueller, Gene A. *The Forgotten Field Marshal: Wilhelm Keitel*. Durham, NC: Moore Publishing Company, 1962.

Mueller-Hillebrand, Burkhart. *Das Heer*. 3 vols. Darmstadt: E. S. Mittler und Sohn, 1954–1969.

Neitzel, Soenke. *Tapping Hitler's Generals*. Geofrrey Brooks, trans. Barnsley, UK: Frontline Books, Ltd., 2007.

Newland, Samuel J. *Cossacks in the German Army, 1941–1945*. New York: Routledge, 1991.

Newton, Steven H. *Hitler's Commander*. Cambridge, MA: Da Capo Press, 2005.

Overy, R. J. *The Air War, 1933–1945*. Briarcliff Manor, NY: Stein and Day, 1980.

Pabst, Helmut. *The Outermost Frontier*. New York: Kimber, 1957.

Plocher, Hermann. "The German Air Force Versus Russia, 1941." United States Air Force Historical Studies Number 153. Manuscript on file at the Air University Archives, Maxwell Air Force Base, Montgomery, Alabama.

Ritgen, Helmut. *The 6th Panzer Division, 1937–1945*. London: Osprey, 1985.

Roemhild, Helmut. *Geschichte der 269. Infanterie-Division*. Bad Nauheim: Podzun-Verlag, 1967.

Schmitz, Peter, Klaus-Juergen Thies, Guenter Wegmann, and Christian Zweng. *Die deutschen Divisionen, 1939–1945*. 3 vols. Osnabrueck: Biblio Verlag, 1993–1997.

Seaton, Albert. *The Battle for Moscow*. 1971. Reprint, New York: Sarpedon Publishers, 1993.

———. *The German Army*. New York: Plume, 1985.

———. *The Russo-German War, 1941–1945*. Westport, CT: Praeger, 1972.

Sydnor, Charles W. *Soldiers of Destruction: The SS Death's Head Division*. Princeton, NJ: Princeton University Press, 1990.

Taylor, Telford. *Sword and Swastika: Generals and Nazis in the Third Reich*. 1952. Reprint, Chicago: Quadrangle Paperbacks, 1969.

Tessin, Georg. *Verbaende und Truppen des deutschen Wehrmacht und Waffen-SS im Zweiten Weltkrieg, 1939–1945*. 16 vols. Osnabrueck: Biblio Verlag, 1979–1986.

Thorwald, Juergen. *Wen Sie Verderben Wollen*. Stuttgart: Steingrueben Verlag, 1951.

Toland, John. *Adolf Hitler*. 1976. Reprint, New York: Ballantine Books,1977.

United States Department of the Army. "The German Campaign in Russia—Planning and Operations (1940–42)." United States Department of the Army *Pamphlet 20-261a*. 1955.

Warlimont, Walter. *Inside Hitler's Headquarters*, R. H. Barry, trans. 1964. Reprint New York: Praeger, 1966.

Wistrich, Robert. *Who's Who in Nazi Germany*. New York: Macmillan, 1982.

Yerger, Mark. *Waffen-SS Commanders*. 2 vols. Atglen, PA: Schiffer Publishing, 1997–1999.

Ziemke, Earl F., and Magna Bauer. *Moscow to Stalingrad: Decision in the East*. Washington, DC: U.S. Army Center of Military History, 1985.

Internet Sources:

Altenburger, Andreas. http://www.lexikon.com.

Collins, Gareth, and Michael D. Miller, webmasters. http://www.geocities.com/~orion47/.

Denniston, Peter, and Patrick Kiser. http://www.gebirgsjaeger.4mg.com.

Düfel, Andreas. http://www.das-ritterkreuz.de

Linzmaier, Jan. http://www.diedeutschewehrmacht.de

Pipes, Jason, webmaster. http://www.feldgrau.com.

Wendell, Marcus, webmaster. http://www.forum.axishistory.com..

www.historic.de/Militar/Personen/ Sponeck/Graf%29Sponeck.htm.

www.ritterkreuztraeger-1939-45.de

INDEX